Reactive Web Applic

Reactive Web Applications

COVERS PLAY, AKKA, AND REACTIVE STREAMS

MANUEL BERNHARDT

MANNING
Shelter Island

For online information and ordering of this and other Manning books, please visit www.manning.com. The publisher offers discounts on this book when ordered in quantity. For more information, please contact

Special Sales Department
Manning Publications Co.
20 Baldwin Road
PO Box 761
Shelter Island, NY 11964
Email: orders@manning.com

Manning Publications Co.
20 Baldwin Road
PO Box 761
Shelter Island, NY 11964

Development editor: Karen Miller
Technical development editor: Kostas Passadis
Copyeditors: Andy Carroll and Benjamin Berg
Proofreader: Katie Tennant
Technical proofreader: Vladimir Kuptsov
Typesetter: Gordan Salinovic
Illustrator: April Milne
Cover designer: Marija Tudor

ISBN 9781633430099
Printed in the United States of America
1 2 3 4 5 6 7 8 9 10 – EBM – 21 20 19 18 17 16

brief contents

contents

foreword

Until four years ago, every major web application that I had written used the tried-and-trusted thread-per-request execution model. A few niche applications that I had been involved with—a chat server and a push notification system—may have used some form of evented I/O, but I would have laughed at the suggestion that that model should be used for general web development. At that time in our industry's history, the word "reactive" was virtually unheard-of.

The switch to reactive applications has been the biggest architectural change since the web itself, and it has swept across our industry at lightning speed. What I considered far-fetched four years ago, I now use every day, and I am lead developer of Play, a framework that embraces it. With the concept evolving from relative obscurity to mainstream best practice in such a short time, it's no wonder that countless web developers are asking the question, "What is reactive?" This is where *Reactive Web Applications* perfectly fills a gap.

Beginning with addressing the question of why we need reactive in the first place, Manuel takes you through the principles of reactive development as it applies to web applications, in the context of the practical grounding of the Play Framework, Akka, and Reactive Streams. You'll be guided through concrete examples and exercises, and you'll come away with a solid understanding of how reactive web applications are architected, developed, tested, and deployed, so you can try it out yourself.

The journey to reactive applications is one in which we're all continually learning. The Reactive Manifesto itself has undergone several revisions in the short time since my colleagues first penned it. Manuel and I have attended many conferences together, and we've chatted often in person and through our dealings in open source software about how reactive development should be realized in web applications. I'm glad to see that Manuel has so articulately captured these leading-edge best practices for web application development in this time of great change in our thinking. The practical application of this book to web development will put you in a great position to produce software for the high demands of today's world.

JAMES ROPER
LEAD DEVELOPER OF THE PLAY FRAMEWORK

preface

I first had the idea for this book in April 2014, after I'd spent the better part of four months assisting a client rebuild their entire application infrastructure using Scala, the Play Framework, and Akka, three technologies I'd already been using extensively for a few years.

The existing application faced two challenges that called for a rebuild: On one hand, the application data was spread across two separate database systems, a few caches, and a few external cloud services such as Amazon EC2, YouTube, SoundCloud, and Mixcloud, making it nearly impossible to keep the data up to date and in sync. On the other hand, the number of users had been increasing, and the flood of requests whenever a new campaign was launched had started to overwhelm the system. It was almost unavailable under load. The new version of the application had to accommodate sudden bursts in traffic in its initial design. And to make things more interesting, the relaunch of the site not only involved migrating, reconsolidating, and updating the data of millions of users and tens of millions of items, but it had to happen over a single weekend.

This project is a perfect example of a new category of web applications—one that has gained increasing importance over the past few years. Reactive web applications need to be able to cope with a varying and potentially large numbers of requests, manage and provide access to large datasets, and communicate with several cloud services in real time. To make things more complicated, all of these tasks need to be carried out while withstanding the inevitable failures that occur in an increasingly complex networked environment. Gone are the days when all of a web application's data was hosted on the same computer or in the same data center—a scenario that often hid the true and messy nature of computer networks. Reactive web applications rely heavily on heterogeneous and distributed services, but paradoxically the margin for user-facing errors is smaller than ever. The tolerance of today's typical user is close to zero. Everyone is used to the service reliability of giants such as Google or Facebook, unaware of the tremendous technical challenges faced by the engineers building and operating these platforms.

Building reactive web applications is no small feat, and it wouldn't be possible without the advances in technology we've witnessed over the past few years. Reactive technologies enable asynchronous programming coupled with first-class failure handling. The Play Framework and the Akka concurrency toolkit are two technologies that combine to offer a solid foundation for building reactive web applications. They both leverage the powerful functional programming concepts provided by the Scala programming language, enabling asynchronous and reactive programming.

This book aims to be a guide to using Scala, the Play Framework, Akka, and a few more powerful and exciting technologies to build reactive web applications. In one way, it's the book I wish I had when starting to work with this stack several years ago. I hope you'll find it useful and wish you a fun ride while reading it!

acknowledgments

You wouldn't be holding this book in your hands today if it weren't for the support, insights, inspiration, encouragement, and feedback from a whole lot of people. To everyone involved: thank you!

I'd first like to thank my friend Peter Brachwitz for the many interesting discussions around the technologies described in this book and for sharing with me his stories from the battlefield. Those meetings have been a continuous source of inspiration, fueling the examples in this book. We should keep on having them in the future!

I would also like to thank Rafael Cordones for kick-starting the Scala community in Vienna in 2013, as well as all the members of the Vienna Scala User Group for the entertaining meetups.

The example applications in this book make use of many technologies and libraries, and their use and related explanations wouldn't have been half as good had I not received help from their developers. Konrad Malawski from the Akka team was instrumental in improving the book's quality by pointing out mistakes and making me aware of best practices used by the Akka team. Lukas Eder, inventor of the jOOQ library, not only provided quick answers to my questions, but also provided useful feedback on all things database-related. Sébastien Doeraene, inventor of Scala.js, was always available to answer my questions about the technology and provided elegant solutions. I'd also like to thank Vincent Munier, author of the sbt-play-scalajs library, as well as Johannes Kastner, author of the scalajs-angulate library. Thanks to Marius Soutier, author of the play-angular-require-seed library, for his feedback and his insights into configuring the JavaScript optimization process with Play. Lastly, Clément Delafargue answered all my questions related to Clever Cloud and was kind enough to give me early access to its then-unreleased API for use in this book. And finally, special thanks to James Roper, lead developer of the Play Framework, for not only patiently answering all my questions and helping me anticipate the evolution in the technology that would affect the book, but also for kindly contributing the foreword and endorsing my book.

I'd also like to thank all the people at Manning who helped me write this book: Karen Miller, my development editor who patiently reviewed chapter after chapter, not minding that they were written in a creative derivation of the English language; Bert Bates, who taught me how to organize my mind for writing in a way useful to readers; acquisitions editor Mike Stephens, who suggested broadening the topic of the book to reactive web applications; and Candace Gillhoolley, for putting the word out there and continuously promoting the book. Finally, I'd also like to extend my thanks to all the people involved in getting this book to production: copyeditors Andy Carroll and Benjamin Berg; proofreader Katie Tennant; project editor David Novak; production manager Janet Vail; and all the other people who worked behind the scenes.

The book wouldn't have reached its current quality if it weren't for the reviewers who took the time to read early versions of the chapters and provide insightful feedback about what could be improved. I'd like to thank Antonio Magnaghi, Arsen Kudla, Changgeng Li, Christian Papauschek, Cole Davisson, David Pardo, David Torrubia, Erim Erturk, Jeff Smith, Jim Amrhein, Kevin Liao, Narayanan Jayaratchagan, Nhu Nguyen, Pat Wanjau, Ronald Cranston, Sergio Martinez, Sietse de Kaper, Steve Chaloner, Thomas Peklak, Unnikrishnan Kumar, Vladimir Kuptsov, Wil Moore III, William E. Wheeler, and Yuri Kushch. Many thanks as well to all the readers of the Early Access Program version, who commented on the Manning Author Forum, pointing out errors in the source code and telling me when something would simply not work: without you, it would have been much more difficult to get the example applications running.

Lastly to Veronika, my friend, partner, and wife: thank you for your support, patience, understanding, and love. This book, as well as so many of my other projects, would not have been remotely possible without your help.

about this book

This book will introduce you to building reactive web applications using the Scala programming language, the Play Framework, and the Akka concurrency toolkit. The Play Framework is now a very popular web framework on the JVM, but few projects take full advantage of its strength and take the necessary steps to make a web application reactive. That's because the steps involved aren't obvious, nor are the advantages. Similarly, Akka is a technology that many developers know of, but they don't always know how to employ it in their projects. This book aims to remedy this situation by showing how these technologies can be used in practice and in combination. The book introduces the conceptual foundation for asynchronous, reactive programming using futures and actors, and it demonstrates how you can configure an application and integrate other technologies to build real-life projects.

Who should read this book

To get the most out of this book, you should be a seasoned programmer and be well acquainted with at least one modern language such as Java or C#. Furthermore, you should know enough about the syntax and main concepts of Scala to read the examples in the book and implement the exercises. Knowledge of functional programming isn't required but is of advantage. Appendix B contains a list of references that you can use to get up to speed with Scala and functional programming.

Given that this book is mainly about building web applications, it's assumed that you know the basics of HTML and JavaScript and are familiar with the Model-View-Controller (MVC) paradigm that most modern web application frameworks use.

Roadmap

Part 1 of this book will teach you the fundamentals of functional programming, on top of which you can build asynchronous applications, as well as the basics of the Play Framework.

Chapter 1 explains why we need reactive web applications. It discusses how the architecture of web applications has evolved and how the concept of reactive web applications came to be.

Chapter 2 throws you into the deep end of reactive web application development. You'll set up the necessary tools to bootstrap your first reactive Play project, and you'll build an asynchronous stream-processing pipeline for the Twitter filter API, resulting in a myriad of tweets being displayed in your browser via a WebSocket connection. By the end of this chapter, you should have a much better idea of what it means to write a reactive web application.

Chapter 3 introduces basic concepts of functional programming that we'll use throughout the book. It introduces immutability, functions, and higher-order functions, and shows how you can use these concepts to manipulate immutable collections much as you'll manipulate asynchronous values further on.

Chapter 4 provides a quick but complete and self-contained introduction to the Play Framework. You'll build a bare-bones Play application, setting up each of the files by hand to get familiar with the structure and the configuration. Along the way, we'll take a peek under the hood to see how Play's request handling is truly reactive.

Part 2 of this book explains the concepts at the core of reactive web applications.

Chapter 5 introduces futures, a key concept used to manipulate and combine short-lived asynchronous computations. First we'll look at the theory behind futures, and then we'll look at how you can design business logic with futures to make it asynchronous and fault tolerant.

Chapter 6 introduces actors, a key concept for modeling long-lived asynchronous computations. You'll see how Akka implements the actor model to provide supervision and recovery, and how it can be used to build applications capable of reacting to failure and to sudden shifts in load.

Chapter 7 demonstrates how you can apply futures and actors to deal with state in a stateless application—that is, in an application where each application node may disappear or reappear at any given time. It explores how you can integrate traditional RDBMSs with a reactive Play application without losing the advantages of the reactive paradigm. Finally, it introduces the Command and Query Responsibility Segregation (CQRS) pattern in combination with Event Sourcing, which is an architectural pattern used for large-scale data handling in reactive applications.

Chapter 8 takes you on a tour of responsive user interface development using Scala.js, enabling you to write Scala for the browser. It shows how you can use existing JavaScript libraries, such as AngularJS, and integrate arbitrary libraries for which there isn't yet any integration with Scala.js. This chapter also points out what precautions need to be taken on the client side to cater to the reactive nature of the application.

Part 3 introduces advanced topics related to building reactive web applications.

Chapter 9 introduces Reactive Streams, a new standard for asynchronous and failure-tolerant stream manipulation on the JVM. You'll see how you can use the Akka implementation of this standard, Akka Streams, to access, split, and filter the Twitter streaming API.

Chapter 10 covers the deployment of reactive Play applications using different approaches. You'll see how you can roll your own deployment using the Jenkins continuous integration server and Docker, and alternatively how to use the managed deployment service Clever Cloud to deploy a simple reactive application.

Chapter 11 explores the aspects of the application that can be tested, and how testing a reactive web application differs from testing a non-reactive one, putting the focus on concerns such as load handling and failure handling. In this chapter you'll see how to make use of the autoscaling capability of Clever Cloud to handle increased service load reactively.

Code conventions and downloads

The source code for the listings in the book can be found on GitHub at https://github.com/manuelbernhardt/reactive-web-applications. Most chapters contain an application that can be executed, and the source code of the final application (including the resolution of any exercises in the chapter) can be found in separate directories, ready to be executed. (You'll need to configure Twitter API credentials and database settings on your own.)

In addition to the full applications, the listings for each chapter can be found in the listings directory.

Author Online

Purchase of *Reactive Web Applications* includes free access to a private web forum run by Manning Publications, where you can make comments about the book, ask technical questions, and receive help from the author and from other users. To access the forum and subscribe to it, point your web browser to http://www.manning.com/books/reactive-web-applications. This page provides information on how to get on the forum once you are registered, what kind of help is available, and the rules of conduct on the forum.

Manning's commitment to our readers is to provide a venue where a meaningful dialog between individual readers and between readers and the author can take place. It is not a commitment to any specific amount of participation on the part of the author, whose contribution to the forum remains voluntary (and unpaid). We suggest you try asking the author some challenging questions lest his interest stray!

The Author Online forum and the archives of previous discussions will be accessible from the publisher's website as long as the book is in print.

About the author

Manuel Bernhardt is a passionate engineer, author, speaker, and consultant with a keen interest in the science of building and operating networked applications. Since 2008, he has guided and trained enterprise teams on the transition to distributed computing. In recent years, he has focused primarily on production systems that embrace the reactive application architecture, using Scala, the Play Framework, and Akka to this end.

Manuel likes to travel and is a frequent speaker at international conferences. He lives in Vienna where he is a co-organizer of the Vienna Scala User Group. Next to thinking, talking about, and fiddling with computers, he likes to spend time with his family, run, scuba dive, and read. You can find out more about Manuel's recent work at http://manuel.bernhardt.io.

about the cover illustration

The figure on the cover of *Reactive Web Applications* is captioned "Chamanne Bratsquienne," or a shaman from the city of Bratsk in Russia. A shaman is a spiritual healer. The illustration is taken from a collection of dress costumes from various countries by Jacques Grasset de Saint-Sauveur (1757–1810), titled *Costumes de Différents Pays,* published in France in 1797. Each illustration is finely drawn and colored by hand. The rich variety of Grasset de Saint-Sauveur's collection reminds us vividly of how culturally apart the world's towns and regions were just 200 years ago. Isolated from each other, people spoke different dialects and languages. In the streets or in the countryside, it was easy to identify where they lived and what their trade or station in life was just by their dress.

The way we dress has changed since then and the diversity by region, so rich at the time, has faded away. It is now hard to tell apart the inhabitants of different continents, let alone different towns, regions, or countries. Perhaps we have traded cultural diversity for a more varied personal life—certainly for a more varied and fast-paced technological life.

At a time when it is hard to tell one computer book from another, Manning celebrates the inventiveness and initiative of the computer business with book covers based on the rich diversity of regional life of two centuries ago, brought back to life by Grasset de Saint-Sauveur's pictures.

Part 1

Getting started with reactive web applications

This part of the book will get you started with reactive web applications by providing you with the foundation you need to understand the concepts discussed later in the book. You'll learn how reactive web applications came to be and why they matter, and then you'll get your hands dirty by building a simple reactive web application. You'll also get a quick introduction to the concepts behind functional programming as well as to the Play Framework, should you not be familiar with those topics already.

1 Did you say reactive?

This chapter covers

- Reactive applications and their origin
- Why reactive applications are necessary
- How Play helps you build reactive applications

Over the past few years, web applications have started to take an increasingly important role in our lives. Be it large applications such as social networks, medium-sized ones such as e-banking sites, or smaller ones such as online accounting systems or project management tools for small businesses, our dependency on these services is clearly growing. This trend is now transitioning to physical devices, and the information technology research and advisory firm Gartner predicts that the Internet of Things will grow to an installed base of 26 billion units by 2020.[1]

Reactive web applications are an answer to the new requirements of high availability and resource efficiency brought by this rapid evolution. Cloud computing and the subsequent emergence of cloud services have shifted web application development from an activity wherein one application tries to solve all kinds of

[1] Gartner, "Gartner Says the Internet of Things Installed Base Will Grow to 26 Billion Units By 2020" (December 12, 2013), www.gartner.com/newsroom/id/2636073.

problems to a process of identifying and connecting to adequate cloud services and only solving those problems that have not been solved beforehand satisfactorily.

We need a new set of tools to help us efficiently deal with the challenges that come with this evolution. The Play Framework has been designed from the ground up to make it possible to build reactive web applications that are capable of providing real-time behavior to users even under high load and in a decentralized setting. At the time of this writing, Play is the only full-stack reactive web application framework available on the Java virtual machine. Embraced by large companies such as Morgan Stanley, LinkedIn, and The Guardian, as well as many smaller players, Play is available as free, open source software, ready to be downloaded to your computer.

In this chapter, we'll look into what reactive web applications are, why you'd want to build such applications, and why the Play Framework is a good tool for this purpose. We'll start by disambiguating the meaning of the word "reactive" and look into how new trends in hardware design and software architecture call for a reconsideration of how to use computational resources. Finally, we'll explore why failure handling plays a crucial role in this context, and how it can be achieved.

1.1 Putting reactive into context

If you're reading this book, chances are that you've heard of concepts such as reactive applications, reactive programming, reactive streams, or the Reactive Manifesto. Even though we can probably agree that all those terms sound a lot more exciting when prepended with *reactive*, you may wonder what *reactive* means in those different contexts. Let's find out by looking at the origins of the word in relation to computer systems.

1.1.1 Origins of reactive

The concept of reactive systems isn't new. In their paper "On the Development of Reactive Systems"[2] (published in 1985), David Harel and Amir Pnueli round up several dichotomies to characterize complex computer systems and propose a novel dichotomy: *transformative* versus *reactive* systems. Transformative systems accept a known set of inputs, transform those inputs, and produce outputs. For example, a transformative system may prompt the user for some input, and then for some more, depending on what the user provided, to finally provide a result. Think, for example, of a pocket calculator, which accepts numbers and performs basic operations to finally return a result when the equals key is pressed. Reactive systems, on the other hand, are continuously stimulated by the external environment, and their role is to continuously respond to these stimuli. For example, a wifi-enabled camera with motion-detection capabilities may notice a burglar enter a room and send an alert to the camera owner's mobile phone, letting them witness helplessly their room being emptied of its precious belongings, as well as later on, the police arriving on the scene.

[2] A PDF version of the article is available at http://mng.bz/p1n3.

A few years later, Gérard Berry refined this definition by introducing the distinction between *interactive* and reactive programs. Whereas interactive programs set the speed at which they interact with the environment themselves, reactive programs are capable of interacting with the environment at the speed dictated by the environment.[3]

Thus, reactive programs

- Are available to continuously interact with their environment
- Run at a speed that is dictated by the environment, not the program itself
- Work in response to external demand

Coming back to present times, the preceding modus operandi of reactive programs looks a lot like how web applications operate or should be operating. Though appealing in theory, it takes quite some effort to fulfill these criteria, and possibly serious hardware resources, depending on the number of users and the nature of what they demand. It's perhaps the lack of widespread high-performance hardware capable of delivering real-time interaction at scale that explains why we haven't heard much of reactive systems until recently, when a set of core aspects that characterize reactive systems were published under the name *Reactive Manifesto*.

1.1.2 The Reactive Manifesto

The first version of the Reactive Manifesto was published in June 2013, and it describes a software architecture with the name *Reactive Applications*. Reactive applications are defined by a set of characteristics, or *traits* as they're called in the manifesto (those traits have nothing to do with Scala's `traits`), that altogether make up for applications that behave in the same way as the reactive programs we talked about earlier: continuously available and readily responding to external demand. Although the Reactive Manifesto may seem like it's describing an entirely new architectural pattern, its core principles have long been known in industries that require real-time behavior from their IT systems, such as financial trading.

The following four traits make up reactive applications:

- *Responsive*—React to users
- *Scalable*—React to load
- *Resilient*—React to failure
- *Event-driven*—React to events

A *responsive* application will satisfy the user's expectations in terms of availability and real-time behavior. Real-time, or near real-time, means that the application will respond within a short or very short time. The time interval between the request and response is called *latency*, and it's one of the key measurements when it comes to assessing how well a system performs.

---

[3] Gérard Berry, "Real-Time Programming: General Purpose or Special-Purpose Languages," *Information Processing* 89 (Elsevier Science Publishers, 1989): 11-18.

In order to continuously interact with their environment, reactive applications must be able to adjust to the load they're facing. Sudden traffic bursts may affect an application; for example, a popular tweet with a link to a news article could cause a rush on a news website. To this end, an application must be *scalable*: it must be able to make use of increased computational capacity when necessary. This means it must be able to make efficient use of the hardware on a single machine (which may have one or more CPU cores), and also be able to function across several computation nodes at its disposal, depending on the load.

NOTE We use the term "computation node" or simply "node" to refer to a resource on which a web application runs. In practice, this may be a physical computer, a virtual machine, or even a logical node on a Platform-as-a-Service provider.

Because even the simplest of software systems are prone to failure (whether software-related or hardware-related), reactive applications need to be *resilient to failure* to meet the demand of continuous availability. The capability of an application to get back on its feet should it encounter a problem is arguably even more important when it comes to scalable systems, which are more complex in nature and distributed, because the likeliness of hardware or network failure is increased.

Event-driven applications based on *asynchronous* communication can help you achieve the previously listed traits. In this setup, the system (or subsystem) reacts to discrete events such as HTTP requests without monopolizing computational resources as it waits for an event to occur. This natural level of concurrency yields better latency than traditional synchronous method calls. Another consequence of writing event-driven programs is that components are loosely coupled, making the software much more maintainable in the longer term.

1.1.3 Reactive programming

Reactive programming is a programming paradigm based on data flows and the propagation of changes. Consider, for example, the spreadsheet represented in table 1.1.

The cell `C1` is defined programmatically in the following way:

```
= A1 * B1
```

Table 1.1 A simple spreadsheet demonstrating the concept of reactive programming

	A	B	C
1	6	7	42
2			
3			

If we were to run the preceding example in spreadsheet software, as soon as either the value of `A1` or `B1` was changed, the result in `C1` would change accordingly. The programming language behind the spreadsheet thus allows us to define relations between the data that result in the propagation of changes across the spreadsheet.

In order to implement a real-time spreadsheet application, such as the one in Google Drive, we'd build on top of lower-level concepts such as events: when the user changes the value of cell `A1`, an event is fired. All the cells interested in the content of `A1`, such as cell `C1` containing our expression, would act on this event by reevaluating themselves and displaying a new value. This process is entirely hidden from the user, who is only concerned with describing the high-level relation among cell values.

In terms of web application development, this technique is increasingly being used for front-end application development: tools such as KnockoutJS, AngularJS, Meteor, and React.js all make use of this paradigm. The developers only need to describe how changes in the data propagate through the user interface; they don't need to concern themselves with the nitty-gritty details of declaring listeners on specific DOM elements, thus greatly simplifying how reactive user interfaces can be implemented. We'll look into reactive user interfaces in chapter 8.

Similar abstractions, wherein events play a central role, can also be found on the server side. A new initiative called *Reactive Streams*, which we'll talk more about in chapter 9, aims at providing a standard interface for working with asynchronous stream processing on the JVM.

1.1.4 The emergence of reactive technologies

Over the years, a number of technologies and frameworks have been developed that share common aspects and can be broadly classified as reactive technologies. Building reactive applications takes more than simply using reactive technologies, as you'll see later, but technologies must satisfy a number of prerequisites to enable reactive behavior, most notably the capacity for *asynchronous* and *event-driven* code execution.

Microsoft's Reactive Extensions (Rx; https://rx.codeplex.com/) is a library for composing asynchronous and event-based programs, available on the .NET platform and other platforms such as JavaScript. Node.js (http://nodejs.org) is a popular platform for building asynchronous, event-driven applications in JavaScript. On the JVM, a number of libraries enable these capabilities, such as Apache MINA (https://mina.apache.org) and Netty (http://netty.io).

Those low-level technologies all offer basic tools for building asynchronous and event-driven applications, but it takes a bit more work to get to the state of a full-blown web application that also has to deal with concerns such as code organization, view templates, inclusion and organization of client-side resources such as stylesheets and JavaScript files, database connectivity, security, and so on. Many so-called full-stack web application frameworks exist, but few of them also include reactive technologies, and very few are built from the ground up using reactive technologies, embracing reactive principles at their core. Full-stack frameworks concern themselves with all the layers required to build and deploy an application: client-side UI technology (or a means to integrate it), server-side business logic, authentication, integration of database access, and various libraries for the most common tasks (such as remote web service calls). In a reactive application, all these layers must furthermore cooperate by following the same principles of asynchronous communication and error recovery.

On the JVM, the only mature full-stack reactive web application framework to this day is the Play Framework. Other full-stack frameworks such as Lift (http://liftweb.net) provide a good alternative for building web applications, but they haven't been designed with asynchronicity, failure resilience, and scalability as primary goals.

Play is built on top of Netty and leverages its reactive behavior by using asynchronous stream handling provided by *Reactive Streams* (see figure 1.1).

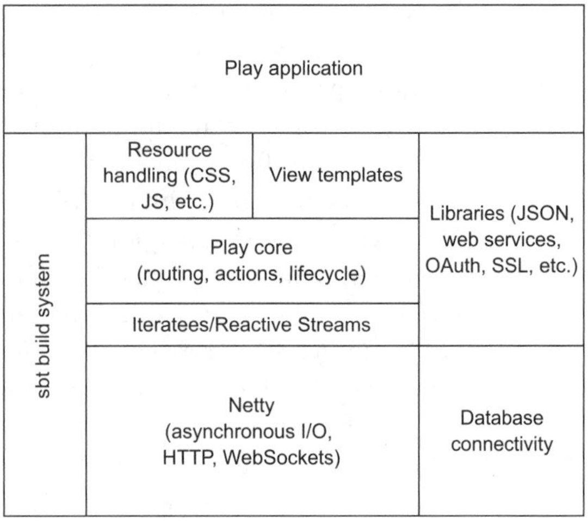

Play application
sbt build system
Resource handling (CSS, JS, etc.)
View templates
Libraries (JSON, web services, OAuth, SSL, etc.)
Play core (routing, actions, lifecycle)
Iteratees/Reactive Streams
Netty (asynchronous I/O, HTTP, WebSockets)
Database connectivity

Figure 1.1 High-level architecture of the Play Framework

Play deals with the typical concerns of web application development such as client-side resource handling, project compilation, and packaging by making use of the sbt build tool. It comes with a number of useful libraries to address common concerns such as JSON handling and web service access and offers access to databases though a range of plugins. Throughout the rest of this book, you'll learn how to use the Play Framework as an effective tool to build reactive web applications.

Let's now take a closer look at how web applications work and how they make use of computational resources to understand why the asynchronous, event-driven behavior of reactive web applications is necessary.

1.2 Rethinking computational resource utilization

To understand the why and how of reactive applications, we need to take a quick look at computers. They have certainly evolved a lot over the past decades, especially in terms of CPU clock speed (MHz to GHz) and memory (kilobytes to gigabytes). The most significant change, however, which has happened in the past few years, is that although the clock speed of CPUs isn't increasing very much, the number of cores each CPU has is changing. At the time of writing, most computers have at least 4 CPU cores, and there are already vendors offering CPUs with 1024 cores. On the other hand, the overall architecture of computers and the mechanism by which programs are executed haven't undergone a significant evolution, so some of the limitations of this architecture, such as the *von Neumann bottleneck*,[4] become more of a problem nowadays. To understand how this evolution affects web application development, let's take a look at the two most popular web server architectures.

[4] John Backus, "Can programming be liberated from the von Neumann style? A functional style and its algebra of programs," *Communications of the ACM* 21 (8) (August 1978): 613-41.

1.2.1 Threaded versus evented web application servers

Roughly speaking, there are two categories of programming models in which web servers can be placed. In the *threaded* model, large numbers of threads take care of handling the incoming requests. In an *evented* model, a small number of request-processing threads communicate with each other through message passing. Reactive web application servers adopt the evented model.

THREADED SERVERS

A threaded server, such as Apache Tomcat, can be imagined as a train station with multiple platforms.[5] The station chief (acceptor thread) decides which trains (HTTP requests) go on which platform (request processing threads). There can be as many trains at the same time as there are platforms. Figure 1.2 illustrates how a threaded web server processes HTTP requests.

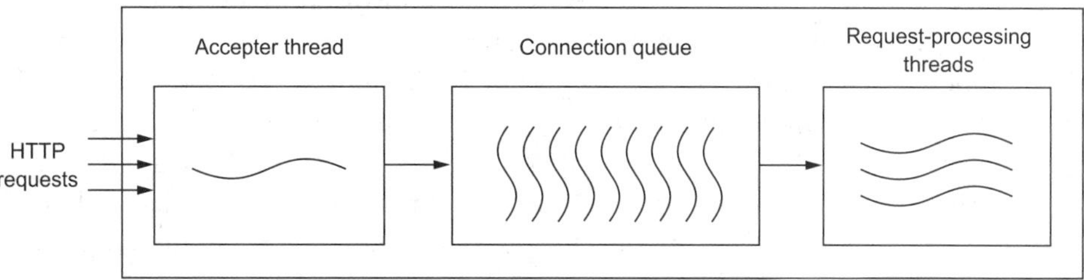

Figure 1.2 Threaded web server

As implied by the name, threaded web servers rely on using many threads as well as on queuing. The analogy between trains and threaded web application servers is depicted in table 1.2.

Table 1.2 Imagining threaded web application servers as train stations

Train station	Threaded server
More trains come in than there are platforms; trains have to queue up and wait.	More HTTP requests reach the server than there are worker threads; users connecting to the application have to wait.
Trains hanging around at the platform for too long may be cancelled.	HTTP requests taking too long to process are cancelled; the user may see a page with *HTTP Error 408 - Request timeout.*
Too many trains queuing up in the station can cause huge delays and passengers to go home.	Too many requests queuing up can cause users to leave the site.

5 See Julian Doherty, "How Your Web Server Works," http://madlep.com/How-your-web-server-works-/.

EVENTED SERVERS

To explain how evented servers work, let's take the example of a waiter in a restaurant.

A waiter can take orders from several customers and pass them on to multiple chefs in the kitchen. The waiter will divide their time between the different tasks at hand and not spend too much time on a single task. They don't need to deal with the whole order at once: first come the drinks, then the entrees, later the main course, and finally dessert and an espresso. As a result, a waiter can effectively and efficiently serve many tables at once.

As I write this book, Play is built on top of Netty. When building an application with Play, developers implement the behavior of the chefs that cook up the response, rather than the behavior of the waiters, which is already provided by Play.

The mechanism of an evented web server is shown in figure 1.3.

In an evented web server, incoming requests are sliced and diced into events that represent the various smaller pieces of work involved in handling the whole request, such as parsing the request body, retrieving a file from disk, or making a call to another web service. The slicing and dicing is done by *event handlers*, which may trigger I/O actions, resulting in new events later on. Say, for example, that you wanted to issue a request for the size of a file on the web server. In this case, the event handler dealing with the request will make an asynchronous call to the disk. When the operating system is done figuring out the size of the file, it emits an interrupt, which results in a new event. When it's the turn of that event to be handled, you'll get a response with the size. While the operating system is taking care of figuring out the size of the file, the event loop can process other events in the queue.

One important implication of the evented programming model is that the time spent on tasks needs to be small. If a chef insisted on cooking the whole order when a waiter simply wanted to place it, there would be many angry unserved customers once the waiter finally got back from the kitchen. The evented model only works if the entire pipeline is *asynchronous*: orders, or HTTP requests, are processed without *blocking*. The term *nonblocking I/O* is often used to refer to input-output operations that don't hold up the current execution thread while doing their work, but instead send a notification when the work is done.

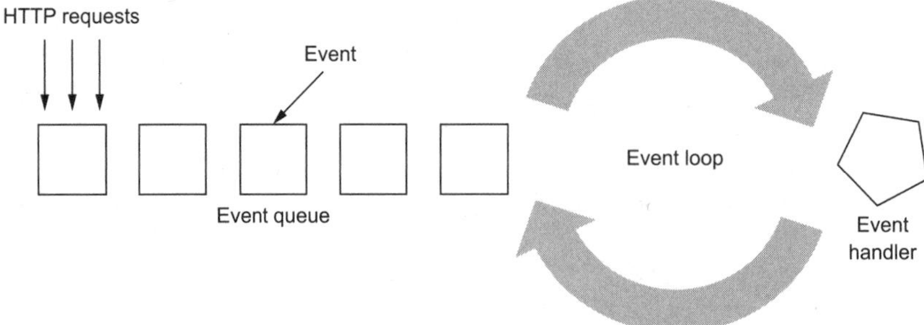

Figure 1.3 Evented web server

MEMORY UTILIZATION IN THREADED AND EVENTED WEB SERVERS

Evented web servers make much better use of hardware resources than threaded ones. Instead of having to spawn thousands or tens of thousands of "train track" worker threads to deal with large numbers of incoming requests, only a few "waiter" threads are necessary. There are two advantages to working with a smaller number of threads: reduced memory footprint and much improved performance due to reduced context switching, thread management time, and scheduling overhead.

Each thread created on the JVM has its own stack space, which is by default 1 MB. The default thread pool size of Apache Tomcat is 200, which means that Apache Tomcat needs to be assigned over 200 MB of memory in order to start. In contrast, you can run a simple Play application with 16 MB of memory. And although 200 MB may not seem like a lot of memory these days, let's not forget that this means that 200 MB are required to process 200 incoming HTTP requests at the same time, without taking into account the memory necessary to perform additional tasks involved in handling these requests. If you wanted to cater to 10,000 requests at the same time, you'd need a lot of memory, which may not always be readily available. The threaded model has difficulty scaling up to a larger number of concurrent users because of its demands on available memory.

In addition to utilizing a lot of memory, the threaded approach results in inefficient use of the CPU.

1.2.2 Developing web applications fit for multicore architectures

Threaded web servers rely on multiple thread pools to distribute the available CPU resources among incoming requests. This mechanism is mostly hidden from developers, letting developers work as though there were only one main thread. Arguably, developing against an abstraction that hides away the increased complexity of dealing with multiple threads may appear simpler at first. Indeed, programming contracts such as the Servlet API provide the illusion that there's only one main thread of execution answering an incoming HTTP request and all the resources in the world to answer it. But the reality is somewhat different, and this leaky abstraction brings its own set of drawbacks.[6]

SHARED MUTABLE STATE AND ASYNCHRONOUS PROGRAMMING

If you've built web applications served by a threaded server, chances are that you've found yourself facing the side effects of a race condition caused by the use of *shared mutable state*. Threads on the JVM, while running in parallel, do not run in isolation: they have access to the same memory space, open file handles, and other shared resources as other threads. One classic example of the problems caused by this behavior is a Java servlet making use of the `DateFormat` class:

```
private static final DateFormat dateFormatter = new SimpleDateFormat();
```

---

6 Joel Spolsky, "The Law of Leaky Abstractions," http://www.joelonsoftware.com/articles/LeakyAbstractions.html.

The problem with the preceding line is that `DateFormat` is not thread-safe. When called by two threads concurrently, it doesn't act differently depending on what thread is calling it, and makes use of the same variables to hold its internal state. This leads to unpredictable behavior and to bugs that are usually hard to understand and analyze. Even experienced developers spend a lot of time trying to understand race conditions, deadlocks, and other strange, funny, or despairing side effects brought about by this unfortunate situation. This isn't to say that applications written in an evented way are immune to the phenomenon of shared mutable state—for the most part, application developers decide whether or not to make use of mutable data structures and what level of exposition to give them. But the design of frameworks such as Play and languages such as Scala discourages developers from making use of shared mutable state.

LANGUAGE DESIGN AND IMMUTABLE STATE

Languages and tools favoring the use of immutable state make it easier to develop web applications that have to deal with concurrent access. The Scala programming language is designed to use immutable values by default, rather than mutable variables. Although it's possible to write programs in an immutable fashion in Java, a lot more boilerplate is involved than in Scala. For example, declaring an immutable value in Scala is done like this:

```
val theAnswer = 42
```

The same result would be achieved in Java by explicitly prepending the `final` keyword:

```
final int theAnswer = 42
```

This may seem like a minor difference, but over the course of writing a large application, it means that the `final` keyword needs to be used many, many times. When it comes to more-complex data structures, such as lists and maps, Scala provides these data structures in both their immutable and mutable versions, favoring the immutable one by default:

```
val a = List(1, 2, 3)
```

Java, on the other hand, doesn't provide immutable data structures in its collection library. You'd have to use third-party libraries such as Google's Guava library (https://github.com/google/guava) to get a useful set of immutable data structures.

LOCKS AND CONTENTION

To avoid the side effects caused by concurrent access to non-thread-safe resources, locks are used to let other threads know that a resource is currently busy. If all goes well, the thread holding the lock will release it and thus inform other possibly waiting threads that they may now access the resource in turn. In some situations, however, threads may wait for one another to release a lock and be stuck in a *deadlock*. If a thread holds on to a resource for too long, this may cause resource *starvation* from the viewpoint of

> **The Scala programming language**
>
> One of the main design goals of the Scala programming language is to enable developers to tackle the complexity of programming multicore and distributed systems. It does so by favoring immutable values and data structures over mutable ones, providing functions and higher-order functions as first-class citizens of the language, as well as easing the use of an expression-oriented programming style. For this reason, this book's examples are written in Scala rather than Java. (It should, however, be noted that Play, Akka, and Reactive Streams all have Java APIs.) We'll review the core concepts of functional programming with Scala in chapter 3.

other threads. When the load on a web application that relies on locks surges, it isn't unusual to observe *lock contention*, which results in decreased performance for the whole application.

The new many-core architecture that CPU vendors have moved toward doesn't make locks look any better. If a CPU offers over 1,000 real threads of execution, but the application relies on locks to synchronize access to a few regions in memory, one can only imagine how much performance loss this mechanism will entail. There is a clear need for a programming model that better suits the multithread and multicore paradigm.

THE APPARENT COMPLEXITY OF ASYNCHRONOUS PROGRAMMING

For a long time, writing asynchronous programs hasn't been popular among developers because it can seem more difficult than writing good old synchronous programs. Instead of the ordered sequence of operations in a synchronous program, a request-handling procedure may end up being split into several pieces when written in an asynchronous fashion.

One of the popular ways of writing asynchronous code is to make use of callbacks. Because the program's flow of execution isn't blocked when waiting for an operation to complete (such as retrieving data from a remote web service), the developer needs to implement a callback method that's executed once the data is available. Proponents of the threaded programming model would argue that when the processing is a bit more complicated, this leads to a style of code known as "callback hell."

Listing 1.1 Example of nested callbacks in JavaScript

```
var fetchPriceList = function() {
    $.get('/items', function(items) {
        var priceList = [];
        items.forEach(function(item, itemIndex) {
            $.get('/prices', { itemId: item.id }, function(price) {
                priceList.push({ item: item, price: price });
                if ( priceList.length == items.length ) {
```

The main function composes a list of items and their prices.

First callback function handles the retrieval of the items

Second callback function is called for each item

Third callback method handles the retrieval of the price of one item

```
                return priceList;
            }
        }).fail(function() {
            priceList.push({ item: item });
            if ( priceList.length == items.length ) {
                return priceList;
            }
        });
    }
}).fail(function() {
    alert("Could not retrieve items");
});
}
```

Fourth callback method performs error handling when a price can't be retrieved

Fifth callback method performs error handling if the items can't be retrieved

It's easy to imagine that if you had to retrieve data from more sources, the level of callback nesting would be further increased and the code harder to understand and maintain. There are dozens of articles about callback hell and even one domain name (http://callbackhell.com) dedicated to this issue, and it's often encountered in larger Node.js (http://nodejs.org) applications.

But writing asynchronous applications doesn't need to be that hard. Callbacks, for all of their merits, are an abstraction that's too low-level to write complex asynchronous flows. JavaScript is only slowly catching up on tools and abstractions enabling a more human approach to asynchronous programming, but languages such as Scala have been designed with these abstractions in mind, leveraging well-known functional programming principles that make it possible to approach the problem from a different angle.

NOVEL WAYS OF WRITING ASYNCHRONOUS PROGRAMS

Tools inspired by functional programming concepts, such as Java 8 lambdas or Scala's first-order functions, greatly simplify the handling of multiple callbacks (as compared to the rather meager options that the JavaScript language provides). On top of this tooling built into the programming languages, abstractions such as *futures* and *actors* are powerful means to write and compose asynchronous request-handling pipelines, largely eliminating the phenomenon of callback hell.

Switching from an imperative, synchronous style of writing applications to a more functional and asynchronous style doesn't happen overnight. We'll discuss the tools, techniques, and mental model of asynchronous programming in chapters 3 and 5.

By adopting an evented request-handling model, Play can make much better use of a computer's resources. But what happens if, despite having an extremely performant request-processing pipeline, you hit the hardware limits of your server? Let's find out how Play can help you *scale horizontally* to several servers.

1.2.3 The horizontal application architecture

When developing a web application, a few fundamental choices have to be made that have a profound impact on how the web application can be operated. Unfortunately, web applications are often developed without considering what happens to the application after the code has been shipped and deployed on the production server. This can lead to profound limitations, such as when it comes to running the application on more than just one computer. If the application wasn't designed for this operational mode from the start, chances are that it won't be practicable to run it this way without significant changes to the code. In the following discussion, we'll explore a few deployment models and consider their benefits and disadvantages. We'll also look at the advantages of the so-called *horizontal deployment model* enabled and embraced by reactive applications.

SINGLE-SERVER DEPLOYMENTS

The single-server deployment is a very common deployment model. Web applications are deployed on a single computer, and often the database is deployed on that same computer, as shown in figure 1.4.

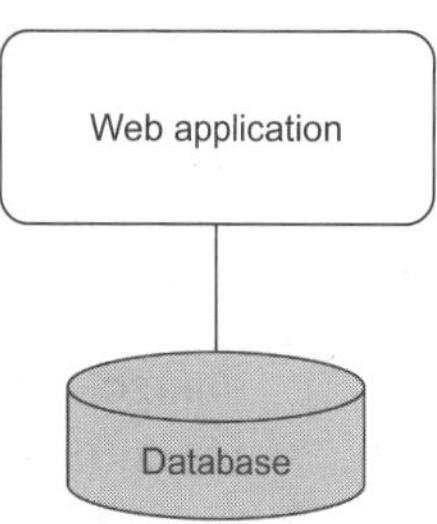

Figure 1.4 Traditional application deployment model

This deployment is widely used because of its relative simplicity, but it comes with a few important limitations. When the load on the server exceeds the capabilities of the hardware, or when the hardware fails, or when security or application upgrades need to be installed, the unavoidable result is that the application becomes unavailable. The usage load that this kind of setup can handle depends to a great extent on the hardware—when there's a need for more performance, a more powerful computer with more memory and faster CPUs is necessary. The process of increasing the load a server can handle by switching to more performant hardware is called *vertical scaling*.

REPLICATED DEPLOYMENTS

For applications that need better availability or performance, a popular setup involves *replication* of the data across two computers, as shown in figure 1.5.

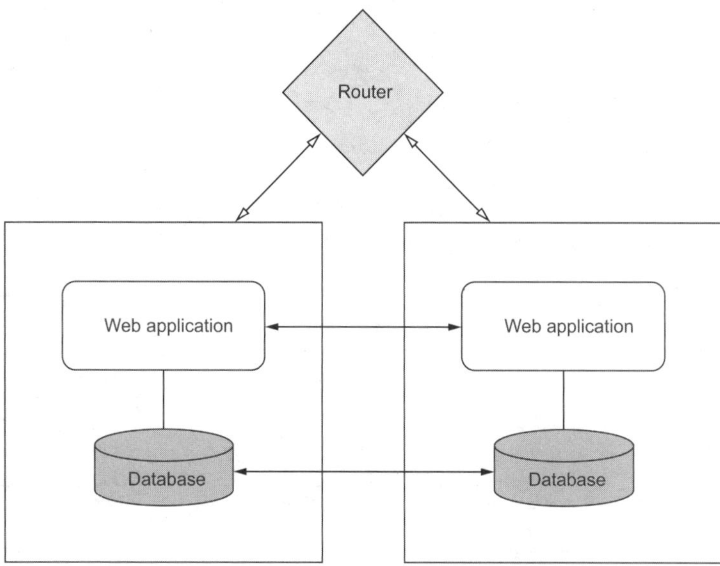

Figure 1.5 Replicated application deployment model

In this kind of setup, both the database and the server-side state, such as server-side user sessions or caches, need to be replicated (by making use of Apache Tomcat's clustering capabilities or similar functionality). On the database level, master-to-master replication can be employed. This solution makes it possible to update one deployment after another, thus allowing uptime during upgrades. But the complexity involved in correctly configuring this kind of setup more often than not limits the number of replicas to two. From a developer's perspective, the web application is still developed as though it were running on a single computer, and the underlying framework or application server takes care of replicating server-side state.

The complexity inherent in a multi-machine setup isn't eliminated but instead pushed to the application server. This makes it more difficult to deal with error states elegantly (without annoying the user too much), given that the error happens at a different level than the application itself and isn't a first-class concern of the application.

HORIZONTAL DEPLOYMENTS

In a horizontal architecture, as shown in figure 1.6, the same version of the web application is deployed across many nodes.

Those nodes may be physical computers or virtual machines, and an important characteristic about them is that they don't know anything about each other and don't share any state. This *share-nothing* principle is at the core of so-called *stateless* architectures, wherein each node is self-contained, and its presence or absence doesn't affect other nodes in any way (except, perhaps, with increased or decreased load, depending on the traffic). The advantage of such an architecture is that the application can be scaled easily by adding new nodes to a front end router, and rolling updates can be performed by bringing up new nodes with the new version and then switching the

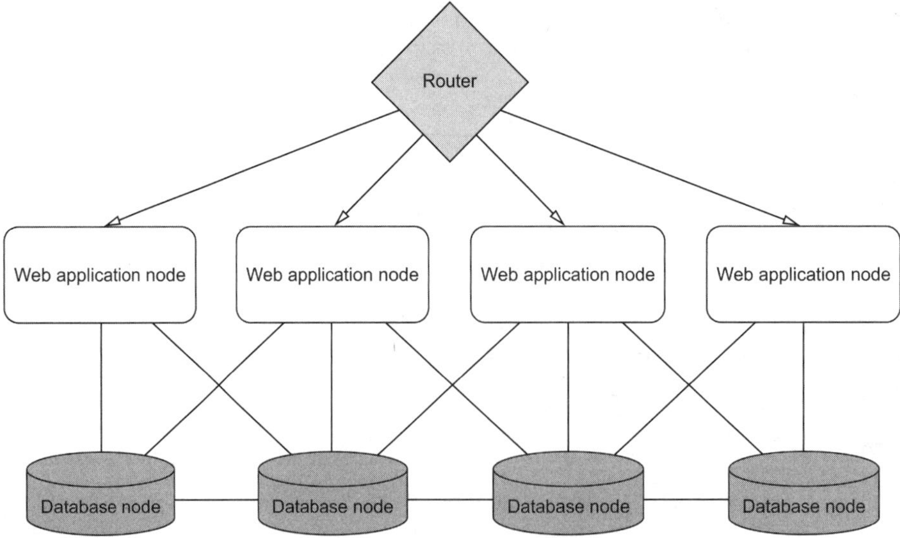

Figure 1.6 Horizontal architecture model

routing layer to point to those new nodes. These so-called *hot redeploy* mechanisms are popular with Platform-as-a-Service (PaaS) providers such as Heroku.

On the storage layer, a good counterpart to a share-nothing web application layer is a storage technology that supports some form of clustering. NoSQL databases such as MongoDB, Cassandra, Couchbase, and new versions of relational databases (such as WebScaleSQL; http://webscalesql.org) are a good fit for such scalable front end layers.

One consequence of using a horizontal architecture is that a user may be connected randomly to one of the front end nodes by the routing layer instead of always ending up on the same node. Given that there's no shared state between nodes, a server-side session (the default in the Servlet Standard and in frameworks built on top of it) can't be used. The Play Framework embraces the share-nothing philosophy at its core and provides a client-side user session based on cookies, which we'll talk about in chapter 8.

Thanks to its low memory footprint, Play is also a good candidate for multi-node deployments through PaaS or on other cloud-based platforms, where the amount of memory available to a single node is typically much lower than on a dedicated server.

1.3 Failure-handling as first-class concern

When the New York Stock Exchange (NYSE) opened at 9:30 AM on August 1, 2012, the automatic trading software of the Knight Capital Group (KCG) started trading stocks automatically, as it had been built to do and had done for many years. A few days earlier, a new version of the application had been rolled out on the servers, enabling customers of the company to participate in the Retail Liquidation Program at the NYSE. But on this August 1, things would be a little different: in the 45 minutes from when the market opened until it was shut down, the application generated a loss of 440 million USD. Oops.[7]

Building applications that don't fail is extremely difficult, and if those applications are meant to be built at a reasonable pace it's close to impossible. Instead of avoiding failure, reactive systems are designed and built from the ground up to embrace failure, leveraging the principle of *supervision*, which if employed might have prevented the fate of KCG. Reactive systems detect failure on their own and spring back into shape automatically, or degrade in such a way as to minimize catastrophic failure.

To cope with failure up front, it's important to understand what can go wrong. Let's look a bit closer at why failure is inevitable (you may not be convinced just yet that this is the case) and at what techniques can be used to cope with it.

1.3.1 Failure is inevitable

Unlike the development teams of the onboard shuttle group, which built the software that ran the space shuttles at a rate of a few lines of code per day,[8] most development

---

[7] Doug Seven, "Knightmare: A DevOps Cautionary Tale," http://dougseven.com/2014/04/17/knightmare-a-devops-cautionary-tale.

[8] Charles Fishman, "They Write the Right Stuff" (December 31, 1996), http://www.fastcompany.com/28121/they-write-right-stuff.

teams will produce software that contains errors (and hopefully, at a higher rate of lines of code per day). Even when employing test-driven development methodologies and achieving a perfect code coverage score, chances are that the software will not be entirely error-free. Applications fail because of human mistakes all the time, and increasing software quality is an iterative process. The difficulty of building failure-tolerant applications is increased many times when it comes to distributed systems running on different computers.

At the ACM Symposium on the Principles of Distributed Computing in July 2000, Eric Brewer gave a keynote speech[9] in which he presented the CAP theorem. CAP stands for *consistency*, *availability*, and tolerance to network *partitions*.

The essence of the theorem is that in the presence of network partitions, depicted in figure 1.7, you can have either *consistency* of data across servers or *availability* of all servers, but not both at the same time.

Suppose we wanted to build an online trading platform to deal with a high volume of orders. To satisfy our expected load, we set up four servers, all connected to the

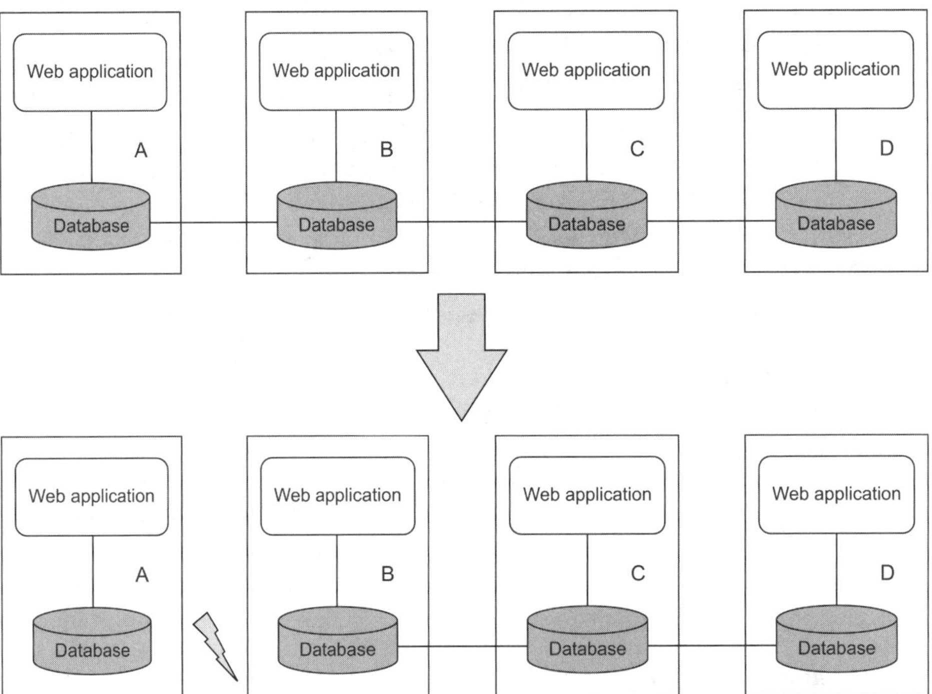

Figure 1.7 Network partition on a system with four servers. When the partition occurs, server A is isolated from the other servers, yet the application running on the server is still reachable from the outside world. Changes occurring on this server will occur in isolation, and once the network partition is over, there may be data inconsistency between server A and servers B, C, and D.

[9] Eric Brewer, "Towards Robust Distributed Systems," www.cs.berkeley.edu/~brewer/cs262b-2004/PODC-keynote.pdf.

internet, and additionally interconnected on a LAN. (Never mind that in practice such a setup wouldn't pass any of the security audits required for online trading. Let's just go with it for this example.) Each server is hosting a web application as well as a database that keeps data changes synchronous via replication on the LAN. When an order is placed on any of the nodes, this information is automatically propagated to all other server instances, thus ensuring the consistency of the data in our small cluster.

Now let's suppose that through an unfortunate turn of events, a member of the office cleaning personnel trips over the LAN cable of server A, thus disconnecting it from the internal network, but not from the internet. If a user now places an order via server A to buy a number of shares, and the order is successfully executed, nothing would prevent another user from placing a buy order for the same shares on any of the other nodes of the system and having it execute correctly. When the network recovers, we'd wind up with node A being in an inconsistent state, and we'd have quite a problem as a result of having sold the same shares twice.

Even if it can be argued that network partitions are rare, they still happen often enough that they can't just be overlooked. Technologies such as Amazon's DynamoDB were built with network partitions as a key part of their design.[10] Using the Command and Query Responsibility Segregation (CQRS) pattern in combination with Event Sourcing, which we'll discuss in chapter 7, is an increasingly popular mix of techniques for achieving *eventual consistency*—ensuring that even though a system may at first not be consistent at all times across all nodes, it will eventually *converge* so that all nodes see the latest version of an update.

To make things even more interesting, network partitions are just one of many things that can go wrong when working with distributed systems. In 1994, Peter Deutsch drafted out seven fallacies of distributed computing, and an additional one was added by James Gosling in 1997. The result is known as the eight fallacies of distributed computing:[11]

1. The network is reliable
2. Latency is zero
3. Bandwidth is infinite
4. The network is secure
5. Topology doesn't change
6. There is one administrator
7. Transport cost is zero
8. The network is homogeneous

As you can see from the length of this list, there are many reasons building a highly available system is difficult. In order for a system to be truly *resilient*, fault-tolerance can't be an afterthought—it must be handled right from the start.

---

[10] Giuseppe DeCandia et al., "Dynamo: Amazon's Highly Available Key-value Store," http://mng.bz/YY5A.
[11] "The Eight Fallacies of Distributed Computing," https://blogs.oracle.com/jag/resource/Fallacies.html.

1.3.2 Building applications with failure in mind

Though failure is unavoidable, there are ways to influence how a system fails and how quickly it recovers. Not every kind of failure needs to render an entire application unavailable.

RESILIENT CLIENTS

Take, for example, the online service Trello, a project-management tool inspired by the Kanban methodology. Trello allows you to create cards and edit their content, drag and drop them from one list to another, and perform a lot more actions. When there's a problem with the network connection, be it on the client side or the server side, the Trello application doesn't simply stop responding but instead exhibits one of the most important behaviors of a reactive web application: resiliency. A user doesn't need to interrupt their work but can continue to use the service, and when the connection is recovered, the actions saved locally are transmitted back to the server. As shown in figure 1.8, users are constantly kept informed about the status of the application and made aware of situations in which their actions can't be saved properly.

BULKHEADING

Watertight bulkhead partitions, used in shipbuilding for centuries, are an effective way to prevent a ship from sinking by compartmentalizing different sections. Should the ship

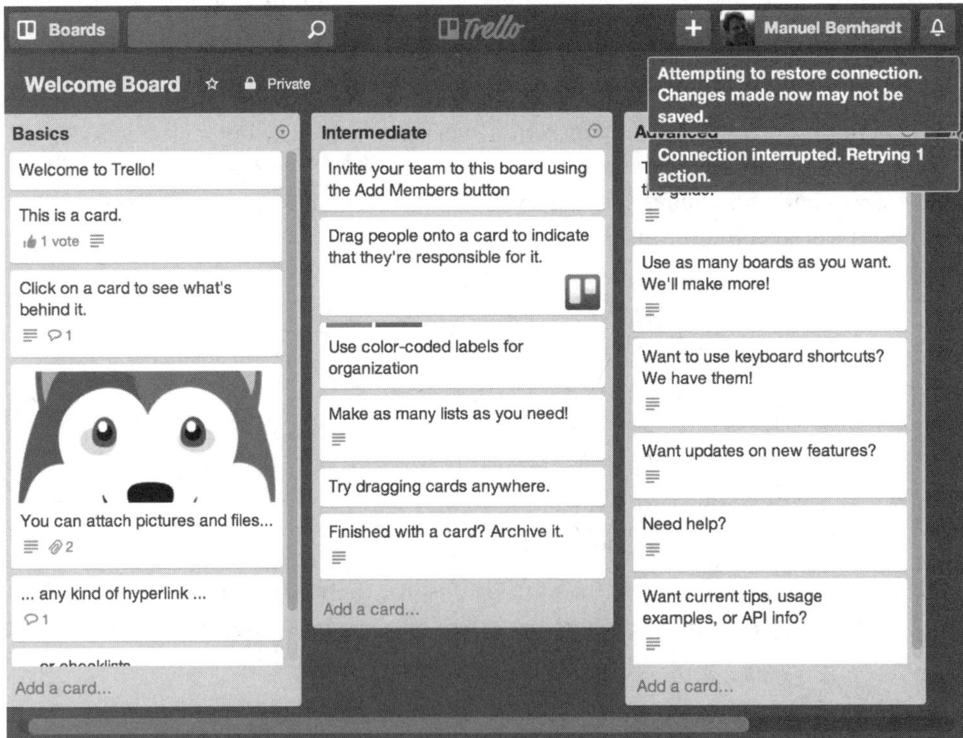

Figure 1.8 Failure handling and user interaction in Trello

hit an iceberg, only the damaged compartments would be flooded—the whole ship would stay afloat if enough compartments remained intact. (It should be noted here that in the case of the Titanic, the bulkheads were not truly watertight, which explains why this mechanism did not work as designed.)

The bulkhead pattern can be used in web applications at different levels. For example, LinkedIn's home page features a lot of information kept in different sections: people you may know, people you recently visited, people who have viewed your profile, people who have viewed your updates, and so on. Those sections appear to be loaded at the same time but are in fact retrieved from various back-end services and composed together asynchronously.[12] When one of the back-end services is unavailable or takes a long time to load, the other sections aren't affected and are loaded on a first-come, first-served basis. Sections that can't get an answer from their service can render themselves differently or hide themselves entirely if necessary.

SUPERVISION AND ACTORS

Supervision is one of the fundamental concepts used by reactive applications in order to be fault-tolerant.

When considering supervision, you might think of adult supervision of children or supervision in a work environment. In both cases, a hierarchical relationship exists—between parent and child or boss and employee. Though different in nature, these human relationships have a few common aspects:

- The supervisor (parent or boss) is responsible for the mistakes the supervised (child or employee) makes.
- The supervisor gets to know about the mistakes of the supervised (this may not always be true in reality, but let's assume it is for the sake of this explanation).
- The supervisor has to decide how to react to those mistakes.

Building on these three aspects, we can say that the core idea of supervision in the context of software systems is one of *separation of concerns*: the responsibility of executing a task is separated from the responsibility of deciding how failures are dealt with and ensuring that they are dealt with.

Joe Armstrong's thesis, "Making reliable distributed systems in the presence of software errors,"[13] introduces the Erlang computing language, designed with the idea that software, no matter how well it may be tested, always has mistakes in it. He goes on to introduce supervision as a means to counteract those mistakes when possible.

When implementing a given task, a developer may not always be able to predict all the errors that may arise. More often than not there's a degree of uncertainty when implementing an application. And even when an error condition is expected, the best reaction to the error may not be clear because it will depend on the current state of the systems. Software systems—especially distributed systems that combine many moving

---

[12] Yevgeniy Brikman, "Play at LinkedIn: Composable and streamable Play apps," http://www.slideshare.net/brikis98/composable-and-streamable-play-apps.

[13] A PDF of the article is available at http://mng.bz/uFsr.

parts—gain in robustness and resilience through experience and by seeing the system behave in reality. By isolating the risky parts of a task into supervised units of code, developers can acknowledge the sometimes unpredictable nature of these systems and factor the unpredictability right into their design.

A popular implementation of supervision can be found in the *actor programming model*, which is at the core of Erlang and is also represented on the JVM by Akka. It revolves around small units of software called *actors*, which, much like humans, can communicate with each other by sending and reacting to messages. Just as in human communication, messages are sent asynchronously, which means that an actor doesn't freeze and wait for a response to a message before it resumes its work.

Actors exist in a supervision hierarchy: each actor has a supervisor and can have one or several child actors for which it is responsible. Unhandled errors raised by a child actor are communicated to the parent actor, which decides to react in one way or another. We'll discuss actors in detail in chapter 6.

1.3.3 Dealing with load

Reactive web applications are designed to cope with varying loads. When building web applications, one critical piece of information that should flow into the design is the expected load in terms of requests per second that the application should be able to handle. This varies depending on the application: a meeting room–scheduling application on a company intranet isn't likely to generate as much interest (or be available to as many users) as a social media site for sharing funny video clips. Often, and especially in the early stages of a project, concerns about performance are dismissed as *premature optimization*, the attitude being, "We'll take care of it when we have enough users." In reality though, if a site gets popular, users won't gently and slowly visit the site turn by turn, giving developers time to come up with a way to increase capacity. Instead, the site may be featured on a popular news feed such as Hacker News, and suddenly tens of thousands of people will rush to it without warning. (Incidentally, Hacker News regularly features stories about the impact of being featured on Hacker News, sometimes including the amount of the Amazon Web Services bill.) The problem with such bursts in the number of visitors is that they are often unpredictable, and not being able to cope with them may well mean a website will lose one of its few chances to get noticed by the general public.

The capability of an application to perform well under load and to scale out to the necessary number of nodes (hardware servers or virtualized ones) can't be an afterthought. Unlike simple features such as the capability to log in using an existing Google, Facebook, or Twitter account, scalability is a *cross-cutting concern* and needs to be factored into the design right from the beginning. Reactive systems often make use of stateless architectures, which we discussed in the section "Horizontal deployments." Let's look at a few tools available for handling increased load on an application.

CAPACITY PLANNING WITH LITTLE'S LAW

Little's law is a formula from queuing theory often used for dimensioning telecommunication infrastructures (such as traditional telephone installations). When applied to the domain of web servers, it states that

```
L = λ * W
```

where

- L is the average number of requests served at the same time
- λ is the average rate at which requests arrive on the system
- W is the average time it takes to process a request

In the case of a meeting room–scheduling application for a company intranet, if there's an average of one request per minute and each request takes 100 ms to process, the average number of concurrent requests will be approximately 0.0017. In other words, there's no need to worry about scaling out for this application.

On the other hand, the site for sharing funny videos may get 10,000 requests per second (many people like to watch those videos instead of working), and if the processing time is 100 ms, the application faces on average 1,000 concurrent requests. In this case we might want to adopt a number of design and deployment decisions that allow for handling 1,000 requests at the same time. If, for example, we know that one node in our system is capable of handling 100 concurrent requests, we'll need 10 such nodes to handle the entire load.

DYNAMICALLY SCALING IN AND OUT

As I've already pointed out, it's hard to predict the effective number of users visiting a website. The time of the day, weather conditions, and mentions via social media services may influence how high the load on the funny video clip site will be. Instead of running at full capacity all the time, it may be worth saving some money by scaling up and down depending on the load.

One approach would be to measure the effective load on the site using a monitoring tool, and then shut down or start up nodes accordingly. But as heroic as it may sound, getting up at 3:00 AM when receiving an SMS alert that the load has increased, and going online to slide the Heroku slider to the right may not be a very good strategy for the health of the website operator. Instead, using Little's law in combination with scripts to automate this process seems more reasonable. We'll look at an example of elastically scaling a Play deployment with Clever Cloud in chapter 10.

BACK PRESSURE PROPAGATION

One of the main features of the web application for sharing funny videos is to show those videos to visitors. If we were to store the videos on a third-party storage service, such as Amazon S3, and display them using a video player on our site, we'd have to stream the video to the client through our server. If, however, the client's bandwidth was not as good as that of our server (which is often the case, especially for mobile devices), we'd need to keep the video in memory on the server for the duration of the streaming. With many users watching videos at the same time, we'd certainly run out of memory very quickly. *Back pressure propagation* is a means of regulating the speed of streams by taking into account the effective consumption speed on the consumer side. Instead of keeping the entire video in memory on our server, a setup involving back pressure would allow us to modulate the speed at which the data is retrieved from Amazon S3 so we'd only buffer a small amount in memory on the server, fetching more of it as the video is played on the user's phone.

The Play Framework builds on the concept of back pressure and utilizes it for core concerns, such as request body parsing and WebSocket handling. The Reactive Streams initiative that we briefly mentioned in the context of reactive programming provides this capability, as you'll see in chapter 9.

CIRCUIT BREAKERS

Sometimes, it may not be possible to scale a service out, such as when communicating with a legacy application (for example, a mainframe system in a banking environment). In this case, we may need a different approach for dealing with load bursts to protect the legacy service from overload and avoid cascading failures.

In an electric circuit, a circuit breaker is an automatic switch that's meant to protect the circuit from overload or short circuits. On an abstract level, it functions as illustrated in figure 1.9.

In the context of a web application, a circuit breaker is configured to check whether the service it protects responds within a certain time frame, and if the service takes longer to answer than this timeout, the circuit trips into an open state. After a certain amount of time (which can also be configured), the circuit goes into a half-open state and a new attempt is made to contact the service. If it responds within the intended time frame, the circuit is closed again; otherwise, it trips into the open state again and waits longer for the service to recover.

Circuit breakers are an effective way to protect legacy services from overloading. Play can easily leverage the circuit breaker implementation provided by Akka, this combination having been employed successfully in a project for the Walmart Canada site.[14]

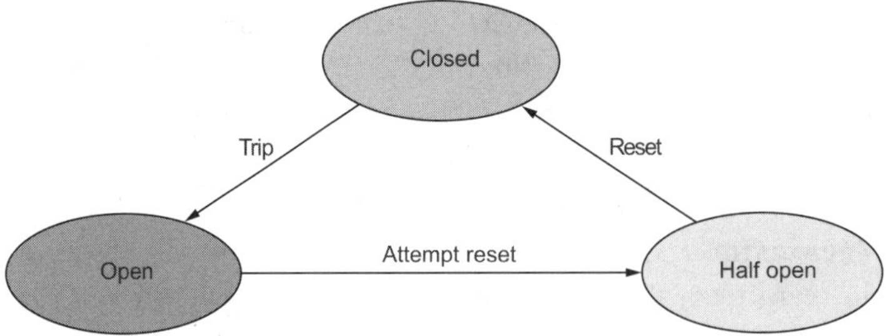

Figure 1.9 Different states of a circuit breaker

[14] Lightbend, "Walmart Boosts Conversions by 20% with Lightbend Reactive Platform," www.lightbend.com/resources/case-studies-and-stories/walmart-boosts-conversions-by-20-with-lightbend-reactive-platform.

1.4 Summary

In this chapter, you were introduced to reactive applications and why they matter. In particular, we looked at

- The meaning and origins of reactive applications and reactive technologies, including the Play Framework
- How threads are executed by a CPU and how an asynchronous, event-driven programming style embraced by evented servers makes better use of resources
- Different deployment models, including stateless, horizontal architectures that scale well under load
- The importance of failure handling and different methods that reactive applications employ to become resilient

In the next chapter, we'll get our hands dirty and build a small reactive web application with Play.

2 Your first reactive web application

This chapter covers

- Creating a new Play project
- Streaming data from a remote server and broadcasting it to clients
- Dealing with failure

In the previous chapter, we talked about the key benefits of adopting a reactive approach to web application design and operation, and you saw that the Play Framework is a good technology for this. Now it's time to get your hands dirty and build a reactive web application. We'll build a simple application that connects to the Twitter API to retrieve a stream of tweets and send them to clients using WebSockets.

2.1 Creating and running a new project

An easy way to start a new Play project is to use the Lightbend Activator, which is a thin wrapper around Scala's sbt build tool that provides templates for creating new projects. The following instructions assume that you have the Activator installed on your computer. If you don't, appendix A provides detailed instructions for installing it.

Let's get started by creating a new project called "twitter-stream" in the workspace directory, using the `play-scala-v24` template:

```
~/workspace » activator new twitter-stream play-scala-2.4
```

This will start the process of creating a new project with Activator, using the template as a scaffold:

```
Fetching the latest list of templates...

OK, application "twitter-stream" is being created using the "play-scala-2.4"
➥ template.

To run "twitter-stream" from the command line, "cd twitter-stream" then:
/Users/mb/workspace/twitter-stream/activator run

To run the test for "twitter-stream" from the command line,
➥ "cd twitter-stream" then:
/Users/mb/workspace/twitter-stream/activator test

To run the Activator UI for "twitter-stream" from the command line,
➥ "cd twitter-stream" then:
/Users/mb/workspace/twitter-stream/activator ui
```

You can now run this application from the project directory:

```
~/workspace » cd twitter-stream
~/workspace/twitter-stream » activator run
```

If you point your browser to http://localhost:9000, you'll see the standard welcome page for a Play project. At any time when running a Play project, you can access the documentation at http://localhost:9000/@documentation.

PLAY RUNTIME MODES Play has a number of runtime modes. In *dev mode* (triggered with the `run` command), the sources are constantly watched for changes, and the project is reloaded with any new changes for rapid development. *Production mode*, as its name indicates, is used for the production operation of a Play application. Finally, *test mode* is active when running tests, and it's useful for retrieving specific configuration settings for the test environment.

Besides running the application directly with the `activator run` command, it's possible to use an interactive console. You can stop the running application by hitting Ctrl-C and start the console simply by running `activator`:

```
~/workspace/twitter-stream » activator
```

That will start the console, as follows:

```
[info] Loading project definition from
         /Users/mb/workspace/twitter-stream/project
[info] Set current project to twitter-stream
         (in build file:/Users/mb/workspace/twitter-stream/)
[twitter-stream] $
```

Once you're in the console, you can run commands such as `run`, `clean`, `compile`, and so on. Note that this console is not Play-specific, but common to all sbt projects. Play adds a few commands to it and makes it more suited to web application development.

Table 2.1 lists some useful commands:

Table 2.1 Useful sbt console commands for working with Play

Command	Description
`run`	Runs the Play project in dev mode
`start`	Starts the Play project in production mode
`clean`	Cleans all compiled classes and generated sources
`compile`	Compiles the project
`test`	Runs the tests
`dependencies`	Shows all the library dependencies of the project, including transitive ones
`reload`	Reloads the project settings if they have been changed

When you start the application in the console with `run`, you can stop it and return to the console by pressing Ctrl-D.

> **AUTO-RELOADING** By prepending a command with ~, such as ~ `run` or ~ `compile`, you can instruct sbt to listen to changes in the source files. In this way, every time a source file is saved, the project is automatically recompiled or reloaded.

Now that you're all set to go, let's start building a simple reactive application, which, as you may have guessed from the name of the empty project we've created, has something to do with Twitter.

What we'll build is an application that will connect to one of Twitter's streaming APIs, transform the stream asynchronously, and broadcast the transformed stream to clients using WebSocket, as illustrated in figure 2.1. We'll start by building a small Twitter client to stream the data, and then build the transformation pipeline that we'll plug into a broadcasting mechanism.

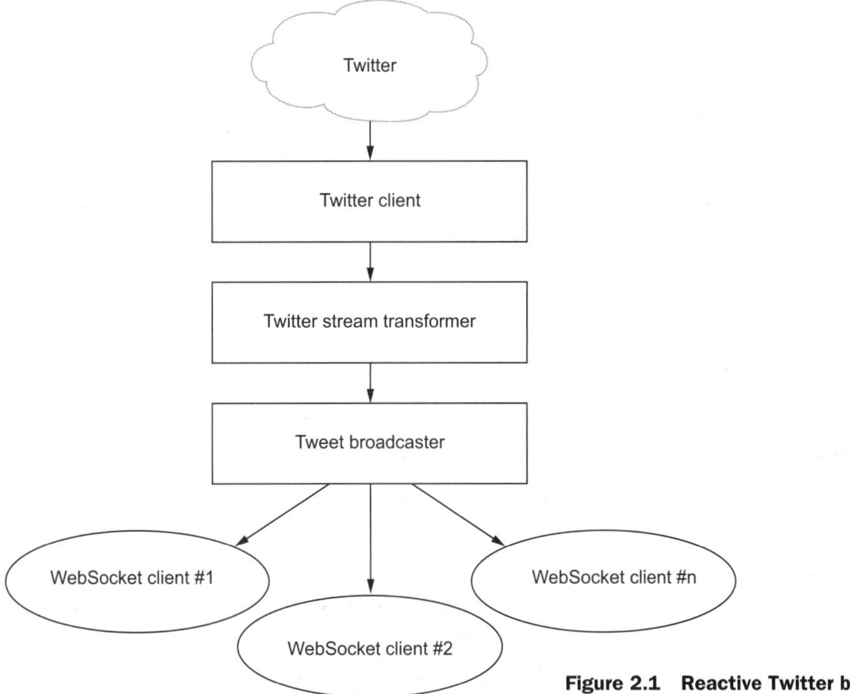

Figure 2.1 Reactive Twitter broadcaster

2.2 Connecting to Twitter's streaming API

To get started, we'll connect to the Twitter filter API.[1] At this point, we'll just focus on getting data from Twitter and displaying it on the console—we'll deal with sending it to clients connecting to our application at a later stage.

Start by opening the project in your favorite IDE. Most modern IDEs have extensions to support Play projects nowadays, and you can find resources on the topic in the Play documentation (www.playframework.com/documentation), so we won't look into setting up various flavors of IDEs here.

2.2.1 Getting the connection credentials to the Twitter API

Twitter uses the OAuth authentication mechanism to secure its API. To use the API, you need a Twitter account and OAuth consumer key and tokens. Register with Twitter (if you haven't already), and then you can go to https://apps.twitter.com where you can request access to the API for an application. This way, you'll get an API key and an API secret, which together represent the consumer key. In addition to these keys, you'll need to generate request tokens (in the Details tab of the Twitter Apps web application). At the end of this process, you should have access to four values:

---

[1] The Twitter API documentation can be found at https://dev.twitter.com/streaming/reference/post/statuses/filter.

- The API key
- The API secret
- An access token
- An access token secret

Once you have all the necessary keys, you'll need to add them to the application configuration in conf/application.conf. This way, you'll be able to retrieve them easily from the application later on. Add the keys at the end of the file as follows:

```
# Twitter
twitter.apiKey="<your api key>"
twitter.apiSecret="<your api secret>"
twitter.token="<your access token>"
twitter.tokenSecret="<your access token secret>"
```

2.2.2 Working around a bug with OAuth authentication

As a technical book author, I want my examples to flow and my code to look simple, beautiful, and elegant. Unfortunately the reality of software development is that bugs can be anywhere, even in projects with a very high code quality, which the Play Framework definitely is. One of those bugs has its origins in the async-http-client library that Play uses, and it plagues the 2.4.x series of the Play Framework. It can't be easily addressed without breaking binary compatibility, which is why it will likely not be fixed within the 2.4.x series.[2]

More specifically, this bug breaks the OAuth authentication mechanism when a request contains characters that need to be encoded (such as the `@` or `#` characters). As a result, we have to use a workaround in all chapters making use of the Twitter API. Open the build.sbt file at the root of the project, and add the following line:

```
libraryDependencies += "com.ning" % "async-http-client" % "1.9.29"
```

2.2.3 Streaming data from the Twitter API

The first thing we'll do now is add some functionality to the existing `Application` controller in app/controllers/Application.scala. When you open the file, it should look rather empty, like this:

```
class Application extends Controller {

  def index = Action {
    Ok(views.html.index("Your new application is ready."))
  }

}
```

The `index` method defines a means for obtaining a new `Action`. Actions are the mechanism Play uses to deal with incoming HTTP requests, and you'll learn a lot more about them in chapter 4.

---

[2] https://github.com/playframework/playframework/pull/4826

Start by adding a new `tweets` action to the controller.

Listing 2.1 Defining a new `tweets` action

```
import play.api.mvc._

class Application extends Controller {
  def tweets = Action {
    Ok
  }
}
```

This action won't do anything other than return a 200 `Ok` response when accessed. To access it, we first need to make it accessible in Play's routes. Open the conf/routes file and add a new route to the newly created action, so you get the following result.

Listing 2.2 Route to the newly created `tweets` action

```
# Routes
# This file defines all application routes
# (Higher priority routes first)
# ~~~~

# Home page
GET     /                   controllers.Application.index
GET     /tweets             controllers.Application.tweets

# Map static resources from the /public folder to the /assets URL path
GET     /assets/*file       controllers.Assets.at(path="/public", file)
```

Now when you run the application and access the /tweets file, you should get an empty page in your browser. This is great, but not very useful. Let's go one step further by retrieving the credentials from the configuration file.

Go back to the app/controllers/Application.scala controller and extend the `tweets` action as follows.

Listing 2.3 Retrieving the configuration

```
import play.api.libs.oauth.{ConsumerKey, RequestToken}
import play.api.Play.current
import scala.concurrent.Future
import play.api.libs.concurrent.Execution.Implicits._

def tweets = Action.async {
  val credentials: Option[(ConsumerKey, RequestToken)] = for {
    apiKey <- Play.configuration.getString("twitter.apiKey")
    apiSecret <- Play.configuration.getString("twitter.apiSecret")
    token <- Play.configuration.getString("twitter.token")
    tokenSecret <- Play.configuration.getString("twitter.tokenSecret")
```

Uses Action.async to return a Future of a result for the next step

Retrieves the Twitter credentials from application.conf

```
  } yield (
    ConsumerKey(apiKey, apiSecret),
    RequestToken(token, tokenSecret)
  )

  credentials.map { case (consumerKey, requestToken) =>
    Future.successful {
      Ok
    }
  } getOrElse {
    Future.successful {
      InternalServerError("Twitter credentials missing")
    }
  }
}
```

Wraps the result in a successful Future block until the next step

Returns a 500 Internal Server Error if no credentials are available

Wraps the result in a successful Future block to comply with the return type

Now that we have access to our Twitter API credentials, we'll see whether we can get anything back from Twitter. Replace the simple `Ok` result in app/controllers/Application.scala with the following bit of code to connect to Twitter.

Listing 2.4 First attempt at connecting to the Twitter API

```
// ...
import play.api.libs.ws._

def tweets = Action.async {
  credentials.map { case (consumerKey, requestToken) =>
    WS
      .url("https://stream.twitter.com/1.1/statuses/filter.json")
      .sign(OAuthCalculator(consumerKey, requestToken))
      .withQueryString("track" -> "reactive")
      .get()
      .map { response =>
        Ok(response.body)
      }
    } getOrElse {
      Future.successful {
        InternalServerError("Twitter credentials missing")
      }
    }
}

def credentials: Option[(ConsumerKey, RequestToken)] = for {
  apiKey <- Play.configuration.getString("twitter.apiKey")
  apiSecret <- Play.configuration.getString("twitter.apiSecret")
  token <- Play.configuration.getString("twitter.token")
  tokenSecret <- Play.configuration.getString("twitter.tokenSecret")
} yield (
  ConsumerKey(apiKey, apiSecret),
  RequestToken(token, tokenSecret)
)
```

The API URL

OAuth signature of the request

Specifies a query string parameter

Executes an HTTP GET request

Play's WS library lets you easily access the API by signing the request appropriately following the OAuth standard. You're currently tracking all the tweets that contain the word "reactive," and for the moment you only log the status of the response from Twitter to see if you can connect with these credentials. This may look fine at first sight, but there's a catch: if you were to execute the preceding code, you wouldn't get any useful results. The streaming API, as its name indicates, returns a (possibly infinite) stream of tweets, which means that the request would never end. The WS library would time out after a few seconds, and you'd get an exception in the console.

What you need to do, therefore, is consume the stream of data you get. Let's rewrite the previous call to `WS` and use an *iteratee* (discussed in a moment) to simply print the results you get back.

Listing 2.5 Printing out the stream of data from Twitter

```
// ...
import play.api.libs.iteratee._
import play.api.Logger

def tweets = Action.async {

  val loggingIteratee = Iteratee.foreach[Array[Byte]] { array =>
    Logger.info(array.map(_.toChar).mkString)
  }

  credentials.map { case (consumerKey, requestToken) =>
    WS
      .url("https://stream.twitter.com/1.1/statuses/filter.json")
      .sign(OAuthCalculator(consumerKey, requestToken))
      .withQueryString("track" -> "reactive")
      .get { response =>
        Logger.info("Status: " + response.status)
        loggingIteratee
      }.map { _ =>
        Ok("Stream closed")
      }
  }
}

def credentials = ...
```

Defines a logging iteratee that consumes a stream asynchronously and logs the contents when data is available

Sends a GET request to the server and retrieves the response as a (possibly infinite) stream

Feeds the stream directly into the consuming loggingIteratee; the contents aren't loaded in memory first but are directly passed to the iteratee

Returns a 200 Ok result when the stream is entirely consumed or closed

QUICK INTRODUCTION TO ITERATEES

An iteratee is a construct that allows you to consume streams of data asynchronously; it's one of the cornerstones of the Play Framework. Iteratees are typed with input and output types: an `Iteratee[E, A]` consumes chunks of `E` to produce one or more `A`'s.

In the case of the `loggingIteratee` in listing 2.5, the input is an `Array[Byte]` (because you retrieve a raw stream of data from Twitter), and the output is of type

`Unit`, which means you don't produce any result other than the data logged out on the console.

The counterpart of an iteratee is an *enumerator.* Just as the iteratee is an asynchronous consumer of data, the enumerator is an asynchronous producer of data: an `Enumerator[E]` produces chunks of `E`.

Finally, there's another piece of machinery that lets you transform streaming data on the fly, called an *enumeratee.* An `Enumeratee[From, To]` takes chunks of type `From` from an enumerator and transforms them into chunks of type `To`.

On a conceptual level, you can think of an enumerator as being a faucet, an enumeratee as being a filter, and an iteratee as being a glass, as in figure 2.2.

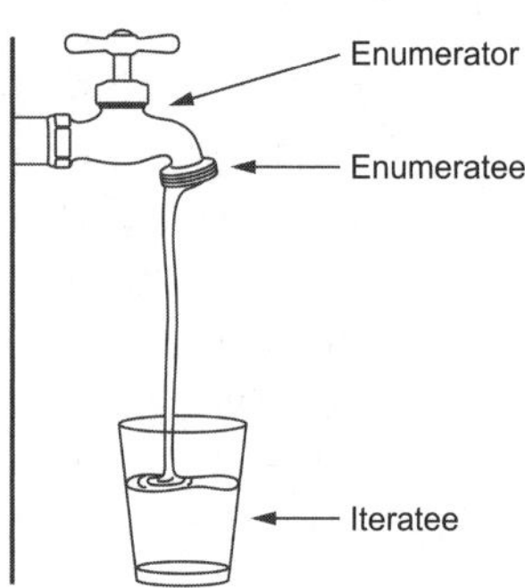

Figure 2.2 Enumerators, enumeratees, and iteratees

Let's go back to our `loggingIteratee` for a second, defined as follows:

```
val loggingIteratee = Iteratee.foreach[Array[Byte]] { array =>
    Logger.info(array.map(_.toChar).mkString)
}
```

The `Iteratee.foreach[E]` method creates a new iteratee that consumes each input it receives by performing a side-effecting action (of result type `Unit`). It's important to understand here that `foreach` isn't a method of an iteratee, but rather a method of the Iteratee library used to create a "foreach" iteratee. The Iteratee library offers many other methods for building iteratees, and we'll look at some of them later on.

At this point, you may wonder how this is any different from using other streaming mechanisms, such as `java.io.InputStream` and `java.io.OutputStream`. As mentioned earlier, iteratees let you manipulate streams of data asynchronously. In practice, this means that these streams won't hold on to a thread in the absence of new data. Instead, the thread that they use will be freed for use by other tasks, and only when there's a signal that new data is arriving will the streaming continue. In contrast, a `java.io.OutputStream` blocks the thread it's using until new data is available.

> **THE FUTURE OF ITERATEES IN PLAY** At the time of writing, Play is largely built on top of iteratees, enumerators, and enumeratees. *Reactive Streams* is a new standard for nonblocking stream manipulation with backward pressure on the JVM that we'll talk about in chapter 9. Although we use iteratees in this chapter and later in the book, the roadmap for the next major release of Play is to gradually replace iteratees with *Akka Streams,* which implement the Reactive Streams standard. Chapter 9 will cover this toolset as well as how to convert from iteratees to Akka Streams and vice versa.

Let's now get back to our application. Our approach to turning the `Array[Byte]` into a `String` is very crude (and, as you'll see later, problematic), but if someone were to tweet about "reactive," we'd be able to see something. If you want to check that things are going well, you can write a tweet yourself, as I just did:

```
[info] application - Status: 200
[info] application - {"created_at":"Fri Sep 19 15:08:07 +0000 2014","id
":512981466662592512,"id_str":"512981466662592512","text":"Writing the
second chapter of my book about #reactive web-applications with #PlayFr
amework. I need a tweet with \"reactive\" for an example.","source":"<a
 href=\"http:\/\/itunes.apple.com\/us\/app\/twitter\/id409789998?mt=12\
" rel=\"nofollow\">Twitter for Mac<\/a>","truncated":false,"in_reply_to
_status_id":null,"in_reply_to_status_id_str":null,"in_reply_to_user_id"
:null,"in_reply_to_user_id_str":null,"in_reply_to_screen_name":null,"us
er":{"id":12876952,"id_str":"12876952","name":"Manuel Bernhardt","scree
n_name":"elmanu","location":"Vienna" ...
```

> **GETTING MORE TWEETS** For all the advantages of reactive applications, the keyword "reactive" is slightly less popular than more common topics on Twitter, so you may want to use another term to get faster-paced data. (One keyword that always works well, and not only on Twitter, is "cat.")

2.2.4 *Asynchronously transforming the Twitter stream*

Great, you just managed to connect to the Twitter streaming API and display some results! But to do something a bit more advanced with the data, you'll need to parse the JSON representation to manipulate it more easily, as shown in figure 2.3.

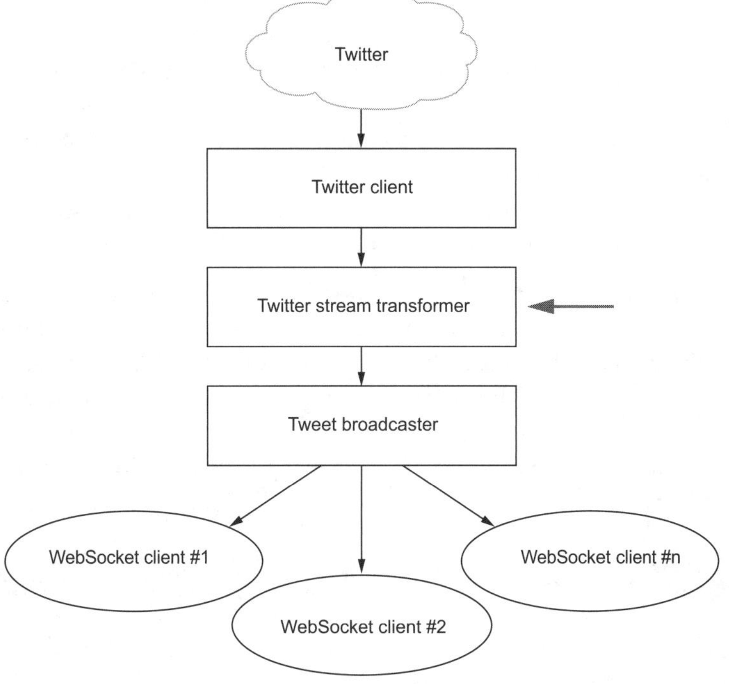

Figure 2.3 Twitter stream transformation step

Play has a built-in JSON library that can take care of parsing textual JSON files into a structured representation that can easily be manipulated. But you first need to pay a little more attention to the data you're receiving, because there are a few things that can go wrong:

- Tweets are encoded in UTF-8, so you need to decode them appropriately, taking into account variable-length encoding.
- In some cases, a tweet is split over several chunks of `Array[Byte]`, so you can't just assume that each chunk can be parsed right away.

These issues are rather complex to solve, and they may take quite some time to get right. Instead of doing it ourselves, let's use the play-extra-iteratees library. Add the following lines to the build.sbt file.

Listing 2.6 Including the play-extra-iteratees library in the project

```
resolvers += "Typesafe private" at
  "https://private-repo.typesafe.com/typesafe/maven-releases"

libraryDependencies +=
  "com.typesafe.play.extras" %% "iteratees-extras" % "1.5.0"
```

To make the changes visible to the project in the console, you need to run the `reload` command (or exit and restart, but `reload` is faster).

Armed with this library, you now have the necessary tools to handle this stream of JSON objects properly:

- `play.extras.iteratees.Encoding.decode` will decode the stream of bytes as a UTF-8 string.
- `play.extras.iteratees.JsonIteratees.jsSimpleObject` will parse a single JSON object.
- `play.api.libs.iteratee.Enumeratee.grouped` will apply the `jsSimpleObject` iteratee over and over again until the stream is finished.

We'll start with a stream of `Array[Byte]`, decode it into a stream of `CharString`, and finally parse it into JSON objects of kind `play.api.libs.JsObject` by continuously parsing one JSON object out of the incoming stream of `CharString`. `Enumeratee.grouped` continuously applies the same iteratee over and over to the stream until it's finished.

You can set up the necessary plumbing by evolving your code in app/controllers/Application.conf as follows.

Listing 2.7 Reactive plumbing for the data from Twitter

```
// ...
import play.api.libs.json._
import play.extras.iteratees._
```

```
def tweets = Action.async {
    credentials.map { case (consumerKey, requestToken) =>
      val (iteratee, enumerator) = Concurrent.joined[Array[Byte]]

      val jsonStream: Enumerator[JsObject] =
        enumerator &>
        Encoding.decode() &>
        Enumeratee.grouped(JsonIteratees.jsSimpleObject)

      val loggingIteratee = Iteratee.foreach[JsObject] { value =>
        Logger.info(value.toString)
      }

      jsonStream run loggingIteratee

      WS
        .url("https://stream.twitter.com/1.1/statuses/filter.json")
        .sign(OAuthCalculator(consumerKey, requestToken))
        .withQueryString("track" -> "reactive")
        .get { response =>
          Logger.info("Status: " + response.status)
          iteratee
        }.map { _ =>
          Ok("Stream closed")
        }
    }
}

def credentials = ...
```

Sets up a joined iteratee and enumerator

Defines the stream transformation pipeline; each stage of the pipe is connected using the &> operation

Plugs the transformed JSON stream into the logging iteratee to print out its results to the console

Provides the iteratee as the entry point of the data streamed through the HTTP connection. The stream consumed by the iteratee will be passed on to the enumerator, which itself is the data source of the jsonStream. All the data streaming takes place in a nonblocking fashion.

The first thing you have to do in this setup is get an enumerator to work with. Iteratees are used to consume streams, whereas enumeratees produce them, and you need a producing pipe so you can add adapters to it. The `Concurrent.joined` method provides you with a connected pair of iteratee and enumerator: whatever data is consumed by the iteratee will be immediately available to the enumerator.

Next, you want to turn the raw `Array[Byte]` into a proper stream of parsed `JsObject` objects. To this end, start off with your enumerator and pipe the results to two transforming enumeratees:

- `Encoding.decode()` to turn the `Array[Byte]` into a UTF-8 representation of type `CharString` (an optimized version of a String proper for stream manipulation, and part of the play-extra-iteratees library)
- `Enumeratee.grouped(JsonIteratees.jsSimpleObject)` to have the stream consumed over and over again by the `JsonIteratees.jsSimpleObject` iteratee

The `jsSimpleObject` iteratee ignores whitespace and line breaks, which is convenient in this case because the tweets coming from Twitter are separated by a line break.

Set up a logging iteratee to print out the parsed JSON object stream, and connect it to the transformation pipeline you just set up using the `run` method of the enumerator.

This method tells the enumerator to start feeding data to the iteratee as soon as some is available.

Finally, by providing the `iteratee` reference to the `get()` method of the WS library, you effectively put the whole mechanism into motion.

If you run this example, you'll now get a stream of tweets printed out, ready to be manipulated for further use.

> **FASTER JSON PARSING** Although the play-extra-iteratees library is very convenient, the JSON tooling it offers isn't optimized for speed; it serves as more of a showcase of what can be done with iteratees. If I wanted to build a pipeline for production use, or where performance matters a lot more than low memory consumption, I'd probably create my own enumeratee and make use of a fast JSON parsing library such as Jackson.

2.3 Streaming tweets to clients using a WebSocket

Now that we have streaming data being sent by Twitter, let's make it available to users of our web application using WebSockets. Figure 2.4 provides an overview of what we want to achieve.

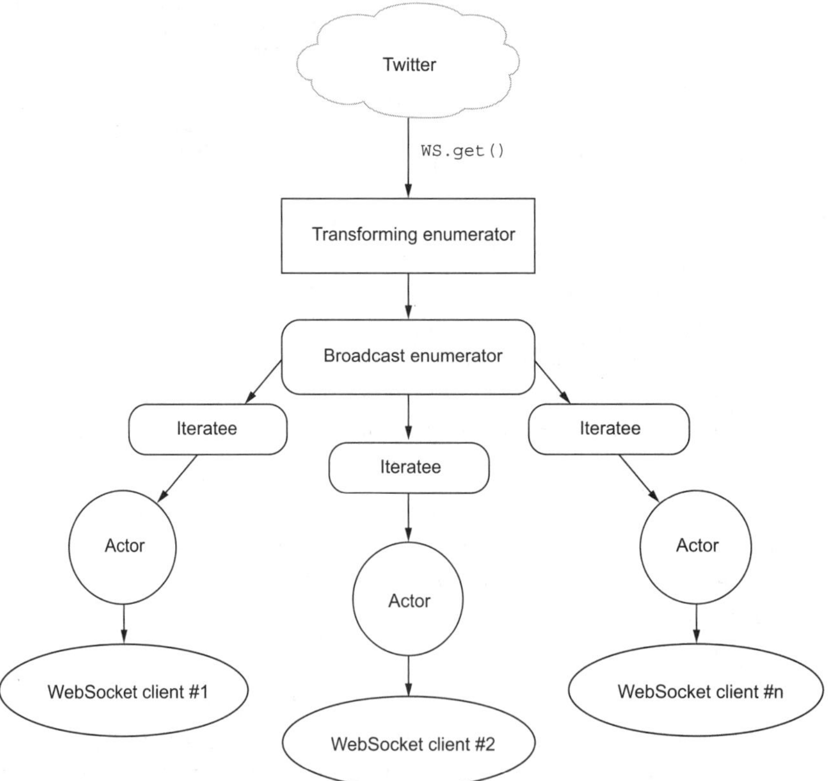

Figure 2.4 Reactive pipeline from Twitter to the client's browser

We want to connect once to Twitter and broadcast the stream we receive to the user's browser using the WebSocket protocol. We'll use an actor to establish the WebSocket connection for each client and connect it to the same broadcasted stream.

We'll proceed in two steps: first, we'll move the logic responsible for retrieving the stream from Twitter to an Akka actor, and then we'll set up a WebSocket connection that makes use of this actor.

2.3.1 Creating an actor

An actor is a lightweight object that's capable of sending and receiving messages. Each actor has a mailbox that keeps messages until they can be dealt with, in the order of reception. Actors can communicate with each other by sending messages. In most cases, messages are sent asynchronously, which means that an actor doesn't wait for a reply to its message, but will instead eventually receive a message with the answer to its question or request. This is all you need to know about actors for now—we'll talk about them more thoroughly in chapter 6.

To see an actor in action, start by creating a new file in the `actors` package, app/actors/TwitterStreamer.scala, with the following content.

Listing 2.8 Setting up a new actor

```
package actors

import akka.actor.{Actor, ActorRef, Props}
import play.api.Logger
import play.api.libs.json.Json

class TwitterStreamer(out: ActorRef) extends Actor {
  def receive = {
    case "subscribe" =>
      Logger.info("Received subscription from a client")
      out ! Json.obj("text" -> "Hello, world!")
  }
}

object TwitterStreamer {
  def props(out: ActorRef) = Props(new TwitterStreamer(out))
}
```

The receive method handles messages sent to this actor.

Handles the case of receiving a "subscribe" message

Sends out a simple Hello World message as a JSON object

Helper method that initializes a new Props object

You want to use your actor to represent a WebSocket connection with a client, managed by Play. You need to be able to receive messages, but also to send them, so you pass the `out` *actor reference* in the constructor of the actor. Play will take care of initializing the actor using the `akka.actor.Props` object, which you provide in the `props` method of the companion object `TwitterStreamer`. It will do so every time a new WebSocket connection is requested by a client.

An actor can send and receive messages of any kind using the `receive` method, which is a so-called *partial function* that uses Scala's pattern matching to figure out which case statement will deal with the incoming message. In this example, you're only concerned with messages of type `String` that have the value `"subscribe"` (other messages will be ignored).

When you receive a subscription, you first log it on the console, and then (for the moment) send back the JSON object { `"message": "Hello, world!"` }. The exclamation mark (`!`) is an alias for the `tell` method, which means that you "fire and forget" a message without waiting for a reply or a delivery confirmation.

SCALA TIP: PARTIAL FUNCTIONS In Scala, a partial function `p(x)` is a function that's defined only for some values of x. An actor's `receive` method won't be able to handle every type of message, which is why this kind of function is a good fit for this method. Partial functions are often implemented using pattern matching with `case` statements, wherein the value is matched against several `case` definitions (like a `switch` expression in Java).

2.3.2 Setting up the WebSocket connection and interacting with it

To make use of your freshly baked actor, you need to create a WebSocket endpoint on the server side and a view on the client side that will initialize a WebSocket connection.

SERVER-SIDE ENDPOINT

We'll start by rewriting the `tweets` method of the `Application` controller (you may want to keep the existing method as a backup somewhere, because we'll reuse most of its parts later on). You'll notice that we're not creating a Play `Action` this time, because actions only deal with the HTTP protocol, and WebSockets are a different kind of protocol. Play makes initializing WebSockets really easy.

Listing 2.9 Setting up the WebSocket endpoint in app/controllers/Application.scala

```
// ...
import actors.TwitterStreamer

// ...

def tweets = WebSocket.acceptWithActor[String, JsValue] {
  request => out => TwitterStreamer.props(out)
}
```

That's it! You don't need to adjust the route in the routes file either, because you're essentially reusing the existing mapping to the /tweets route.

The `acceptWithActor[In, Out]` method lets you create a WebSocket endpoint using an actor. You specify the type of the input and output data (in this case, you want to send strings from the client and receive JSON objects) and provide the `Props` of the actor, given the `out` actor reference that you're using to communicate with the client.

SIGNATURE OF THE ACCEPTWITHACTOR METHOD The `acceptWithActor` method has a slightly uncommon signature of type `f: RequestHeader => ActorRef => Props`. This is a function that, given a `RequestHeader`, returns another function that, given an `ActorRef`, returns a `Props` object. This construct allows you to access the HTTP request header information for purposes such as performing security checks before establishing the WebSocket connection.

CLIENT-SIDE VIEW

We'll now create a client-side view that will establish the WebSocket connection using JavaScript. Instead of creating a new view template, we'll simply reuse the existing view template, app/views/index.scala.html, as follows.

Listing 2.10 Client-side connection to the WebSocket using JavaScript

```
@(message: String)(implicit request: RequestHeader)

@main(message) {
    <div id="tweets"></div>
    <script type="text/javascript">
        var url = "@routes.Application.tweets().webSocketURL()";
        var tweetSocket = new WebSocket(url);

        tweetSocket.onmessage = function (event) {
            console.log(event);
            var data = JSON.parse(event.data);
            var tweet = document.createElement("p");
            var text = document.createTextNode(data.text);
            tweet.appendChild(text);
            document.getElementById("tweets" ).appendChild(tweet);
        };

        tweetSocket.onopen = function() {
            tweetSocket.send("subscribe");
        };
    </script>
}
```

Initializes the WebSocket connection using a URL generated by Play

The container in which the tweets will be displayed

The handler called when a message is received

The handler called when the connection is opened

Sends a subscription request to the server

You start by opening a WebSocket connection to the `tweets` handler. The URL is obtained using Play's built-in reverse routing and resolves to ws://localhost:9000/tweets. Then you add two handlers: one for handling new messages that you receive, and one for handling the new WebSocket connection once a connection with the server is established.

USING URLS IN VIEWS It's also possible to make use of reverse routing natively in JavaScript. We'll look into that in chapter 10.

When a new connection is established, you immediately send a subscribe message using the `send` method, which is matched in the `receive` method of the `Twitter-Streamer` on the server side.

Upon receiving a message on the client side, you append it to the page as a new paragraph tag. To do this, you need to parse the `event.data` field, as it's the string representation of the JSON object. You can then access the `text` field, in which the tweet's text is stored.

There's one change you need to make for your project to compile, which is to pass the `RequestHeader` to the view from the controller. In app/controllers/Application .scala, replace the `index` method with the following code.

Listing 2.11 Declaring the implicit `RequestHeader` to make it available in the view

```
def index = Action { implicit request =>
  Ok(views.html.index("Tweets"))
}
```

You need to take this step because in the index.scala.html view you've declared two parameter lists: a first one taking a message, and a second implicit one that expects a `RequestHeader`. In order for the `RequestHeader` to be available in the implicit scope, you need to prepend it with the `implicit` keyword.

Upon running this page, you should see "Hello, world!" displayed. If you look at the developer console of your browser, you should also see the details of the event that was received.

Scala tip: implicit parameters

Implicit parameters are a language feature of Scala that allows you to omit one or more arguments when calling a method. Implicit parameters are declared in the last parameter list of a function. For example, the index.scala.html template will be compiled to a Scala function that has a signature close to the following:

```
def indexTemplate(message: String)(implicit request: RequestHeader)
```

When the Scala compiler tries to compile this method, it will look for a value of the correct type in the implicit scope. This scope is defined by prepending the `implicit` keyword when declaring anonymous functions, as here with `Action`:

```
def index = Action { implicit request: RequestHeader =>
  // request is now available in the implicit scope
}
```

You don't need to explicitly declare the type of `request`; the Scala compiler is smart enough to do so on its own and to infer the type.

2.3.3 *Sending tweets to the WebSocket*

Play will create one new `TwitterStreamer` actor for each WebSocket connection, so it makes sense to only connect to Twitter once, and to broadcast our stream to all connections. To this end, we'll set up a special kind of broadcasting enumerator and provide a method to the actor to make use of this broadcast channel.

We first need an initialization mechanism to establish the connection to Twitter. To keep things simple, let's set up a new method in the companion object of the `TwitterStreamer` actor in app/actors/TwitterStreamer.scala.

Listing 2.12 Initializing the Twitter feed

```
object TwitterStreamer {
  def props(out: ActorRef) = Props(new TwitterStreamer(out))

  private var broadcastEnumerator: Option[Enumerator[JsObject]] = None

  def connect(): Unit = {
    credentials.map { case (consumerKey, requestToken) =>
      val (iteratee, enumerator) = Concurrent.joined[Array[Byte]]

      val jsonStream: Enumerator[JsObject] = enumerator &>
        Encoding.decode() &>
        Enumeratee.grouped(JsonIteratees.jsSimpleObject)

      val (be, _) = Concurrent.broadcast(jsonStream)
      broadcastEnumerator = Some(be)

      val url = "https://stream.twitter.com/1.1/statuses/filter.json"
      WS
        .url(url)
        .sign(OAuthCalculator(consumerKey, requestToken))
        .withQueryString("track" -> "reactive")
        .get { response =>
          Logger.info("Status: " + response.status)
          iteratee
        }.map { _ =>
          Logger.info("Twitter stream closed")
        }

    } getOrElse {
      Logger.error("Twitter credentials missing")
    }
  }
}
```

Initializes an empty variable to hold the broadcast enumerator

Sets up a joined set of iteratee and enumerator

Sets up the stream transformation pipeline, taking data from the joined enumerator

Initializes the broadcast enumerator using the transformed stream as a source

Consumes the stream from Twitter with the joined iteratee, which will pass it on to the joined enumerator

With the help of the broadcasting enumerator, the stream is now available to more than just one client.

> **A WORD ON THE CONNECT METHOD** Instead of encapsulating the `connect()` method in the `TwitterStreamer` companion object, it would be better practice to establish the connection in a related actor. The methods exposed in the `TwitterStreamer` connection are publicly available, and misuse of them may seriously impact your ability to correctly display streams. To keep this example short, we'll use the companion object; we'll look at a better way of handling this case in chapter 6.

You can now create a `subscribe` method that lets your actors subscribe their WebSocket clients to the stream. Append it to the `TwitterStreamer` object as follows.

Listing 2.13 Subscribing actors to the Twitter feed

```
object TwitterStreamer {

  // ...

  def subscribe(out: ActorRef): Unit = {
    if (broadcastEnumerator.isEmpty) {
      connect()
    }
    val twitterClient = Iteratee.foreach[JsObject] { t => out ! t }
    broadcastEnumerator.foreach { enumerator =>
      enumerator run twitterClient
    }
}
```

In the `subscribe` method, you first check if you have an initialized `broadcastEnumerator` at your disposal, and if not, establish a connection. Then you create a `twitterClient` iteratee, which sends each JSON object to the browser using the actor reference.

Finally, you can make use of this method in your actor when a client subscribes.

Listing 2.14 `TwitterStreamer` actor subscribing to the Twitter stream

```
class TwitterStreamer(out: ActorRef) extends Actor {
  def receive = {
    case "subscribe" =>
      Logger.info("Received subscription from a client")
      TwitterStreamer.subscribe(out)
  }
}
```

When running the chain, you should now see tweets appearing on the screen, one after another. You can open multiple browsers or tabs to see more client connections being established.

This setup is very resource-friendly given that you only make use of asynchronous and lightweight components that don't block threads: when no data is sent from Twitter, you don't unnecessarily block threads waiting or polling. Instead, each time new data comes in, the parsing and subsequent communication with clients happen asynchronously.

PROPER DISCONNECTION HANDLING One thing we haven't done here is properly handle client disconnections. When you close the browser tab or otherwise disconnect the client, your `twitterClient` iteratee will continue trying to send new messages to the `out` actor reference, but Play will have closed the WebSocket connection and stopped the actor, which means that messages will be sent to the void. You can observe this behavior by seeing Akka complain in the log about "dead letters" (actors sending messages to no-longer-existing endpoints). To properly handle this situation, you'd need to keep track of subscribers and check if each actor is still in the list of subscribers prior to sending each message. You can find an example of how this is done in the source code for this chapter, available on GitHub.

2.4 Making the application resilient and scaling out

We've built a pretty slick and resource-efficient application to stream tweets from our server to many clients. But to meet the failure-resilience criterion of a reactive web application, we need to do a bit more work: we need a good mechanism to detect and deal with failure, and we need to be able to scale out to respond to higher demand.

2.4.1 Making the client resilient

To be completely resilient, our application would need to be able to deal with a multitude of failure scenarios, ranging from Twitter becoming unavailable to our server crashing. We'll look into a first level of failure handling on the client side here, in order to alleviate the pain inflicted on our users if the stream of tweets were to be interrupted. We'll cover the topic of responsive clients in depth in chapter 8.

If the connection with the server is lost, we should alert the user and attempt to reconnect. This can be achieved by rewriting the <script> section of our index.scala.html view, as follows.

Listing 2.15 Resilient version of the JavaScript

```
function appendTweet(text) {
    var tweet = document.createElement("p");
    var message = document.createTextNode(text);
    tweet.appendChild(message);
    document.getElementById("tweets").appendChild(tweet);
}

function connect(attempt) {
    var connectionAttempt = attempt;
    var url = "@routes.Application.tweets().webSocketURL()";
    var tweetSocket = new WebSocket(url);
    tweetSocket.onmessage = function (event) {
        console.log(event);
        var data = JSON.parse(event.data);
        appendTweet(data.text);
    };
    tweetSocket.onopen = function() {
        connectionAttempt = 1;
        tweetSocket.send("subscribe");
    };
    tweetSocket.onclose = function() {
        if (connectionAttempt <= 3) {
```

Encapsulates the WebSocket connection logic in a reusable function

The onclose handler, called when the WebSocket connection is closed (→ `tweetSocket.onclose`)

Attempts up to three connection retries (→ `if (connectionAttempt <= 3)`)

```
            appendTweet("WARNING: Lost server connection,
        attempting to reconnect. Attempt number " + connectionAttempt);
            setTimeout(function() {
                connect(connectionAttempt + 1);
            }, 5000);
        } else {
            alert("The connection with the server was lost.");
        }
    };
}
connect(1);
```

Executes the wrapped function call after a delay of 5000 milliseconds

Attempts reconnection and increments the number of retries

In case of failure, alerts the user with a more prominent alert

Initiates the first connection attempt

To avoid repeating the same code twice, you start by moving the logic for displaying a new message into the appendTweet method and the logic for establishing a new WebSocket connection into the connect method. The latter now takes as its argument the connection attempt count, so you know when to give up trying and can then inform the user about the progress.

The onclose handler of the WebSocket API is invoked whenever the connection with the server is lost (or can't be established). This is where you plug in your failure-handling mechanism: when the connection is lost, you inform the user in an unobtrusive manner (by appending a warning message to the existing tweet stream) and then attempt to reconnect after a waiting period of five seconds. If you haven't succeeded after three reconnection attempts, you alert the user in a more direct fashion (in this example, by using a native browser alert). If you succeed at reconnecting, you reset the connection attempt count to 1.

FURTHER COPING MECHANISMS It's not uncommon for a web application to lose connection with the server. One popular mechanism implemented in many clients, such as Gmail, is to wait for increasing amounts of time between two reconnection attempts (first a few seconds, then a minute, and so on), while still informing the user and also giving them a means to reestablish the connection manually by clicking a link or button. This disconnection scenario is quite frequent with mobile devices and laptops, so it's good for an application to have an automated reconnection mechanism in place to optimize the user experience.

SERVER-SIDE FAILURE HANDLING So far we've only handled failures on the client side; we haven't looked into mechanisms to deal with failure handling on the server side. This is not, unfortunately, because there are no failures on the server side, but rather because this topic is too big to cover in this chapter's example application. Don't worry, though. We'll revisit this aspect of the application in detail in chapters 5 and 6.

2.4.2 *Scaling out*

We now have a pretty slick and resource-efficient application that can stream tweets to many clients. But what if we were to build a fairly popular application, and we wanted

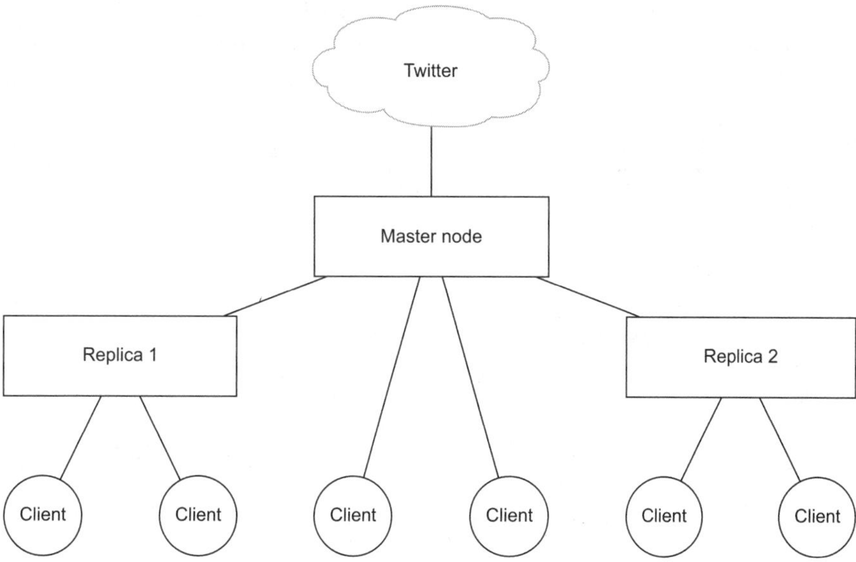

Figure 2.5 Scaling out using replica nodes

to handle more connections than a single node could manage? One mechanism we'll consider is *replica nodes* that could replicate our initial connection, as shown in figure 2.5.

Let's say we wanted to reuse the same connection to Twitter (because Twitter doesn't let us reuse the same credentials many times, and we don't want to create a new user and get new API credentials for each node). We already have a mechanism in place that lets clients view the stream using WebSockets, and we also have a mechanism to broadcast an incoming Twitter stream to WebSocket clients. The only thing we need in order to have working replica nodes that connect to a master node is a means to configure them and get them to connect to our master node instead of Twitter.

To achieve this, we'll set up a new subscription mechanism that allows other nodes to consume data from the initial stream (the one coming from Twitter). We'll set up a new controller action to stream out the content and make the necessary modifications to run the application in *replica* mode.

First, you need to set up a means for the `controller` method to subscribe to the stream.

Listing 2.16 Subscribing other nodes to the broadcast Twitter feed

```
def subscribeNode: Enumerator[JsObject] = {
  if (broadcastEnumerator.isEmpty) {
    connect()
  }
  broadcastEnumerator.getOrElse {
    Enumerator.empty[JsObject]
  }
}
```

This method, like the existing `subscribe` method, first makes sure that the connection to Twitter is initialized, and then simply returns the broadcasting enumeratee. You can now use the enumeratee in a controller method in your `Application` controller.

Listing 2.17 Streaming the replicated Twitter feed in the controller

```
class Application extends Controller {

  // ...

  def replicateFeed = Action { implicit request =>
    Ok.feed(TwitterStreamer.subscribeNode)
  }
}
```

The `feed` method simply feeds the stream provided by the enumerator as an HTTP request.

You now need to provide a new route for this action in conf/routes:

```
GET     /replicatedFeed          controllers.Application.replicateFeed
```

If you now visit http://localhost:9000/replicatedFeed, you'll see the stream of JSON documents displayed with continuous additions to the page.

You now have almost everything in place to set up a replica node. The last thing you need to do is connect to the master node instead of the original Twitter API. You can do this very easily by replacing the URL used in a replica node with the master node's URL. In a production setup, you'd use the application configuration for this. To keep things simple for this example, we'll use a JVM property that can easily be passed along. Add the following logic in the `connect()` method of the `TwitterStreamer` companion object, replacing the existing URL declaration:

```
val maybeMasterNodeUrl = Option(System.getProperty("masterNodeUrl"))
val url = maybeMasterNodeUrl.getOrElse {
  "https://stream.twitter.com/1.1/statuses/filter.json"
}
```

Now, start a new terminal window and start another Activator console (don't close the existing running application):

```
activator -DmasterNodeUrl=http://localhost:9000/replicatedFeed
```

Then run the application on another port:

```
[twitter-stream] $ run 9001
```

Upon visiting http://localhost:9001, you'll see the stream from the other node. You can start more of those nodes on different ports to check if the replication works as expected. Given how the setup works, you can also chain more replicating nodes by passing the URL of a replicating node as `masterNodeUrl` to another node.

FAILURE HANDLING IN A REPLICATED SETUP Although scaling out makes your application capable of handling a higher demand in terms of connections, it also makes failure handling quite a bit more complicated. Given the limitation of only one node being able to connect to Twitter, you're in a situation where there is a single point of failure—if this node were to go down, you'd be in trouble. In a real system, you'd seek to avoid having a single point of failure, and instead have a number of master nodes. You'd also need to devise a mechanism to cope with the loss of a master server.

2.5 Summary

In this chapter, we built a reactive web application using Play and Akka. We used a few key techniques for reactive applications:

- Using asynchronous actions for handling incoming HTTP requests
- Streaming and transforming tweets asynchronously using iteratees, enumeratees, and enumerators
- Establishing WebSocket connections using an Akka actor and connecting it to the stream
- Dealing with failure on the client side
- Scaling out using a simple replication model

Throughout the remainder of the book, we'll explore these topics in more depth. In the next chapter, we'll visit one building block of reactive web applications by looking into functional programming concepts.

3 Functional programming primer

> **This chapter covers**
> - Core functional programming principles
> - Practical tools for working with immutable state and data structures

Before going further into the realm of Play, let's take a detour and talk about a few functional programming fundamentals at the core of asynchronous programming in Scala. If you're already familiar with functional programming concepts and their application in Scala, you may want to skip over this chapter or skim through it quickly. If you're a newcomer to functional programming, this chapter will help you get up to speed with the most important principles and tools that you'll need to understand and write asynchronous code in Scala.

3.1 A few words on functional programming

Functional programming is a vast topic, and there are entire books dedicated to the topic.[1] I won't try to present all aspects of functional programming in just one

[1] See, for example, *Functional Programming in Scala* by Paul Chiusano and Rúnar Bjarnason (Manning, 2014) or *Scala in Action* by Nilanjan Raychaudhuri (Manning, 2013).

chapter, nor will we get to the core of it. In this chapter we'll only look at the most important concepts that you'll need to get started with asynchronous programming: immutability, functions, and manipulating immutable collections.

When thinking about functional programming, the first definition that may come to mind is "to program with functions." This definition is a bit vague, however, and doesn't point out the difference between functional and imperative programming. For what follows, let's use the following definition from "Uncle Bob" Martin:[2]

Functional programming is programming without assignment statements.

If you've been working mostly in an imperative programming style (such as Java), the preceding statement may be quite bewildering because it's hard to imagine how programming would look without assignment statements. If you're a functional programming aficionado, you may find the definition somewhat too shallow—I hear you say "there's so much more to functional programming than this!" And you are right—but for the purpose of this chapter, this definition will suit our needs as it brings us right to the one concept that's perhaps the hardest to understand when transitioning from an imperative programming style: *immutability*. Saying that there are no assignment statements is equivalent to saying that you can't change the value of a variable once it has been declared. In Java, this would be similar to using the `final` keyword everywhere, and only working with collections that can't be changed after they've been initialized with a given set of elements.

3.2 Immutability

Immutability in terms of programming languages means that a "thing" that can be referenced—be it a simple value such as a number, or a more complex one such as a collection or an object—can't be changed once it has been declared. To understand how this rather interesting restriction can be of benefit, we first need to take a look at the standard state representation of imperative languages: mutable state.

3.2.1 The fallacy of mutable state

The conceptual model of the world that object-oriented languages have been using for the longest time is flawed. What we do in object-oriented languages such as Java is mix up two things: we try to represent processes that occur in real life by describing entities, and then also try to represent how these entities evolve over time by mutating them. I say "try," because in reality what we do is create the illusion that we have somehow encoded the passing of time into a mutable object, but this illusion falls apart as soon as someone else looks at our object from a different reference point. Let's take the example of a car moving on a road, as shown in figure 3.1.

We may want to represent the movement of the car by changing its position, like so:

```
car.setPosition(0);
car.setPosition(10);
```

[2] Robert C. Martin, Functional Programming Basics, https://pragprog.com/magazines/2013-01/functional-programming-basics.

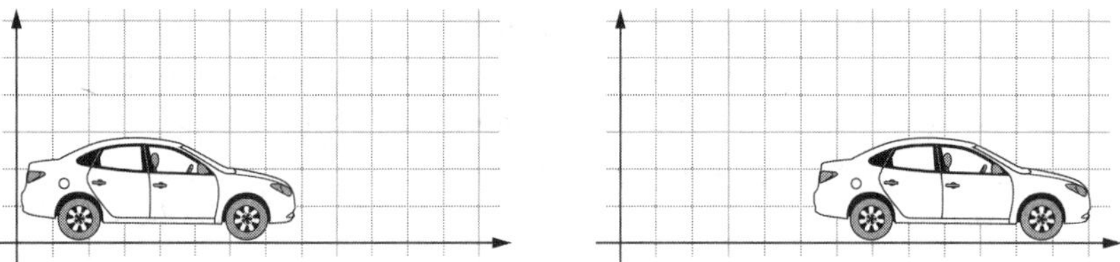

Figure 3.1 Car moving on a road, at one instant and the next

After running these two statements, we'd expect the position of the car to be 10, and `car.getPosition()` should return 10. If we are making those changes in a controlled environment where nobody else can see the car (and provided we're not subject to a space-time anomaly wherein time runs backwards), we may even be right. But as soon as this is not true anymore, as in figure 3.2, we run into problems.

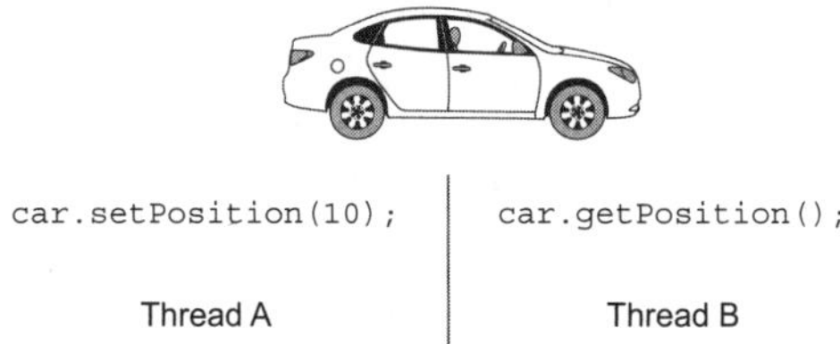

Figure 3.2 Two threads accessing the same mutable car at the same time

At what position will the car be for thread B? Is it at 0? Or is it already at 10? We can't tell because we don't know for sure *when* thread B is going to be called—it may be before or after thread A has changed the value. So we have a rather big problem: at the root of this conceptual model, we find ourselves confronted with uncertainty about the value of the object we're working with. This uncertainty brought about by mutable state doesn't need to involve multiple threads. Even if we were working with one thread and we built a sufficiently complex program, in which we passed mutable objects around, it would become increasingly difficult to know what the value of an object was going to be at any given point in time. Debuggers have helped us walk through the jungle of mutable state for a long time, but there are better ways to spend our time than debugging programs, trying to figure out what value a variable has at a certain point.

To get back to the multithreaded scenario, you may object and point out that it's possible to bring order to chaos by having threads A and B talk to each other about when it would be appropriate for B to retrieve the position of the car, rather than looking at it without considering A's efforts to change the position of the car. In this civilized world, with a bit of dialogue, there would be no indeterminism. This workaround might even succeed, but it comes at a high cost: threads A and B now need to know about each other, talk, and wait on one another before going about their usual business with the car. This has two direct consequences on our program:

- Performance suffers (because B needs to wait until A tells it that it is done moving the car).
- We (the developers) have to suddenly deal with an additional layer of complexity caused by the communication between A and B.

And as if things weren't bad enough with two threads, CPU vendors look at us with a smile on their face and a new processor model featuring 1,000 cores in their hand. To increase the performance of our programs, they say, we have no choice but to let many more threads work on the data at the same time. Just imagine 1,000 threads arguing about whose turn it is to have a look at the car—no, this is not going to turn out well either for us developers or for the car.

If we want to build applications that are future-proof, we need to utilize a conceptual model that doesn't lie about the value of an object. Let's have a look at the reasoning behind programming with immutable state.

3.2.2 Immutable values as snapshots of reality

An immutable value, as its name indicates, doesn't change. In a program, immutable values are declared once and their values are always the same throughout the execution of the program, or until they are no longer needed and are discarded.

This doesn't mean that we can't change our view of the world if we're using immutable state. To take the example of the car we talked about previously, this is how we would move the car:

```
case class Car(brand: String, position: Int)

val car = Car(brand = "DeLorean", position = 0)
val movedCar = car.copy(position = 10)
```

Instead of pretending that `car` is still the same, we now have two values: the original `car` at position 0, and a `movedCar` at position 10. `movedCar` is still the same DeLorean as the one at position 0, with the difference that it's now at a new position.

`car` and `movedCar` are snapshots of the car at two instants in time. You don't need to know *when* the snapshot was taken, because if an external observer were to read either of the values, they would be sure of the meaning: once defined, the values never change, and the `car` value will always represent the car before it went on its way. We could have 1,000 threads read the car's position and not need to be worried about causing any harm when creating a new moved version of it.

By embracing immutable values as a way to represent an object (or a data structure in general), we entirely eliminate the problem of not being quite sure about what value an observer will see. What it also means for us as developers is that we have to be explicit about passing values around, instead of passing references to variables that may change behind the scenes. Functions are a great way to manipulate immutable values and data structures. But before we talk about functions, there's another concept that goes hand in hand with immutable state and that is a cornerstone of functional programming languages: *expression-oriented programming*.

3.2.3 Expression-oriented programming

In expression-oriented programming languages, programs are written using *expressions* that return a value, rather than by writing *statements* that execute code but don't return anything. To perform a computation, statements will typically mutate the state of one or more variables outside the scope of the statement itself, whereas expressions return a value containing the result of the computation and don't change any state outside the expression while doing so.

For example, the following method is a statement.

Listing 3.1 A statement that removes an element from a list

```
public void removeElement(List<String> list, String toRemove) {
    for(Iterator<String> it = list.iterator(); it.hasNext();) {    // Iterates over the original list
        String s = it.next();
        if (s.equals(toRemove)) {
            it.remove();    // Removes values from the original list
        }
    }
}
```

In this statement, you pass in a list of strings and the value of the element you want to remove. The method then proceeds to remove this element from the list you have given it.

In contrast, the following expression achieves the same result, but without altering the initial list.

Listing 3.2 An expression that filters a list and removes a specific element

```
public List<String> filterNot(List<String> list, String toRemove) {
    List<String> filtered = new LinkedList<>();    // Creates a new list to contain the filtered results
    for(String s : list) {    // Iterates over the original list
        if (!s.equals(toRemove)) {
            filtered.add(s);    // Adds any results that match the filter text to the new filter list
        }
    }
    return filtered;    // Returns the new filter list
}
```

In this example, the data still gets mutated, but the mutation takes place inside the `filterNot` method, and it's visible only to that method. You can think of building a program as working with Lego blocks, putting together small expressions to build code of increasing complexity and size. All purely functional programming languages are expression-oriented.

EXPRESSION-ORIENTED PROGRAMMING AT THE CORE OF SCALA

Writing in an expression-oriented style in Java is not very comfortable. But Scala is designed around the concept of expressions, and besides featuring first-class functions, which we'll talk about soon, many of the language constructs such as control structures and pattern matching are expressions.

For example, a more generic version of the `filterNot` method example in listing 3.2 is available by default on all standard Scala collections:

```
val list = List("a", "b", "c")
val filtered = list.filterNot(letter => letter == "b")
```

Control structures such as conditional `if-else` statements are also expressions in Scala:

```
scala> val greeting: String = if(true) "Hello" else "Goodbye"
greeting: String = Hello
```

The preceding construct may look familiar if you've been working with Java, as there's an equivalent notation:

```
String greeting = true ? "Hello" : "Goodbye";
```

Scala's match expressions also allow you to manipulate data in a concise manner without having to make use of mutable state. The following example transforms a number given as input into its string representation.

Listing 3.3 Simple match expression spelling out a few numbers

```
def spellOut(number: Int): String = number match {
  case 1 => "one"
  case 2 => "two"
  case 42 => "forty-two"
  case _ => "unknown number"
}

val fortyTwo = spellOut(42)
```

- The match statement is applied against the number integer.
- Each branch is represented by a case expression.
- The wildcard pattern represented by the underscore matches all cases.

In imperative programming languages, it's not uncommon to see large blocks of logic, such as large `if-else` statements, reasoning about data and modifying variables and mutable data structures declared outside of their scope. The idea of expression-oriented programming is to keep the different flows of logic small and to combine small "reasoning machines" together to build a complex mechanism. An essential ingredient for achieving this is functions, which we're finally going to take a closer look at now.

3.3 Functions

Just like in mathematics, functions in programs take a number of inputs and return an output, as shown in figure 3.3.

In this section we'll see that functions haven't been used at their full potential in object-oriented languages, and we'll look at how they can be useful in working with immutable state.

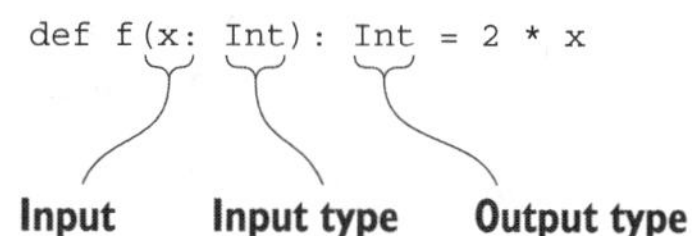

Figure 3.3 Example of a function in Scala

3.3.1 Functions in object-oriented programming languages

One of the main principles of object-oriented programming languages as we know them is *encapsulation*: data and methods for manipulating this data are encapsulated together in one object. The original idea behind encapsulation was to reduce the visibility of data as much as possible, as this would yield more reliable and maintainable code, especially in large codebases. Prior to languages that supported encapsulation, large codebases had problems related to identically named variables and to code organization in general (encapsulation made it possible to group related methods together).

In practice, encapsulation is often misunderstood: Java objects are often cluttered with getters and setters, effectively exposing to the whole world the inner state of an object, which was supposed to be protected by encapsulation. But even if encapsulation were strictly applied, it wouldn't solve the problems of mutable state that we've already discussed. Mutable state (encapsulated or not) means that it's very difficult to reason about data when working in a multithreaded setting, and to reason about what the state of an object is in general.

The perhaps larger implication of encapsulation in a language such as Java is that functions have been degraded to a means of mutating data inside a specific type of object. The methods encapsulated in an object are effectively tied to that specific family of objects, which greatly limits the reuse of similar behavior across a broader variety of objects. Inheritance can only partially undo this hard link—entities that share a set of characteristics and are otherwise entirely unrelated aren't likely to be found in the same inheritance hierarchy. As a side effect of this limitation, it's not uncommon to see several utility classes consisting of `public static` methods in larger Java projects. In Java projects, the `utils` package is a niche in which most of the functions used in those projects are to be found.

And yet, functions can do much more! In essence, functions encode behavior. They define to a large degree what happens with data and, if used at their full potential, can tremendously simplify the maintenance of a program. Let's see what full-fledged functions can do for us, and how we can get the most out of them.

3.3.2 Functions as first-class values

In functional programming languages in general, and in Scala in particular, functions are treated as first-class citizens of the language, and are not restricted to living as a method tied to a particular type. Just like any other object, functions can be passed around as parameters to other methods or functions. Functions, unlike methods encapsulated in objects, don't need to be executed right away. Instead, the behavior they hold can be moved around and applied when it's needed.

DECLARING FUNCTIONS IN SCALA

In Scala, functions can be defined in multiple ways. The most common way is to use the `def` keyword, which is the equivalent of traditional methods in object-oriented languages:

```
def square(x: Int): Int = x * x
```

Another way of defining a function in Scala is to use a *function literal*:

```
val square = (x: Int) => x * x
```

Function literals are objects of type `Function1`, `Function2`, and so on (depending on the number of parameters), that can be passed around just like any other object instance.

The full type of the square function literal is written as follows:

```
val square: Function1[Int, Int] = (x: Int) => x * x
```

> **PURE FUNCTIONS** Functions that take inputs and produce outputs without producing any side effects (such as printing a statement on the console or causing input/output operations such as filesystem access or network access) are said to be *pure*. Whenever possible, you should favor working with pure functions, as there are no surprises related to side effects.

3.3.3 Moving behavior around

Usually, I favor using method definitions rather than function literals, given that their syntax looks more natural, especially when it comes to more-complex parameter declarations. It's possible to turn a method into a function literal by telling the compiler that you don't want to call the method but rather treat it as a value.

For example, let's turn the `square` method into a function literal:

```
scala> def square(x: Int): Int = x * x
square: (x: Int)Int

scala> val squareLiteral = square _
squareLiteral: Int => Int = <function1>
```

The underscore in the preceding example tells the compiler that you don't wish to execute the method, but rather to *partially apply* it: instead of providing a concrete value for the parameter `x`, you use the underscore as a placeholder, resulting in a function literal that can be passed around and executed only once a parameter is provided (as opposed to the default behavior of expecting an argument to be provided when referencing it).

Being able to defer the execution of a function is key to some applications, such as callbacks in asynchronous programming. Before the introduction of lambdas in Java 8, the means to emulate the behavior of functions was to define an interface with the function signature. For example, this is how you would implement a `Runnable`:

```
public class AsynchronousTask implements Runnable {
    public void run() {
        System.out.println("This task is running asynchronously");
    }
}
```

AsynchronousTask acts as a container for the behavior executed when calling the run() method. The first-class equivalent of that would be a simple function literal in Scala:

```
val asynchronousTask =
  () => println("This task is running asynchronously")
```

Just like a new instance of the AsynchronousTask in Java, the asynchronousTask function literal in Scala can be moved around. For example, it can be used as a parameter to another function.

3.3.4 Composing functions

Let's come back to the square function literal we defined earlier on:

```
val square: Function1[Int, Int] = (x: Int) => x * x
```

You can use this literal as a parameter to another function, such as to calculate the fourth power of a number by building on the square function:

```
def fourth(x: Int, squarer: Function1[Int, Int]): Int =
  squarer(squarer(x))
```

See what I did there? squarer is a regular parameter of the new fourth function that expects a function from Int to Int that will square its input.

There is a nicer syntax for the type of the squarer parameter that's used commonly in Scala programs (in fact, it's fairly unusual to see the Function1 notation in programs):

```
def fourth(x: Int, squarer: Int => Int): Int = squarer(squarer(x))
```

The type Int => Int with the arrow notation is pronounced "from Int to Int."

You can call the fourth function by passing in a number and the square function literal we just defined, as follows:

```
val twoToThePowerOfFour = fourth(2, square)
```

Having a function as one of its parameters makes fourth a so-called *higher-order function*. Higher-order functions are a powerful way to abstract similar operations. For example, let's say we also wanted a function to calculate the double of a number:

```
def double(x: Int): Int = 2 * x
```

If we wanted to calculate the quadruple, we could call double twice by passing it in as a parameter:

```
def quadruple(x: Int, doubler: Int => Int): Int = doubler(doubler(x))
```

This last definition is very similar to the fourth function defined earlier. In fact, except for the name, these functions are identical and perform the same operation. We can therefore infer an abstraction:

```
def applyTwice(x: Int, f: Int => Int): Int = f(f(x))
```

We can now rewrite our fourth and quadruple functions:

```
def fourth(x: Int) = applyTwice(x, y => y * y)
def quadruple(x: Int) = applyTwice(x, y => 2 * y)
```

ANONYMOUS FUNCTION DECLARATIONS In the two rewritten function definitions fourth and quadruple, instead of passing in references to the square or double functions that we had already defined, we directly pass in their definitions. Functions that are declared like this on the spot, without being given a name, are called *anonymous functions.*

3.3.5 The size of functions

One characteristic of functions that's important concerning readability and code maintainability is their size. The more complex the behavior you're encoding, the longer the function may become. It's easy to get carried away while programming and end up with a function that spans many lines of code, declaring a group of values on the way, but not necessarily making it very clear what happens.

Finding the right size for a function is harder than it may sound. In terms of execution or performance, it doesn't hurt a program to have long functions, but it does makes it harder to maintain and understand the program. Let's consider the following example, in which we want to compute simple statistics about advertisement clicks.

Listing 3.4 Function to compute advertisement clicks on a per-month basis

```
case class Click(timestamp: DateTime, advertisementId: Long)
case class Month(year: Int, month: Int)

def computeYearlyAggregates(clickRepository: ClickRepository):
  Map[Long, Map[Month, Int]] = {
    val pastClicks =
      clickRepository.getClicksSince(DateTime.now.minusYears(1))   <- Retrieves clicks over the past year
    pastClicks.groupBy(_.advertisementId).mapValues {   <- Groups the clicks by advertisementId
      case clicks =>
        val monthlyClicks = clicks
          .groupBy(click =>
            Month(
              click.timestamp.getYear,
              click.timestamp.getMonthOfYear   <- Groups the clicks by month
            )
          ).map { case (month, groupedClicks) =>
            month -> groupedClicks.length   <- Computes the click count for a month
          }.toSeq
        monthlyClicks
    }
}
```

You may be able to read this example, and perhaps with a bit of practice it may become easier to understand this kind of code quickly. But even though this code may be easy to write, after some time it may not be very easy to put yourself back into context and make sense out of all the imbricated `groupBy` and `map` blocks.

This is a situation where it makes sense to reduce the overall complexity of the `computeYearlyAggregates` function by cutting it into several small functions. Scala lets us declare functions pretty much anywhere, even inside of other functions. Let's make use of this feature to rewrite the code with smaller functions that we can then tie together.

Listing 3.5 Refactored function to compute advertisement clicks on a per-month basis

```
def computeYearlyAggregates(clickRepository: ClickRepository):
  Map[Long, Seq[(Month, Int)]] = {

  def monthOfClick(click: Click) =
    Month(click.timestamp.year, click.timestamp.month)

  def countMonthlyClicks(monthlyClicks: (Month, Seq[Click])) =
    monthlyClicks match { case (month, clicks) =>
      month -> clicks.length
    }

  def computeMonthlyAggregates(clicks: Seq[Click]) =
    clicks.groupBy(monthOfClick).map(countMonthlyClicks).toSeq

  val pastClicks =
    clickRepository.getClicksSince(DateTime.now.minusYear(1))

  pastClicks
    .groupBy(_.advertisementId)
    .mapValues(computeMonthlyAggregates)
}
```

Function that extracts the month of a click

Function that counts all the clicks in a month

Function to compute monthly aggregates of a set of clicks

Function that ties all the computations together

Notice how this code is a lot easier to read. Problems are broken into small functions, and their purpose can easily be identified through their names. What's more, those small functions are only visible in the scope of the `computeYearlyAggregates` function, which makes sense because their utility might be limited outside of that scope. Notice how the functions are combined to build up increasingly complex behavior; for example, the `computeMonthlyAggregates` function combines both the `monthOfClick` and `countMonthlyClicks` functions.

OMITTING FUNCTION ARGUMENTS It's possible to omit parameters when working with functions. In the `computeMonthlyAggregates` function, the `monthOfClick` function is passed as an argument to `groupBy` directly, without explicitly wiring in the arguments of `groupBy`. `groupBy` is a higher-order function that, in this case, expects a function of the kind `Click => T` where `T` is the type of the element to group the collection by. Because the `monthOfClick` function has the expected type, it's suitable as an argument to `groupBy`.

As you can see, writing small, focused functions makes the code easier to understand and maintain. The fact that Scala lets you omit the function parameters (in some cases, at least) helps you further focus on the functions alone—on the behavior you want to apply to the data rather than on the somewhat secondary task of passing data from one function to another.

One rule of thumb that can be useful when trying to identify what granularity the functions should have is to clearly identify the responsibility of the function. It should be possible to infer the one thing a function does from its name—if you can't find a good name for a function, that may be an indication that the function does too many things.

3.4 Manipulating immutable collections

One of the first issues that arises when trying to make the switch from mutable to immutable data structures is working with collections. In a mutable world, loops are the tool of choice for rearranging collections. In the following pages you'll see how you can go about manipulating immutable collections with higher-order functions instead.

3.4.1 Transformations instead of loops

Let's say we wanted to split a list of users by age into minors and majors. In a mutable world, we'd most likely go about it using the following loop.

Listing 3.6 Splitting users into minors and majors using a loop and two mutable collections

```
List<User> minors = new ArrayList<User>();
List<User> majors = new ArrayList<User>();

for(int i = 0; i < users.size(), i++) {
    User u = users.get(i);
    if(u.getAge() < 18) {
        minors.add(u);
    } else {
        majors.add(u);
    }
}
```

In this example, two mutable lists are populated from within the loop. The iteration over the list relies on an index and retrieving each element by index, as opposed to the behavior of an iterable.

In contrast, let's see how you could go about achieving the same result in a functional fashion.

Listing 3.7 Splitting users into minors and majors using a higher-order function

```
val (minors, majors) = users.partition(_.age < 18)
```

In this example, you use the `partition` function, which expects as its argument a *predicate* function (returning a Boolean value). This function is executed for each value of the source collection, the result being a tuple of two immutable lists containing the values partitioned according to the predicate.

There are several things we can observe when comparing the second approach to the first:

- The loop is not explicit.
- Functions, oftentimes predicate functions, play a central role in this kind of manipulation.
- There's no need for mutable state because the result is provided right away, as an immutable data structure.

The second approach is said to be *declarative*: we describe the result we want, rather than how to get it. In the first approach, said to be *imperative*, we explicitly specify how we want to get the result. By operating at a different level of abstraction, the declarative approach, supported by the powerful higher-order functions, lets us focus on describing the results of our program rather than worrying too much about the implementation details. Eventually, a loop will be executed, but it's not necessary to concern ourselves with it—especially since loops are a well-understood mechanism.

Another advantage of declaring operations on a higher level of abstraction is that the implementation can be switched out rather easily. Scala's collection library is built around the two traits `scala.collection.Traverseable` and `scala.collection.Iterable`, which contain many methods useful for working with traversable or iterable data structures. The standard library offers a few flavors of collections, mainly immutable and mutable collections, but also a parallel flavor that executes the computations on the collection across several threads.

Before looking further at a few ways of programming in a declarative fashion, let's first look at the tools we'll use for this purpose.

3.4.2 *Higher-order functions for manipulating collections*

As you've seen, higher-order functions are very helpful when it comes to declaratively specifying how you want a collection to be transformed. By expecting functions as arguments (expecting behavior as arguments to be applied to the data), the developer can focus on describing behavior rather than fiddling with the state itself.

In this section we'll talk about some of the most powerful transformation functions available for manipulating Scala collections and for transforming data structures through expressions in general.

MAP AND FLATMAP

`map` is a function that walks through all the elements of a collection and applies a function to them, returning a new *mapped* collection as a result (the original collection doesn't change). Here's an example:

```
scala> val list1 = List(1, 2, 3)
list1: List[Int] = List(1, 2, 3)

scala> val doubles = list1.map(_ * 2)
doubles: List[Int] = List(2, 4, 6)
```

map operates as depicted in figure 3.4.

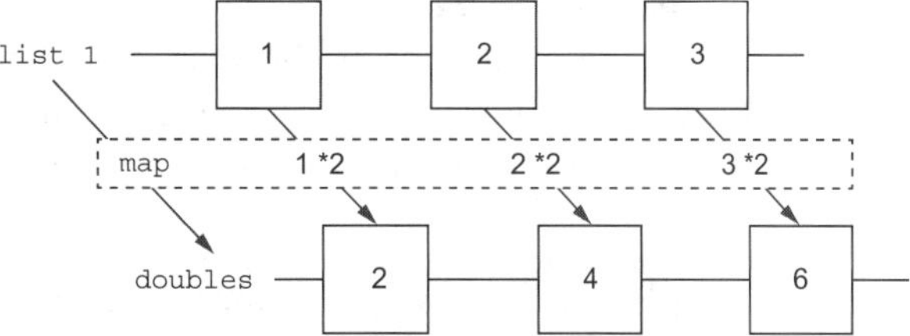

Figure 3.4 Applying map to a list of integers

That's simple, isn't it? map just takes each element of the collection, applies the function it has been called with, and returns a new collection. Note that you're not limited to returning integers: if your function were to return another type, you'd end up with the same kind of collection, but with a different type of elements.

Let's move on to something more complicated: flatMap. flatMap is a function that expects a function that returns a collection of elements. Like map, it then applies that function to all elements of the collection it has been called from. But unlike map, it takes one more step and *flattens* the resulting groups of collections into the original collection. This all sounds somewhat complicated, so let's look at an example:

```
scala> def f(i: Int) = List(i * 2, i * i)
f: (i: Int)List[Int]

scala> val flatMapped = list1.flatMap(f)
flatMapped: List[Int] = List(2, 1, 4, 4, 6, 9)
```

You define a function that takes an integer and turns it into a list, and then apply this function to your existing list1 with flatMap, as shown in figure 3.5.

You can reproduce this process of cutting the flatMap operation into two parts by first mapping the values and then flattening them:

```
scala> val mapped = list1.map(f)
mapped: List[List[Int]] = List(List(2, 1), List(4, 4), List(6, 9))

scala> val flatMapped = mapped.flatten
flatMapped: List[Int] = List(2, 1, 4, 4, 6, 9)
```

FOREACH One other method worth mentioning here is foreach. Like map, it iterates over each element of a collection, but it doesn't return any value—instead, it creates a side effect, for example by printing out a line on the console. Under the hood, map and flatMap are implemented using foreach.

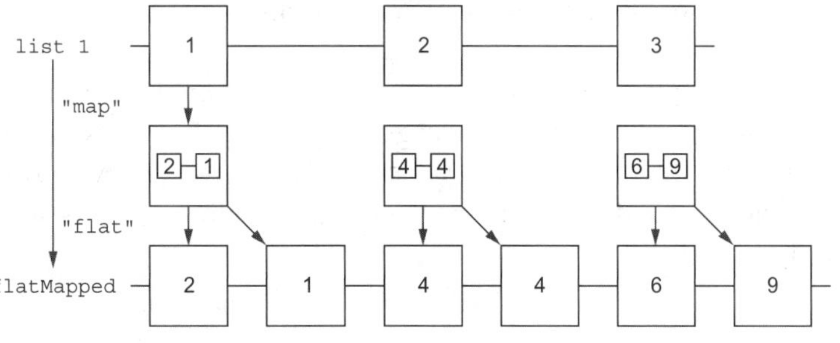

Figure 3.5 Applying flatMap to a list of integers

FOR COMPREHENSIONS

A `for` comprehension is the Swiss army knife for working with collections. It allows you to combine your work on several collections and to filter the results in a very versatile manner. Consider the following example.

Listing 3.8 Example of a simple `for` comprehension

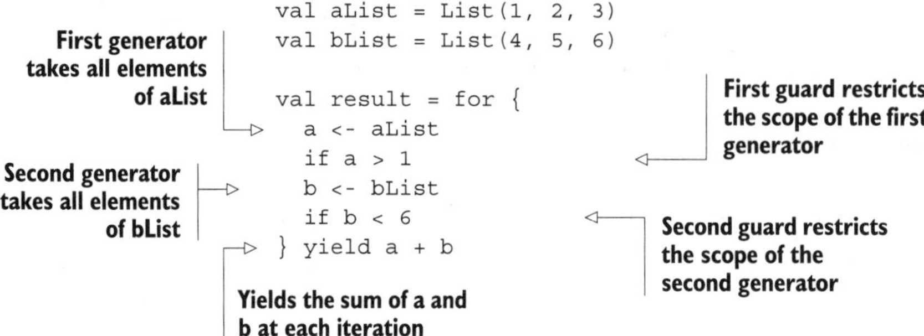
First generator takes all elements of aList
Second generator takes all elements of bList
Yields the sum of a and b at each iteration
First guard restricts the scope of the first generator
Second guard restricts the scope of the second generator

```
val aList = List(1, 2, 3)
val bList = List(4, 5, 6)

val result = for {
  a <- aList
  if a > 1
  b <- bList
  if b < 6
} yield a + b
```

A `for` comprehension is made out of *generators* such as `a <- aList`, and *guards* such as `if a > 1`. Generators produce values at each iteration, and guards can be used to filter the values. You can picture multiple generators as behaving like imbricated lists, the first generator wrapping the second one, and so on.

Internally, Scala will turn `for` comprehensions into a sequence of `flatMap`, `map`, and `withFilter` calls. For example, the preceding `for` comprehension would be turned into the following:

```
val result = aList
  .withFilter(_ > 1)
  .flatMap { a =>
    bList
      .withFilter(_ < 6)
      .map { b =>
        a + b
      }
  }
```

USING MAP, FLATMAP, AND FOR COMPREHENSIONS WITH THE OPTION TYPE

To gain a wider appreciation for the tools we've just talked about, let's look at how they can be used in combination with one of Scala's more popular data structures: the `Option` type.

An `Option` is Scala's solution to the `NullPointerException` that haunts Java developers (and developers of other similar languages) to this day. It represents a value that may or may not be available. Saying that `Option`s are widely used in Scala would be an understatement: they're the de facto standard notation in libraries for passing around values that may be undefined.

There are two ways to look at an Option, as depicted in figure 3.6: either as a box that contains something or not, or as a list that has at most one element.

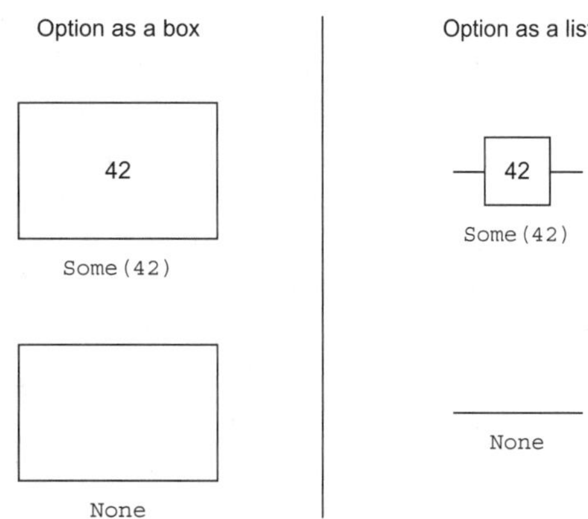

Figure 3.6 An `Option` represented as a box or a list

`Option[T]` has two subtypes, `Some[T]` and `None`, representing the two possible states an `Option` can take. The main implications of working with `Option`s instead of nullable values is that you have to ask yourself every time you want to access the value of the `Option` what you'll do if it's not there. It's easy to forget to deal with this possibility when manipulating nullable values, but it certainly isn't a very good idea, as the resulting `NullPointerExceptions` are very annoying and time-consuming (Tony Hoare, who introduced null references back in the day, called them his "billion dollar mistake").[3] Options make it more difficult for the programmer to forget a nullable value check, given that a value has to be explicitly retrieved rather than just passed around by reference.

OPTION AS A BOX—IMPERATIVE ACCESS TO AN OPTION'S CONTENT

There are several ways to check whether an `Option` contains anything:

```
scala> val box = Option("Cat")
box: Option[String] = Some(Cat)

scala> box.isEmpty
res0: Boolean = false

scala> box.isDefined
res1: Boolean = true

scala> box == None
res2: Boolean = false
```

One way of working with `Option`s in this paradigm is to write code as follows:

```
if (box != None) {
  val contents = box.get
  process(contents)
} else {
  reportError()
}
```

[3] See the "Apologies and retractions" section of the Wikipedia article on Tony Hoare: http://en.wikipedia.org/wiki/Tony_Hoare#Apologies_and_retractions.

If you remember what we talked about in section 3.4, you may already recognize that this code isn't at all expression-oriented. If you adopt a functional programming style and work with it for a while, this kind of code may make you itch (it does so for me at least). The advantage of using `Options` over nullable values also becomes less obvious—the `box != None` check is quite similar to checks like `value != null`. Finally, if you forget to check whether an `Option` is defined and call the `get` method on a `None`, Scala will throw a `java.util.NoSuchElementException` (which isn't much more useful than a `NullPointerException`).

An interesting alternative—from the point of view of functional programming—is to use the tools we talked about previously to manipulate collections, and consider an `Option` to be a list that can have at most one element.

OPTION AS A LIST—FUNCTIONAL ACCESS TO AN OPTION'S CONTENT

If you picture an `Option` as a list, you can use `map` to access and transform each of its elements:

```
val user: Option[User] = User.findById(42)
val fullName: Option[String] = user.map { u =>
  u.fullName
}
```

With `map` you can access the contents of an `Option` without "unboxing" it. If the `Option` isn't defined, your operation won't be applied. After the transformation, however, you're still left with another `Option` and no concrete value. Depending on the situation, you may want to provide a default value if none can be retrieved. You can do this using the `getOrElse` method:

```
val user: Option[User] = User.findById(42)
val fullName: String = user.map { u =>
  u.fullName
} getOrElse {
  "Unknown user"
}
```

`map` is a powerful tool for working with `Options`, but it sometimes has limits. For example, let's say we wanted to retrieve a user's address, instead of just their name, by calling the `findById` method of `Address`, which returns an `Option` of an `Address`:

```
val user: Option[User] = User.findById(42)
val address: Option[Option[Address]] = user.map { u =>
  Address.findById(u.addressId)
}
```

We've now created an `Option` of an `Option` of an `Address`, and that's not a very good place to be. Luckily, we have another tool at our disposal for dealing with this kind of situation: `flatMap` lets us inline the result of a mapped list into one flat list. We can do the exact same thing with imbricated `Options`:

```
val user: Option[User] = User.findById(42)
val address: Option[Address] = user.flatMap { u =>
  Address.findById(u.addressId)
}
```

Sometimes, even `flatMap` isn't a good enough solution for composing operations on `Option`s, in the sense that we may need to compose many values as part of one operation. Consider the following example, in which we want to update a user's first name.

Listing 3.9 Using a `for` comprehension to compose multiple `Option`s

```
def updateFirstName(userId: Long) = Action {
  implicit request =>
    val update: Option[Result] = for {
      json <- request.body.asJson
      user <- User.findOneById(userId)
      newFirstName <- (json \ "firstName").asOpt[String]
      if !newFirstName.trim.isEmpty
    } yield {
      User.updateFirstName(user.id, newFirstName)
      Ok
    }

  update.getOrElse {
    BadRequest(Json.obj("error" -> "Could not update your " +
      "first name, please make sure that it is not empty"))
  }
}
```

- **Attempts to retrieve the request's body as JSON object**
- **Attempts to find the user given its identifier**
- **Attempts to extract the first name from the JSON object**
- **Makes sure that the first name isn't empty**
- **Returns an error if it can't retrieve all the data necessary to do the update**

Using a `for` comprehension makes your code more readable, as it becomes very clear which values need to be available to perform an operation. The alternative of writing out the imbricated `flatMap` and `map` statements makes for less-readable code. If you're just starting to work with `for` comprehensions, you may find that they're somewhat less intuitive than `map` and `flatMap`: when manipulating `Option`s (or other types of data that support this kind of operation), you may find that you use `map` on the optional value, then use the result to retrieve a second optional value, and then come back to change the outer `map` into a `flatMap` to get rid of the nesting. Only after having implemented the whole chain by hand may it become clear that a `for` comprehension is a better way to compose various `Option`s. Don't worry about this, though. You'll get used to it as you go.

One disadvantage of using `for` comprehensions in combination with `Option`s is that they hide the origin of the resulting nondeterminism: in the previous example, if you don't get a result, it may be due to the request body not containing a valid JSON encoding, the user with this identifier not being available, the JSON object not containing a `firstName` string field, or the first name being empty. In my experience, however, what matters most is writing code that's resilient to all of those mishaps and that handles the most probable error causes (in this case, that the user hasn't provided a value for the first name). If any of the other steps were invalid along the path, there isn't much you could do to help your user anyway, so giving them the exact reason why the system couldn't update their first name likely wouldn't make them a lot happier.

CARRYING ON UNDEFINED VALUES Using `map`, `flatMap`, and `for` comprehensions lets you write code in which you carry on the undefined state of an `Option` or several `Options` until you've finished dealing with the "normal" case in which all values are defined. You can then deal with undefined values, error conditions, and so on in one place instead of having to constantly check if a value is defined or not.

MONADIC OPERATIONS Scala's `Option` is a so-called *monad*, and `map`, `flatMap`, and `withFilter` are called *monadic* operations. In category theory, a monad is a construct that obeys a certain set of laws and exhibits interesting properties, such as the composability we've just worked with. A few of the other most popular types in Scala are also monads and provide monadic operations, such as `Try`, `Either`, and `Future`. As you'll see, this means that these types can also be combined and generally be manipulated with ease.

3.5 Making the switch to a declarative programming style

It would be very convenient if reading a few pages on the principles of immutability, higher-order functions, and tools for manipulating collections were sufficient for you to drop your perhaps years-old habit of imperative programming and immediately replace it with functional programming. I'm afraid this won't be the case, as it takes time for our brains to unlearn the habits ingrained by imperative programming practice and to apply novel ways of thinking to our daily programming.

I've found that what most helps people make the switch to functional programming is to practice it—to work on a project with a functional programming language such as Scala. If you're reading this book, chances are that you're interested in learning the tools of the trade precisely in order to work with these technologies, and I can only encourage you to try applying functional programming principles as soon as possible. In this section, I'll give you a few pointers that may help you accelerate the switch.

Most APIs that you'll encounter when working with Scala, Play, and Akka are designed to be used in a functional manner. As such, you'll often encounter the `Option` type, as well as other types that are composable in nature.

There are four practical pieces of advice that I've used myself to embrace a more functional approach to programming:

- Never use the `get` method on an `Option`.
- Only use immutable values and data structures.
- Aim for small and crisp functions.
- Iterate and refine your functional style.

3.5.1 Never use the get method on an Option

By applying this rule, your preferred means of manipulating `Options` will be one of the functional approaches we've talked about earlier: using `map`, `flatMap`, or `for` comprehensions every time you want to manipulate a value inside an `Option`. One of the first things you'll notice when adopting this rule is that much of your logic will be wrapped inside of a callback (or inside of a specialized function that you'll provide as input to `map` or to any other collection method).

If you're connecting to Java APIs, one trick you can use to shield yourself against `NullPointerExceptions` is to wrap unsafe input (input that can be nullable according to the API you're using) inside of an `Option`, like so:

```
val unsafeInput = Option(myJavaAPI.getValue)
```

If the value provided by the API is `null`, the resulting `Option` will be `None`.

3.5.2 Only use immutable values and data structures

This rule is likely going to be one of the harder ones to follow, especially if you're still reaching out for a loop instead of one of the collection methods to work with data, and you'll often be tempted to use a `var` instead of a `val` when declaring variables. Your IDE may be able to point out when `var` is used needlessly.

Note that there are a few cases where mutable state is "allowed," or where its use is of benefit. For example, when integrating with an existing Java API, it may not make much sense to go against the imperative design of the API. If you can't get your code `var`-free from the beginning, don't despair. Asking a colleague or friend who is more versed in functional programming to take a look may also be a good way to get a faster start.

3.5.3 Aim for small and crisp functions

Once you start getting the hang of writing your code in a functional structure (building one transformation after another, rather than loops and imperative code that changes existing state), it's a good exercise to revisit your code and factor out small bits and pieces into functions, as you saw in listing 3.5. During this process, finding meaningful names for each function is of high importance; after all, you want to be able to understand what you've done when you revisit the code later on.

One suggestion for naming functions: if possible, always aim at describing the semantics of what a function is doing, rather than the way it works. In other words, including technical details such as type names in a function name may not be very helpful; the type annotations of a function should already encode which types are to be expected as input and output. Say you're retrieving a database cursor that you want to use in multiple other functions (before effectively executing the call that will fetch the data from the database):

```
def findAllUsersCursor: DBCursor[DBObject] =
  find(DBQuery("{}"))
```

This method signature repeats the `Cursor` type both in its name and signature. A better alternative would be to describe what the functions does, which is to provide a means to iterate over a result set:

```
def iterateOverAllUsers: DBCursor[DBObject] =
  find(DBQuery("{}"))
```

3.5.4 Iterate and refine your functional style

If you sit down in front of your computer with the aim of applying the preceding advice all at once, chances are that you won't get very far. Instead of trying to get everything right from the very first step, it may be helpful to start by writing your code the way you're used to, with mutable `var`s instead of `val`s, mutable collections, and using loops. Once you've fleshed out what your code should do, start thinking about how you want to achieve the behavior. Take the time to revisit the code bit by bit, making it immutable one piece at the time, replacing loops with collection methods, and slowly fleshing out incrementally smaller functions.

3.6 Summary

In this chapter we looked at some of the most important functional programming concepts used in the remainder of the book. These concepts are very useful for writing asynchronous code with Scala's Futures API. In particular, we talked about

- Functional programming, functions, and higher-order functions
- Immutable state and expression-oriented programming
- Scala's immutable collections and how to work with them

Now that you have the necessary tooling, let's go one level deeper and look at how to use the Play Framework in combination with these tools and build reactive applications.

4 Quick introduction to Play

This chapter covers

- The structure of a Play application
- The core concepts of Play, including HTTP actions and WebSocket handlers
- A few advanced features, such as customization mechanisms for error handling and custom request filters

The Play Framework is a web application framework inspired in its design by Model-View-Controller (MVC) frameworks such as Ruby on Rails and Django. Unlike most JVM-based web application frameworks, Play doesn't build on top of the Servlet standard, but instead has its own lightweight abstraction of the HTTP and WebSocket protocols. It's stateless at its core (it doesn't hold server-side state) and it's built around the concept of asynchronous request handling. Along with providing a high-performance framework, Play is also guided by the idea of rapid development and prototyping, allowing you to see changes almost instantly after having made them in code.

You saw some of the elements of Play in chapter 2, but we didn't take any time to discuss how they work or why they matter. In this chapter you'll learn the ropes of creating a new Play application and finding your way around existing Play applications. This chapter won't make you an expert in all things Play, but you will get an overview of what you can do with Play and how the main mechanisms work under the hood so that we have some common ground to explore reactive web application design and development with Play in the remainder of this book. If at any time you'd like to take a deep dive into the Play Framework and explore all of the features it has to offer in detail, I recommend taking a look at the official framework documentation at http://playframework.com/documentation.

4.1 Play application structure and configuration

In chapter 2 we set up Play using a template from the Lightbend Activator as a quick way to get started. To better understand how a Play application is structured and what the different files do, we'll now set up a minimal project and create the required files by hand. Don't worry, the files aren't too big, so there won't be that much typing involved.

To illustrate the main concepts of the Play Framework, we'll use a simple REST-based application as an example.

4.1.1 Introducing the Simple Vocabulary Teacher

In this chapter we'll build an application that can quiz users on the vocabulary of a certain language. It's up to the user to tell the application about the vocabulary in the first place. Once the application knows some vocabulary, it will pick a random word in one language and ask the user to translate it. Figure 4.1 gives an overview of the intended functionality and workflow.

In this first version of the Simple Vocabulary Teacher, we won't create a user interface but instead set up a REST interface and communicate with the application using curl. This will give us direct insight into what kind of responses Play is sending us.

The source and target languages need to be specified by the user with each request.

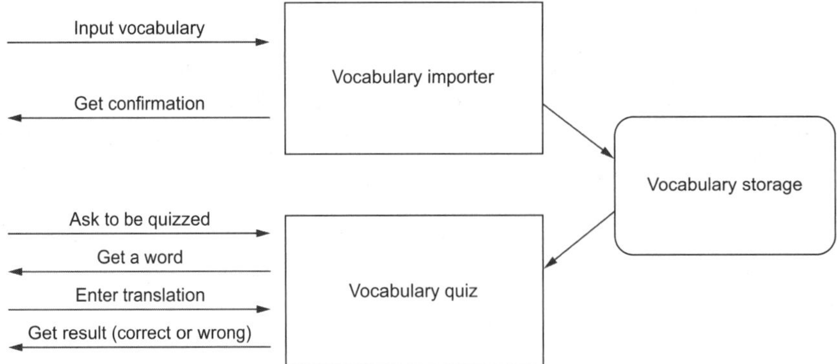

Figure 4.1 Functional overview of the Simple Vocabulary Teacher application

4.1.2 Creating a minimal Play application scaffold

This is the minimal set of files and directories we'll use for the project:

```
├── app
│   ├── controllers
│   │   ├── Import.scala
│   │   └── Quiz.scala
│   └── models
│       └── Vocabulary.scala
│   └── services
│       └── VocabularyService.scala
├── build.sbt
├── conf
│   ├── application.conf
│   └── logback.xml
└── project
      ├── build.properties
      └── plugins.sbt
```

If you compare this to the directory listing you obtained when working through chapter 2, you'll notice that some elements are missing here, especially anything related to views and public assets. This is in line with making a REST back end without a user interface. Play will create the directories it's missing when the application is first started.

APPLICATION CONFIGURATION

Let's start by creating the conf/application.conf file, which holds the configuration of our application.

Listing 4.1 Minimal application configuration in conf/application.conf

```
play {
  crypto.secret="changeme"
  i18n.langs="en"
}
```

The application secret used for encryption and signing

Comma-separated list of languages supported by the application

The application.conf file employs the HOCON notation, which stands for "Human-Optimized Config Object Notation." The idea is to keep the semantics of JSON for tree structure, types, and encoding, but to make it more friendly for humans to read and edit. Play uses the Lightbend Config library (https://github.com/typesafehub/config) to read its configuration files. A nice feature of HOCON is that it makes it possible to include configuration files, so you can, for example, separate the technical configuration in application.conf from more business-related configuration.

Lightbend Config also supports a flat format, wherein the trees are flattened into keys. In the remainder of this book, we'll use both of those notations in combination, because sometimes the flat notation makes more sense (such as when there's only one or very few values in the same branch).

As you can see in listing 4.1, the minimal set of values required in the configuration is rather small. There are several other concerns that are usually covered in the application configuration:

- Database access configuration
- Automatic database evolution configuration
- Mail server configuration
- Akka actor system configuration
- Thread pool configuration

THE APPLICATION SECRET Play uses an application secret to sign session cookies and CSRF tokens, and to provide built-in encryption tools. It's very important not to make this secret publicly available, as this makes it possible for attackers to forge their own sessions, among other things. We'll generate a fresh application secret later using one of Play's built-in utilities.

DEVELOPMENT CONFIGURATION You can leverage the configuration's inclusion mechanism to set up the development configuration for various members of your team. For example, each developer may have a different setup (such as database configuration) or focus on the project for which they'd like to enable or disable specific services in the application. By including a development.conf file in the main application.conf, and also adding this file to the exclusion mechanism of your version control system (for example, `.gitignore`), you make it possible for each member of your team to override specific configuration settings. (Be careful that you only ever override values in this file, and don't specify new ones, which would become problematic in production.) The following syntax is used to include this file:

```
include "development.conf"
```

LOGGING CONFIGURATION

Play uses the logback library (http://logback.qos.ch) for logging, expecting to find a logback.xml file on the classpath (in the conf directory). Logback lets you fine-tune the logging configuration, such as by configuring rotating log files, which is recommended for production deployment.

The following listing shows a minimal logback configuration for our project.

Listing 4.2 Defining a minimal logback configuration in conf/logback.xml

```
<configuration>
  <conversionRule
    conversionWord="coloredLevel"
    converterClass="play.api.Logger$ColoredLevel" />

  <appender name="STDOUT" class="ch.qos.logback.core.ConsoleAppender">
    <encoder>
      <pattern>
```

Specifies a conversion rule provided by Play that adds color to the console output

Configures the logging to standard output by creating an appender

```
        %coloredLevel - %logger - %message%n%xException
      </pattern>
    </encoder>
  </appender>

  <logger name="play" level="INFO" />
  <logger name="application" level="DEBUG" />

  <root level="ERROR">
    <appender-ref ref="STDOUT" />
  </root>

</configuration>
```

Defines the pattern in which messages are logged (see the logback documentation for customizing options)

Configures the level for each logger; you can add more loggers here to customize the log level of third-party libraries

Defines which appenders should be used for logging

You can check the source code for this chapter to see a more advanced logback configuration example that features rotating log files.

4.1.3 Building the project

To build, run, and package a Play project, you'll need the sbt build tool (www.scala-sbt.org). Follow the instructions provided on the sbt website to install it on your computer if you haven't done so already.

> **SBT VERSUS ACTIVATOR** The Activator is a small wrapper on top of sbt that extends sbt's capabilities, allowing you to create new projects based on templates as well as to run an interactive user interface by issuing the `activator ui` command. It's intended for first-time users of the technology platform provided by Lightbend. In this chapter we want to get to the core of things, so we'll use sbt directly without additional features. Feel free to use either one of the tools for the remainder of the book—I personally like to use sbt directly, but Activator makes it easy to bootstrap a new project from a template, as you saw in chapter 2.

A minimal sbt project only requires a single build.sbt file at the root of the project. To use Play, however, you'll need the Play *sbt plugin*, and we'll specify which version of sbt to use.

Start by creating the project/build.properties file:

```
sbt.version = 0.13.9
```

It's possible to do without this file, but if you were to install a new version of sbt, running the build tool against your project would then use the new version by default, even if it weren't compatible with your project for one reason or another. It's best to always indicate which version of sbt the project expects to be built with.

Next, you need to specify which plugins you want to use for your project by creating the project/plugins.sbt file.

Listing 4.3 The plugins.sbt file declaring which plugins to use for this build

```
addSbtPlugin("com.typesafe.play" % "sbt-plugin" % "2.4.3")          <-- The Play plugin

addSbtPlugin("com.typesafe.sbt" % "sbt-scalariform" % "1.3.0")      <-- The scalariform plugin used for code formatting
```

There are many plugins that can augment the capabilities of a standard sbt project. For example, there are plugins for diverse tasks such as code coverage, static analysis, and specific release mechanisms, all available as community plugins.[1] In combination with the sbt web plugin (https://github.com/sbt/sbt-web), Play leverages the plugin mechanism to make the assets pipeline extensible and integrate various front-end technologies such as CoffeeScript, LESS, React, and JSHint, to name but a few.

The final piece that you need to start the build is the build.sbt file at the root of the project. This is the file that describes how the project is built.

Listing 4.4 The build.sbt file declaring the configuration of the project

```
name := "simple-vocabulary-teacher"                <-- The name of the project

version := "1.0"                                   <-- The version of the project

scalaVersion := "2.11.7"                           <-- The Scala version to use

lazy val `simple-vocabulary-teacher` =
  (project in file(".")).enablePlugins(PlayScala)  <-- The configuration of the main project

routesGenerator := InjectedRoutesGenerator         <-- Uses dependency injection in the Play router

com.typesafe.sbt.SbtScalariform.scalariformSettings  <-- The default settings for the scalariform code formatting tool
```

sbt uses a declarative domain-specific language (DSL) for its configuration, implemented in Scala. It's through the build.sbt file that library dependencies are declared, repositories for publishing are specified, multi-module configurations are set up, and many aspects of the build can be customized. This example application is quite straightforward, so we won't see any of these features in action here, but there will be plenty of opportunities to see them in the remainder of the book.

At this point, you can start sbt! Fire up a console, navigate to your project's directory, and start sbt simply by typing `sbt`:

```
~/book/CH04 ±master » sbt
Picked up JAVA_TOOL_OPTIONS: -Dfile.encoding=UTF8 -Xmx2048m
[...]
[simple-vocabulary-teacher] $
```

[1] See the sbt Community Plugins page: www.scala-sbt.org/release/docs/Community-Plugins.html.

Now that sbt is running, you can get a new application secret by running the `playUpdateSecret` command. This will generate a new secret and automatically update the conf/application.conf file.

At this point, you're all set to run the Play application using the `run` command. If you check the application at http://localhost:9000, you'll get a result from Play. But the page you'll be greeted with will start with the welcoming words "Action not found" and the explanation "No router defined." This is because you haven't defined any routes yet. Worse, you haven't even created the conf/routes file, which is the default location of the application routes.

Don't worry, we'll get around to this shortly. Before talking about routes, though, we'll take a more detailed look at the request lifecycle in Play.

4.2 Request handling

Play is a web framework, so it's going to primarily deal with HTTP requests, as well as, increasingly, WebSocket connections, and in the future HTTP/2 connections. In this section we'll look at how Play deals with these protocols (except for HTTP/2, which has just been released) and at how Play structures the different elements of the processing pipeline.

4.2.1 The request lifecycle

A typical HTTP request-response lifecycle in a Play application is represented in figure 4.2.

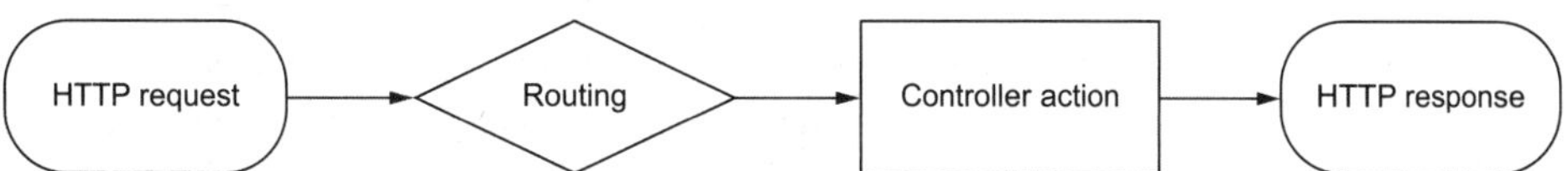

Figure 4.2 High-level stages of a typical request-response lifecycle in Play

There are three steps in the process:

1. The HTTP request is passed from the Netty back end to Play and transformed appropriately.
2. Depending on the parameters in the request, it's routed to the appropriate `Action` by the router.
3. The core of the work is carried out by an `Action`, which turns a request into a response, which is then sent back to the client.

Play is built on top of Netty, an asynchronous event-driven framework that supports a wide range of protocols and standards and is highly performant. Netty allows for a very fine-grained level of detail when it comes to deciding exactly how requests are being handled and responses are generated, in order to tune for performance. But when developing a web application, we're not interested in fine-tuning each and every request—it would be much nicer to have this done for us. This is where Play comes in:

it uses a subset of the large array of capabilities and protocols that Netty supports (mainly HTTP and WebSocket) and deals with all the low-level nitty-gritty details involved in handling requests “the right way.”

To get started with request handling in Play, let’s look a bit closer at an HTTP request. I’m sure you already know what a request is, but let’s walk through the theory once again to make sure we’re talking about the same thing.

At its core, an HTTP request is composed of a *header* and an optional *body* for certain kinds of requests. For example, a request may look like this:

```
GET /welcome HTTP/1.1
Host: localhost
Connection: keep-alive
Cache-Control: max-age=0
Accept: text/html,application/xhtml+xml,application/xml;q=0.9
User-Agent: Mozilla/5.0 (Macintosh; Intel Mac OS X 10_9_4)
          AppleWebKit/537.36 (KHTML, like Gecko) Chrome/36.0.1985.125
          Safari/537.36
DNT: 1
Accept-Encoding: gzip,deflate,sdch
Accept-Language: en-US,en;q=0.8,de;q=0.6,fr;q=0.4,nl;q=0.2
```

The first line is particularly interesting. It consists of the *method* (`GET`), the *path* (`/welcome`), and the *protocol* (`HTTP/1.1`). The rest of the header is a collection of header fields that can be used for various purposes, such as content negotiation, compression, internationalization, and so on.

In the Scala Play API, all of this core information is represented by the `play.api.mvc.RequestHeader` trait. The `RequestHeader` is one of the cornerstones of Play, and it’s both used by Play internally and available to us for interpreting and responding to requests. It also plays a central role when it comes to deciding which piece of code will handle a request at routing time.

The `RequestHeader` exposes all the information in a developer-friendly fashion, and it mainly consists of the following:

- The request path
- The method
- The query string
- The request headers
- The cookies, including the client-side session cookie and a special “flash” cookie that we’ll talk about later
- A number of convenience methods that help make sense of some of the headers for content negotiation

Let’s do a quick experiment to get a closer look at a `RequestHeader`. We’ll hook into the method of Play that decides what to do when a *request handler* isn’t found, which is the current case (given that we have no routes, controller, or actions defined yet).

Create the file app/ErrorHandler.scala with the following content.

Listing 4.5 Customizing Play's behavior when request handlers aren't found

```
import javax.inject._
import play.api.http.DefaultHttpErrorHandler
import play.api._
import play.api.mvc._
import play.api.mvc.Results._
import play.api.routing.Router
import scala.concurrent._

class ErrorHandler @Inject() (
    env: Environment,
    config: Configuration,
    sourceMapper: OptionalSourceMapper,
    router: Provider[Router])
  extends DefaultHttpErrorHandler(env, config, sourceMapper, router) {

  override protected def onNotFound(
    request: RequestHeader, message: String
  ): Future[Result] = {
    Future.successful {
      NotFound("Could not find " + request)
    }
  }
}
```

Defines an ErrorHandler discoverable via dependency injection

Extends the DefaultHttpErrorHandler trait, which is the hook to error-handling customization in Play

Overrides the onNotFound method to intercept Play's default behavior when an error occurs during communication with the client

Returns a 404 Not Found result with a message containing the String representation of the result

If a handler isn't found, Play's standard behavior is to display a developer-friendly error message in development mode (as you may have seen) or a simple 404 error message in production mode. In listing 4.5 you override this default mechanism by overriding Play's `DefaultHttpErrorHandler`, which is an entry point for customizing the default error-handling concerns. As you'll see further on, there are a few more of these kind of traits that you can use to customize Play's request-handling lifecycle.

In the example in listing 4.5, you just return the `String` representation of the `RequestHeader`.

Let's look at the result using the `curl` command in a terminal window (curl is available by default on Unix-based operating systems; if you use Windows, you can download it at http://curl.haxx.se).

```
~ » curl -v http://localhost:9000
* Rebuilt URL to: http://localhost:9000/
* Hostname was NOT found in DNS cache
*   Trying ::1...
* Connected to localhost (::1) port 9000 (#0)
> GET / HTTP/1.1
> User-Agent: curl/7.37.1
> Host: localhost:9000
> Accept: */*
>
```

```
< HTTP/1.1 404 Not Found
< Content-Type: text/plain; charset=utf-8
< Content-Length: 20
<
* Connection #0 to host localhost left intact
Could not find GET /
```

According to this result, the `String` representation of the `RequestHeader` is `GET /`. That's a good start, but as mentioned earlier, there's a lot more data in the `RequestHeader`. To appreciate all of its richness, let's debug this method at the line where we return the result.

To do this, you need to run sbt with the JVM debug agent enabled. Quit the currently running sbt process and relaunch it like this:

```
sbt -jvm-debug 5005
```

5005 is the port on which the debug agent listens for connections from a debugging tool, provided in most IDEs. Once you've started sbt in this way, launch the application again with `run`, and debug the application with your favorite IDE to explore the structure in depth.

EXERCISE 4.1

Use curl to explore what effect different types of request methods and request headers have on the `RequestHeader`. Add a cookie to see how it's represented.

Quick curl reference

curl supports the following flags:

- `-v` or `--verbose`—Prints verbose output, recommended for the examples in this chapter.
- `-b` or `--cookie`—Adds a cookie to the request. Specify a cookie as key=value pairs; for example, `-b user=123`.
- `-H` or `--header`—Adds a custom header to the request; for example, `-H "X-My-Header:Hi"`.

Now that you know a bit more about incoming requests, let's take a look at how requests are distributed to the various processing components of a Play application.

4.2.2 Request routing

HTTP requests are analyzed and forwarded by the *router* to the appropriate action, as shown in figure 4.3.

The router looks at the `RequestHeader` and analyzes the method, URI, and query string to decide which action to pass the request to. A router is composed of many

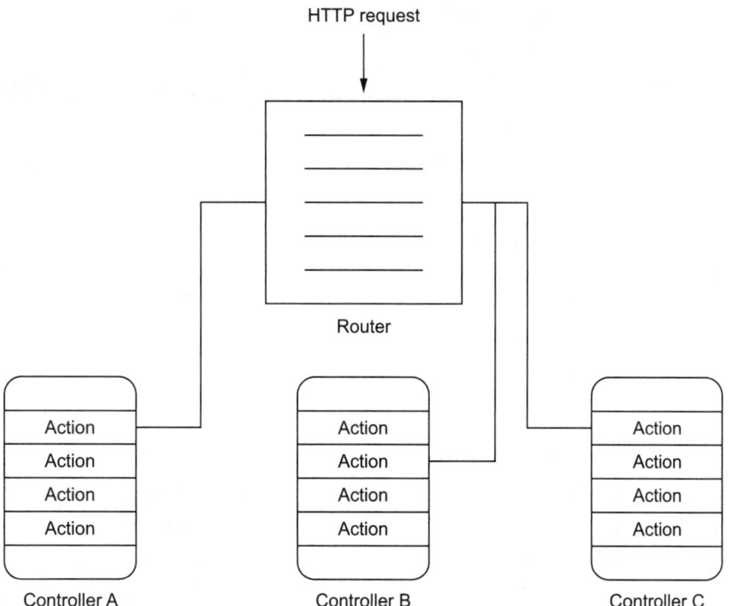

Figure 4.3 The router directs requests to the appropriate controller and action.

different *routes*, which can be thought of as individual request matchers. Play has its own textual format for defining routes, located in the conf/routes file.

To define the routes for your project, create the conf/routes file with the following content:

```
GET         /test        controllers.Test.testAction
```

Save the file and refresh the application. You should now get a compilation error. Play compiles the routes file, which means that each route (and, as you'll see later, each route parameter) is checked against the targeted *action generation method* to see if they're indeed compatible. The action generation method is responsible for creating a Play *action*, which is in charge of handling an HTTP request.

> **ACTIONS VERSUS ACTION GENERATION METHODS** Methods that result in the creation of a Play action are called action generation methods, as they're methods whose result is a Play action. In practice, they're commonly referred to as "actions" instead of "action generation methods."

If you'd like to fix the preceding route, you could point it to the `controllers.Default.todo` method, which will simply return a 501 Not Implemented page. But rather than continuing to work with a dummy route, let's go ahead and create the routes for the vocabulary import controller.

Create the controller at app/controllers/Import.scala with the following contents.

Listing 4.6 The scaffold of the vocabulary import controller

```
package controllers

import play.api.mvc._

class Import extends Controller {
  def importWord(
    sourceLanguage: String,
    targetLanguage: String,
    word: String,
    translation: String
  ) = TODO
}
```

We'll revisit the semantics and the structure of controllers a bit later. For the moment, what matters is that you've created two methods and implemented them using the `TODO` shortcut (which points at the `controllers.Default.todo` action).

Let's now wire these methods in the router. Replace the existing test route with the one defined in the following listing, making sure you write it in one line.

Listing 4.7 Route definition for importing vocabularies

```
PUT /import/word/:sourceLang/:word/:targetLang/:translation
   controllers.Import.importWord(sourceLang, word,
   targetLang, translation)
```

Great! You're now all set to send requests that will be routed to the appropriate location. You may notice that you're also passing data from the request URI to the `importWord` method. It's possible to mark each path fragment as a value to be passed as an argument to the action generation method. Those named URI fragments are called *path parameters.*

There's just one problem with the preceding example: it contains a mistake. You may have noticed that I inverted the order of parameters between the method definition and its invocation, mixing up words and languages. By default, each path parameter is assumed to be of type `String` and there's no need to type it out. For longer method definitions like this one, it's easy to mix up arguments if you're not careful. Thankfully, it's possible to type the path parameters and have Play automatically convert them to the right type, which can help you avoid such mistakes during development, but it also ensures the validity of a path parameter at runtime.

Let's fix the mistake and use the built-in `Lang` class to represent languages. Update the controller method to match the following definition.

Listing 4.8 Controller method using a type-safe representation for languages

```
import play.api.i18n.Lang
def importWord(
  sourceLanguage: Lang,
  word: String,
  targetLanguage: Lang,
  translation: String
) = TODO
```

Now you need to tell the router that you are indeed expecting the `Lang` type for the two language path parameters, as follows, again all typed on one line.

Listing 4.9 Route using type-safe path parameters for languages

```
PUT /import/word/:sourceLang/:word/:targetLang/:translation
  controllers.Import.importWord(
    sourceLang: play.api.i18n.Lang,
    word,
    targetLang: play.api.i18n.Lang,
    translation
  )
```

Finally, you need to tell Play how to read a path parameter of type `play.api.i18n.Lang`. To do so, you need to create a `PathBindable`. Create the file app/binders/PathBinders.scala with the following contents.

Listing 4.10 A `LangPathBindable` to read the `Lang` type as part of a path

```
package binders

import play.api.i18n.Lang
import play.api.mvc.PathBindable

object PathBinders {

  implicit object LangPathBindable extends PathBindable[Lang] {
    override def bind(key: String, value: String):
      Either[String, Lang] =
        Lang.get(value).toRight(s"Language $value is not recognized")

    override def unbind(key: String, value: Lang): String = value.code
  }

}
```

- Places all binders in one object to simplify importing them into the router (`object PathBinders`)
- Declares the PathBindable as an implicit object so it's resolved implicitly by the router (`implicit object LangPathBindable`)
- Implements the bind method to read a query fragment as a type (`override def bind`)
- Encodes the result of a binding as Either[String, Lang], which means the result of a binding is either an error message, or the successfully read Lang value (`Either[String, Lang]`)
- Checks if there's a language for the input value; otherwise returns an error message (`Lang.get(value).toRight`)
- Implements the unbind method to write a type as a path fragment (`override def unbind`)

Now you need to do one more thing to use the type-safe binding mechanism: let the router know about the binding by adding `routesImport += "binders.PathBinders._"` to the build.sbt file. This will add an import statement to the generated router file.

Play's route file is turned into a Scala source file and then compiled alongside the sources of the application. When the Scala compiler finds a route that specifies a given type, it will try to find the appropriate `PathBindable` for that type and will complain if it can't find one. If the application compiles, you can be sure that the appropriate bindings can be performed.

> **RELOADING THE BUILD SYSTEM AFTER CHANGES TO BUILD.SBT** When making changes to build.sbt, like adding the `routesImport` statement in the previous example, don't forget to reload the sbt console by running the `reload` command. Otherwise the changes won't be visible, and the compilation will continue to fail.

> **QUERY STRING PARAMETERS** The request path isn't the only way to convey parameters to an action—query parameters are also supported and there are also `QueryStringBindables` that allow you to bind a specific type. We'll look at query parameter handling later on.

> **THE EITHER TYPE** Scala's `Either[A, B]` type makes it possible to encode results that can have either of two results. The left type (`A`) is often used to encode the error case, while the right type (`B`) is the type of the expected result.

You can now test if things work as expected with curl. First, check if you get routed appropriately using valid languages:

```
curl -v -X PUT http://localhost:9000/import/word/en/hello/fr/bonjour
```

This should produce a 501 Not Implemented result (because you have a `TODO` action and no real implementation). Then check out an invalid language:

```
curl -v -X PUT http://localhost:9000/import/word/en/hello/foo/bonjour
```

This should produce a 400 Bad Request because `foo` is not a valid language.

> **REVERSE ROUTING** Any route defined in the routes file also has a reverse equivalent that yields a URI and is very useful when used in view templates or emails. For example, you could create a link for importing a certain word using the `routes.Import.importWord(Lang("en"), "hello", Lang("fr"), "salut").url()` method. The advantage of reverse routing over using handwritten URLs is that there's no danger of getting a wrong link because it's always generated by Play from the single source of truth that the router represents.

Alright! Now that you have the first routes set up and working, we'll move on and implement some of the actions.

4.2.3 *Controllers, actions, and results*

A Play application can be seen as a collection of request-processing functions, the *actions*. As in any MVC framework, those actions are organized in various controllers that group related actions. In our example, we have two controllers: the `Import` controller dealing with adding new vocabulary, and the `Quiz` controller that will quiz us for it.

CREATING ACTIONS AND RETURNING RESULTS

Let's continue where we left off and implement the functionality for importing a single word. First we'll need a way to store and query words. Normally you'd do this with a specialized database of some kind, but for this example application we'll simply store things in memory.

Create the models/Vocabulary.scala file with the following contents.

Listing 4.11 Simple model for defining vocabulary entries

```
package models

import play.api.i18n.Lang

case class Vocabulary(
  sourceLanguage: Lang,
  targetLanguage: Lang,
  word: String,
  translation: String)
```

That was easy enough, but we can't get anything done with the model alone. Let's build a simple service to store the vocabulary.

Listing 4.12 Simple in-memory vocabulary storage

```
package services

import javax.inject.Singleton
import play.api.i18n.Lang

@Singleton
class VocabularyService {

  private var allVocabulary = List(
    Vocabulary(Lang("en"), Lang("fr"), "hello", "bonjour"),
    Vocabulary(Lang("en"), Lang("fr"), "play", "jouer")
  )

  def addVocabulary(v: Vocabulary): Boolean = {
    if (!allVocabulary.contains(v)) {
      allVocabulary = v :: allVocabulary
      true
    } else {
      false
```

Specifies that the VocabularyService class has singleton scope, which means the same instance will be injected in all classes having a dependency on it

Bootstraps the list with a minimal vocabulary because the list will be lost with each application reload

Only adds vocabulary that doesn't exist yet, and returns a Boolean

```
        }
    }
}
```

You now have a simple in-memory storage system, which will do just fine for the moment. The `addVocabulary` method is extremely rudimentary and returns a simple `Boolean`, which is enough for this example, but it wouldn't be sufficient for a real-life application because it doesn't give any details about why an item couldn't be stored. We'll use this system to implement the `importWord` action of the `Import` controller.

> **NOTE** This storage implementation is so simple that it's not even thread-safe! Several clients could potentially access this service simultaneously, which could cause the same entry to be added twice or new entries to be lost. A more elaborate implementation of this service would make use of a thread-safe collection or leverage some of the concurrency mechanisms that we'll be exploring in chapters 5 and 6.

Before you implement the `importWord` action of the `Import` controller, you must tell the controller how to get to a `VocabularyService`. Play uses the annotations defined in JSR 330 (https://www.jcp.org/en/jsr/detail?id=330) for dependency injection, and we'll use this to inject the `VocabularyService` in all the controllers that need it. Modify the constructor of the `Import` controller as follows:

```
import javax.inject.Inject

class Import @Inject() (vocabulary: VocabularyService)
  extends Controller {
  // ...
}
```

All you've done here is declare that the `Import` class requires a `VocabularyService` to be constructed, and that its constructor is dependency-injected by using the `@Inject()` annotation. You're now ready to implement the `importWord` action.

Listing 4.13 Implementing the action to add a single word

```
def importWord(
  sourceLanguage: Lang,
  word: String,
  targetLanguage: Lang,
  translation: String
) = Action { request =>
  val added = vocabulary.addVocabulary(
    Vocabulary(sourceLanguage, targetLanguage, word, translation)
  )
  if (added)
    Ok
  else
    Conflict
}
```

Uses the Action constructor to build a simple Action

If adding was successful, returns a 200 Ok response

If adding didn't work (because you already added this word), returns a 409 Conflict response

You can now test if things work according to plan by using curl:

```
~ » curl -v -X PUT http://localhost:9000/import/word/en/hello/fr/ \
\ bonjour
* Hostname was NOT found in DNS cache
*   Trying ::1...
* Connected to localhost (::1) port 9000 (#0)
> PUT /import/word/en/hello/fr/bonjour HTTP/1.1
> User-Agent: curl/7.37.1
> Host: localhost:9000
> Accept: */*
>
< HTTP/1.1 409 Conflict
< Content-Length: 0
```

Because "hello" was already part of the initial vocabulary set, this result is as expected.

> **DEPENDENCY INJECTION IN PLAY** Play aims at providing dependency injection without limiting the approaches to it. All native Play components can be instantiated using plain constructors or factory methods, and Play employs an abstraction that allows any kind of JSR 303 implementation to be plugged in. By default, Play uses and provides Guice (https://github.com/google/guice) out of the box.

Now all you have to do is implement the quiz controller. Let's start by adding a bit more functionality to the `VocabularyService`.

Listing 4.14 Extending the `Vocabulary` model to retrieve and check random vocabulary

```
def findRandomVocabulary(sourceLanguage: Lang, targetLanguage: Lang):
  Option[Vocabulary] = {
    Random.shuffle(allVocabulary.filter { v =>
        v.sourceLanguage == sourceLanguage &&
        v.targetLanguage == targetLanguage
      }).headOption
}

def verify(
  sourceLanguage: Lang,
  word: String,
  targetLanguage: Lang,
  translation: String): Boolean = {
    allVocabulary.contains(
      Vocabulary(sourceLanguage, targetLanguage, word, translation)
    )
}
```

Randomly shuffles the subset of the vocabulary that matches the desired languages

Verifies if a proposed translation is correct by looking for a Vocabulary that matches

Next, you'll need to implement the Quiz controller, which will provide a word and check if a proposed translation is appropriate. Create the quiz controller in the app/controllers/Quiz.scala file and implement two methods:

- `def quiz(sourceLanguage: Lang, targetLanguage: Lang)`—An action that will use `findRandomVocabulary` and return a 200 Ok result that wraps a random word if there is one, and a 404 Not Found result otherwise.
- `def check(sourceLanguage: Lang, word: String, targetLanguage: Lang, translation: String)`—An action that verifies the word and returns a 200 Ok result if the translation is correct, and a 406 Not Acceptable result otherwise. (406 Not Acceptable is the closest to what we want to express, and even though it may not have exactly the same semantic meaning as in the HTTP specification, it will do fine for this example.)

If you encounter difficulties implementing these methods, you can always check the source code for the chapter, but this shouldn't be too difficult.

The only thing you need now are the appropriate routes. Open the conf/routes file and add the following routes. Again, make sure you write these routes on one line each.

Listing 4.15 Additional routes for the quiz

```
GET /quiz/:sourceLang
  controllers.Quiz.quiz(sourceLang: play.api.i18n.Lang,
  targetLang: play.api.i18n.Lang)

POST /quiz/:sourceLang/check/:word
  controllers.Quiz.check(sourceLang: play.api.i18n.Lang, word,
  targetLang: play.api.i18n.Lang, translation)
```

Just as when you implemented the routes for the `Import` controller, here you use path parameters to provide some of the data to your actions. But unlike previously, there are some parameters in the action method invocation that don't have an obvious origin. If you compile the project now, you'll get a hint as to where Play tries to fetch them from through the compilation error:

```
No QueryString binder found for type play.api.i18n.Lang.
Try to implement an implicit QueryStringBindable for this type.
```

Any parameter that's passed to the action generation method and isn't specified as a path parameter is inferred to be part of the request's query string. Just as with path parameters, query string parameters can be typed, and unknown types need to have a `QueryStringBindable` that's available to the router.

Go ahead and implement a `QueryStringBindable` for `Lang`. Don't forget to add the necessary `import` to build.sbt and to reload the build system afterwards.

You can now check if things work as intended:

```
~ » curl -v http://localhost:9000/quiz/en\?targetLang\=fr
* Hostname was NOT found in DNS cache
*   Trying ::1...
* Connected to localhost (::1) port 9000 (#0)
```

```
> GET /quiz/en?targetLang=fr HTTP/1.1
> User-Agent: curl/7.37.1
> Host: localhost:9000
> Accept: */*
>
< HTTP/1.1 200 OK
< Content-Type: text/plain; charset=utf-8
< Content-Length: 4
<
* Connection #0 to host localhost left intact
play%

~ » curl -v -X POST
  http://localhost:9000/quiz/en/check/play
  \?targetLang\=fr\&translation\=jouer
* Hostname was NOT found in DNS cache
*   Trying ::1...
* Connected to localhost (::1) port 9000 (#0)
> POST /quiz/en/check/play?targetLang=fr&translation=jouer HTTP/1.1
> User-Agent: curl/7.37.1
> Host: localhost:9000
> Accept: */*
>
< HTTP/1.1 200 OK
< Content-Length: 0
<
* Connection #0 to host localhost left intact
```

As you can see, you can specify french as a target language when retrieving a word to be quizzed with while submitting your answer.

THE DEFAULT ACTIONBUILDER So far you've implemented actions using the `Action` notation, such as by writing `Action { request => … }`. Behind the scenes, `Action` is an `ActionBuilder`, which is a helper mechanism provided by Play to implement more-advanced `Action` blocks.

REQUEST VERSUS IMPLICIT REQUEST Often you'll see actions written out as `Action { implicit request => … }`. This is because many libraries and convenience methods that Play offers need to know about the request, so they expect it as an *implicit parameter*. Scala's implicit parameters are a means to pass along parameters based on their types without having to write them out in the method invocation. Scala will try to find an implicit value in different scopes (local definition, inherited members, imported objects, package objects, and so on) to pass it on to the method that requires it.

EXERCISE 4.2

So far we've extracted the target language for the quiz-related actions from the query string. As an exercise, try reading them from the custom `X-Target-Language` header instead.

A LOOK UNDER THE HOOD OF ACTIONS

We've used actions but we haven't yet looked at how they work internally. For most of the things you'll do with Play, you won't need to work at this low level, but it's worth taking a look at things in more detail to appreciate what happens when a request is received by Play. This section will be a bit more theoretical and complicated than what we've done so far, so I invite you to grab a cup of coffee (or tea) before reading further.

Ready? Let's dive into it by looking at the definitions of an `Action` and a `Request`:

```
trait Action[A] extends EssentialAction {
  def parser: BodyParser[A]
  def apply(request: Request[A]): Future[Result]
}

trait Request[+A] extends RequestHeader {
  def body: A
}
```

At its core, an HTTP request's body is just a bunch of raw bytes. In Play, `Actions` and `Requests` are typed with the type of the body of the request (`A` in the preceding code). Play has a mechanism that transforms the raw bytes of an HTTP request body into a type that's easy to manipulate, such as `String`, `JsValue`, `java.io.File`, or any other type for which there is a *body parser*.

At this point, you may wonder where the raw bytes that characterize the body of an HTTP request are stored. The `request` parameter of the `apply` method of an `Action` is already a `Request[A]`, which means that it already has been parsed and the body turned into a nicer Scala type. To see where the raw data is hidden, we need to take a closer look at the `EssentialAction` trait:

```
trait EssentialAction
  extends (RequestHeader => Iteratee[Array[Byte], Result])
  with Handler
```

This signature may seem a bit bewildering at first sight, but there's no dark magic at work. Let's decipher it piece by piece:

- `with Handler`—This code snippet at the end simply means that the `EssentialAction` is a `Handler`, which is a type used in Play to indicate that an object is capable of handling a request (be it an HTTP or a WebSocket request).
- `(RequestHeader => Iteratee[Array[Byte], Result])`—This notation defines a function that takes a `RequestHeader` parameter and produces an `Iteratee[Array[Byte], Result]`.

You already know what a `RequestHeader` is: the expected input of the function is just the essential information about a request (method, path, request headers). But what about the strange-looking `Iteratee[Array[Byte], Result]`? In chapter 2 we quickly looked into iteratees, but let's revisit them. An `Iteratee[E, A]` is a tool for working with streams of data; it consumes chunks of `E` to produce one or more `A`s. In this case, the input is an `Array[Byte]` (the raw body of the HTTP request—that's where it was hiding) and the output is a single Play `Result`. So an `Iteratee` consumes many chunks of the HTTP request body and eventually produces a `Result` as an output.

Still here? Great! Let's summarize what an `EssentialAction` is. It's a function that takes as input a `RequestHeader` and produces an `Iteratee`, which, when fed the bytes of a request body, will produce a `Result`. You can think of an action as a mechanism that works in multiple steps:

1. The `Action` is given the `RequestHeader`, from which it infers which `BodyParser` to use to handle the body.
2. Once everything is in place, the body is passed in as a stream of bytes, producing a `Request[A]`.
3. You can easily work with the `Request` to produce a `Result`.

This looks quite complicated, so why does Play go to such lengths for a task seemingly as trivial as parsing a request body? The answer is that Play does everything in an asynchronous, nonblocking fashion. The purpose of iteratees is precisely to enable asynchronous stream manipulation: they consume data sent by the browser without blocking threads, so that when there's a pause in the transfer, no resources are wasted waiting for the transfer to continue. At the same time, using iteratees for body parsing means that the parsing can begin as soon as data is received. This is especially important for large files, because loading everything in memory before starting to parse isn't really an option.

4.2.4 WebSockets

By maintaining two-way communication with the server, WebSockets are a great tool for building interactive web applications. As depicted in figure 4.4, Play deals with WebSockets in a special way. A WebSocket connection is established in two steps: First, the client sends a normal `GET` request that contains a special `Upgrade` header. Then, if the server supports the WebSocket protocol, it replies with the details of the WebSocket connection, and the client can switch to that protocol. To this end, Play doesn't make use of actions but instead uses a special type of `Handler` that will initiate the WebSocket connection. There is support for using WebSockets in combination with actors and in combination with iteratees. When it comes to maintaining an interactive dialogue between clients and the server, actors offer a much more compelling alternative to iteratees because they're built on the idea of asynchronous message-passing.

You already set up a WebSocket connection in chapter 2 for streaming tweets, but at that time you weren't communicating in both directions. Let's step through this process once more and build the interactive quiz endpoint represented in figure 4.4.

Figure 4.4 A WebSocket connection for an interactive vocabulary quiz. Play takes care of creating the quiz actor when a WebSocket connection is requested by the client.

You first need to build a `QuizActor` that will chat with the client about words and translations.

Listing 4.16 The `QuizActor` interacts with a WebSocket client

```
class QuizActor(out: ActorRef,
                sourceLang: Lang,
                targetLang: Lang,
                vocabulary: VocabularyService)
  extends Actor {

  private var word = ""

  override def preStart(): Unit = sendWord()

  def receive = {
    case translation: String
      if vocabulary.verify(
        sourceLang, word, targetLang, translation
      ) =>
        out ! "Correct!"
        sendWord()
    case _ =>
      out ! "Incorrect, try again!"
  }

  def sendWord() = {
    vocabulary
      .findRandomVocabulary(sourceLang, targetLang).map { v =>
      out ! s"Please translate '${v.word}'"
      word = v.word
    } getOrElse {
      out ! s"I don't know any word for ${sourceLang.code} " +
```

Annotations:
- Creates the actor based on the desired languages as well as the reference to the outgoing channel, out
- Keeps track of which word you're currently asking for a translation of
- When starting up, sends a new word to translate
- If a correct translation was provided, asks for a new word
- Sets the requested word so you know what to check against

```
            " and ${targetLang.code}"
        }
      }
    }
```

When a new WebSocket connection is established, Play will automatically create a new instance of your actor and provide it with an actor reference that represents the outgoing channel. Incoming messages are sent by the client, and you can react to them in the actor's `receive` method. Don't worry too much about the details of how an actor works yet; we'll visit them in depth in chapter 6.

The most important part of the plumbing when setting up a WebSocket endpoint is telling Play how it can create a new instance of the actor. For this purpose, we'll first create a small utility method that returns the `Props` of an actor, which are essentially a means of explaining how an actor can be built.

Listing 4.17 Utility method for creating the `Props` of a `QuizActor`

```
object QuizActor {
  def props(out: ActorRef,
                   sourceLang: Lang,
                   targetLang: Lang,
                   vocabulary: VocabularyService): Props =
    Props(classOf[QuizActor], out, sourceLang, targetLang, vocabulary)
}
```

Now the only thing you need is to create the handler method that will upgrade the incoming `GET` request from the client to a WebSocket connection. Add the following code to the `Quiz` controller.

Listing 4.18 The WebSocket handler method

```
def quizEndpoint(sourceLang: Lang, targetLang: Lang) =
  WebSocket.acceptWithActor[String, String] {
    request =>
      out =>
        QuizActor.props(out, sourceLang, targetLang, vocabulary)
}
```

- Languages are provided as parameters to the handler method.
- Incoming and outgoing messages are both Strings.
- RequestHeaders of the incoming request can be used to check whether the connection should be established.
- The actor reference out represents the outgoing channel to the client.
- The call to the helper method that returns the Props of the QuizActor to be created

To correctly set up the WebSocket connection, Play needs to know what the encoding of the messages is going to be, which is why you need to provide it with the type of the incoming and outgoing messages. This is also the type of messages that you can expect to receive (or send) in the actor. In chapter 2 we used JSON for communicating between client and server (using the `JsValue` type), but in this example we'll settle for simple Strings.

If needed, there are other handler methods available for establishing a connection, such as `WebSocket.tryAcceptWithActor`, which are useful when dealing with connection-time concerns such as authentication.

Last but not least, you need a route in order to accept the initial `GET` request from the client. Add the following code to the conf/routes file.

Listing 4.19 The `GET` route to establish a WebSocket connection

```
GET   /quiz/interactive/:sourceLang/:targetLang
  controllers.Quiz.quizEndpoint(
  sourceLang: play.api.i18n.Lang,
  targetLang: play.api.i18n.Lang)
```

You're now all set to try out your brand new WebSocket endpoint. curl isn't going to tell you much more than whether or not a connection could be established, so you can make use of a browser extension to test the connection, such as the Simple WebSocket Client extension for Chrome (https://github.com/hakobera/Simple-WebSocket-Client), the result being shown in figure 4.5.

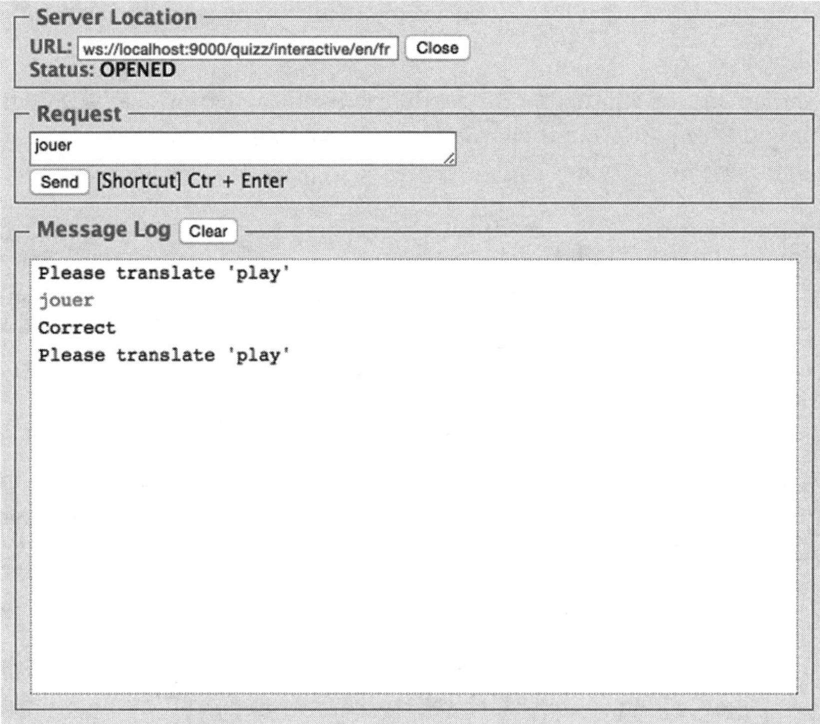

Figure 4.5 Testing the WebSocket endpoint with a browser extension

And that's it! Play takes care of all the internal details of figuring out how to format the data sent across the WebSocket wire and lets you focus on providing the functionality.

4.2.5 Altering the default request-handling pipeline

Play allows you to alter the default behavior of an application in different ways. More often than not, you'll want to add custom error handling and handle cross-cutting concerns (especially security-related ones). In the following subsections, we'll look at how to implement those scenarios with Play.

CUSTOM ERROR HANDLING

Overriding Play's `DefaultErrorHandler` makes it possible to customize how errors are dealt with and displayed to the user. You already saw how to customize handlers for the 404 Not Found response in listing 4.5. But there's more! The `DefaultErrorHandler` provides default behavior through these methods:

- `onBadRequest`—Handles 400 Bad Request client errors
- `onForbidden`—Handles 403 Forbidden client errors
- `onNotFound`—Handles 404 Not Found client errors
- `onOtherClientError`—Handles any other type of client errors
- `logServerError`—Specifies how to log server errors
- `onDevServerError`—Specifies how to display server errors during development
- `onProdServerError`—Specifies how to display server errors in production mode

You can (and should) use these hooks to adapt the error handling to the needs of your application. For example, if you're interested in errors happening in a certain part of your application, you could choose to send an email or trigger a monitoring service of some kind. All the preceding methods give you access to the `RequestHeader`, which gives you fine-grained control over how your app reacts.

> **400 BAD REQUEST** A 400 Bad Request result can be triggered either by returning it explicitly from a controller, or if an appropriate handler has been found but the parsing of the path parameters, the query string, or the request body has failed. You saw such a case earlier when trying to submit a new word using `foo` as a language.

FILTERS

Play offers you the option to set up one or more filters to be applied on requests and results, as shown in figure 4.6.

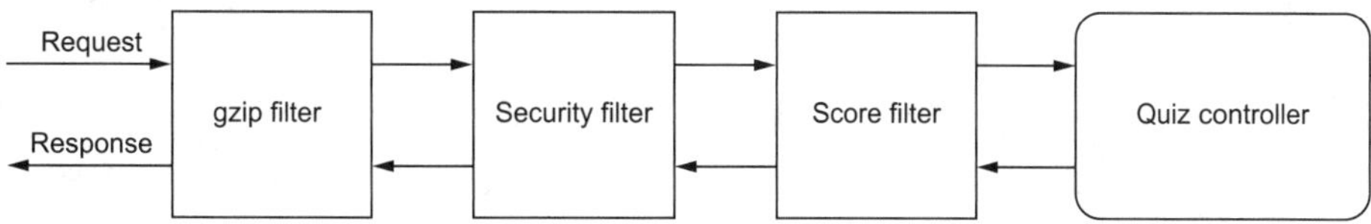

Figure 4.6 Filter chain that alters the default behavior on requests or results

A filter is nothing more than a small component that gets access to the request headers and, if necessary, to the result of the filter that follows it in the filter chain. The most convenient way of setting up a filter chain is to define an implementation of the `HttpFilters` trait and let it be injected by Play.

Before you can use the filters that ship with Play, you'll need to add the following dependency in build.sbt:

```
libraryDependencies += filters
```

Then you can set up a filter chain as shown in the following listing by creating a `Filters` class in the root package.

Listing 4.20 Setting up a few filters to make our application faster and more robust

```
import javax.inject.Inject
import play.api.http.HttpFilters
import play.filters.gzip.GzipFilter
import play.filters.headers.SecurityHeadersFilter

class Filters @Inject() (
  gzip: GzipFilter
) extends HttpFilters {
  val filters = Seq(gzip, SecurityHeadersFilter())
}
```

- **Injects the GzipFilter, which gzips responses sent to the client to speed things up a little** (points to `gzip: GzipFilter`)
- **The HttpFilters trait sets up a filter chain with the filters you specify.** (points to `extends HttpFilters`)
- **Specifies the filters you'd like to apply in the order they should be applied. Play's SecurityHeadersFilter adds a number of header-based security checks and policies.** (points to `val filters`)

Filters are useful when it comes to dealing with cross-cutting concerns, which are more easily handled by hooking them into the request-processing pipeline than dealing with them for each action.

Let's build our own filter! Because this is a vocabulary-teaching application, let's encourage users by reminding them of their score at every request, such as when they submit a new word or answer to the quiz. Create the file app/filters/ScoreFilter.scala with the following contents.

Listing 4.21 A simple filter that prints the current score at each request

```
class ScoreFilter extends Filter {
  override def apply(
    nextFilter: (RequestHeader) => Future[Result]
  )(rh: RequestHeader):
  Future[Result] = {

    val result = nextFilter(rh)
    import play.api.libs.concurrent.Execution.Implicits._
```

- **The nextFilter function represents the next request handler in the chain, which is usually a filter.** (points to `nextFilter`)
- **Provides the request header of the current request as well** (points to `(rh: RequestHeader)`)
- **Applies the request header to the next filter to get the result of the operation** (points to `val result = nextFilter(rh)`)
- **Imports an ExecutionContext to run the Future request** (points to the `import` line)

```
          result.map { res =>
            if (res.header.status == 200 || res.header.status == 406) {
              val correct = res.session(rh).get("correct").getOrElse(0)
              val wrong = res.session(rh).get("wrong").getOrElse(0)
              val score = s"\nYour current score is: $correct correct " +
                s"answers and $wrong wrong answers"
              val newBody =
                res.body andThen Enumerator(score.getBytes("UTF-8"))
              res.copy(body = newBody)
            } else {
              res
            }
          }
        }
      }
```

Only deals with Ok or Not Acceptable requests

Concatenates the existing response body and your score result

Returns a copy of the result containing the modified body

Since filters are usually chained one after another, the `apply` method of a `Filter` provides a function that represents the next filter in the filter chain, or if there is no filter, the next request handler that will take care of turning the request into a result.

This filter reads out the current score from Play's session and then prints it by appending it to the existing body. Because the body is an asynchronous stream of bytes, you use the `andThen` method to compose the two streams handled by enumerators.

> **PLAY'S CLIENT-SIDE SESSION** Unlike many traditional web application servers, Play's session is a client-side session, which means that it's represented as a cookie. This means the client can switch from one node to another without problem, which makes it much easier to scale Play applications horizontally. Play session cookies are signed with the application's secret key. We'll talk about them in chapter 7 when we deal with state in Play.

Now the only thing you need is to keep score. Bring up app/controllers/Quiz.scala and make the adjustments shown in the following listing.

Listing 4.22 Adjustments to the Quiz controller check action to keep the score

```
def check(
  sourceLanguage: Lang,
  word: String,
  targetLanguage: Lang,
  translation: String) = Action { request =>
    val isCorrect =
      vocabulary
        .verify(sourceLanguage, word, targetLanguage, translation)
    val correctScore =
      request.session.get("correct").map(_.toInt).getOrElse(0)
    val wrongScore =
      request.session.get("wrong").map(_.toInt).getOrElse(0)
      if (isCorrect) {
        Ok.withSession(
          "correct" -> (correctScore + 1).toString,
    "wrong" -> wrongScore.toString
```

Reads the previous score from the session and converts the counts from String to Int

Sets a new session with an adjusted score

```
      )
    } else {
      NotAcceptable.withSession(
        "correct" -> correctScore.toString,
        "wrong" -> (wrongScore + 1).toString
      )
    }
}
```

Finally, don't forget to add the brand-new filter to the filter chain in the `Filters` class.

Let's see if this works! First off, let's make one request:

```
~ » curl -v -X POST http://localhost:9000/quiz/en/check/play
  \?targetLang\=fr\&translation\=jouer
* Hostname was NOT found in DNS cache
*   Trying ::1...
* Connected to localhost (::1) port 9000 (#0)
> POST /quiz/en/check/play?targetLang=fr&translation=jouer HTTP/1.1
> User-Agent: curl/7.37.1
> Host: localhost:9000
> Accept: */*
>
< HTTP/1.1 200 OK
< Content-Security-Policy: default-src 'self'
< Set-Cookie: PLAY_SESSION="c...f-correct=1&wrong=0"; Path=/; HTTPOnly
< X-Content-Type-Options: nosniff
< X-Frame-Options: DENY
< X-Permitted-Cross-Domain-Policies: master-only
< X-XSS-Protection: 1; mode=block
< Content-Length: 62
<

* Connection #0 to host localhost left intact
Your current score is: 1 correct answers and 0 wrong answers%
```

There are a few interesting things to observe here:

- Given that the response contains the indication of the current score, the custom `ScoreFilter` works.
- Given the response headers (`X-Content-Type-Options`, `X-Frame-Options`, and so on), the security filter works as well.
- You get a cookie back (in the `Set-Cookie` header, which contains the Play session).

For the session-cookie-based scoring mechanism to work, you need to send back the cookie on subsequent requests. You can do this with curl by using the `--cookie` parameter and copying and pasting the content of the cookie that you received:

```
~ » curl -v --cookie "PLAY_SESSION=\"c...f-correct=1&wrong=0\""
  -X POST http://localhost:9000/quiz/en/check/play\?targetLang\=fr
  \&translation\=jouer
```

By passing in the updated cookie at each request (which a browser would do automatically), you can see the score-appending mechanism at work.

4.3 Summary

In this chapter we explored some of the basic mechanisms and concepts that Play is built on and that it uses to enable the creation of web applications:

- Routes, path bindables, and query string bindables are used to route and parse some elements of the request and pass them on to a controller action.
- Controllers and actions are Play's main mechanisms for handling requests.
- WebSockets provide an interactive dialogue between client and server.
- Mechanisms for customizing the default request pipeline, such as custom error handling and filters.

You now have the tools in hand to use the basics of Play. It's time to move ahead and explore how you can use those tools in a reactive manner. To this end, let's take a closer look at futures.

Part 2

Core concepts

This part of the book explains the concepts at the core of reactive web applications. You'll start by learning about futures and actors, two concepts used for modelling and manipulating asynchronous computations with failure tolerance in mind. Next you'll learn how to apply those tools to handle state in reactive applications. Finally you'll learn how to apply the reactive mindset to user interfaces.

5 Futures

This chapter covers

- Manipulating futures and handling their failure
- Using futures correctly in the context of Play
- Splitting business logic into small pieces suitable for implementing with futures

Futures are at the foundation of asynchronous and reactive programming in Scala: they allow you to manipulate the results of a computation that hasn't happened yet and to effectively deal with the failure of such computations, enabling more efficient use of computational resources. You'll encounter futures in many of the libraries you'll work with in Play and other tools.

This chapter has two parts. First we'll look at how to work with futures both on a standalone basis and within the context of Play. Second, we'll take an example of business logic and turn it into multiple futures that can be combined to parallelize their execution. Let's go!

5.1 Working with futures

Just like an `Option`, which we briefly discussed in chapter 3, a `Future` is a monadic data structure, which means, amongst other things, that it can easily be composed with other futures. Futures are a layer of abstraction on top of the familiar concept of callbacks. In chapter 1 we briefly looked at the problem of "callback hell," which plagues languages like JavaScript (such as when working with the server-side asynchronous Node.js platform) and stems from the fact that there hasn't been a proper abstraction over the low-level work of manipulating results of asynchronous tasks, invoking complex callback chains, and properly dealing with errors along that chain.

Futures help address the problem of programming in an asynchronous fashion in several ways:

- They encapsulate the result of asynchronous computations in a composable data structure.
- They transparently handle failure cases, propagating them along chained futures.
- They provide a mechanism for scheduling the execution of asynchronous tasks on a thread pool.

In this first part of the chapter, we'll make use of Play's WS library (which we used a bit in chapter 2) to make calls to a few websites related to the Play Framework. The WS library is asynchronous and returns future results, which is just what we need to get our hands dirty.

5.1.1 Future fundamentals

A `scala.concurrent.Future[T]` can be thought of as a box that will eventually contain a value of type `T` if it succeeds, as shown in figure 5.1. If it fails, the `Throwable` at the origin of the failure will be kept. A `Future` is said to have *succeeded* once the computation it's waiting for has yielded a result or *failed* if there was an error during the computation. In either case, once the `Future` is done computing, it's said to be *completed.*

As soon as a `Future` is declared, it will start running, which means that the computation it tries to achieve will be executed asynchronously. For example, you can use Play's WS library to execute a `GET` request against the Play Framework website:

```
val response: Future[WSResponse] =
  WS.url("http://www.playframework.com").get()
```

This call will return immediately and let you continue to do other things. At some point in the future, the call will have been executed, at which point you can access the result to do something with it. Unlike Java's `java.util.concurrent.Future<V>`, which lets you check whether a `Future` is done or block the calling thread while retrieving it, the `get()` method for Scala's `Future` makes it possible to specify what you want to do with the result of an execution.

To register a callback with a `Future`, you can use the `onComplete` handler, which exposes success or failure:

```
import scala.util.{Success, Failure}

response onComplete {
  case Success(response) => println(s"Success: response.body")
  case Failure(t) => t.printStackTrace()
}
```

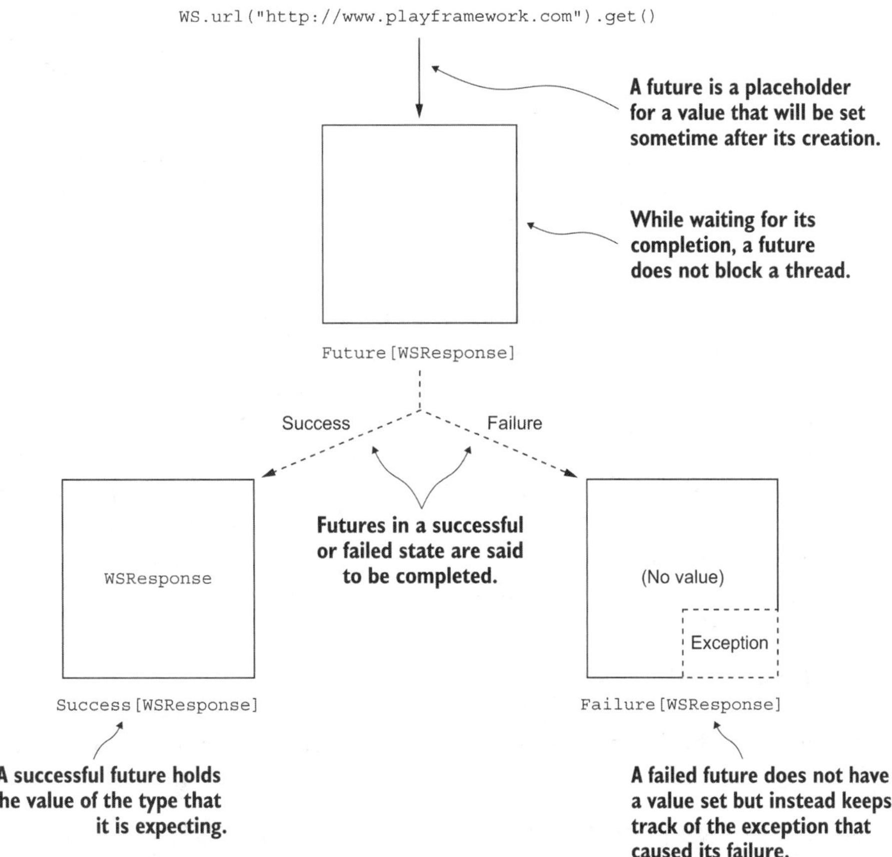

Figure 5.1 Lifecycle of a `Future`: it can either succeed or fail

The `onComplete` handler takes a callback of type `Try[T] => U`. The success and failure of the `Future` are encoded using the `Success` and `Failure` case classes, which are the two possible implementations of `Try`.

TRANSFORMING FUTURES

A frequent use case that arises when working with a library is transforming the library's result into a type that's more appropriate to the task at hand. Whether it's one call producing a future, or several calls producing futures holding different types of results, being able to transform the content of a future without having to wait for it to complete is key to building more complex asynchronous computation pipelines.

Let's take a look at how a future can be transformed.

Listing 5.1 Successful execution and transformation of a future

```
val response: Future[WSResponse] =
  WS.url("http://www.playframework.com").get()
```

Declares the initial future by making a GET call to the Play site

```
val siteOnline: Future[Boolean] = response.map { r =>
  r.status == 200
}

siteOnline.foreach { isOnline =>
  if(isOnline) {
    println("The Play site is up")
  } else {
    println("The Play site is down")
  }
}
```

Transforms the Future[WSReponse] with the map function into a Future[Boolean]

Acts upon the successful completion of the siteOnline future

In this example, you check the status of the response to see if the `GET` request succeeded. It's important to understand that although you're declaring what to do with the `WSResponse` result inside the `map` operation, this doesn't mean it must be completed. The function attached to the initial `response` future only gets executed once and only if the future succeeds. If the future were to fail, the function wouldn't be executed.

In the spirit of expression-oriented programming, futures are primarily meant to be transformed and combined in one or more small steps. The example in listing 5.1 shows that it's also possible to use the side-effecting `foreach` operation (which returns a result of type `Unit`), but you'll see that it's much more useful to transform futures than to perform side-effecting operations on them.

RECOVERING A FAILED FUTURE

Futures don't always succeed. If it fails, a future will remember the cause of its failure rather than throw an exception right away. Instead of wrapping your code in `try...catch` blocks, you have full control over when you want to deal with failures.

Listing 5.2 Recovering the failure of a future

```
val response: Future[WSResponse] =
  WS.url("http://www.playframework.com").get()

val siteAvailable: Future[Option[Boolean]] = response.map { r =>
  Some(r.status == 200)
} recover {
  case ce: java.net.ConnectException => None
}
```

Return a Future[Option[Boolean]] because you can't always say whether the site is available

Handle recovery with the recover function

Return None if you don't have internet access

The `recover` function takes a partial function as a parameter, allowing you to match against different kinds of exceptions and handle them accordingly. In this example, you return an `Option[Boolean]` instead of a Boolean to express that you can't always say whether a site is available or not, especially if you're not online.

> **ENCODING FAILURE** It may not always be adequate to encode the semantics of a failure in an `Option[Boolean]` type. When more than one type of failure can happen, it may be better to work as if the future will succeed and then plug in a failure-handling strategy at the end of the computation pipeline. We'll look at how to do this in section 5.2.

COMPOSING FUTURES

One of the nicest features of Scala's futures is that you can compose them.

Say, for example, that you wanted to check not one but several sites related to Play for their availability. Instead of waiting for the check on one call to finish and then check another one, you could execute both requests concurrently as shown in figure 5.2.

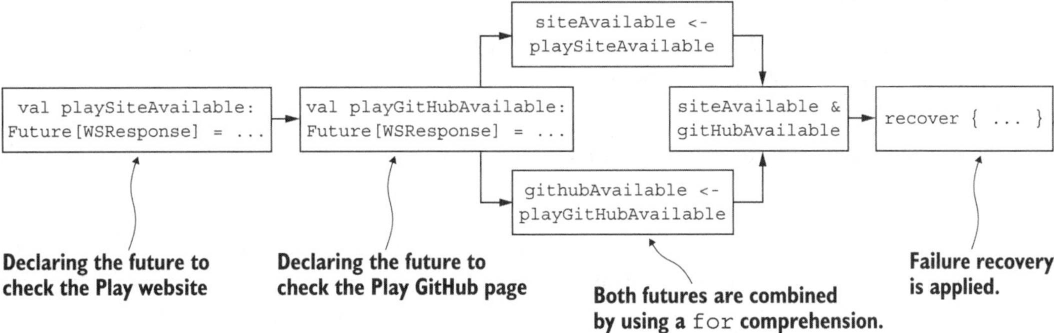

Figure 5.2 Two futures composed together so results and failure handling can be combined

As you saw in listing 5.1, futures have access to the same type of monadic operations as options. You could use the `map` and `flatMap` operations we talked about in chapter 3, but it's even more convenient to employ a `for` comprehension, because this produces more readable source code, as follows.

Listing 5.3 Composing multiple futures with a `for` comprehension

```
def siteAvailable(url: String): Future[Boolean] =
  WS.url(url).get().map { r =>
    r.status == 200
}

val playSiteAvailable =
  siteAvailable("http://www.playframework.com")
val playGithubAvailable =
  siteAvailable("https://github.com/playframework")

val allSitesAvailable: Future[Boolean] = for {
  siteAvailable <- playSiteAvailable
  githubAvailable <- playGithubAvailable
} yield (siteAvailable && githubAvailable)
```

Helper method checks the availability of one site

Future holds the availability of the Play website

Future holds the availability of the Play GitHub page

Composes the futures in a for comprehension so they run concurrently

When both futures have completed, checks if all sites are available

Here you start by declaring two futures, one for each site you want to check. You then compose these two futures with a `for` comprehension and return `true` only if both sites are available. What's important in this example is that you declare the futures *outside* of the for comprehension. This is because futures start to run as soon as they're declared. If you were to declare them inside the for comprehension, the second future would only execute after the first one had completed, which would defeat the purpose.

At this point, you could also add a recovery mechanism on the composed allSitesAvailable future:

```
val overallAvailability: Future[Option[Boolean]] =
  allSitesAvailable.map { a =>
    Option(a)
  } recover {
    case ce: java.net.ConnectException => None
  }
```

Rather than having to handle failure individually on each call, you can add the failure handling at the end of the computation chain. In this way, the failure-handling logic is at one place in the code, which makes it easier to read and maintain. The advantages of this approach may not be obvious now, but we'll take a closer look at this kind of failure handling in section 5.2.

RUNNING FUTURES

There's one last thing we need to look into before we go on to make use of futures in Play. In order to run, a future needs to have access to an ExecutionContext, which takes care of running the asynchronous tasks. An ExecutionContext is typically backed by a plain old ThreadPool.

If you tried to run the code from the previous examples in this chapter, you'll have encountered a compilation error prompting you to provide an execution context. Scala's concurrent library provides a default global execution context, and Play also has a default execution context that can be imported as follows:

```
import play.api.libs.concurrent.Execution.Implicits._
```

In fact, it's pretty easy to create your own execution context if you want to explore how it works.

Listing 5.4 Declaring a custom execution context and running a simple future block on it

```
import scala.concurrent._
import java.util.concurrent.Executors

implicit val ec = ExecutionContext.fromExecutor(
  Executors.newFixedThreadPool(2)
)

val sum: Future[Int] = Future { 1 + 1 }
sum.foreach { s => println(s) }
```

Creates an ExecutionContext based on Java's Executor API

Declares a fixed ThreadPool with 2 threads

Creates a simple future that sums two numbers

In this example, the `ec` execution context is declared as an implicit value. One advantage of this API is that you don't need to tell each future individually which execution context it should be using. But there's one caveat: it's pretty tempting to import one default execution context and then forget about it until, for one reason or another, you need to adjust and fine-tune the execution contexts in use. For example, if you were to use your custom execution context in a real application by importing it in each compilation unit, chances are that at some point it would be exhausted. You'd then need to revisit the whole codebase and check whether or not it makes sense to use this execution context in each situation.

Although it may be handy to use a default execution context for running futures when you're getting started with a project, a better strategy for avoiding trouble later on is to design your service APIs in such a way that an execution context can be passed to them. We'll talk further about this in a moment.

WHEN TO CREATE FUTURES?

In most cases, you'll use futures provided by some library (such as Play's WS library). Unfortunately, asynchronous libraries or wrappers aren't always available for all the tools you might be using.

Futures should primarily be used when there's a blocking operation happening. Blocking operations are mainly I/O bound, such as network calls or disk access. As you've already briefly seen in listing 5.4, Scala provides a simple way to create futures.

Listing 5.5 Creating a future over a blocking operation

```
import scala.concurrent._
import scala.concurrent.ExecutionContext.Implicits.global
import java.io.File

def fileExists(path: String): Future[Boolean] = Future {
  new java.io.File(path).exists
}
```

Note that this won't magically turn the blocking code into something asynchronous! The `java.io.File` API call will still be blocking. But now you can run this code on a different execution context, which means that it won't use the threads of your default application's execution context, which is important to keep in mind, especially when working with Play.

> **FUTURE BLOCK** A future block doesn't just create a new future; it schedules its execution against an execution context.

You shouldn't create futures to wrap purely CPU-bound operations. This doesn't help anyone—CPU-bound operations aren't blocking (with one exception: long-lasting CPU operations that take a long time to do complicated calculations can be considered blocking). Unless you're writing code that should run several calculations in parallel (and where you need these calculations to run simultaneously), creating a future is a costly operation because it involves switching the computation to another execution context and paying the cost of context switching.

Asynchronous code doesn't equal faster code

A dangerous preconception about asynchronous code is that it's fast. That's far from the truth. Asynchronous code is nonblocking, which means that it won't monopolize threads while waiting for a result. There are costs associated with asynchronicity due to the overhead introduced by context switching. Depending on how often the context is switched, this overhead can be more or less important, but it's always there. A very good explanation of this phenomenon can be found in James Roper's talk on the topic of performance.[1]

Telling the execution context about blocking code

There's a `blocking` marker that allows you to tell the execution context that a certain portion of code is blocking. This is useful because the execution context will then be able to respond appropriately, such as by creating more threads (in the case of a fork-join `ThreadPool`). The other advantage to using this marker is that it becomes clear to other developers (as well as to your future self) that a given portion of code is blocking. The example of listing 5.5 would be rewritten as follows:

```
import scala.concurrent._
import scala.concurrent.ExecutionContext.Implicits.global
import java.io.File

def fileExists(path: String): Future[Boolean] = Future {
  blocking {
    new java.io.File(path).exists
  }
}
```

Now that we've talked at length about futures in general, let's take a look at how to use them efficiently in Play.

5.1.2 Futures in Play

Play follows the event-driven web-server architecture, so its default configuration is optimized to work with a small number of threads. This means that to get good performance from a Play application, you need to write asynchronous controller actions. Alternatively, if you really can't write the application by adhering to asynchronous programming principles, you'll need to adjust Play's configuration to another paradigm.

In the following sections we'll look at how to write asynchronous actions and how to adjust Play's thread pool configuration to meet our needs.

---

1 James Roper at the Ping Conference 2014: www.ustream.tv/recorded/42801712.

BUILDING ASYNCHRONOUS ACTIONS

Play has a dedicated mechanism for producing asynchronous controller actions that expect a `Future` as a result. Let's put our previous example in an asynchronous action.

Listing 5.6 Asynchronous action to check if the Play site is online

```
import play.api.libs.ws._
import scala.concurrent._
import play.api.libs.concurrent.Execution.Implicits._
import play.api.Play.current

def availability = Action.async {
  val response: Future[WSResponse] =
    WS.url("http://www.playframework.com").get()
  val siteAvailable: Future[Boolean] = response.map { r =>
    r.status == 200
  }
  siteAvailable.map { isAvailable =>
    if(isAvailable) {
      Ok("The Play site is up.")
    } else {
      Ok("The Play site is down!")
    }
  }
}
```

- Uses the Action.async builder to create an asynchronous action (at `def availability = Action.async {`)
- Maps the resulting Future to produce a Result (at `siteAvailable.map { isAvailable =>`)

Upon invocation, this action will check the status of the Play website and return a short message indicating whether the site is up or down, based on whether the status code is 200 Ok or not. The `Action.async` builder expects to be given a function of type `Request => Future[Result]`. Actions declared in this fashion are not much different from plain `Action { request => ... }` calls, as we discussed in chapter 4—the only difference is that Play knows that `Action.async` actions are already asynchronous, so it doesn't wrap their contents in a future block. That's right—Play will by default schedule any `Action` body to be executed asynchronously against its default web worker pool by wrapping the execution in a future. The only difference between `Action` and `Action.async` is that in the second case, we're taking care of providing an asynchronous computation.

This Play behavior means that you have to be careful when it comes to using blocking code inside of an `Action`.

Blocking and nonblocking controller actions

As you've just seen, the `Action.async` builder is useful when implementing actions that perform blocking I/O or CPU-intensive operations that take a long time to execute. By contrast, the normal `Action` builder doesn't expect an underlying future, but Play will run the body of a normal action against the default web worker pool, assuming that it's nonblocking. The following action does nothing but produce a `Result`. It's therefore purely CPU-bound.

```
def echoPath = Action { implicit request =>
  Ok(s"This action has the URI ${request.path}")
}
```

The next action, however, is problematic, given its use of the blocking `java.io.File` API:

```
def listFiles = Action { implicit request =>
  val files = new java.io.File(".").listFiles
  Ok(files.map(_.getName).mkString(", "))
}
```

Here the `java.io.File` API is performing a blocking I/O operation, which means that one of the few threads of Play's web worker pool will be hijacked while the OS figures out the list of files in the execution directory. This is the kind of situation you should avoid at all costs, because it means that the worker pool may run out of threads.

Realizing when code is blocking is one of the more important aspects of writing reactive web applications. Many database drivers, for example, are still blocking, and you'll see in chapter 7 how to deal with this.

REACTIVE AUDIT TOOL The reactive audit tool, available at https://github.com/octo-online/reactive-audit, aims to point out blocking calls in a project.

RESILIENT ASYNCHRONOUS ACTIONS

Because futures have a built-in mechanism for failure recovery, it's only natural to apply it to asynchronous actions.

Custom error handlers

As you saw in chapter 4, Play has a default error-handling mechanism that can be customized, such as by extending the `DefaultHttpErrorHandler`. In some cases, however, it may be useful to configure custom handlers, such as when you're building a REST API. In this situation it's useful to centralize the error handling in one method.

Listing 5.7 Custom error handler attached to a set of futures

Defines an error handler as a partial function taking as input a Throwable and producing a recovered Result

Addresses the UserNotFoundException, which will yield a 404 Not Found result

```
def authenticationErrorHandler: PartialFunction[Throwable, Result] = {
  case UserNotFoundException(userId) =>
    NotFound(
      Json.obj("error" -> s"User with ID $userId was not found")
    )
  case UserDisabledException(userId) =>
    Unauthorized(
      Json.obj("error" -> s"User with ID $userId is disabled")
    )
  case ce: ConnectionException =>
    ServiceUnavailable(
```

Addresses the UserDisabledException, which will yield a 401 Unauthorized result

Addresses the ConnectionException, which will yield a 503 Service Unavailable result

```
        Json.obj("error" -> "Authentication backend broken")
      )
  }

  val authentication: Future[Result] = ???

  val recoveredAuthentication: Future[Result] =
    authentication.recover(authenticationErrorHandler)
```

Plugs the recovery handler into the future using the recover method

Executes a method that should yield an authentication Result (the ??? marker is valid Scala syntax and will throw a scala.NotImplementedError if executed)

In this example, you define one common recovery handler that knows how to deal with different types of exceptions that may arise when invoking an authentication service. Encapsulating this recovery mechanism in a partial function allows it to be reused. For example, if you were to allow different authentication possibilities using an email-password combination or a social network authentication mechanism, you could use the same recovery handler in all cases.

> **CHAINING RECOVERY HANDLERS** It's possible to chain multiple recovery handlers by calling `recover` multiple times. This way, you can define "last resort" handlers and apply them after your existing handlers in case a more severe error occurs.

Properly handling timeouts

When working with third-party services, it's a good idea to cap the maximum time a request can take, and to fall back to another behavior instead of keeping the user waiting for a long time (2 minutes by default in Play). In an ideal world, everything would run quickly and smoothly, but as we discussed at length in chapter 1, we don't live in an ideal world. The internet is a dangerous place, and calls to remote services may time out.

Listing 5.8 explicitly declares how long we're willing to wait for a service to answer and defines an alternative response in case of timeouts, allowing the client to respond appropriately (perhaps by retrying the authentication call after some delay).

Listing 5.8 Handling timeouts

```
import play.api.libs.concurrent.Promise
import scala.concurrent.duration._

case class AuthenticationResult(success: Boolean, error: String)

def authenticate(username: String, password: String) = Action.async {
  implicit request =>
    val authentication: Future[AuthenticationResult] =
      authenticationService.authenticate(username, password)
    val timeoutFuture = Promise.timeout(
      "Authentication service unresponsive", 2.seconds
    )
    Future.firstCompletedOf(
      Seq(authentication, timeoutFuture)
    ).map {
```

Creates a Promise that times out after 2 seconds

Calls whichever of the two futures completes first

```
      case AuthenticationResult(success, _) if success =>
        Ok("You can pass")
      case AuthenticationResult(success, error) if !success =>
        Unauthorized(s"You shall not pass: $error")
      case timeoutReason: String =>
        ServiceUnavailable(timeoutReason)
    }
}
```

PROMISES The `Promise` used in the previous example is a utility provided by Play and shouldn't be confused with a Scala `Promise`, which would be of type `scala.concurrent.Promise`.

CORRECTLY CONFIGURING AND USING EXECUTION CONTEXTS

As I briefly mentioned earlier, Play has a default execution context for the application that can be imported using the `import play.api.libs.concurrent.Execution.Implicits._` statement. This is not to be confused with Scala's global execution context defined in `scala.concurrent.ExecutionContext.Implicits.global`. Play's default execution context is backed by an Akka dispatcher and is configured by Play itself.

AKKA DISPATCHERS Akka is a toolkit for concurrent programming. We already used Akka actors in chapter 2 and we'll talk about them in chapter 6. But Akka is not limited simply to actors. One of the other tools it provides is dispatchers, which provide a way to configure diverse thread execution strategies in detail. Play uses this configuration facility to configure its own web worker pool.

Because Play follows the evented server model, the number of hot threads available on the default execution context is relatively limited. By default, the dispatcher is set up to create one thread per CPU core, with a maximum of 24 hot threads in the pool, as shown in the following extract from Play's reference configuration:

```
akka {
  actor {
    default-dispatcher {
      fork-join-executor {
        parallelism-factor = 1.0
        parallelism-max = 24
        task-peeking-mode = LIFO
      }
    }
  }
}
```

This configuration is well suited if the application is built in a truly asynchronous manner, without blocking I/O or CPU operations (long computations are blocking in the sense that they keep the CPU busy for a long time, compared to traditional operations). Given that a maximum of 24 hot threads is allowed in the pool, it's easy to imagine what happens if just one action misbehaves under load.

For your reactive application to perform well under load, it's important to ensure that your application is entirely asynchronous, or, if that isn't possible, to adopt a different strategy for dealing with blocking operations. Let's look at a few scenarios.

Falling back to a threaded model

If you're in a situation where much of your code is synchronous, and you can't do much about it or don't have the resources to do so, the easiest solution might be to give up and fall back to a model with many threads. Although this is likely not the most appealing of solutions because of the performance loss incurred by context switching, this approach may come in handy for existing projects that haven't been built with asynchronous behavior in mind. In practice, configuring your application for this approach can provide it with the necessary performance boost while giving the team time to change to another approach.

To configure Play for a highly synchronous application, all you need to do is increase the number of threads:

```
akka {
  akka.loggers = ["akka.event.slf4j.Slf4jLogger"]
  loglevel = WARNING
  actor {
    default-dispatcher = {
      fork-join-executor {
        parallelism-min = 300
        parallelism-max = 300
      }
    }
  }
}
```

This configuration creates a pool of 300 threads, which should be enough for most synchronous operations. By comparison, Tomcat has 200 threads in its worker pool by default. Chances are high that the performance of such an application won't be as good as a purely asynchronous application with a much smaller pool, but this approach might be helpful if there's no other option or you don't have high performance requirements.

> **MEMORY USAGE** Increasing the number of threads available also increases the amount of memory the application needs.

Specialized execution contexts

It's common to have an application that's mostly asynchronous, except for a few expensive CPU operations or calls to synchronous libraries. If you can identify the special cases that require blocking access, a good approach is to configure a few capped execution contexts, and use them in those places.

> **BLOCKING DATABASE DRIVERS** Accessing databases with blocking drivers (which still includes most JDBC drivers) is another case, and we'll talk about that in chapter 7.

Deciding what execution contexts to create and how to cap them isn't the easiest task, and there's little sense in trying to go about it until the application reaches a certain size and complexity and reveals potential bottlenecks. After all, it's hard at design time to predict exactly which libraries will cause trouble, because there's often no strict plan as to which libraries will be used to build an application. Note that this kind of fine-grained execution context configuration affects only small portions of an entire application, as opposed to upfront infrastructure decisions such as which database to use. Those important decisions need to be taken up front and should have an overall impact on the execution context configuration.

For example, let's say your application makes use of a graph database to generate a specialized kind of report, and it uses a third-party service for resizing images. Those libraries might be performing blocking I/O operations, so it may be a good idea to isolate their impact on the default pool so they don't affect the performance of the application.

The first thing you need to do is configure those contexts accordingly in conf/application.conf.

Listing 5.9 Custom execution context configuration in conf/application.conf

```
contexts {
    graph-db {
        thread-pool-executor {
          fixed-pool-size = 2
        }
    }
    image-resizer {
        thread-pool-executor {
            core-pool-size-factor = 10.0
            max-pool-size-max = 50
        }
    }
}
```

Uses the thread-pool-executor for the pool

Defines the number of threads

Defines the core pool size factor; the number of threads will be a multiple of the number of cores and this factor

max-pool-size-max = 50

Next, you need to materialize those execution contexts in your application, such as in a `Contexts` object.

Listing 5.10 Declaring custom execution contexts

```
object Contexts {
  val graphDb: ExecutionContext =
    Akka.system.dispatchers.lookup("contexts.graph-db")
  val imageResizer: ExecutionContext =
    Akka.system.dispatchers.lookup("contexts.image-resizer")
}
```

Finally, you can use the context in the places where they were designed to be used. We were talking about querying a graph database and resizing images using a specialized service—let's look at how you would use your custom context in the reporting service.

Listing 5.11 Using a custom execution context

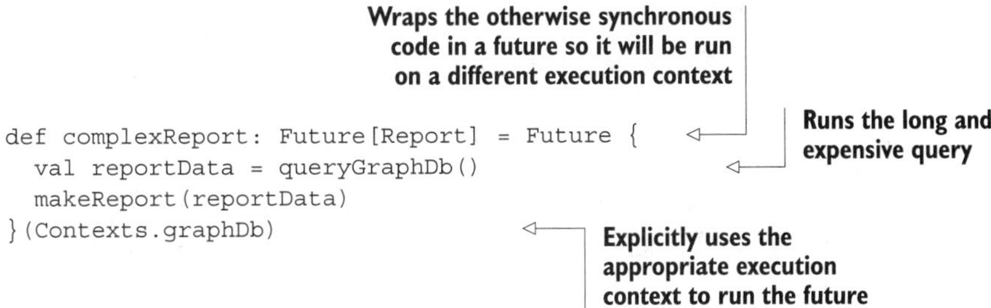


```
def complexReport: Future[Report] = Future {
  val reportData = queryGraphDb()
  makeReport(reportData)
}(Contexts.graphDb)
```

To cap the size of a custom execution context, it's useful to consider the use case and the hardware the application will be running on.

First, it's always good to keep the number of threads as low as possible to reduce the amount of context switching and to save some memory. It's also good to consider what happens when the pool is exhausted. In the case of a report that's only used by a few power users a few times a month, waiting a little while for a report may not be too dramatic. On the other hand, a function that allows new users to resize their profile pictures needs to be available and quick.

If we assume that our hypothetical application will be deployed on a machine with a quad-core CPU, we'll start with 40 threads available for the image-resizing process during signup (given that the preceding code sets up a factor of 10.0, which is the number of threads per core used by the thread pool). If the image-resizing process takes 1 second, we can perform 40 resizes per second, with a limit of 50 resizes per second in total (given the `max-pool-size-max` value) for one machine.

If we were to launch our new application with four machines, we'd have a bandwidth of 200 concurrent resizes at the start. Even if more than 200 users signed up at the same time, they probably wouldn't upload their profile pictures at the same time, so the number of effective users that can sign up at once is likely more than 200, which might be sufficient.

If the application were to go viral and we had many more users signing up at the same time, we'd need to be prepared to scale out elastically onto more nodes. We'll discuss this topic in chapter 9.

Execution contexts and virtualized environments

If your application is going to be deployed on a cloud infrastructure platform, it will be trickier estimating a good thread pool size, because you can no longer be sure whether the cores on the machine are real or virtual. Capping a thread pool under the assumption that you have a quad-core CPU might have nasty side effects on the performance of your application if in reality there are only two cores on the machine. It's a good idea to start by experimenting with the deployment before running a production application on virtual-ized infrastructure.

> **Capping execution context sizes**
>
> To figure out how to cap a custom execution context, you can use the following guidelines:
>
> - Keep in mind that your aim is to protect the overall application from resource exhaustion.
> - Consider the consequences of exhaustion for that specific context.
> - Know the hardware you're running on, and specifically how many cores you have at your disposal.
> - Be aware of the maximum time that tasks running on this context may require.

Bulkheading based on business functions

Depending on the nature of your application, you may take a different approach to organizing your execution contexts and use the bulkhead pattern we briefly mentioned in chapter 1. In this approach, instead of dedicating specialized contexts to technical aspects (database, special third-party services, and so on), you set up contexts based on the functionality of your application.

In figure 5.3, you can see the different business concerns of an e-commerce site. It's these concerns that the application's context configuration will be based on. In such a setup, each module uses its own dedicated context across all the technical stack, including blocking database calls or blocking third-party calls.

Setting up such a configuration and using it consistently across the application takes more effort up front, but the advantage is that critical services can't be affected by resource exhaustion caused by other services. For example, a bug in the reporting module that eats up many threads won't be able to affect the payment service.

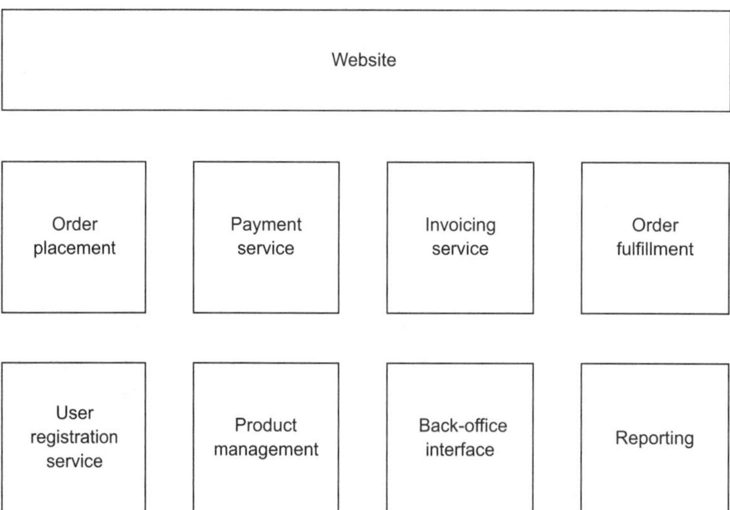

Figure 5.3 Organizing contexts with bulkheads based on the functionality of an e-commerce site

5.1.3 Testing futures

Services that return future results are a bit more tricky to test than plain old synchronous results. Luckily most testing libraries have accepted that futures are here to stay and have included a few useful helpers. In the following examples we'll look at how you can test futures with the specs2 library (http://etorreborre.github.io/specs2/), which is bundled by default with Play.

WHICH BEHAVIOR TO TEST

Before looking into implementing tests with specs2, let's take a moment to consider what behavior we'd like to test. After all, a future is a special abstraction that's directly related to the passage of time. In this respect, we may want to test more than just the usual cases we'd test for synchronous code (more than whether a service responds to a certain set of timing constraints, for example). Figure 5.4 shows the different properties of an asynchronous service implemented with futures that we may want to test.

Synchronous services are mainly tested for the *correctness* of their behavior ❶—whether they behave as expected for a certain set of inputs. In contrast, asynchronous services also need to be tested for *timeliness* ❷. This behavior can, in turn, be influenced by the timeliness of external dependencies, so a third behavior to test is how services respond to delays in those dependencies ❸.

HOW TO USE SPECS2 TO TEST FUTURES

To make it easy to test futures, you should make the execution context configurable. This is good practice for working with futures in general.

```
trait AuthenticationService {
  def authenticateUser(email: String, password: String)
    (implicit ec: ExecutionContext): Future[AuthenticationResult]
}
```

When using specs2's support for futures, a single-threaded executor is used for the tests, available by default in the tests. It's possible to override this configuration or to pass in a specialized executor depending on the test case.

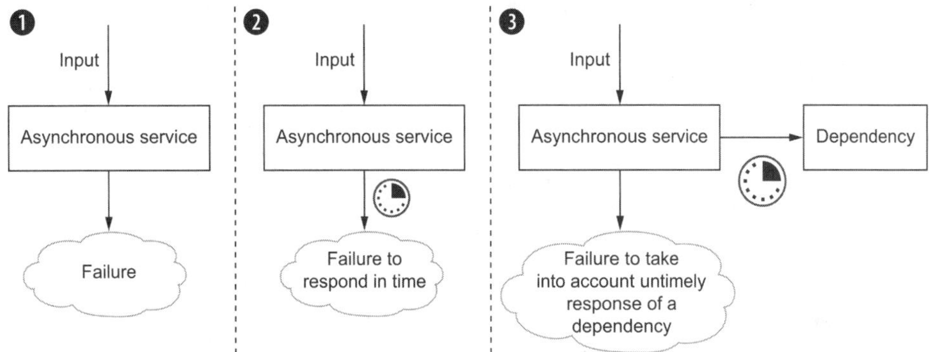

Figure 5.4 Asynchronous services require testing for more types of behavior than whether they do the right thing. You also need to make sure they do the right thing at the right time.

Let's write a few tests for the authentication service.

Listing 5.12 Testing futures with specs2

```
import scala.concurrent.duration._

class AuthenticationServiceSpec extends Specification {

  "The AuthenticationService" should {
    val service = new DefaultAuthenticationService

    "correctly authenticate Bob Marley" in {
      implicit ee: ExecutionEnv =>
        service.authenticateUser("bob@marley.org", "secret")
        must beEqualTo (AuthenticationSuccessful).await(1, 200.millis)
    }

    "not authenticate Ziggy Marley" in { implicit ee: ExecutionEnv =>
      service.authenticateUser("ziggy@marley.org", "secret")
      must beEqualTo (AuthenticationUnsuccessful).await(1, 200.millis)
    }

    "fail if it takes too long" in { implicit ee: ExecutionEnv =>
      service.authenticateUser("jimmy@hendrix.com", "secret")
      must throwA[RuntimeException].await(1, 600.millis)
    }
  }
}
```

spec2's ExecutionEnv provides an execution context for executing futures.

The await method turns any normal matcher for type T into a matcher for Future[T].

The throwA matcher tests if a future fails.

A nice feature of specs2 is that all the usual matchers (`beEqualTo`, `throwA`, and so on) are available when working with futures. The only change compared to the usual use of specs2 matchers is that the last part of the assertion statement that uses a matcher needs to be suffixed with `await`, optionally indicating the number of retries and the timeout duration.

Testing individual futures is useful when writing unit tests. We'll talk in depth about testing an entire reactive web application in chapter 11.

5.2 Designing asynchronous business logic with futures

Futures are a great tool, but using them efficiently requires a bit of planning and thinking ahead. In the following sections we'll build the functionality for a service that provides statistics to Twitter users regarding their follower and friend counts. The simple service that we'll build is shown in figure 5.5.

When asked to do so by a user, the service will look up the latest follower and friend counts using the Twitter API, compare that result to previous counts stored in a database, and finally publish a message telling the user how their statistics changed compared to last time. It will also save the new counts in the database to respond to future requests.

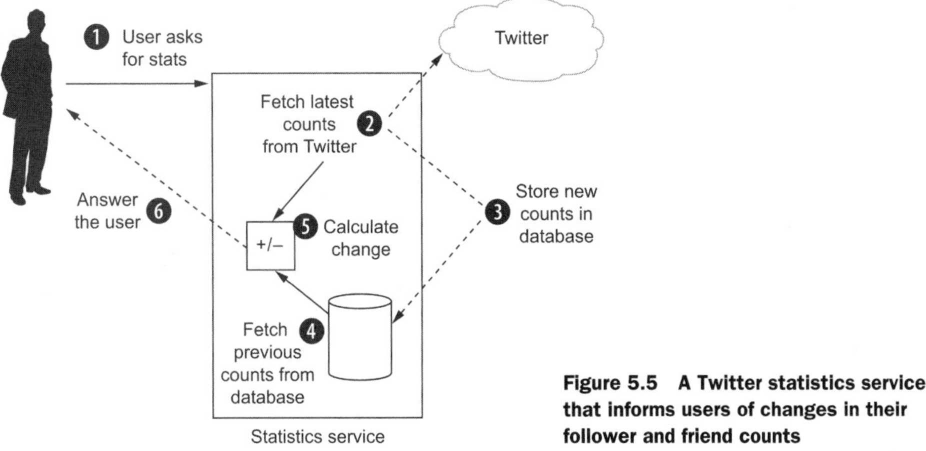

Figure 5.5 A Twitter statistics service that informs users of changes in their follower and friend counts

5.2.1 *Identifying parallelizable elements*

If we were to implement the steps required for the service to function in a naive, straightforward way, we might end up with something like figure 5.6.

The time that the entire process takes to execute is called *latency*, and it's determined by adding the duration of each of the sequential steps. Our goal is to reduce the latency to make for happier users, as they'll get a faster answer.

> **FINDING THE RIGHT LEVEL OF GRANULARITY** Notice how each step of figure 5.6 does one thing only. I didn't group seemingly related items into one step, such as "Fetch the previous counts from the database and save the new ones." What we really want to achieve at this stage is to cut the entire process into steps that are as small as possible and that have the same level of granularity. Once we understand the nature of each step and how they can be rearranged, we may be able to optimize the process by combining closely related steps.

Once the process is divided into separate pieces, we can put on our asynchronous glasses and identify those elements that perform I/O or network operations. We want to identify those steps first because they'll give us a good indication of what elements need to run asynchronously. Remember, we don't want those operations to block a thread while it waits for them to complete. Looking at figure 5.6, it's easy to see that

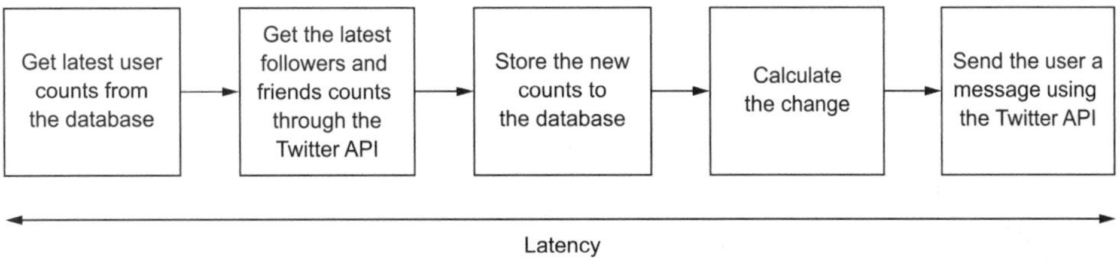

Figure 5.6 The steps involved in the basic Twitter statistics reporting service, executed sequentially. The total time all steps take to run is the latency.

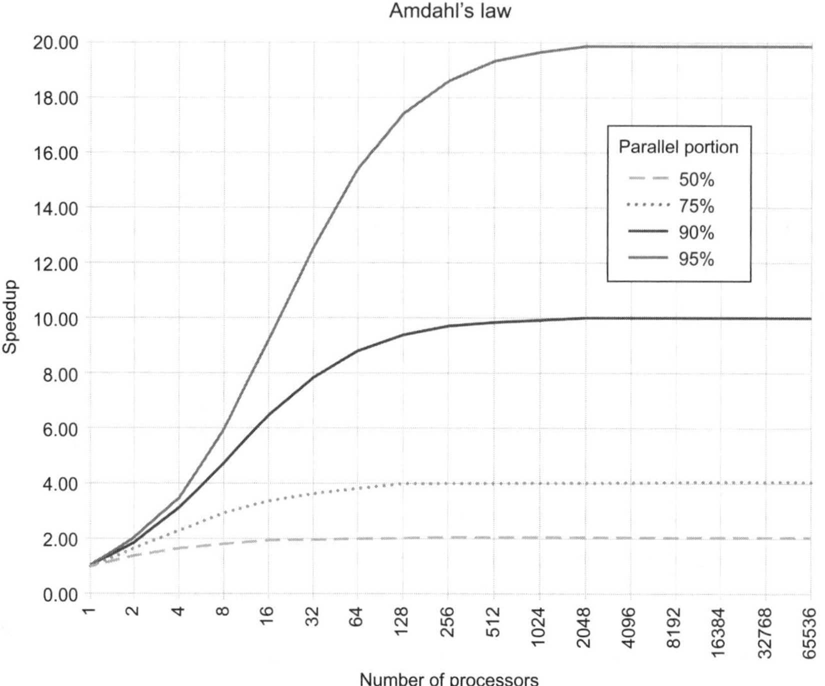

Figure 5.7 Amdahl's law shows that to obtain a high level of speedup, the individual steps of a process need to have as high a degree of parallelism as possible.

almost all the steps perform an I/O operation of some kind, except for the "calculate the change" step, which is purely CPU-bound.

To reduce the latency of the overall process, we want to execute as many of the steps in parallel as possible. Ideally, all of our steps would run in parallel, because in that case the latency of the entire process would be reduced to the execution duration of the longest step. Amdahl's law (http://en.wikipedia.org/wiki/Amdahl's_law) shows in detail how the speed of a process is affected by the degree of parallelization of its individual steps (see figure 5.7).

Let's get back to our Twitter statistics service and take a critical look at the steps to see what we could possibly parallelize. For our rather simple use case, you probably can already see some of the dependencies between the steps. For example, we can't calculate the changes before having retrieved both the previous counts from the database and the current counts from Twitter. This example is simple enough that you can do this kind of dependency analysis, but it won't always be this obvious for more complex processes. Luckily, there's a method to trying to parallelize as much as possible.

Let's write down all of our steps as pseudocode to clarify the inputs and outputs of each step. Figure 5.8 shows the result.

```
def retrievePreviousCountsFromDatabase(userName):
  (previousFollowersCount, previousFriendsCounts)

def fetchRelationshipCountFromTwitter(userName):
  (currentFollowersCount, currentFriendsCount)

def storeCounts(
  userName, currentFollowersCount, currentFriendsCount
)
def calculateChange(
  previousFollowersCount, previousFriendsCounts,
  currentFollowersCount, currentFriendsCount):
    (followersDifference, friendsDifference)

def sendMessageToUser(
  userName, followersDifference, friendsDifference
)
```

Figure 5.8 Pseudocode that clarifies dependencies among the steps

Once expressed in terms of inputs and outputs, the dependencies between the different steps (which really are just functions) become much more obvious. By "unwinding" these dependencies, we now can represent a parallelized version of the execution flow, as in figure 5.9.

GROUPING STEPS I've grouped the two steps related to calculating the changes and sending a message to the user. This was possible for two reasons: no other step was consuming the output of the "calculate the change" step, and this step itself is not asynchronous (as it is only CPU-bound).

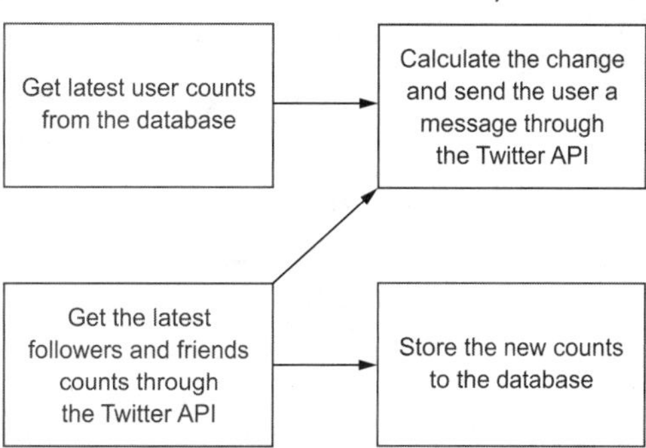

Figure 5.9 Parallelized version of the Twitter statistics service process

5.2.2 *Composing the service's futures*

As you saw briefly in section 5.1.1, one of the most important features that the future abstraction offers over the use of simple callbacks is the possibility to compose them. In the following sections you'll see how to make use of this property.

DEFINING SERVICE INTERFACES

To implement our service, we'll use a few traits to describe the behavior of various components. First, we need a way to store and to retrieve previously stored statistics.

Listing 5.13 Interface of the repository used to store and retrieve statistics locally

```
trait StatisticsRepository {

  def storeCounts(counts: StoredCounts)
    (implicit ec: ExecutionContext): Future[Unit]
```

Method to store newly retrieved counts

```
  def retrieveLatestCounts(userName: String)
    (implicit ec: ExecutionContext): Future[StoredCounts]

}

case class StoredCounts(
  when: DateTime,
  userName: String,
  followersCount: Long,
  friendsCount: Long
)
```

Method to retrieve the most recent entry

Case class holding follower and friend counts at a given time for a given user

Next, we need a means of communicating with Twitter to retrieve the current status of followers and friends, and to send messages to our users.

Listing 5.14 Interface for communicating with the Twitter API

```
trait TwitterService {

  def fetchRelationshipCounts(userName: String)
    (implicit ec: ExecutionContext): Future[TwitterCounts]

  def postTweet(message: String)
    (implicit ec: ExecutionContext): Future[Unit]

}

case class TwitterCounts(followersCount: Long, friendsCount: Long)
```

Method to fetch latest follower and friend counts from Twitter

Method to post a tweet

Case class holding the latest counts

Last but not least, let's create a simple interface for our core statistics service.

Listing 5.15 Simple interface for our statistics service

```
trait StatisticsService {
  def createUserStatistics(userName: String)
    (implicit ec: ExecutionContext): Future[Unit]
}
```

In this last interface method, the return type is a rather awkward `Future[Unit]`. The truth is, however, that this service method won't return any useful value. It will perform a (rather useful) side effect by retrieving data and sending it off again, but it won't provide any useful data as result of the execution, so there's no reason to define a return type. If anything, defining a return type might be more confusing than helpful: at least when a method returns a `Unit` or `Future[Unit]`, it's clearly stating "I am a side-effecting method." You might say that it could be useful to indicate whether the execution succeeded or not, which is a valid point; we'll talk about how to deal with failure shortly.

As you may have noticed, all of our defined methods expect an implicit `ExecutionContext` parameter to be available when they're called. This is in line with what we discussed in section 5.1.1: we shouldn't tightly couple the execution of asynchronous methods to a fixed execution context. We want to be able to easily switch out which configuration we'll use in practice.

Now that we have our most important interfaces ready, let's move on and use them! We won't look at the detailed implementations of the interfaces in this chapter, but you can check the book's source code if you're interested.

RETRIEVING THE COUNTS

The first thing we need to do to calculate the statistics for a user is retrieve the previous and current counts of followers and friends. We'll do this by using the statistics repository and the Twitter service we previously defined, as shown in figure 5.10.

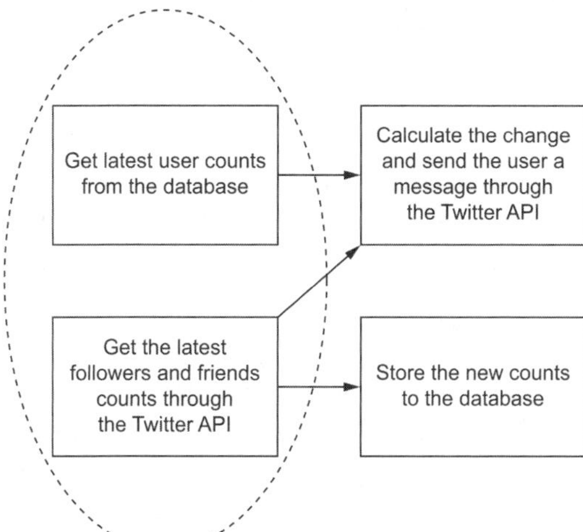

Figure 5.10 First step: retrieving the counts from Twitter and the local database

Listing 5.16 Retrieving the previous and current counts in parallel

```
class DefaultStatisticsService(
  statisticsRepository: StatisticsRepository,
  twitterService: TwitterService) extends StatisticsService {

  override def createUserStatistics(userName: String)
    (implicit ec: ExecutionContext): Future[Unit] = {

      val previousCounts: Future[StoredCounts] =
        statisticsRepository.retrieveLatestCounts(userName)
      val currentCounts: Future[TwitterCounts] =
        twitterService.fetchRelationshipCounts(userName)

      val counts: Future[(StoredCounts, TwitterCounts)] = for {
        previous <- previousCounts
        current <- currentCounts
      } yield {
```

Calls the methods to retrieve previous and current counts so that they start their execution

Uses a for comprehension to run the futures concurrently

```
        (previous, current)                     <— Groups the results in a tuple
      }

    Future.successful({})                       <— For now, returns a
  }                                                successful Unit result so
                                                   the method will compile
```

This first step isn't too complicated. All you need to do is call the respective services to retrieve past and current counts. What's important here is to declare the futures up front, before the `for` comprehension. As I mentioned at the start of this chapter in section 5.1.1, a future starts executing as soon as it's declared.

It would be tempting to shorten the code and write the following:

```
val counts: Future[(StoredCounts, TwitterCounts)] = for {
  previous <- statisticsRepository.retrieveLatestCounts(userName)
  current <- twitterService.fetchRelationshipCounts(userName)
} yield {
  (previous, current)
}
```

What would happen in this case, however, is quite the opposite of what you want to achieve: the first generator of the `for` comprehension would wait until the future is completed before it moves on to the second one, ruining your attempt to run the two methods in parallel.

USING THE COUNTS

The second part of our service method will deal with storing the newly acquired counts in the database for later reuse, as well as informing the user about their statistics (see figure 5.11). Just as in the first step, we'd like these operations to be run in parallel. What makes the second step more interesting than the first is that our input is already a future, and the operations we'll run are also going to be generating future results. If

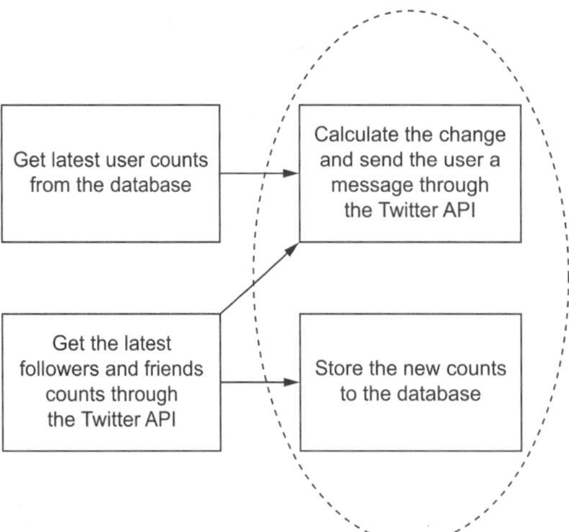

Figure 5.11 Second step: saving the new counts and sending a message to the user

we're not careful, we'll end up having imbricated futures, which is not a nice situation to be in.

Instead of concerning ourselves with this issue, let's move on for the moment and implement the two remaining steps—we'll come back and fix this composition issue later on.

Listing 5.17 Methods to store the fresh counts and publish a statistics message

```
def storeCounts(counts: (StoredCounts, TwitterCounts)): Future[Unit] =
  counts match { case (previous, current) =>
    statisticsRepository.storeCounts(StoredCounts(
      DateTime.now,
      userName,
      current.followersCount,
      current.friendsCount
    ))
  }

def publishMessage(counts: (StoredCounts, TwitterCounts)):
  Future[Unit] =
    counts match { case (previous, current) =>
      val followersDifference =
        current.followersCount - previous.followersCount
      val friendsDifference =
        current.friendsCount - previous.friendsCount
      def phrasing(difference: Long) =
        if (difference > 0) "gained" else "lost"
      val durationInDays =
        new Period(previous.when, DateTime.now).getDays

  twitterService.postTweet(
    s"@$userName in the past $durationInDays you have " +
    s"${phrasing(followersDifference)} $followersDifference " +
    s"followers and ${phrasing(followersDifference)} " +
    s"$friendsDifference friends"
  )
}
```

Takes the tuple of counts as input and matches against it to easily extract and work with them

Computes the differences of followers, friends, and elapsed time as part of the message publishing

Mentions the user on Twitter to attract their attention

You now have two methods, each one dealing with one step. As I mentioned before, these two methods are themselves asynchronous and consume the output of asynchronous methods, so their result is in the future of the future, as illustrated in figure 5.12.

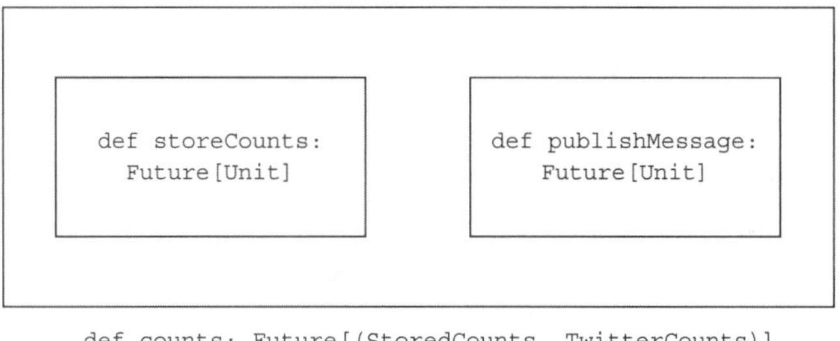

Figure 5.12 Results of the `storeCounts` and `publishMessage` futures are dependent on future results themselves and are therefore nested.

Luckily for us, we have a tool that lets us flatten out this imbrication: `flatMap`. As you may remember from chapter 3, `flatMap` does the same thing as `map` in that it applies a function to each element of a structure (in our case, the result of the first future) and then flattens out the chain. Let's use this to combine our two steps.

Listing 5.18 Combining both steps

```
// first group of steps: retrieving previous and current counts
val previousCounts: Future[StoredCounts] =
  statisticsRepository.retrieveLatestCounts(userName)
val currentCounts: Future[TwitterCounts] =
  twitterService.fetchRelationshipCounts(userName)

val counts: Future[(StoredCounts, TwitterCounts)] = for {
  previous <- previousCounts
  current <- currentCounts
} yield {
  (previous, current)
}

// second group of steps: using the counts in order to store them
// and publish a message on Twitter
val storedCounts: Future[Unit] = counts.flatMap(storeCounts)
val publishedMessage: Future[Unit] = counts.flatMap(publishMessage)

for {
  _ <- storedCounts
  _ <- publishedMessage
} yield {}
```

Combines the results of the first step into one as soon as both futures are available

Uses flatMap to consume the result of the first step and avoid nesting

Combines the execution of both futures into one

The underscore notation means that you don't care about the result of this generator statement, but you want it to be executed.

Returns a Unit result

Here you use `flatMap` in combination with the result of the first `for` comprehension to get rid of nesting. You then combine both resulting futures (`storedCounts` and `publishedMessage`) into one using another `for` comprehension. This way you can return a single `Future[Unit]` from your method, which will be useful when it comes to error handling.

5.2.3 *Propagating and handling errors*

Our service is now ready to be released in the wild and used. Or is it? One thing we haven't dealt with yet are all the different things that could go wrong:

- The database might not be reachable.
- The Twitter API might not be reachable (because of a network problem or because the credentials don't work or aren't defined).
- The user might not exist on Twitter.

These are but a few of the issues a user could encounter while using our service. In fact, more often than not, we're oblivious to how exactly our program may fail. Instead of trying to catch exceptions early on and handle them on the spot, another

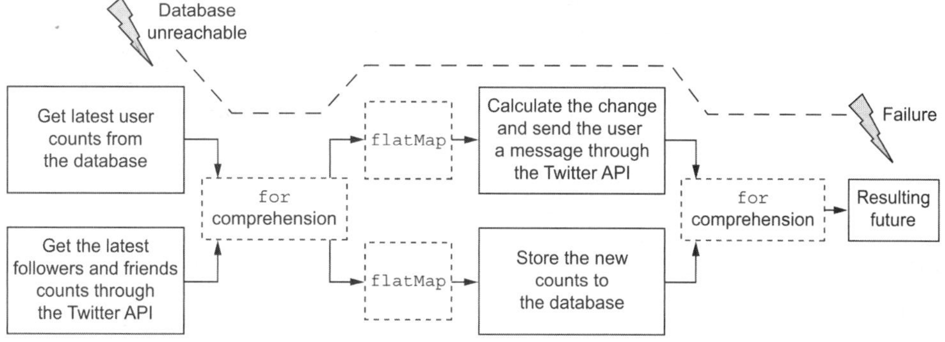

Figure 5.13 If an exception should happen, it will be propagated along the chain of composed futures.

approach enabled by the use of futures is to let them propagate along the asynchronous execution chain, as illustrated in figure 5.13.

What we've done so far combines futures through various means (`for` comprehensions and `flatMap`), which means that the final result we get from our service will carry any exception that may occur along the path. Rather than starting the recovery early in the chain, we can deal with it at the very end.

IDENTIFYING DIFFERENT TYPES OF ERRORS

For our recovery mechanism to take the appropriate actions or to at least provide the user with an accurate error message, it must be able to identify errors correctly. Even if we don't deal with the errors right away, we need to make sure they're encoded appropriately. Let's look at an example in an implementation of the `StatisticsRepository` that uses the ReactiveMongo driver (http://reactivemongo.org), as shown in the following listing (the full example is in the source code for this chapter).

> **WHY MONGODB?** You might wonder why I'm using MongoDB here. The primary reason is simply that its asynchronous driver (ReactiveMongo) is mature and a good fit for the subject matter of this chapter. Furthermore, it has a simple query API and it's easily available on various platforms, which should make it easy to use.

Listing 5.19 Implementation of `StatisticsRepository`

```
class MongoStatisticsRepository @Inject()
  (reactiveMongo: ReactiveMongoApi) extends StatisticsRepository {
  private val StatisticsCollection = "UserStatistics"

  private lazy val collection =
    reactiveMongo.db.collection[BSONCollection](StatisticsCollection)

  override def storeCounts(counts: StoredCounts)
    (implicit ec: ExecutionContext): Future[Unit] = {
    collection.insert(counts).map { lastError =>
```

The insert method returns a future containing the error status returned by MongoDB.

```
      if(lastError.inError) {
        throw CountStorageException(counts)
      }
    }
  }

  override def retrieveLatestCounts(userName: String)
    (implicit ec: ExecutionContext): Future[StoredCounts] = {
    val query = BSONDocument("userName" -> userName)
    val order = BSONDocument("_id" -> -1)
    collection
      .find(query)
      .sort(order)
      .one[StoredCounts]
      .map { counts =>
        counts getOrElse StoredCounts(DateTime.now, userName, 0, 0)
      } recover {
        case NonFatal(t) =>
          throw CountRetrievalException(userName, t)
        }
  }
}

case class CountRetrievalException(userName: String)
  extends RuntimeException("Could not read counts for " + userName)

case class CountStorageException(counts: StoredCounts)
  extends RuntimeException
```

If there's an error, throw a customized CountStorageException, giving client code the chance to decide what to do.

Recovers any exception that may occur from attempting to query counts

If no counts are found, don't treat this as an error. Instead return an empty statistic.

The NonFatal matcher matches any exceptions that aren't fatal, such as OutOfMemoryError and other system-level exceptions.

In the preceding example, there are three different cases of dealing with errors.

The first case can occur when you're trying to store new counts. The ReactiveMongo API won't throw an exception if an error occurs in that case. Instead, you proactively check whether the returned error state is an error. If you're not familiar with MongoDB, this last statement may sound somewhat odd, but I assure you that I'm not making things up. This is how the MongoDB error-reporting mechanism is designed. If you face an error, you throw your custom `CountStorageException` containing the counts you wanted to save, giving the client code that uses the service a chance to decide what to do.

In the second case, the error is that you can't find any counts for user. This will happen the first time a user uses the service. Instead of treating this as an error case and returning an exception, you simply pretend that all counts are at 0.

Finally, in the third case, you explicitly recover any exception that may occur while trying to query the database, and wrap it in a custom `CountRetrievalException`.

> **USING NONFATAL TO CATCH EXCEPTIONS** You may have noticed that instead of catching the exception directly in listing 5.19, you're catching it while it's wrapped in `scala.control.NonFatal`. As a result, this won't match errors like `VirtualMachineError`, `OutOfMemoryError`, and `StackOverflowError`, as well as special types of exceptions used for Scala's control structures. These kinds of errors and throwables should be escalated as far as possible, because they're pretty much impossible to recover from anyway.

RECOVERING IT ALL IN ONE PLACE

To shield the client code from everything that could go wrong in our `StatisticsService`, we should try to recover from exceptions. If there isn't anything we can do, we should fail with a message that's easily usable outside.

Let's start by intercepting all the things that could go wrong and revisit the end of our example from listing 5.18 using the mechanism outlined in the following listing.

Listing 5.20 Recovering failures before handing the result over to the service's clients

```
class DefaultStatisticsService(
  statisticsRepository: StatisticsRepository,
  twitterService: TwitterService) extends StatisticsService {

  // ...

  val result = for {
    _ <- storedCounts
    _ <- publishedMessage
  } yield {}

  result recoverWith {
    case CountStorageException(countsToStore) =>
      retryStoring(countsToStore, attemptNumber = 0)
  } recover {
    case CountStorageException(countsToStore) =>
      throw StatisticsServiceFailed(
        "We couldn't save the statistics to our database. "
        + "Next time it will work!"
      )
    case CountRetrievalException(user, cause) =>
      throw StatisticsServiceFailed(
        "We have a problem with our database. Sorry!", cause
      )
    case TwitterServiceException(message) =>
      throw StatisticsServiceFailed(
        s"We have a problem contacting Twitter: $message
      )
     case NonFatal(t) =>
      throw StatisticsServiceFailed(
        "We have an unknown problem. Sorry!"
      )
  }

}

class StatisticsServiceFailed(cause: Throwable)
  extends RuntimeException(cause) {
    def this(message: String) = this(new RuntimeException(message))
    def this(message: String, cause: Throwable) =
      this(new RuntimeException(message, cause))
}
object StatisticsServiceFailed {
  def apply(message: String): StatisticsServiceFailed =
```

Uses recoverWith to provide a Future result that can handle an exception

If you can't store the retrieved counts, retries by calling a function

Recovers all exceptions that you don't want to handle and returns a unified exception

If you couldn't recover the CountStorageException, apologizes here

Declares a custom exception type that provides a uniform view on all known failures of the statistics service

```
      new StatisticsServiceFailed(message)
    def apply(message: String, cause: Throwable):
      StatisticsServiceFailed =
        new StatisticsServiceFailed(message, cause)
}
```

There are two things you can do with an exception that occurs. You can try to recover from the failure and take measures to do so, or you can give up and pass the failure on to your clients in a more presentable way. In the preceding example, you only try to recover storage exceptions; for all other errors, you simply wrap them in a special kind of exception and provide a human-readable message. This way, anyone using the service doesn't need to concern themselves with the underlying technical cause of the failure, which isn't likely to be very relevant for the user anyway.

To recover from storage exceptions, you retry storing a few times, using the `retryStoring` function.

Listing 5.21 Recursive function that attempts to store counts three times before giving up

```
private def retryStoring(counts: StoredCounts, attemptNumber: Int)
  (implicit ec: ExecutionContext): Future[Unit] = {
  if (attemptNumber < 3) {
    statisticsRepository.storeCounts(counts).recoverWith {
      case NonFatal(t) => retryStoring(counts, attemptNumber + 1)
    }
  } else {
    Future.failed(CountStorageException(counts))
  }
}
```

Attempts to store the counts 3 times

Calls the storage function again and recovers the call

Recurses by calling the retryStorage method itself and increases the retry count

If things don't work, fails with the initial kind of exception

This function tries to store the counts again, and calls itself in case of failure. After three attempts it gives up and fails with the same type of exception that the storage repository returned. This is why you also check for this kind of exception in the `recover` part of listing 5.20.

5.3 Summary

Throughout this chapter, you've seen how futures work in theory and in practice. Most importantly, you've seen that

- Futures can either succeed or fail, and failures are propagated up a chain of futures.
- Futures can be composed, which is essential for building more-complex asynchronous tasks.
- Working with futures requires you to handle timeouts, and that should be tested for, to ensure that an asynchronous service is resilient.

In addition to learning about the fundamentals of futures, we discussed how to best use them in the context of Play and how to configure the execution contexts of the framework to ensure the smooth execution of the application. In particular, it is essential to

- Be aware that blocking operations have an impact on Play's default minimal thread pool. They should be executed on specialized thread pools or the configuration should be adapted to cater to a mostly synchronous application.
- Avoid hardcoding the execution context used in the application by importing execution contexts; instead, define them as implicit parameters on service interface functions.
- Think ahead about which strategy you want to employ when it comes to the configuration and layout of an application's execution contexts.

In the next chapter, we'll look at another essential tool for building complex asynchronous applications: actors.

6 Actors

This chapter covers

- Creating actors and actor hierarchies
- Sending messages and handling failure the Akka way
- Reacting to load with control messages and circuit breakers

The actor-based concurrency model[1] was popularized by the Erlang programming language and is implemented on the JVM by the Akka concurrency toolkit (http://akka.io). This chapter provides an introduction to the wonderful world of actors. As you'll see, actors are a very effective tool for building scalable and resilient applications. As Akka is available out of the box in Play, we can use it to implement more-advanced asynchronous logic.

Actors are a vast topic, and we'll only look at the most important aspects to get started using them. If you want to get a deeper understanding of actors, I recommend looking at Akka's excellent documentation (http://akka.io/docs) as well as at

[1] Carl Hewitt, Peter Bishop, and Richard Steiger, "A universal modular ACTOR formalism for artificial intelligence," in *Proceedings of the 3rd international joint conference on artificial intelligence* IJCAI'73 (Morgan Kaufmann Publishers, 1973), 235-245.

a book dedicated to the topic, such as Kuhn and Allen's *Reactive Design Patterns* (Manning, 2016) or *Akka in Action* by Roestenburg, Bakker, and Williams (Manning, 2016).

In one way, the actor model is object orientation done right: the state of an actor can be mutable but never exposed directly to the outside world. Instead, actors communicate with each other via asynchronous message passing, in which the messages themselves are immutable. An actor can only do one of three things:

- Send and receive any number of messages
- Change its behavior or state in response to a message
- Start new child actors

The actor decides what state it's ready to share and when to mutate it. This model makes it easier to write concurrent programs that aren't riddled with race conditions or deadlocks that are introduced by accidentally reading or writing outdated state or using locks to avoid the latter.

6.1 Actor fundamentals

You've already worked with actors in chapters 2 and 4, using them to deal with WebSocket connections. So far the actors you've set up have been very simple, and we haven't spent much time explaining their different parts.

In chapter 5 we built a workflow based on futures to calculate statistics about Twitter followers. In this chapter we'll expand on the idea of a Twitter analytics service. This chapter's version will use a combination of futures and actors, letting us take an in-depth look at different ways actors can be used.

6.1.1 A simple Twitter analytics service

In this chapter we'll build a simple service that provides users with basic analytics about their activity on Twitter, as illustrated in figure 6.1. The first use case we'll explore is computing the "reach" of a tweet by looking at how many times it was retweeted and how many people potentially saw it.

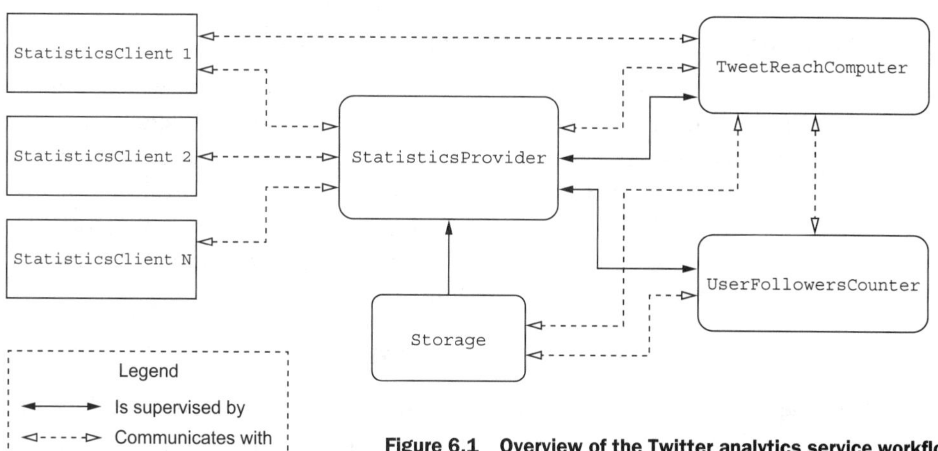

Figure 6.1 Overview of the Twitter analytics service workflow

To provide a robust service, we'll have to be able to deal with storage service problems and take into account Twitter's API rate limits.

Actors should have a single responsibility, which makes them easy to implement and understand. They should cooperate in groups to fulfill their mission, whatever that may be. Table 6.1 lists the actors we'll build.

Table 6.1 Overview of the actors and their responsibilities

Actor	Responsibilities	Supervisor	Talks with
`StatisticsClient`	Represents a WebSocket client connection, forwards messages and results	Actor provided by Play itself	`StatisticsProvider`
`StatisticsProvider`	Supervises all statistics services and forwards messages from clients	Akka User Guardian	`StatisticsClient`, `TweetReachComputer`
`TweetReachComputer`	Computes the reach of one tweet	`StatisticsProvider`	`StatisticsProvider`, `StatisticsClient`, `UserFollowersCounter`, `Storage`
`UserFollowersCounter`	Provides the number of followers of one user	`StatisticsProvider`	`TweetReachComputer`
`Storage`	Stores data	`StatisticsProvider`	`TweetReachComputer`

In what follows, we'll walk through each of the steps of building this service, first setting up something barely functional and then improving on our implementation as we go.

6.1.2 Laying out the foundation: actors and their children

At the core of our service will be the `StatisticsProvider`, which will receive the requests from clients and see to it that those requests get fulfilled.

Start by creating a new Play project with the Activator: run the `activator new twitter-service play-scala-2.4` command and the Play Scala template. Alternatively, you could copy the structure of the example we created in chapter 4. In either case, don't forget to include the workaround for the OAuth bug mentioned in chapter 2 by adding the following line to build.sbt:

```
libraryDependencies += "com.ning" % "async-http-client" % "1.9.29"
```

You'll also need to declare the latest version of Akka as a dependency in build.sbt because we'll use a few of its features, along with the library for logging:

```
libraryDependencies +=
  "com.typesafe.akka" %% "akka-actor" % "2.4.0",
  "com.typesafe.akka" %% "akka-slf4j" % "2.4.0"
```

Once you're set up, go ahead and create the scaffold of the `StatistcsProvider`.

Listing 6.1 Scaffold of the `StatisticsProvider` actor

```
package actors

import akka.actor.{Actor, ActorLogging, Props}

class StatisticsProvider extends Actor with ActorLogging {
  def receive = {
    case message => // do nothing
  }
}
object StatisticsProvider {
  def props = Props[StatisticsProvider]
}
```

Implements the receive method, which is the only method an actor needs to implement

Implements the Actor trait and mixes in the ActorLogging trait, which provides nonblocking logging capabilities

Handles any kind of incoming message by literally doing nothing

Defines how the actor can be instantiated by providing the Actor's Props

Finally, for logging to work correctly, it requires a bit of configuration. First you need to tell Akka where to log by adding the following configuration in conf/application.conf.

Listing 6.2 Configuring logging bindings

```
akka {
  loggers = ["akka.event.slf4j.Slf4jLogger"]
  loglevel = "DEBUG"
  logging-filter = "akka.event.slf4j.Slf4jLoggingFilter"
}
```

We're using the SLF4J logger (http://slf4j.org) provided by Akka. Because Play already includes logback (http://logback.qos.ch), we'll use it as the SLF4J back end, which means we need to configure it appropriately. Adjust the conf/logback.xml file that's generated when using the Activator, as follows.

Listing 6.3 Adjusting the logback configuration to display actor logs

```
<configuration>

  <!-- ... -->

  <logger name="play" level="INFO" />
  <logger name="akka" level="INFO" />
```

Logs the Play logs at INFO level

Logs the Akka logs at INFO level

```
  <logger name="application" level="DEBUG" />
  <logger name="actors" level="DEBUG" />

  <root level="ERROR">
    <appender-ref ref="STDOUT" />
  </root>

</configuration>
```

Logs the application logs at DEBUG level

Logs the actors package logs at DEBUG level

This configuration makes sure that log messages will be recorded for all the actors we're going to build in the `actors` package.

MAIN ACTOR CONCEPTS

Actors, just like cinematographic celebrities with their mobile phones, have the capability to send and receive messages. By default, messages are handled in the order they're received, and until they're processed they queue up in the actor's mailbox. There are different types of mailboxes, with the default actor mailbox being *unbounded*, which means that if messages aren't dealt with fast enough and keep accumulating, the application will eventually run out of memory. An example of two actors communicating with each other is shown in figure 6.2.

When you implement an actor, you don't get direct access to the mailbox. The key to communicating with the outside world is the partial function `receive`. As its name indicates, this function receives incoming messages and the *actor context* (which can be accessed through the `context` reference, as you'll see later on). This context provides the necessary means for communicating with the outside world. Actors are part of an `ActorSystem`, which takes care of handling the resource management, allowing actors to do their work.

After it's created, an actor will just wait for a message to come in, process it, and then move on to the next message (or do nothing if the mailbox is empty). For actors to process their messages, they need to have a *dispatcher* that will allow them to execute the processing logic. A dispatcher is also an `ExecutionContext`, which means you can use it to execute futures inside an actor (we'll get to this later on). By default, the same dispatcher will be used for the entire `ActorSystem`, and it will be backed by a fork-join executor (the one we used in chapter 5).

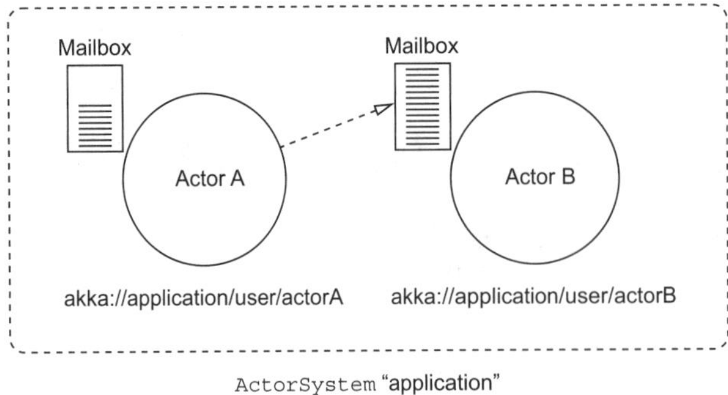

Figure 6.2 Two actors communicating with each other, each having its own mailbox and actor reference

Actors aren't threads, but they need threads to do their work. An actor is usually a long-lived and very lightweight component that reacts to various events (represented by incoming messages), and it will execute the work associated with those events using threads. The default dispatcher uses a shared thread pool, and an actor will execute its work using whatever thread the pool gives it. This separation between actor and thread makes for good resource utilization: an actor that has no work to do won't hold on to any threads. There are also different types of dispatchers, such as the `PinnedDispatcher`, which provides each actor with its own thread pool with a single thread in it, ensuring that each actor will always have a thread ready and waiting when needed. Which kind of dispatcher you use depends largely on the kind of work the actor system does.

Instead of an actor being exposed directly, it's reached through its *actor reference*. Like a phone number, the actor reference is a pointer to an actor. If the actor is restarted (such as because of a crash) and replaced by a new *incarnation*, the reference remains valid; it isn't dependent on the identity of one particular incarnation. This is just like when your expensive smartphone stops working after two years (shortly after the warranty expires) and you replace it—none of the people trying to call you will be affected by this change.

ADVANTAGES OF THE ACTOR REFERENCE It may not be entirely obvious why an actor reference is used instead of talking to the actor directly. There are two important advantages to this indirection. First, changes in the lifecycle of the actor (such as an actor crashing) are hidden from anyone wanting to talk to the actor. Second, because the only means of communicating with an actor is via the actor reference, its methods can't be called directly. This eliminates a lot of non-thread-safe calls—the actor has full control over how its state is affected when a message is received. It's almost as if the inner workings of an actor are taking place in a single-threaded environment.

At this point, our actor from listing 6.1 is just an actor class—we can't yet talk to it. Only once we start it will we be able to obtain an actor reference that will allow us to communicate with it.

CREATING ACTORS

So far our actor doesn't do anything. In fact, it doesn't exist yet! We'll let Play's dependency injection mechanism create it when the application is initialized by setting up a module in app/modules/Actors.scala.

Listing 6.4 Creating the `StatisticsProvider` straight from the `ActorSystem`

```
package modules

import javax.inject._
import actors.StatisticsProvider
import akka.actor.ActorSystem
import com.google.inject.AbstractModule
```

```
class Actors @Inject()(system: ActorSystem)
  extends ApplicationActors {
  system.actorOf(
    props = StatisticsProvider.props,
    name = "statisticsProvider"
  )
}

trait ApplicationActors

class ActorsModule extends AbstractModule {
  override def configure(): Unit = {
    bind(classOf[ApplicationActors])
      .to(classOf[Actors]).asEagerSingleton
  }
}
```

Injects the ActorSystem in the module implementation so it can create actors

Creates the root actor

Defines a marker trait for the actor's module

Implements the actor's Guice module

Defines the binding as eager, so it's initialized when the application is wired up and is available to any component in the app without explicitly depending on it

You also need to enable the module in application.conf for Play to know about it:

```
play.modules.enabled += "modules.ActorsModule"
```

LETTING PLAY CREATE AND INJECT ACTORS Play's dependency injection mechanism allows it to create actors and inject actor references wherever needed. You'll see how to do this in chapter 7. Here we use the approach that you'd take when working solely with Akka.

There are essentially two ways of creating an actor: either by asking the actor system to create an instance, or by creating a child actor using an existing actor's context.

Actors don't merely exist in the wild but instead are part of an *actor hierarchy*, and each actor has a parent. Actors that you create are supervised by the user guardian of the application's `ActorSystem`, which is a special actor provided by Akka that's responsible for supervising all actors in user space. The role of a supervising actor is to decide how to deal with the failure of a child actor and to act accordingly.

The user guardian is supervised by the root guardian (which also supervises another special actor internal to Akka), and the root guardian is itself supervised by a special actor reference. Legend says that this reference was there before all other actor references came into existence and that it's called "the one who walks the bubbles of space-time" (if you don't believe me, check the official Akka documentation).

ALWAYS AIM FOR A HIERARCHY You should be careful not to create too many top-level actors in your application; otherwise, you lose the ability to control supervision. Additionally, top-level actors are expensive to create because doing so involves some synchronization on the user guardian's end. Always aim at designing an actor system with few top-level actors, and build up a hierarchy inside one of your own actors so you are in full control of handling any failures.

ACTORS ACROSS ACTOR SYSTEMS Actors inside of the same `ActorSystem` can communicate with each other, and it's possible to allow actors running on separate JVMs to communicate with each other via remoting or clustering. In those configurations, all the concepts that we've talked about are still valid, and message passing happens using actor references regardless of *where* the actors are running.

As you may have seen in listing 6.4, we're not directly instantiating the `Actor` class; instead we instruct Akka's `ActorSystem` to do so using `Props`. `Props` are a way to tell Akka how to initialize an `Actor` class, and they're serializable. If your `StatisticsProvider` class had any constructor parameters, the `Props` would look like this:

```
val extendedProps = Props(classOf[StatisticsProvider], arg1, arg2)
```

Where to put the props

When they get a bit more elaborate, it's good practice to define the props in a companion object alongside an actor class. Here's an example:

```
object StatisticsProvider {
  def props(arg1: String, arg2: Int) =
    Props(classOf[StatisticsProvider], arg1, arg2)
}
```

ACTOR LIFECYCLE

We've created a new actor and it happily hums along once Play is started. Don't believe me? Let's make it talk!

Override the `preStart` lifecycle method of the `StatisticsProvider` actor in app/actors/StatisticsProvider.scala by adding the following snippet:

```
override def preStart(): Unit =
  log.info("Hello, world.")
```

Now if you restart the application, you'll see something along these lines on your console:

```
[INFO] [04/03/2015 07:44:47.026]
  [application-akka.actor.default-dispatcher-2]
  [akka://application/user/$a] Hello, world.
```

The actor emitting this message is running on `default-dispatcher-2` and the absolute actor path of the actor is akka://application/user/$a. The $a portion of the name has been generated by Akka because we didn't specify a name ourselves. Let's correct that by slightly altering listing 6.4:

```
val providerReference: ActorRef =
  Akka.system.actorOf(
    Props[StatisticsProvider], name = "statisticsProvider"
)
```

Upon restarting, the new path will be akka://application/user/statisticsProvider.

The `preStart` method is just one of many lifecycle methods. The full list is shown in table 6.2.

Table 6.2 Actor lifecycle and methods involved

Phase	Triggered by	Lifecycle methods involved	Description
Start	Call to `actorOf`	`preStart`	The actor's path is reserved, the actor instance is created, and the `preStart` hook is called.
Resume	A supervisor, if it decides to do so		If an actor crashes (by throwing an exception), the supervision process kicks in and the actor is suspended. The supervisor may decide to resume an actor's execution.
Restart	A supervisor, if it decides to do so	`preRestart` and `postRestart`	The default behavior of a supervisor is to restart an actor that fails. In this case, the actor path remains the same and a new instance is created to replace the old one (these are called *incarnations* of an actor). Messages in the actor's inbox are still there, but any state of the actor instance is flushed out (because an entirely new instance takes its place).
Stop	Call to `context.stop()` or reception of a `PoisonPill`	`postStop`	When an actor is stopped, actors who watch the now-stopped actor will receive a `Terminated` message.

An actor is said to fail (or to crash) if it throws an exception. In this case, its supervisor needs to decide what happens next, as you'll see a bit later when we talk about actor supervision.

CHILDREN OF AN ACTOR

Let's lay out the foundation of our service by creating a few child actors. Just as you created the `StatisticsProvider`, create the actor classes `UserFollowersCounter`, `TweetReachComputer`, and `Storage`.

To create the child actors, we'll use the `StatisticsProvider` actor context. Replace the existing `preStart` method with the following implementation.

Listing 6.5 Creating children during the startup of `StatisticsProvider`

```
var reachComputer: ActorRef = _
var storage: ActorRef = _
var followersCounter: ActorRef = _

override def preStart(): Unit = {
  log.info("Starting StatisticsProvider")
  followersCounter = context.actorOf(
    Props[UserFollowersCounter], name = "userFollowersCounter"
  )
```

```
  storage = context.actorOf(Props[Storage], name = "storage")
  reachComputer = context.actorOf(
    TweetReachComputer.props(followersCounter, storage),
    name = "tweetReachComputer")
  )

}
```

Actors created using the `context.actorOf` method become children of that actor. Inside a supervising actor, all children are accessible through the `context.children` collection or by their name with the `context.child(childName)` method.

The child actors need to be created in the `preStart` method of the parent actor to ensure that they'll be re-created if the parent actor crashes (when a parent crashes, all children are terminated as well).

MESSAGE PASSING

The purpose of actors is to model asynchronous processes by passing messages. Like humans in an organizational structure, actors pass each other information and react to certain types of messages. Unlike humans, actors will only reply to the set of messages that are handled in their `receive` method. If no wildcard case has been defined, they'll boldly ignore a message for which no reaction has been defined, without so much as a log message. (This behavior can be quite distressing when you're getting started with actors, so it's a good idea to log any unhandled messages.) As you can see, one of the most important tasks of building an actor system is getting the message protocol right.

> **Dealing with unhandled messages**
>
> You can log any unhandled messages in an actor by overriding the `unhandled` method, like so:
>
> ```
> class SomeActor extends Actor with ActorLogging {
>   override def unhandled(message: Any): Unit = {
>     log.warn(
>       "Unhandled message {} message from {}", message, sender()
>     )
>     super.unhandled(message)
>   }
> }
> ```

We'll start with a minimal protocol to model the most important interactions:

- Between client and `StatisticsProvider` regarding the request to compute the reach of a tweet
- Between `StatisticsProvider` and `UserFollowersCounter`
- Between `StatisticsProvider` and `Storage`

Create the app/messages/Messages.scala file with the following content.

Listing 6.6 Initial message protocol

```
package messages

case class ComputeReach(tweetId: BigInt)
case class TweetReach(tweetId: BigInt, score: Int)

case class FetchFollowerCount(user: String)
case class FollowerCount(user: String, followersCount: Int)

case class StoreReach(tweetId: BigInt, score: Int)
case class ReachStored(tweetId: BigInt)
```

As you can see, this minimal protocol consists of a set of request-response pairs, and it's very optimistic—there's no message dealing with failure here (rest assured that we'll have to create a few of those cases as well).

> **IMMUTABILITY OF MESSAGES** Messages sent from one actor to another should be immutable; indeed, there'd be nothing more annoying than having the contents of one message change "under the hood" when it has already been sent to another actor. This would break the principle of encapsulation of actor state, wherein only an actor can change its own state.

There are several ways to send messages from one actor to another:

- `tell` (also known as `!`) sends messages in a fire-and-forget fashion, returning right after the message has been sent. It's by far the most popular means of sending messages and it promotes loose coupling.
- `ask` (also known as `?`) returns a `Future` and expects an answer within a given timeout (which must be provided). One popular use case is for communication at the boundaries of the actor system, when a request sent by a non-actor can't be received through a `receive` method.
- `forward` is like `tell`, but it will maintain the original sender of the message so that the recipient can reply directly to it.
- `pipeTo` is a special message-sending pattern that allows the result of a `Future` to be sent to an actor upon completion. For this pattern to be available, you need to import `akka.pattern.pipe`.

Let's start sending messages around by implementing the core of our machinery, the `TweetReachComputer`, illustrated in figure 6.3. Upon receiving a request to compute the reach of a tweet from the `StatisticsProvider` ❷, we contact Twitter and fetch the retweets ❸, and for each retweet, we fetch the followers count for each user ❺, respond to the client ❾, and store the count ❿.

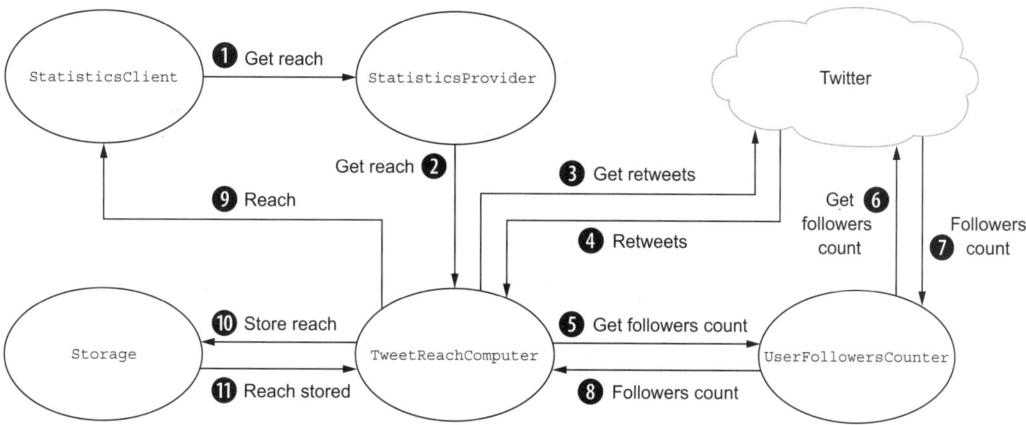

Figure 6.3 The flow of actions required to compute the reach of a tweet

Those actions are largely asynchronous, so in addition to dealing with asynchronous message passing, we'll also have to deal with futures inside of our actor. Let's look at a possible implementation of the `TweetReachComputer`.

Listing 6.7 Implementation of the `TweetReachComputer`'s core flow

```
class TweetReachComputer(
  userFollowersCounter: ActorRef, storage: ActorRef
) extends Actor with ActorLogging {
  implicit val executionContext = context.dispatcher

  var followerCountsByRetweet =
    Map.empty[FetchedRetweet, List[FollowerCount]]

  def receive = {
    case ComputeReach(tweetId) =>
      fetchRetweets(tweetId, sender()).map { fetchedRetweets =>
        followerCountsByRetweet =
          followerCountsByRetweet + (fetchedRetweets -> List.empty)
        fetchedRetweets.retweeters.foreach { rt =>
          userFollowersCounter ! FetchFollowerCount(tweetId, rt)
        }
      }

    case count @ FollowerCount(tweetId, _, _) =>
      log.info("Received followers count for tweet {}", tweetId)
      fetchedRetweetsFor(tweetId).foreach { fetchedRetweets =>
        updateFollowersCount(tweetId, fetchedRetweets, count)
      }
    case ReachStored(tweetId) =>
      followerCountsByRetweet.keys
        .find(_.tweetId == tweetId)
```

Annotations:
- **Passes the reference to other actors as a constructor parameter**
- **Uses the actor's dispatcher as an ExecutionContext against which to execute futures**
- **Sets up a cache to store the currently computed follower counts for a retweet**
- **Fetches the retweets from Twitter and acts upon the completion of this future result**
- **Asks for the followers count of each user that retweeted the tweet**

```
        .foreach { key =>
          followerCountsByRetweet =
            followerCountsByRetweet.filterNot(_._1 == key)
        }
    }

    case class FetchedRetweets(
      tweetId: BigInt, retweeters: List[String], client: ActorRef
    )

    def fetchedRetweetsFor(tweetId: BigInt) =
      followerCountsByRetweet.keys.find(_.tweetId == tweetId)

    def updateFollowersCount(
      tweetId: BigInt,
      fetchedRetweets: FetchedRetweet,
      count: FollowerCount) = {
        val existingCounts = followerCountsByRetweet(fetchedRetweets)
        followerCountsByRetweet =
          followerCountsByRetweet.updated(
            fetchedRetweets, count :: existingCounts
          )
        val newCounts = followerCountsByRetweet(fetchedRetweets)
        if (newCounts.length == fetchedRetweets.retweeters.length) {
          log.info(
            "Received all retweeters followers count for tweet {}" +
            ", computing sum", tweetId
          )
          val score = newCounts.map(_.followersCount).sum
          fetchedRetweets.client ! TweetReach(tweetId, score)
          storage ! StoreReach(tweetId, score)
        }
      }

    def fetchRetweets(tweetId: BigInt, client: ActorRef):
      Future[FetchedRetweets] = ???
  }
```

Annotations: Removes the state once the score has been persisted; Updates the state of retrieved follower counts; Checks if all follower counts were retrieved; Replies to the client with the final score; Asks for the score to be persisted; Fetches retweets—this implementation is left as an exercise

Upon receiving the `ComputeReach` message, you contact Twitter to fetch the retweets for a given tweet (the implementation of the `fetchRetweets` method is left as an exercise—by now you should be pretty familiar with making `WS` calls to the Twitter API). Based on the retweets, you then ask the `UserFollowersCounter` to tell you how many followers the author of a retweet has. Once you've received that piece of information for all users, you then reply to the client and store the retweets.

This is all well and good, but the preceding example contains a potential race condition. In the `ComputeReach` case, you wait for the `fetchRetweets` future to complete, and then you close over the mutable `followerCountsByRetweet` state, which you update to contain a new empty `List` of `FollowerCount` at the beginning of your computation. The problem is that because this all happens asynchronously, your actor is free to receive more messages in the meantime, including another `ComputeReach` message. This, in turn, may cause the execution of another `fetchRetweets` future that could potentially mutate the `followersCountByRetweet` at the same time as the first future.

So how do you go about this? As you may have guessed, blocking the future and waiting for a result isn't a good idea—you really shouldn't block inside of an actor. Remember the pipe pattern I mentioned previously? Let's make use of that pattern to fix the race condition!

> **ACTOR STATE—VARS VERSUS VALS** When choosing how to encode the state of your actor, always prefer an immutable data structure held by a `var` rather than a mutable data structure held by a `val`. If you (or a teammate) mistakenly decides to send a `var` state around, at least it will be immutable, and the risk of mutating the state of the actor from outside will be considerably reduced. Passing mutable state to the outside world, on the other hand, would risk having that piece of internal state mutated by someone else, with unknown consequences.

PIPING FUTURES AND ACTORS

The pipe pattern lets you automatically send the result of a future to an arbitrary actor when it has completed. This allows you to turn potentially concurrent operations affecting the actor's state into well-ordered operations, eliminating race conditions.

Let's rewrite the first part of the `receive` method.

Listing 6.8 Piping `fetchRetweets` to `TweetReachComputer`

```
import akka.pattern.pipe                    <-- Imports the pipe pattern

def receive = {
  case ComputeReach(tweetId) =>
    fetchRetweets(tweetId, sender()) pipeTo self          <-- Pipes the fetchRetweets future to the actor
  case fetchedRetweets: FetchedRetweets =>                 <-- Receives the result of the future
    followerCountsByRetweet += fetchedRetweets -> List.empty
    fetchedRetweets.retweets.foreach { rt =>
    userFollowersCounter ! FetchFollowerCount(
      fetchedRetweets.tweetId, rt.user
    )
  }
  ...
}
```

Upon successful completion of the future, the result (an instance of `FetchedRetweets`) will be sent to the actor, and you can treat it as yet another message.

The one thing to look out for with this approach is the case in which the future fails. If you don't change anything in the way you deal with the failure, a message of type `akka.actor.Status.Failure` will be sent to the actor, containing the `Throwable` responsible for the failure, but not providing any useful context. When you're working with the pipe pattern, it's a good idea to define appropriate messages for handling success and failure, or at least failure, as in the following listing.

Listing 6.9 Transforming the failure of the future before piping it

```
case class RetweetFetchingFailed(
  tweetId: BigInt, cause: Throwable, client: ActorRef
)

def receive = {
  val originalSender = sender()
  case ComputeReach(tweetId) =>
    fetchRetweets(tweetId, sender()).recover {
      case NonFatal(t) =>
        RetweetFetchingFailed(tweetId, t, originalSender)
    } pipeTo self
    ...
}
```

Defines a case class to hold the context of the failure

Handles the recovery of the failure of the future

Wraps the cause of the failure together with some context in the case class designed for this purpose

Pipes the "safe" future

In this way, if the future fails, you'll receive a `RetweetFetchingFailed` message containing the context necessary for correctly handling the failure. You'll be able to, for example, inform the client that its request couldn't be fulfilled.

CAPTURING THE ORIGINAL SENDER You may have noticed that because we now want to capture the sender in the `RetweetFetchingFailed` message, we capture it outside of the future. As described earlier, this is because we need to make sure we use the correct sender, which might have changed by the time the future has failed.

COMMON BEGINNER MISTAKES

There are a few mistakes that are very common when people start to use actors in combination with futures. These can really make you want to throw your computer out the nearest window.

Don't close over mutable state!

Even though working with actors may provide the illusion that everything happens in an orderly fashion, one message being handled after another, there are cases where race conditions can occur. As you've seen, mixing futures and actors is such a case—closing over the state of an actor inside a future is to be avoided at all costs.

Don't close over the sender!

Another common mistake when working with futures in actors is to close over the sender of a message. It's always possible to retrieve the sender of the message that's currently being processed by using the `sender()` method. The problem that arises when working with futures is that the future may not complete fast enough to still be part of the handling of that message, and calling `sender()` in the completion callback of the future may retrieve the wrong sender. In one way, this is a special case of closing over mutable state, but it can be overlooked because the sender is provided by Akka itself.

Suppose in listing 6.7 that we were to retrieve the sender inside the closure in which we're making calls to `UserFollowersCounter`. If another client had requested a tweet's reach to be computed in the meantime, we'd end up answering the wrong client.

Don't close over the context!

The actor context is only valid inside the actor; it can't be used in other threads. Closing over the context when using a future, for example, is a very bad idea:

```
class Nitrogliceryn(service: ExplosionService) extends Actor {
  def receive = {
    case Explode =>
      import Contexts.customExecutionContext
      val f: Future[Boom] = service.fetchExplosion
      // closing over the actor context is dangerous
      // since the context relies on running on the same thread
      // than its actor - DO NOT TRY THIS AT HOME
      f.map { boom =>
        context.actorSelection("surroundings") ! boom
      }
  }
}
```

This example won't work as intended because the future is very likely to be executed in another thread provided by `customExecutionContext`. As a result, the actor's context, which expects to always run in the context of its actor, won't be able to function correctly.

> **WHEN TO USE FUTURES AND WHEN TO USE ACTORS** Futures are a one-off tool for computing single results. You should use futures when you have a specific task in mind, like getting a result from a database or a web service.
>
> Actors are meant to be used for more-advanced processes. They can hold state, and the messages sent between actors cause state changes to happen in a distributed and potentially more elaborate network of objects. The logic encapsulated in an actor hierarchy is meant to be called on many times within the lifespan of that actor, and actors can make decisions based on past state. Once completed, a future is done, whereas an actor continues to hum along as long as it's needed.

6.2 Letting it crash—supervision and recovery

Before going any further, let's quickly summarize what we've done so far:

- We've created the `StatisticsProvider` actor and are bootstrapping it in Play's `Global` object when the application starts.
- We've created the `TweetReachComputer`, `UserFollowersCounter`, and `Statistics-Provider` actors as children of `StatisticsProvider`.
- We're reacting to and sending a few different messages in `TweetReachComputer`, in some cases as a result of the completion of a future.

What's sorely lacking in our current implementation is any kind of failure-handling mechanism. In chapter 5 we took a closer look at error-handling strategies when futures were involved, using the `recover` and `recoverWith` handlers. In the case of actors, the approach to failure handling is a little different.

The idea of letting a system, or components thereof, crash and then recover is one of the cornerstones of the Erlang programming language. It's designed for systems that need to be able to run for a very long time without human intervention.

The Akka community blog is appropriately titled "Let it crash" (http://letitcrash.com). Indeed, the core idea of the actor model is to divide the problem to be solved into layers of actors, ideally reaching a level of granularity wherein each leaf actor has the best possible focus (a very well-defined scope of work)—and then to rely on the supervision mechanism to deal with any unforeseen issues. Therefore, besides being a nice title for a blog, "Let it crash" sums up the design philosophy of actor-based systems—design around the ideas that individual components will crash, and that the system will know how to heal itself.

As I mentioned in chapter 1, it's almost impossible to predict all the ways in which a software system can fail. Instead of focusing on *avoiding* failure, the focus in actor systems is on *recovering* from failure in the most effective way. In practice, this means not trying to catch exceptions, but instead letting them flow and letting the supervisor of a crashed actor decide what to do next. It may be a bit bewildering to let go of a defensive programming style (like the style promoted by checked exceptions), but once you're used to it, it can feel very liberating.

6.2.1 Robust storage

To get a better understanding of Akka's failure and recovery mechanism and philosophy, let's build the `Storage` actor. Just as in chapter 5, we'll use the ReactiveMongo driver to store the computed tweet reach in MongoDB. Unlike chapter 5, we'll handle the connection initialization ourselves.

Let's start by setting up the actor and initializing the connection. Create the actor as in the following listing.

Listing 6.10 Initializing the `Storage` actor and a connection to MongoDB

```
class Storage extends Actor with ActorLogging {

  val Database = "twitterService"
  val ReachCollection = "ComputedReach"

  implicit val executionContext = context.dispatcher

  val driver: MongoDriver = new MongoDriver())
  var connection: MongoConnection = _
  var db: DefaultDB = _
  var collection: BSONCollection = _
  obtainConnection()

  override def postRestart(reason: Throwable): Unit = {
    reason match {
      case ce: ConnectionException =>
        // try to obtain a brand new connection
        obtainConnection()
```

Overrides the postRestart handler to reinitialize the connection after restart if necessary

Handles the case where you've restarted because of a ConnectionException

```
    }
    super.postRestart(reason)
  }

  override def postStop(): Unit = {
    connection.close()
    driver.close()
  }

  def receive = {
    case StoreReach(tweetId, score) => // TODO
  }

  private def obtainConnection(): Unit = {
    connection = driver.connection(List("localhost"))
    db = connection.db(Database)
    collection = db.collection[BSONCollection](ReachCollection)
  }
}

case class StoredReach(when: DateTime, tweetId: BigInt, score: Int)
```

Tears down connection and driver instances when the actor is stopped

Declares MongoConnection as the state of the actor

To be able to function, ReactiveMongo requires a driver that's based on an Akka `ActorSystem` itself, as well as a `MongoConnection`, which represents a connection pool to MongoDB. (Depending on the MongoDB configuration, several logical connections may be handled over a single physical connection to the MongoDB server.) Upon starting the `Storage` actor, you initialize those components, and you clean up after yourself when the actor is stopped.

> **USING MUTABLE STATE IN ACTORS** It's perfectly legitimate to use mutable state (such as the `connection` var in listing 6.10) inside of actors as long as it's not shared with the outside world. If only the actor has access to its state, it doesn't run the risk of concurrent access. You should, however, be careful not to directly expose this mutable state to the outside world by doing something like referencing it directly in a message to another actor, which would break this safe-harbor paradigm. Be especially careful when using mutable state in combination with asynchronous operations through futures, because race conditions can occur at this point.

When you receive a message, you should ask the driver to store it, and reply with a `ReachStored` message. Implement this optimistic scenario using the `collection.insert` method. Take a look at the ReactiveMongo documentation (http://reactivemongo.org), or look at how this was done in chapter 5 if you get stuck.

Once this optimistic scenario is dealt with, it's time to focus on the harsh reality of things. Roughly speaking, there are two types of failures that can happen: the ones you kind of expect, and the ones you didn't know could happen. In any case, failures arising in an actor result in the crash of that actor. It's up to the supervisor to decide what to do next. An example of a supervision hierarchy is shown in figure 6.4.

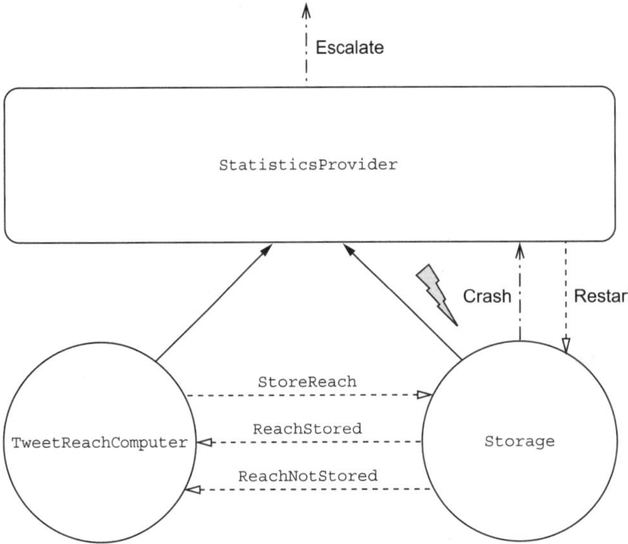

Figure 6.4 Supervision and recovery

When it comes to expected errors (not failures!), you can leverage the error-handling mechanism of the ReactiveMongo driver: MongoDB returns the state of the last operation that was executed, and this is encoded in the driver as a result of the `insert` operation. Based on this state, you could, for example, retry saving it a few times until the insertion is confirmed, just as we did in chapter 5. It's important to understand that this is a form of error handling: you explicitly have to check the state returned by ReactiveMongo's `insert` operation to see if all went well. Doing so is part of the normal business logic pertaining to storing something in a database.

Failures, on the other hand, are a different concept entirely—they actively disrupt the normal flow of operations of a component. In what follows, we'll tackle an expected failure in which the connection dies on you. This could happen at any time, and checking if the connection is alive before each call to `insert` makes little sense. ReactiveMongo throws a `ConnectionException` when the driver encounters this problem, so let's leverage that bit of knowledge.

6.2.2 *Letting it crash*

Rather than trying to catch the `ConnectionException` in action, we'll let it destroy the incarnation of our `Storage` actor. When that happens, the `StatisticsProvider` supervisor will need to decide on the fate of the actor.

Akka defines the *supervisor strategy* for this kind of decision making. There are two families of supervision strategies:

- `AllForOneStrategy` means that all children of an actor will be given the same treatment if one child fails.
- `OneForOneStrategy` will just affect the one child that misbehaved.

Which strategy you choose to use largely depends on the kind of work that's done by the child actors. For example, if your child actors are working together to compute an elaborate result and communicate with each other for this purpose, with their states being intricately linked, you might choose `OneForAll`. If one of them crashes, it would be quite tiresome to have all the siblings try to figure out exactly which pieces of information are missing after restart. Simply stopping and re-creating all children using the `OneForAll` strategy would be easier. In other cases, when siblings work mainly on their own, re-creating just the one that failed might make more sense.

In our case, the siblings are cooperating but are mostly stateless, so let's go ahead and define a `OneForOne` supervisor strategy in the `StatisticsProvider`.

Listing 6.11 Defining a custom supervisor strategy to deal with different exceptions

Restarts the actor if faced with a ConnectionException

Uses a OneForOneStrategy, retrying up to 3 times within 2 minutes before stopping the actor

```
override def supervisorStrategy: SupervisorStrategy =
  OneForOneStrategy(maxNrOfRetries = 3, withinTimeRange = 2.minutes) {
    case _: ConnectionException =>
      Restart
    case t: Throwable =>
      super.supervisorStrategy.decider.applyOrElse(t, _ => Escalate)
  }
```

Applies the default supervisor strategy for any other kind of failure, escalating it if that strategy doesn't handle the failure

Using the `OneForOneStrategy` means that we'll restart only the child actor that crashed (as opposed to restarting all child actors, as with the `AllForOneStrategy`). We only do this in the case of a `ConnectionException` that we hope to be able to recover from, and we'll escalate any other kind of failure.

The default supervisor strategy provides sensible defaults for dealing with an actor's demise, taking special care of cases where the child actor can't be initialized, and restarting the child actor when an `Exception` is thrown. Any other kind of `Throwable` that can't be dealt with is escalated further up the actor hierarchy. In our example, "further up" means escalating to the user guardian, because we created the `StatisticsProvider` using the `ActorSystem` itself. Escalation is the strategy of choice when dealing with unimagined failures of an actor—when you don't know that an actor can fail with an unhandled type of exception, you ask your own supervisor to decide what to do next.

USER GUARDIAN SUPERVISION STRATEGY The user guardian's default strategy is to restart its children in the case of an exception, except for a few special cases in which the actor was meant to shut down (when an actor can't be initialized or was killed deliberately).

6.2.3 Watching actors die and reviving them

Despite this section's heading, we're not going to look at the basics of necromancy but rather at a different supervision model. Akka's `SupervisorStrategy` provides a sensible mechanism for intercepting and dealing with all kinds of child actor failures, but in some cases this supervision mechanism may not be the most useful. In our example, any unforeseen problem with the storage will result in the `Storage` child actor being stopped once the maximum number of retries has failed within the configured time range. If there is no storage, the service won't function as intended, so we may want to explicitly tell any clients that it's currently unavailable.

To do this, we'll use another type of supervision that involves watching the death of an actor and then taking the necessary steps for recovery. In this process, we'll also make use of a very interesting feature of actors: we'll alter their default reaction to messages, effectively overriding their behavior temporarily until things (hopefully) get better.

Akka lets you monitor the lifecycle of an actor so you're notified of its termination. This is usually referred to as "DeathWatch" in Akka, because it's implemented in the `DeathWatch` component.

Let's look at how we can make use of these features.

Listing 6.12 Specialized supervision of the `Storage` child actor

```
class StatisticsProvider extends Actor with ActorLogging {
  // ...

  override def preStart(): Unit = {
    // ... initialization of the children actors
    storage = context.actorOf(Props[Storage], name = "storage")
    context.watch(storage)
  }

  def receive = {
    case reach: ComputeReach =>
      reachComputer forward reach
    case Terminated(terminatedStorageRef) =>
      context.system.scheduler
        .scheduleOnce(1.minute, self, ReviveStorage)
      context.become(storageUnavailable)
  }

  def storageUnavailable: Receive = {
    case ComputeReach(_) =>
      sender() ! ServiceUnavailable
    case ReviveStorage =>
      storage = context.actorOf(Props[Storage], name = "storage")
      context.unbecome()
  }
}
```

Annotations:

- Registers to the lifecycle monitoring of the Storage child actor (`context.watch(storage)`)
- Reacts to the termination. Because you only subscribed to the Storage actor notifications, it must be that actor that terminated. (`case Terminated(terminatedStorageRef)`)
- Schedules to send itself a ReviveStorage message after a minute (`.scheduleOnce(1.minute, self, ReviveStorage)`)
- Switches to a newly defined behavior
- Responds to ComputeReach requests by telling the client the service is unavailable (`sender() ! ServiceUnavailable`)
- Revives the Storage child actor
- Switches back to the original behavior (`context.unbecome()`)

```
object StatisticsProvider {
  case object ServiceUnavailable
  case object ReviveStorage
}
```

Right after creating the `Storage` child actor, you subscribe to notifications as to its death using the `context.watch()` method, which takes an `ActorRef`. If that `Storage` child actor were to be terminated permanently (most likely because the supervision strategy prompted it to do so after trying to restart it unsuccessfully), you'd be notified, giving you the chance to set up an alternative means to react to incoming messages. If the actor simply crashed and restarted, you wouldn't be notified and you'd continue to watch the lifecycle of the actor.

In this example, you wait for a minute, hoping that things will fix themselves. If they don't, you re-create a new `Storage` child actor. In real life, you might want to try a more elaborate strategy. For example, you could temporarily switch to a different type of storage entirely, using an alternative database host, or write your data to the local filesystem as a last resort, and synchronize it with the database once it's available again. It all depends on what the failure of the service means and how badly you want to keep it available under the most complicated situations.

EXPONENTIAL BACKOFF In this example we use a very simple back-off strategy that waits one minute prior to attempting the re-creation of a `Storage` actor. A more elaborate strategy is often used in networked systems: the supervisor will wait exponentially increasing amounts of time before trying to contact the child again. Akka persistence offers a `BackoffSupervisor` that implements such behavior.[2]

6.3 Reacting to load patterns for monitoring and preventing service overload

A truly reactive application isn't only capable of reacting appropriately to software or hardware issues through supervision, but is also capable of degrading gracefully if the system is overloaded. In the following sections we'll look into a few mechanisms that can prevent our service from becoming entirely unresponsive.

6.3.1 Control-flow messages

At the core of the internet as we know it, the TCP/IP protocol guarantees safe delivery of messages across heterogeneous, wild, and scary network topologies around the globe. One of the main mechanisms TCP/IP uses is acknowledging the receipt of messages. Unless the sender receives an acknowledgment of a message from a client within a certain time frame, the packet is retransmitted.

---

[2] See "Delayed restarts with the BackoffSupervisor pattern" in the "Supervision and Monitoring" chapter of the Akka documentation: http://doc.akka.io/docs/akka/2.4.4/general/supervision.html#backoff-supervisor.

Let's imagine that, for one reason or another, our database became overloaded or temporarily unavailable, and some of the computed scores weren't inserted. It would be useful to have a mechanism that confirmed that a score had been inserted, using a mechanism similar to (but less elaborate than) TCP/IP. In listing 6.7 I hinted at this mechanism. The `ReachStored` message is in itself an acknowledgement that the computed reach has been received and stored by `Storage`. That being said, we haven't done anything to deal with the unfortunate case in which we don't receive an acknowledgment.

Let's build a simple mechanism for dealing with unacknowledged storage requests. This is what we need to do:

- Resend messages that haven't been acknowledged in a given window of time
- Not store the same reach twice if we send a few retries
- Become aware of the larger issue with storage and react accordingly

Let's take these one by one.

CHECKING FOR UNACKNOWLEDGED MESSAGES

The first step is to check regularly whether there are unacknowledged messages. We'll start by adding a scheduler mechanism.

Listing 6.13 Setting up a scheduler for unacknowledged messages

```
class TweetReachComputer(
  userFollowersCounter: ActorRef, storage: ActorRef
) extends Actor with ActorLogging with TwitterCredentials {
  // ...
  val retryScheduler: Cancellable = context.system.scheduler.schedule(
    1.second, 20.seconds, self, ResendUnacknowledged
  )
  override def postStop(): Unit = {
    retryScheduler.cancel()
  }
  def receive = {
    // ...
    case ResendUnacknowledged =>
      val unacknowledged = followerCountsByRetweet.filterNot {
        case (retweet, counts) =>
          retweet.retweeters.size != counts.size
      }
      unacknowledged.foreach { case (retweet, counts) =>
        val score = counts.map(_.followersCount).sum
        storage ! StoreReach(retweet.tweetId, score)
      }
  }

  case object ResendUnacknowledged
}
```

Initializes the scheduler for resending unacknowledged messages every 20 seconds

Cancels the scheduler when the actor is stopped

Filters out the cases for which all counts have been received

Sends a new StoreReach message to the storage

IMPROVING ON TIME-BASED SCHEDULING In this simple example, we assume that the database will be the component in trouble. But what if the service was under heavy load at the same time (or the database was under heavy load as a result of the service being heavily used)? In this case, it may make sense to check for unacknowledged messages for a given number of received `ComputeReach` messages—indeed, our `ResendUnacknowledged` messages may be lost somewhere among a lot of incoming requests. This is the perfect case for using the exponential back-off strategy I mentioned earlier.

AT-LEAST-ONCE DELIVERY SEMANTICS Guaranteeing that a message will be received at least once is hard, and chances are that the naive implementation we've used in this example won't do very well in a real system if, for example, the JVM were to crash. Akka persistence offers at-least-once delivery semantics,[3] so if you need this kind of guarantee in your system, you may be better off using that implementation rather than rolling your own.

AVOIDING STORING DUPLICATES

If we resend a command for storing a computed score but had in fact already stored it, we shouldn't store that same element twice.

Let's use a simple mechanism for detecting such duplicates in the `Storage` actor.

Listing 6.14 Avoiding storing duplicate messages

```
class Storage extends Actor with ActorLogging {
  // ...
  var currentWrites = Set.empty[BigInt]

  def receive = {
    case StoreReach(tweetId, score) =>
    log.info("Storing reach for tweet {}", tweetId)
    if (!currentWrites.contains(tweetId)) {
      currentWrites = currentWrites + tweetId
      val originalSender = sender()
      collection
        .insert(StoredReach(DateTime.now, tweetId, score))
        .map { lastError =>
          LastStorageError(lastError, tweetId, originalSender)
      }.recover {
        case _ =>
          currentWrites = currentWrites - tweetId
      } pipeTo self
    }
  case LastStorageError(error, tweetId, client) =>
    if(error.inError) {
      currentWrites = currentWrites - tweetId
    } else {
      client ! ReachStored(tweetId)
    }
```

Annotations:
- Keeps track of the identifiers you're currently trying to write
- Checks whether you're already trying to write the score for this tweet, and only goes ahead if you're not
- Adds the tweet identifier to the set of current writes prior to saving it
- Removes the tweet identifier from the set of current writes in the case of failure
- Removes the tweet identifier from the set of current writes in the case of write error

[3] See the "At-Least-Once Delivery" section of the "Persistence" chapter in the Akka documentation: http://doc.akka.io/docs/akka/2.4.4/scala/persistence.html#At-Least-Once_Delivery.

```
    }
  }

  object Storage {
    case class LastStorageError(
      error: LastError, tweetId: BigInt, client: ActorRef
    )
  }
```

Using this mechanism, you can keep track of the messages you're currently trying to write, avoiding attempts to save the score for the same tweet twice. You also gather a history of all the previous writes. This is useful, because your `ReachStored` message might only be processed after a call to `ResendUnacknowledged`, so it makes sense to keep those messages around for a bit. This being said, in a real-world application you'd need to make sure you clean the history periodically to avoid running out of memory.

EXERCISE 6.1

Implement the cleanup of past `currentWrites`. One way to achieve this would be to flag those identifiers that have been saved, and to periodically remove them from the set.

LIMITS OF THIS "WRITE ONCE" IMPLEMENTATION With this implementation, you won't always be able to guarantee that the computed reach will be saved exactly once. If the `Storage` actor crashes, the state kept in `currentWrites` will be lost, allowing some messages to be stored twice after restarting. This method also has another drawback—it effectively means that a score can only be saved once, regardless of whether the tweet is retweeted in the future. Another approach would be to save the computation time along with the score, allowing for more values to be available.

REACTING TO AN INCREASE OF UNACKNOWLEDGED MESSAGES

If too many storage requests go unacknowledged, resending them again will make things even worse. In this situation, it would make sense to alter the default behavior and stop processing incoming requests, or at least to slow down.

One drastic way to do so would be to throw a special kind of exception, informing the supervisor that something is wrong and switching into a Service Unavailable mode. In this case, we'd do better to propagate the unacknowledged storage requests as part of the exception, so we'd have a chance to store them when things recover.

This "red flag" approach may be effective, but it isn't very subtle. The database might be fine processing more messages, only at a slower pace. This is where the concept of *reactive back pressure* comes in. In this context, back pressure means that we're signaling the producer (`StatisticsProvider` in this example) that we're not able to process the messages at such a high speed and we need to slow down. The `StatisticsProvider` would then have the opportunity to force a slowdown by rejecting requests at an appropriate rate, effectively reducing the load on the service but not entirely suspending it.

Implementing truly reactive back pressure by means of controlling the flow of messages is quite a complicated topic, and it's too much to look at in this chapter. We'll look at a technology that embodies this mechanism in chapter 9 when we talk about Reactive Streams.

As an alternative to reactive back pressure, we can use message priorities to alert upstream actors when the system becomes overloaded. Let's take a look at this approach.

6.3.2 Prioritizing messages

At the beginning of this chapter, I mentioned that each actor has a mailbox. By default, the `UnboundedMailbox` is used, which is a mailbox backed by a `java.util.concurrent.ConcurrentLinkedQueue` and which queues messages in the order of their arrival. As its name indicates, it isn't bounded, meaning that it will keep growing. This means that the JVM could run out of memory if messages aren't processed fast enough. That's why it's a good idea to get a sense of when this is the case.

Akka provides quite a few types of mailboxes, one of which is the `ControlAware-Mailbox`, which we'll look at now to deal with something we've thus far completely ignored: Twitter's API rate limits. Twitter's API tracks how many times it has been called within a given time window and disallows further calls against the API if a threshold has been reached. If our service were to receive more requests than the allowed threshold, the rate limits would prevent us from responding to all of those requests. As such, Twitter's rate limits might be a lot more troublesome for our service than the storage layer being overloaded—in fact, it's safe to say that with Twitter's standard rate limits, the chance of our storage layer being overwhelmed is pretty close to zero, because Twitter will stop providing us with data first.

DETECTING WHEN YOU'RE ABOUT TO HIT THE RATE LIMIT

Twitter communicates the rate limit for a particular kind of request using response headers. In our case, two of those headers are particularly interesting: `X-Rate-Limit-Remaining` describes how many requests are left in the current window, and `X-Rate-Limit-Reset` indicates the UTC timestamp at which the window will be reset.

EXERCISE 6.2

In the `UserFollowersCounter`, check the value of the `X-Rate-Limit-Remaining` header in the response of calls to Twitter. If the value is lower than 10, send a `Twitter-RateLimitReached` message to the supervisor.

This message is defined as follows:

```
import akka.dispatch.ControlMessage
     case class TwitterRateLimitReached(reset: DateTime)
       extends ControlMessage
```

You can use the `context.parent` reference to send a message to an actor's parent.

SETTING UP A CONTROLAWAREMAILBOX

A `ControlAwareMailbox` is a special type of mailbox that passes on messages of type `ControlMessage` immediately. The first thing you need to do to use a `ControlAwareMailbox` is to configure a dispatcher to use one. Add the following bit of configuration to conf/application.conf:

```
control-aware-dispatcher {
  mailbox-type = "akka.dispatch.UnboundedControlAwareMailbox"
}
```

Next you need to tell Akka that you want to use this dispatcher for your `StatisticsProvider` actor. Adjust the `Actors` component so as to bootstrap your actor hierarchy with a custom dispatcher, as shown in the following listing.

Listing 6.15 Using a custom dispatcher

```
class Actors @Inject()(system: ActorSystem)
  extends ApplicationActors {
  Akka.system.actorOf(
    props = StatisticsProvider.props
      .withDispatcher("control-aware-dispatcher"),
    name = "statisticsProvider"
  )
}
```

Specifies the custom dispatcher you set up in the configuration

Finally, you need to indicate that you're unavailable until Twitter lets you resume work by handling the `TwitterRateLimitReached` message in the `StorageProvider`.

Listing 6.16 Handling the unfortunate case of being rate-limited by Twitter

```
def receive = {
  // ...
  case TwitterRateLimitReached(reset) =>
    context.system.scheduler.scheduleOnce(
      new Interval(DateTime.now, reset).toDurationMillis.millis,
      self,
      ResumeService
    )
    context.become({
      case reach @ ComputeReach(_) =>
        sender() ! ServiceUnavailable
      case ResumeService =>
        context.unbecome()
    })

case object ResumeService
```

Schedules a message to remind you when you've reached the window reset

Rejects all incoming requests

Resumes the service by cancelling the temporary behavior

With this mechanism you can effectively avoid overloading Twitter with requests, which will keep you from being rate-limited for longer than necessary.

6.3.3 Circuit breakers

Unfortunately, not all services are as good as Twitter at preventing user overloads by means of a rate-limiting service. As a result, those services slow down considerably as load increases. Chances are that you've had to use such a system in the past. For some reason, these systems tend to be the ones responsible for performing tedious tasks, such as entering travel expenses, uploading a meeting report, or reporting the time spent on a project.

When it comes to interacting with slow systems, one of the dangers is that the slowness and unresponsiveness of the system may propagate to the otherwise snappy, modern, responsive application you're happily building. This is where the circuit breaker pattern comes in to save the day. It's illustrated in figure 6.5.

A circuit breaker is typically included in electric circuits to protect from overload or short circuits. You can usually hear them clicking when you're running the dishwasher, washing machine, kettle, and toaster at the same time. But unlike the simple circuit breakers you have at home, the ones we'll talk about here are a little more sophisticated in that they attempt to reset themselves.

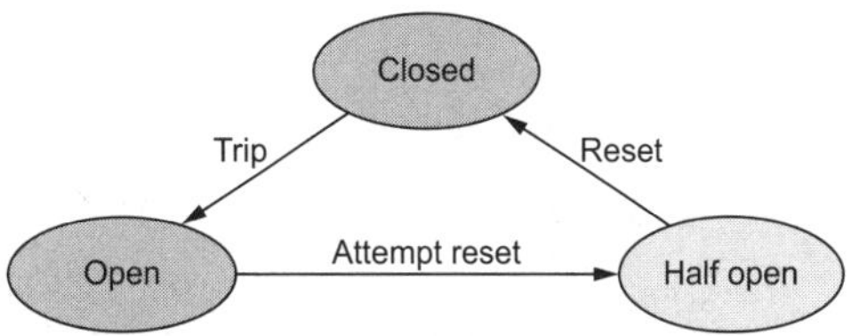

Figure 6.5 Diagram of a circuit breaker

A circuit breaker functions as follows:

1. When everything is fine, it's in a *closed* state, letting electricity (or data) flow.
2. When an overload or a short circuit is detected, the breaker *trips* and is in an *open* state, not letting anything pass. That's when the lights go out and you realize it wasn't a good idea to run all those machines (or pass all that data) at the same time.
3. After a bit, the breaker will put itself in *half-open* state, probing to see if things are back to normal. If the current (or data) flows, the breaker puts itself back into open state.

Akka provides an implementation of the circuit breaker pattern in the `akka.pattern.CircuitBreaker` class. This kind of circuit breaker is designed to work with operations that time out, such as a call to a remote web service or the completion of a `Future`. It works much like the abstract circuit breaker just described, with the following rules regarding its state changes:

- In closed state, the breaker counts the number of exceptions or calls that exceed a configured `callTimeout`. If the number of failures reaches a configured value (`maxFailures`), it trips. Any successful call that happens before the maximum is reached resets the counter to 0.
- In open state, the breaker idles until the configured `resetTimeout` is reached, and then it enters half-open state.
- In half-open state, if the first attempt to make a call fails, it again waits until the `resetTimeout` is reached to retry.

That's enough theory for now. Let's see how to use one of these things in practice. Because Twitter likely won't time out, let's build a dumb future that will sleep for a while every time the number of requests allowed by Twitter's rate-limit mechanism gets lower than 170. The rate-limit mechanism starts with allowing 180 requests, so by starting to throttle our own service once only 170 requests are allowed, you'll quickly be able to see the mechanism in action.

In `UserFollowersCounter`, declare a circuit breaker as shown in the following listing.

Listing 6.17 Declaring a circuit breaker that logs state changes

```
val breaker =
  new CircuitBreaker(context.system.scheduler,
    maxFailures = 5,
    callTimeout = 2.seconds,
    resetTimeout = 1.minute
  ).onOpen(
      log.info("Circuit breaker open")
    ).onHalfOpen(
      log.info("Circuit breaker half-open")
    ).onClose(
      log.info("Circuit breaker closed")
    )
```

- maxFailures: Configures the maximum number of consecutive failures or timeouts allowed before the breaker trips
- callTimeout: Configures the timeout for a call before it's counted as a failure
- resetTimeout: Configures the time before a reset is attempted

Next, alter the code you wrote previously so that it sleeps for 10 seconds if the number of available requests (the one provided by the `X-Rate-Limit-Remaining` header) gets lower than 170. You can use a `Thread.sleep` statement here, although this kind of deliberate blocking should be avoided at all costs in a real application.

Finally, you need to plug the brand-new circuit breaker into the circuit. You could put it in the `receive` method of `UserFollowersCounter` as shown here.

Listing 6.18 Plugging in a circuit breaker

```
class UserFollowersCounter extends Actor with ActorLogging {
  implicit val ec = context.dispatcher
  val breaker = ...
  private def fetchFollowerCount(tweetId: BigInt, userId: BigInt):
    Future[FollowerCount] = ...
  def receive = {
    case FetchFollowerCount(tweetId, user) =>
      breaker
        .withCircuitBreaker(fetchFollowerCount(tweetId, user))
        pipeTo sender()
  }
}
```

- implicit val ec: Reuses the actor's dispatcher as ExecutionContext for the pipe
- fetchFollowerCount: Defines the fetchFollowerCount method that makes the call to Twitter
- withCircuitBreaker: Plugs in the circuit breaker, which wraps the Future result of the call to Twitter
- pipeTo sender(): Pipes the result to send it back to the TweetReachComputer

Alright, you're all set to go! If you now make a request with a tweet that contains, say, 15 retweets with a fresh quota, the following will happen:

1. The first 10 calls to `fetchFollowerCount` will work without problem.
2. Starting from the 11th call, the thread will sleep for 10 seconds, producing a failure due to timeout.
3. After 5 such failed requests, the breaker will trip.
4. After 1 minute of waiting, the process will continue. Because you've "recovered" one request every 5 seconds (you're allowed 180 requests in a 15-minute window), you'll have enough quota to get started again.

EXERCISE 6.3

There are some finishing touches that you can add to make this mechanism fully functional:

- When the breaker trips, the `TweetReachComputer` should be informed and directly reply to the client instead of just sitting there until its client times out.
- When the breaker goes into open state, the supervisor should be informed to not accept any more incoming requests.
- When the breaker goes into closed state again, the supervisor should be informed to accept incoming requests again.

6.4 Summary

In this chapter you had a crash course in All Things Actors, ranging from their initialization and lifecycle to supervision and special cases related to system overload:

- We looked at the main parts required for an actor to work (mailbox, actor reference, actor context).
- We explored the actor lifecycle and how it's influenced by supervision.
- We made use of Akka's supervision strategy and of the Erlang-inspired lifecycle-monitoring mechanism.
- We saw how system overload can be mitigated by using flow-control messages and circuit breakers.

I personally find actors and actor systems to be a fascinating topic. As you've seen throughout this chapter, there are many ways in which a system can be built, and many cases to think of. We've only scratched the surface (although I hope I've sparked your curiosity enough that you'll want to learn more about this topic). In combination with futures, actors are a very powerful tool for building reactive applications, and we'll make use of them in the rest of this book.

7 Dealing with state

This chapter covers

- Configuring Play for an optimal connection to a relational database, and accessing the database with jOOQ
- Creating custom requests and actions and using them with the client-side session
- Command and Query Responsibility Segregation and Event Sourcing (CQRS/ES)

One of the biggest practical hurdles of switching from a traditional application-server development model to a scalable model such as Play is solving the problem of *working with state in a stateless architecture.* The server-side deployment of a Play application is meant to be stateless—it doesn't keep any state in memory other than that for the requests currently being processed. This is in keeping with the philosophy of reactive web applications:

- Stateless server nodes can be interchanged at will without having to worry about keeping client state or other state alive, making it much easier to switch out faulty nodes.
- The overall memory consumption—and, as a result, throughput—of stateless server nodes is much better than that of stateful counterparts.

But where is the state kept, then? Client-side state in Play is pushed to the client (using cookies and possibly other storage local to the client, such as HTML5 storage). Server-side state is typically stored in a database of some kind, and server-side caches are dealt with using dedicated, networked caching technologies.

On the database end of things, object-relational mapping (ORM) tools have long been popular and widely accepted tools for accessing databases. ORMs aim at hiding away SQL as a means of interacting with databases and instead offer an abstracted object-oriented representation of the relational database model. Unfortunately, the use of this abstraction, which brings with it the *object-relational impedance mismatch*, often leads to serious performance issues that can only be addressed by an expert in the particular ORM technology and a time-consuming optimization process.[1]

Throughout this chapter we'll look at where state is kept in a reactive Play application that may scale in or out at any moment, and we'll see how to attend to the practical details of working with relational databases. We'll further explore a paradigm that's increasingly popular for its capacity to handle larger loads and because it introduces immutability to data storage: Command and Query Responsibility Segregation and Event Sourcing (CQRS/ES).

7.1 Working with state in a stateless Play web application

A stateless web application can keep its state in several places, as shown in figure 7.1.

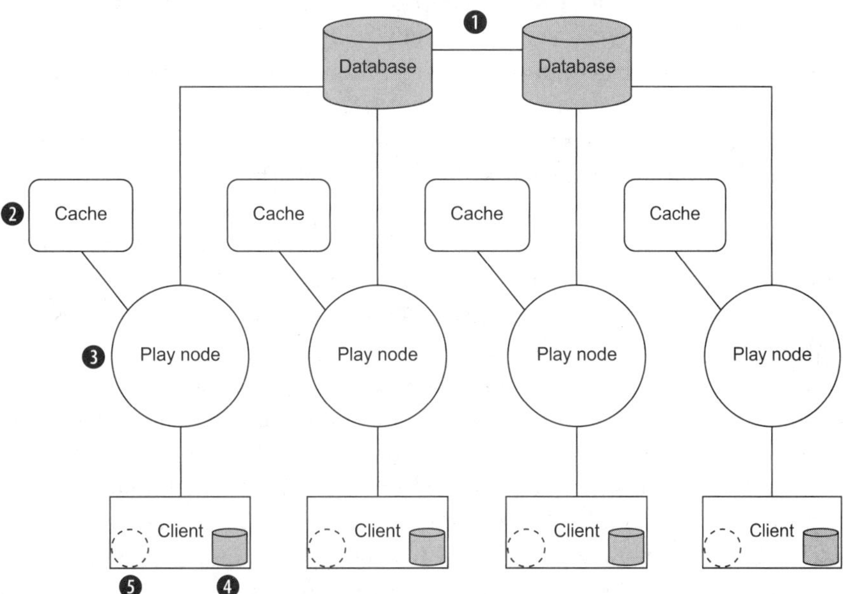

Figure 7.1 Location of state in a stateless web application

[1] For a discussion of the object-relational impedance mismatch, see "The Vietnam of Computer Science" on Ted Neward's blog (26 June 2006), http://blogs.tedneward.com/2006/06/26/The+Vietnam+Of+Computer+Science.aspx.

Traditionally, most data is kept in a (relational) database ❶, which may or may not be replicated. Many applications also make use of a memory-based caching layer ❷ using technologies such as memcached (http://memcached.org) or Redis (http://redis.io). In a stateless application, traditional *server-side state* ❸ should be avoided because a node may go up or down at any time. But you'll see that there are some exceptions to this if the state is managed in such a way that it can be recovered after a crash or when a node comes up.

Client-side state plays an important role in modern web applications. HTML5 introduced local storage ❹, which can be very useful in making an application resilient during temporary network outages, and a cookie-based client-side session ❺ acts as a substitute for the server-side session typically found in a Java `HttpSession`.

Let's look at how we can make use of these different mechanisms by exploring a very simple and yet extremely common use case: user authentication.

7.1.1 Databases

As I've already hinted at in previous chapters, we need to take certain precautions when communicating with databases. Some may have asynchronous drivers that will fit nicely into our asynchronous application model, but others may not—in which case we have to configure things properly.

A WORD ON ASYNCHRONOUS DATABASE ACCESS

Asynchronous database access helps improve the thread and memory usage of the client application wanting to access the database. It further allows you to take advantage of the asynchronous data manipulation techniques we talked about in chapter 5.

The availability of asynchronous drivers for a database largely depends on the database itself. Younger DBMSs, such as MongoDB and CouchBase (http://couchbase.com), have asynchronous drivers, such as ReactiveMongo (http://reactivemongo.org) and ReactiveCouchbase (http://reactivecouchbase.org). If such drivers are available, their use is pretty simple, as you saw in chapters 5 and 6. They offer APIs that rely on futures to provide asynchronous query and statement interfaces.

For some of the more traditional RDBMSs, such as MySQL and PostgreSQL, the mysql-async and posgresql-async community drivers (both found at https://github.com/mauricio/postgresql-async) offer asynchronous alternatives to the blocking JDBC counterparts. These two drivers don't influence how DBMSs work (the communication isn't truly asynchronous on the server side), but they make use of Netty to offer asynchronous communication between the client and the server, which has the advantage of not hogging threads while the database executes a query or statement. Other RDBMSs, such as Microsoft's SQL Server, support asynchronous operations natively and offer asynchronous drivers (https://msdn.microsoft.com/en-us/library/ms131395.aspx).

Finally, another alternative for asynchronous access is offered by Slick 3 (http://slick.typesafe.com), which leverages the Reactive Streams API to stream data from the database while building on top of existing (blocking) JDBC drivers.

As I write this book, asynchronous database drivers for the most popular RDBMSs are still in development and aren't feature-full. They may not provide the richness of features that these systems have to offer. Instead of exploring these technologies, which are prone to rapid change, let's instead focus on a more common use case: accessing relational databases optimally with a solid toolset.

CONFIGURING PLAY FOR SYNCHRONOUS DATABASE ACCESS

As of version 2.4, Play uses HikariCP (http://brettwooldridge.github.io/HikariCP) as a connection pool to manage database connections. A connection pool is used to optimize the costs associated with establishing and maintaining connections with a database. Most relational databases (or their drivers) are synchronous in their communication via a connection—you send a query and get back a result on that same connection. This means that a thread on the JVM, executing one statement, is coupled to one database connection. It's not possible to have more than one thread talk to a database connection at the same time; the database would be confused about what the client wants if it were to send a new statement before the previous query had been answered, and you wouldn't be able to figure out which query a result set belonged to.

Threads that issue statements to a database are short-lived in comparison to the lifespan of a database connection. Because those connections are expensive to create, it makes sense to reuse them across threads (one after another), which is exactly what a pool like HikariCP does.

When it comes to figuring out how many threads you should provide to a context that will interact with a database, you first have to consider how large the database connection pool itself should be—after all, there's likely going to be a relation between those two figures. There is an excellent article in HikariCP's documentation that discusses connection pool sizing.[2] The findings have many parallels in our discussion of thread pool sizes in chapter 1, and the article comes to a similar conclusion: although seemingly counterintuitive, it's more performant to have a small connection pool than a large one because the real number of parallelizable operations across these connections depends on the real number of CPU cores.

Until many-core architectures become mainstream, the connection pool size is going to remain rather small. The PostgreSQL project discusses this subject and proposes a formula that provides a starting point for establishing a connection pool size:[3]

```
connections = ((core_count * 2) + effective_spindle_count)
```

where

- `connections` is the size of the pool
- `core_count` is the real number of cores, without taking hyperthreading into account
- `effective_spindle_count` is the number of hard drives (spindles)

---

2 Brett Wooldridge, "About Pool Sizing," https://github.com/brettwooldridge/HikariCP/wiki/About-Pool-Sizing.

3 "How to Find the Optimal Database Connection Pool Size" in the PostgreSQL wiki, https://wiki.postgresql.org/wiki/Number_Of_Database_Connections#How_to_Find_the_Optimal_Database_Connection_Pool_Size.

According to that formula, if you have a server with a quad-core CPU and one hard drive (or a RAID 1 setup), a good starting point for the connection pool is (4 x 2) + 1 = 9 connections.

To quote the PostgreSQL documentation,

> *A formula which has held up pretty well across a lot of benchmarks for years is that for optimal throughput the number of active connections should be somewhere near ((core_count * 2) + effective_spindle_count). Core count should not include HT [hyperthreaded] threads, even if hyperthreading is enabled. Effective spindle count is zero if the active data set is fully cached, and approaches the actual number of spindles as the cache hit rate falls. ... There hasn't been any analysis so far regarding how well the formula works with SSDs.*

The consequence this has for our thread pool configuration, or for the `ExecutionContext` we're going to use in Play, is that we'll configure a dedicated thread pool sized for the maximum available number of connections. The reason is simple: if you have fewer threads than available connections, fewer of them could be used, and if you had more, threads would potentially be contending for the same connection (which would also negatively impact performance).

> **ON REAL-WORLD CONNECTION POOL SIZING** Although this formula should help you get started quickly, it doesn't replace tuning connection pool size for your specific application and deployment. In this regard, the FlexyPool tool (https://github.com/vladmihalcea/flexy-pool) can be quite useful, as it offers the ability to monitor pools and resize them dynamically.

Let's get started by creating a new Play project. Once you've got it set up, edit the conf/application.conf file as shown in the following listing.

Listing 7.1 Database configuration example

```
db.default.driver="org.postgresql.Driver"
db.default.url="jdbc:postgresql://localhost/chapter7"   <-- The JDBC connection string
db.default.user=user
db.default.password=secret
db.default.maximumPoolSize=9                            <-- The maximum connection pool size

contexts {
    database {
        fork-join-executor {
          parallelism-max=9                             <-- The maximum amount of hot threads in the pool
        }
    }
}
```

To use the configured context, create an app/helpers/Contexts.scala file with the following contents.

Listing 7.2 Database `ExecutionContext` configuration

```
package helpers

import play.api.libs.concurrent.Akka
import scala.concurrent.ExecutionContext

object Contexts {
  val database: ExecutionContext =
    Akka.system.dispatchers.lookup("contexts.database")
}
```

Using this context, you can run database statements on an optimally sized pool.

> **A WORD ON VIRTUALIZED ENVIRONMENTS** If you're running your application in a virtualized environment, it's important to know how many real CPU cores a node has access to. If there are 4 virtual cores but only 1 real core, it isn't going to be very helpful if you use a connection and thread pool of size 10.

> **A WORD ON MULTI-NODE ENVIRONMENTS** If you're planning on deploying your application on several front-end nodes, possibly in an elastic fashion, wherein you'll be adding or removing nodes to allow for increased load, it's important to keep in mind that the database server should be able to cope with the total number of connections.

Now that you've set up the infrastructure for connecting to a relational database, let's go ahead and use it!

CREATING AND EVOLVING THE SCHEMA OF A DATABASE

Let's now use our setup to track users of the service we started building in previous chapters. I'll use a PostgreSQL database in these examples and let Play handle the evolution of the schema; you're welcome to use another database, but make sure you adjust the connection string accordingly, as well as the required connection drivers. I'm using PostgreSQL because it's the most advanced open source database.

As a first step, you need to make sure that you have the right dependencies in your build.sbt file: Play's `jdbc` support and the PostgreSQL connector (adjust the version of the connector to the version of the database you're running):

```
libraryDependencies ++= Seq(
  jdbc,
  "org.postgresql" % "postgresql" % "9.4-1201-jdbc41"
)
```

Next, make sure that you create the `chapter7` database. Using the PostgreSQL command-line client, you can do so with this command:

```
create database chapter7;
```

Now all you need to do is create the database schema. Play offers support for managing schema evolutions, which is very useful when working in a team (or even when working alone and switching back and forth between branches). Create the file conf/evolutions/default/1.sql with the following contents.

Listing 7.3 Evolution file to create the initial database schema with the `user` table

```
# --- !Ups
CREATE TABLE "user" (
    id bigserial PRIMARY KEY,
    email varchar NOT NULL,
    password varchar NOT NULL,
    firstname varchar NOT NULL,
    lastname varchar NOT NULL
);

# --- !Downs
DROP TABLE "user";
```

Statements to run when updating to this version of the schema (annotation on `# --- !Ups`)

Statements to run when downgrading from this version of the schema (annotation on `# --- !Downs`)

If you now run the application and try to access it in a browser, you'll be prompted by Play as to whether or not you want to apply those evolutions.

All subsequent files should be named in sequence (2.sql, 3.sql, 4.sql, and so on). Play will use the file number to apply non-applied evolutions or to downgrade to a previous version of the schema. If you intend to use test data, it's a good idea to also handle insertion or deletion of the data through the evolutions file, as this data is likely to be dependent on the current shape of the schema.

SETTING UP JOOQ CODE GENERATION

To execute statements against the database, we'll use the jOOQ library (http://jooq.org). There are plenty of database access libraries available, but the single most important criterion for database access performance in a multi-tier application remains the same: the number and quality of SQL queries sent to the server. Even if the entire communication chain is fully asynchronous, it's the aggregated query execution time that matters most, and this directly depends on how many queries are executed and how well they perform.

Many libraries provide abstractions on top of the SQL dialect, missing the fact that databases are different from each other and offer plenty of features for data manipulation and retrieval that often outperform application-level transformation of the data. Worse yet, the automatically generated queries resulting from those abstractions may be of such poor quality that their execution time may be orders of magnitude off compared to a non-generated, carefully crafted query.

Here are a few more reasons why it isn't a very good idea to use generic queries and then to transform the resulting data outside of the database:

- Having to transfer data from the database to the application has a negative impact on latency, which is directly proportional to the size of the data at hand.

- Blindly retrieving data (for example, by performing a `SELECT *` statement or by retrieving all the columns of a table because they've been mapped this way automatically) prevents the database from performing a number of optimizations, such as the ones enabled by a cost-based optimizer.[4]
- Metadata that could have been used to improve the speed of certain manipulations in the database memory isn't available.
- The opportunity for capturing statistics regarding data manipulation performance is no longer available—databases can use these statistics to automatically optimize the execution of statements.

We're very much concerned about our system performing well under load, so we'll pay attention to this oft-overlooked aspect of the application stack.

jOOQ offers a type-safe means of writing SQL for any kind of database dialects. Instead of abstracting over SQL, it offers a fluent API that mimics SQL as closely as possible and has specialized versions of the DSL depending on the database at hand, to cater to vendor-specific statements. To use the API, we must first set up the jOOQ code generation, which will generate the necessary code for describing tables and fields in the DSL.

As a first step, add jOOQ to your project by adding the following dependencies to build.sbt:

```
libraryDependencies ++= Seq(
  // ...
  "org.jooq" % "jooq" % "3.7.0",
  "org.jooq" % "jooq-codegen-maven" % "3.7.0",
  "org.jooq" % "jooq-meta" % "3.7.0")
```

Next, set up the configuration for the code generator. Create the file conf/chapter7.xml with the following contents.

Listing 7.4 Code generator configuration

```
<?xml version="1.0" encoding="UTF-8" standalone="yes"?>
<configuration xmlns="http://www.jooq.org/xsd/jooq-codegen-3.7.0.xsd">
  <jdbc>
    <driver>org.postgresql.Driver</driver>
    <url>jdbc:postgresql://localhost/chapter7</url>
    <user>user</user>
    <password>secret</password>
  </jdbc>
  <generator>
    <name>org.jooq.util.ScalaGenerator</name>
    <database>
      <name>org.jooq.util.postgres.PostgresDatabase</name>
      <inputSchema>public</inputSchema>
```

[4] See the "Introduction to the Optimizer" in the *Oracle9i Database Performance Tuning Guide and Reference*, http://mng.bz/4nCV.

```
      <includes>.*</includes>
      <excludes></excludes>
    </database>
    <target>
      <packageName>generated</packageName>
      <directory>app</directory>
    </target>
  </generator>
</configuration>
```

Finally, to generate code, set up build.sbt by creating your own generation task as shown in the following listing.

Listing 7.5 Configuring an sbt task for code generation

```
val generateJOOQ = taskKey[Seq[File]]("Generate JooQ classes")

val generateJOOQTask = (baseDirectory, dependencyClasspath in Compile,
  runner in Compile, streams) map { (base, cp, r, s) =>
    toError(r.run(
      "org.jooq.util.GenerationTool",
      cp.files,
      Array("conf/chapter7.xml"),
      s.log))
    ((base / "app" / "generated") ** "*.scala").get
}

generateJOOQ <<= generateJOOQTask
```

- Declares the generateJOOQ sbt task
- Defines the implementation of the task, with dependencies on the context (base directory, classpath, and so on)
- Runs the GenerationTool and provides the configuration file as an argument
- Returns the generated files so that you can use this task as an sbt source generator
- Wires the implementation of the task to the task key

Now that you're all set, run the freshly created `generateJOOQ` task on the sbt command line. You should see something like this:

```
[CH07] $ generateJOOQ
[info] Updating {file:/Users/manu/Book/public-code/CH07/}ch07...
[info] Resolving jline#jline;2.11 ...
[info] Done updating.
[info] Running org.jooq.util.GenerationTool conf/chapter7.xml
[success] Total time: 2 s, completed May 4, 2015 10:30:54 AM
```

Additionally, you'll now see a number of source files generated in app/generated.

This isn't very verbose though. To get a better insight into what's going on, you can add the jOOQ logger to the logging configuration in conf/logback.xml like so:

```
<logger name="org.jooq" level="INFO" />
```

This will give you more details as to what the code generation is doing.

INSERTING SOME DATA WITH JOOQ

We now have a database and a jOOQ DSL ready to be used—the only ingredient lacking is data! Let's remedy this by inserting a default user record into the database at startup time if none are available.

Create the file app/modules/Fixtures.scala with the following contents.

Listing 7.6 Inserting a sample user with jOOQ at startup

```
package modules

import javax.inject.Inject
import com.google.inject.AbstractModule
import org.jooq.SQLDialect
import org.jooq.impl.DSL
import play.api.db.Database
import play.api.libs.Crypto
import generated.Tables._

class Fixtures @Inject() (val crypto: Crypto, val db: Database)
  extends DatabaseFixtures{
  db.withTransaction { connection =>
    val sql = DSL.using(connection, SQLDialect.POSTGRES_9_4)
    if (sql.fetchCount(USER) == 0) {
      val hashedPassword = crypto.sign("secret")
      sql
      .insertInto(USER)
      .columns(
        USER.EMAIL, USER.FIRSTNAME, USER.LASTNAME, USER.PASSWORD
      ).values(
        "bob@marley.org", "Bob", "Marley", hashedPassword
      )
      .execute()
    }
  }
}

trait DatabaseFixtures

class FixturesModule extends AbstractModule {
  override def configure(): Unit = {
    bind(classOf[DatabaseFixtures])
      .to(classOf[Fixtures]).asEagerSingleton
  }
}
```

Annotations:
- Imports the generated Table classes in order to use them in the DSL
- Obtains a transaction from Play's DB helper
- Creates a jOOQ DSLContext using the JDBC connection
- Checks the number of existing users with jOOQ
- Builds the INSERT statement using jOOQ's fluent DSL
- Executes the statement

Now add the module to application.conf by adding the following line:

```
play.modules.enabled += "modules.FixturesModule"
```

And voilà! After restarting the application, you'll have a user inserted in the database! Note how we used Play's built-in `Crypto` library to hash the password—the application secret defined in application.conf is used for this purpose, so don't lose it if you want to use this library. (You may want to use a more robust approach for storing the password, such as the blowfish cipher.)

WRITING YOUR FIRST JOOQ QUERY

The purpose of setting up a user database is, of course, to be able to authenticate users. Let's write an action capable of checking whether a user exists, based on their credentials. Add the following `login` action to the controllers/Application.scala controller as follows.

Listing 7.7 Querying for users in the `login` method

```
import play.api.db._
import play.api.i18n.{MessagesApi, I18nSupport}
import org.jooq.SQLDialect
import org.jooq.impl.DSL
import generated.Tables._
import generated.tables.records._

class Application(val db: Database, val messagesApi: MessagesApi)
  extends Controller with I18nSupport {
    def login = Action { request =>
      db.withConnection { connection =>
        val sql: DSLContext =
          DSL.using(connection, SQLDialect.POSTGRES_9_4)
        val users = context.selectFrom[UserRecord](USER).fetch()
        Ok(users.toString)
      }
    }
}
```

Initializes a database connection using Play's built-in Database API

Creates a jOOQ DSLContext using the transaction

Fetches all users into classes of the type UserRecord, generated by jOOQ

Displays the result as a response

The first query you place isn't very elaborate. You simply list all users to get a sense of what jOOQ is returning. Add the corresponding route to your conf/routes file:

```
GET     /login          controllers.Application.login(email, password)
```

Now access the action in the browser. You should get a nicely formatted result from the query:

```
+----+--------------+--------------------------+---------+--------+
|  id|email         |password                  |firstname|lastname|
+----+--------------+--------------------------+---------+--------+
|   1|bob@marley.org|14E65567ABDB5D0CFD9A76...EE7|Bob      |Marley  |
+----+--------------+--------------------------+---------+--------+
```

SETTING UP A LOGIN FORM AND PERFORMING AUTHENTICATION

Now that we're out of the starting gate, let's build a simple login form. Start by creating the app/views/login.scala.html file as shown in the following listing.

Listing 7.8 Implementation of the login form page

```
@(form: Form[(String, String)])(implicit messages: Messages)

@form.globalError.map { error =>
    <p>@error.message</p>
}

@helper.form(controllers.routes.Application.authenticate()) {
    @helper.inputText(form("email"))
    @helper.inputPassword(form("password"))
    <button type="submit">Login</button>
}
```

- Passes the form as an input parameter and the Messages API as an implicit parameter
- Displays global form errors
- Defines a form that will call the authenticate action

Next, define the `login` action and the `loginForm` in the `Application` controller as follows.

Listing 7.9 Defining the login action and form

```
import play.api.data._
import play.api.data.Forms._

class Application(val db: Database, val messagesApi: MessagesApi)
  extends Controller with I18nSupport {
    // ...

    def login = Action { implicit request =>
      Ok(views.html.login(loginForm))
    }

    val loginForm = Form(
      tuple(
        "email" -> email,
        "password" -> text
      )
    )
}
```

- Defines the login form with email and password fields

Next, add the `login` action to the routes file, and change the method of the `authenticate` method from `GET` to `POST`. At this point, you should be able to display and submit the form, but without any real functionality yet.

All that's left is to evaluate the submission to the form and to issue a query against the database with the provided email and password. Adjust the `Application` controller to check the form submission, as in the following listing.

Listing 7.10 Authenticating against the database using the provided credentials

```
def authenticate = Action { implicit request =>
  loginForm.bindFromRequest.fold(
    formWithErrors =>
      BadRequest(views.html.login(formWithErrors)),
```

- Binds the submitted form based on the request's body
- Displays the login form again with validation errors

```
            login =>
              db.withConnection { connection =>
                val sql = DSL.using(connection, SQLDialect.POSTGRES_9_4)
                val user = Option(sql
                  .selectFrom[UserRecord](USER)
                  .where(USER.EMAIL.equal(login._1))
                  .and(USER.PASSWORD.equal(crypto.sign(login._2)))
                  .fetchOne())

                user.map { u =>
                  Ok(s"Hello ${u.getFirstname}")
                } getOrElse {
                  BadRequest(
                    views.html.login(
                      loginForm.withGlobalError("Wrong username or password")
                    )
                  )
                }
              }
          )
        }
```

Executes the query that looks for the first user with the provided credentials

Sets a global error if there are no users with the provided credentials

That's it! You simply query the database to check for a matching record, and if one is found, display the user's first name.

As you can see, writing SQL queries with jOOQ is pretty straightforward—the API follows SQL itself. If you need database-specific functions, you can support the corresponding DSL (such as `org.jooq.util.postgres.PostgresDSL`)—or you can always fall back on plain SQL.[5]

USING THE CORRECT EXECUTIONCONTEXT

You may already have noticed that in the previous code listings I haven't made use of the `ExecutionContext` that we set up in listing 7.2. This is, of course, suboptimal because the database query is now running on Play's default context, which we'd like to avoid because we know that this type of call is blocking.

To make use of our carefully devised configuration, we need to switch the code block that accesses the database to the specialized `database` execution context. Let's create a helper method to do so—and because we're using jOOQ's `DSLContext` for querying the database, we can also choose to only expose that one to the client code.

Listing 7.11 Defining a helper query method

```
package helpers

import java.sql.Connection
import play.api.Play.current
import scala.concurrent.Future

class Database @Inject() (db: play.api.db.Database) {
  def query[A](block: DSLContext => A): Future[A] = Future {
```

Defines higher-order function parameterized in A that takes a function from Connection to A as argument and returns a Future[A]

[5] See the "Plain SQL" page in the *The jOOQ User Manual:* http://mng.bz/IP42.

```
    db.withConnection { connection =>
      val sql = DSL.using(connection, SQLDialect.POSTGRES_9_4)
      block(sql)
    }
  }(Contexts.database)
}
```

Creates the jOOQ DSLContext

Invokes the function in the context of a database connection

Explicitly passes the custom database ExecutionContext so that the future will be executed against it

This helper will cause the wrapped code to be executed against the `database` execution context rather than any other `ExecutionContext` in scope. The advantage of this is twofold: the database operations will execute in a context that has the appropriate size, and using a separate execution context dedicated to database operations ensures that the rest of the operations in the application won't be affected should all connections, for one reason or another, block indefinitely.

Use this helper as a replacement for the direct call to `DB.withConnection` in the `authenticate` method of the `Application` controller. Make sure you remove the `import play.api.db.Database` statement to inject the new `Database` helper instead, and adjust the `authenticate` action to use `Action.async`, because the brand-new `Database.query` helper now returns a `Future`.

A word of warning on JDBC connections and asynchronous operations

As we discussed at the beginning of this chapter, a JDBC connection isn't thread-safe in the sense that the database will likely not know what to do if several threads happened to talk to the same connection concurrently. If you want to use a JDBC connection in combination with futures, make sure you access the connection inside of the future and not the other way around, like so:

```
val futureResult = Future {
  db.withConnection { connection =>
    // do something with the connection
  }
}
```

Don't do this:

```
val futureResult = db.withConnection { connection =>
  Future { connection =>
    // do something with the connection
  }
}
```

7.1.2 Client-side state using the Play session

To keep our users logged in once they've correctly filled out the form, we need to store somewhere the fact that they've logged in. Play has a client-side session that's signed with the application's secret (defined in the conf/application.conf file), which we'll use for this purpose.

In chapter 4, we talked about a way to customize Play's standard request-handling pipeline using filters. Another very popular approach is to create custom requests and actions as we'll do now. Append the code in the following listing to the end of the app/controllers/Application.scala file.

Listing 7.12 Defining a custom request and action for requiring authentication

```
case class AuthenticatedRequest[A](
  userId: Long, firstName: String, lastName: String
)

object Authenticated extends ActionBuilder[AuthenticatedRequest]
  with Results {

  override def invokeBlock[A]
    (request: Request[A],
     block: (AuthenticatedRequest[A]) => Future[Result]
    ): Future[Result] = {
    val authenticated = for {
      id <- request.session.get(USER.ID.getName)
      firstName <- request.session.get(USER.FIRSTNAME.getName)
      lastName <- request.session.get(USER.LASTNAME.getName)
    } yield {
      AuthenticatedRequest[A](id.toLong, firstName, lastName)
    }

    authenticated.map { authenticatedRequest =>
      block(authenticatedRequest)
    } getOrElse {
      Future.successful {
        Redirect(routes.Application.login()).withNewSession
      }
    }
  }
}
```

Defines the custom request, which has to be parameterized to account for different types of request bodies

Defines a new action using the ActionBuilder defined by Play

Mixes in the Results trait in order to use the Redirect result later on

Implements the invokeBlock, which is called by Play when an action is called

Uses the code generated by jOOQ to fetch field names

Builds an AuthenticatedRequest based on the contents found in the session

Invokes the body of the AuthenticatedAction by passing in an AuthenticatedRequest

Redirects to the login page if the session doesn't contain the required parameters, with an entirely new session, invalidating any erroneous session that may have existed

The custom request is parameterized to allow for the different types of request bodies—in chapter 4 you saw that Play encodes the content type of a request using the type system. The `ActionBuilder` mechanism lets you define custom actions, optionally using custom requests, which can be useful for storing per-request state that needs to be readily available.

Now that we have a means to explicitly require a user to be authenticated, let's use it to build the `index` action. Start by writing a simple index view template in app/views/index.scala.html:

```
@(firstName: String)

Hello @firstName !
```

Then add the `index` action to the `Application` controller:

```
def index = Authenticated { request =>
  Ok(views.html.index(request.firstName))
}
```

Don't forget to add the appropriate route to / in the conf/routes file.

The last thing you need to do for this mechanism to work properly is initialize the session on login. In the existing `authenticate` method, swap out the result of a successful login with the following result:

```
Redirect(routes.Application.index()).withSession(
  USER.ID.getName -> u.getId.toString,
  USER.FIRST_NAME.getName -> u.getFirstname,
  USER.LAST_NAME.getName -> u.getLastname
)
```

The `withSession` method allocates a new session with a set of key-value pairs that can be retrieved.

That's it! If you now access the application's root, you should be redirected to the login page. Once logged in, you'll be redirected to the index page and Play's session cookie will be set.

CORRECTLY USING SESSIONS

Play's session expiration can be controlled in the configuration. For example, if you want the session to expire after two hours, add `session.maxAge=2h` to application.conf.

The size of Play's client-side session is limited by the size of a cookie, which is to say 4 KB. Hence, the session isn't suited to act as a cache, as is sometimes the case for server-side sessions. In general, you should aim to keep the client-side session as thin as possible—you'll see in a minute how to use a server-side cache.

> **SESSION SECURITY** Play uses the application secret defined in application.conf to sign the session cookie. This protection mechanism makes it impossible to tamper with the contents of the cookie, or worse, to forge a cookie. Make sure you never disclose the application secret publicly, such as by checking it into a public source code repository!

7.1.3 *Server-side state using a distributed cache*

So far we've stored a few key facts about the user in the client-side session. But what if we needed to access more data, and the user model grew in complexity over time? We could, of course, query the database to fetch this data, but chances are that our application performance would suffer as a result—having one database query tied to every kind of request a user makes doesn't sound optimal.

To cache data within a Play application, it's important to remember the share-nothing philosophy of reactive web applications. A node may disappear at any time and for various reasons (scaling, crashing, and so on), so any kind of data stored on the server side needs to be visible to all nodes, not only this node.

Play provides a cache plugin that can have several different implementations. The default implementation is based on EHcache, but we're going to use memcached (http://memcached.org), a high-performance in-memory cache. It may not sound as hip as some younger in-memory caches or key-value stores, but it has the advantage of being readily available and very easy to install. Luckily for us, there's a `play2-memcached` plugin available to easily integrate memcached (https://github.com/mumoshu/play2-memcached).

Start by adding the following dependencies in build.sbt:

```
resolvers += "Spy Repository" at "http://files.couchbase.com/maven2"

libraryDependencies += Seq(
  // ...
  cache,
  "com.github.mumoshu" %% "play2-memcached-play24" % "0.7.0"
)
```

Next, adjust Play's configuration to disable the default plugin and set up the connection to memcached:

```
play.modules.enabled+=
  "com.github.mumoshu.play2.memcached.MemcachedModule"

# To avoid conflict with Play's built-in cache module
play.modules.disabled+="play.api.cache.EhCacheModule"

# Well-known configuration provided by Play
play.modules.cache.defaultCache=default
play.modules.cache.bindCaches=
  ["db-cache", "user-cache", "session-cache"]

# Tell play2-memcached where your memcached host is located at
memcached.host="127.0.0.1:11211"
```

Now that the configuration is in place, you can use the cache to store the whole user.

In the `Authenticated` object that you created in listing 7.12, add a `fetchUser` method.

Listing 7.13 Method to fetch the user from the cache, or the database if there's a cache miss

```
import play.api.cache.Cache

def fetchUser(id: Long) =
  Cache.getAs[UserRecord](id.toString).map { user =>
    Some(user)
```

Retrieves the user from the cache using the identifier as a key

```
} getOrElse {
  DB.withConnection { connection =>
    val sql = DSL.using(connection, SQLDialect.POSTGRES_9_4)
    val user = Option(
      sql
        .selectFrom[UserRecord](USER)
        .where(USER.ID.equal(id))
        .fetchOne()
    )
    user.foreach { u =>
      Cache.set(u.getId.toString, u)
    }
    user
  }
}
```

Queries for a user in the database in the case of a cache miss

Sets the retrieved user in the cache

You first try to fetch the user record from the cache, and in case of a cache miss, you query it in the database and set its value in the cache (to avoid querying the next time).

EXERCISE 7.1

Adjust the `AuthenticatedRequest` to contain the `UserRecord` instead of just the first and last name, and use the `fetchUser` method to retrieve the user in the implementation of the `Authenticated` action.

CACHE NAMESPACING In a flat key-value cache, it's a good idea to namespace the keys. For example, if you plan on caching other types of elements than users in the cache, it would be good to prefix user entries with `user.`, such as `user.42`. This is especially true for incremental identifiers, which are likely to collide across different record types.

7.2 Command and Query Responsibility Segregation and Event Sourcing

In this second part of the chapter, we'll explore an architectural pattern that has been gaining in popularity for building high-throughput applications. The Command and Query Responsibility Segregation and Event Sourcing (CQRS/ES) model makes it easier to scale out by separating writing and reading data into separate processes and storage systems.[6] The effect of this reduced contention on data storage systems makes for much better performance but sacrifices consistency of reads, which are not instantly up to date with the data that has been written, leading to a state of *eventual consistency*.

This model is therefore not suitable for all kinds of applications—for example, you wouldn't want to run an online banking system without credit limits using eventual

[6] Martin Fowler explains CQRS, and how ES can be used with it, on his blog in the "CQRS" entry (14 July 2011), http://martinfowler.com/bliki/CQRS.html.

consistency—but it's suitable in a fair number of cases. As you'll see, another case for using CQRS—next to the one of scaling out to a large number of concurrent reads and writes—is getting an audit trail of all changes made to the data, thanks to the use of an immutable, insert-only event store.

7.2.1 The Twitter SMS service

In chapters 5 and 6 we started to build a Twitter analytics service capable of computing simple statistics and providing insights into how a user's follower numbers evolve over time and how much reach a tweet has. To monetize our service, let's extend it to provide a solution for professional Twitter addicts who can't stay completely out of touch with the Twitterverse, even when on vacation trekking the Sahara desert (or something along those lines). In those situations, internet connectivity may be sparse, and the only connection to the outside world may be a satellite phone with SMS. It wouldn't be very useful to have each and every tweet forwarded to said satellite phone—instead, the service needs to be able to perform certain types of aggregations on the power-user's timeline and let the user specify the notifications they'd like to receive.

An extensive market study has shown that there'd be potentially millions of users wanting to use our service, so we'd like to be able to scale it out by using the CQRS/ES architecture, as shown in figure 7.2.

For this purpose, we'll use

- MongoDB to store incoming events (because we already used it in previous chapters)
- PostgreSQL to act as a read store
- Akka persistence to implement Event Sourcing
- Akka IO to simulate an SMS interface with Telnet (it's not the real deal, but it has the same kind of retro feel to it)

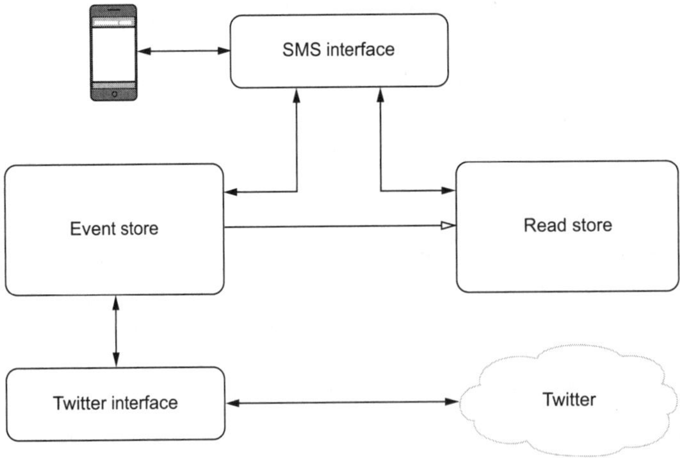

Figure 7.2 Twitter SMS service for highly addicted users

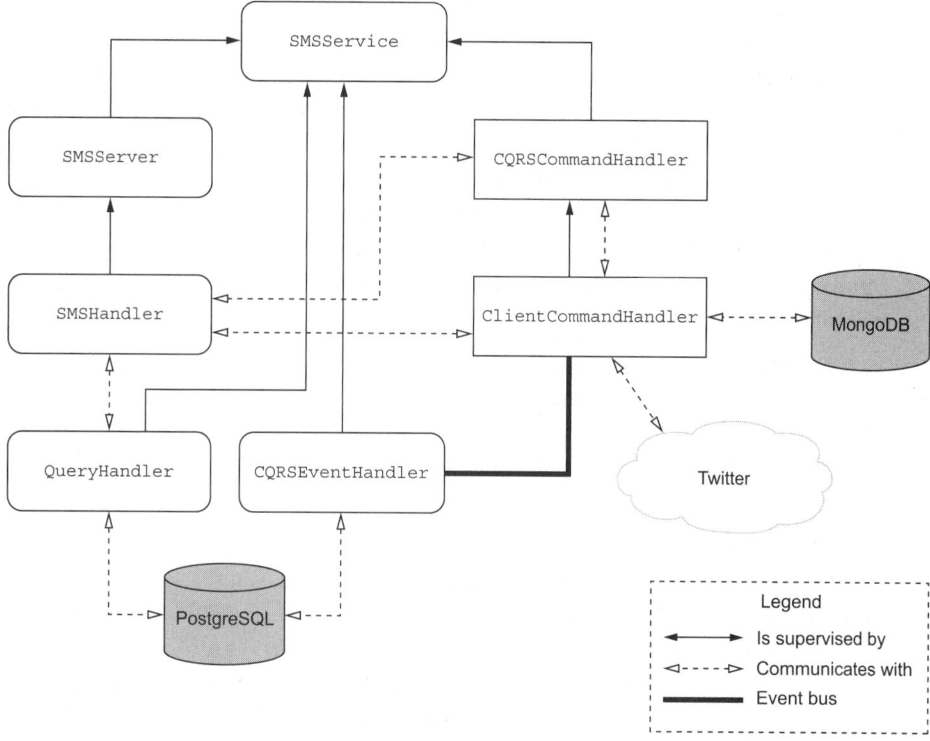

Figure 7.3 Actor hierarchy of our CQRS system

The resulting actor hierarchy is shown in figure 7.3.

APPLICATION SETUP AND SUPERVISION

The `SMSService` is the supervising actor and will be a parent to most components of the system. It deals with their failure if necessary.

INCOMING CLIENT CALLS

The SMS exchange is simulated by simple socket connections. The `SMSServer` will listen to incoming connections. For each new client connection (which we'll establish using Telnet), it creates a new `SMSHandler` child actor that will handle the communication for one particular connection (meaning there can be several instances of `SMSHandler` in the system—this isn't shown in figure 7.3 because the figure would get too crowded). This part will be implemented using the Akka IO library, which takes care of the low-level connection details.

COMMAND HANDLING

A Telnet client can send commands to our service, such as a request to subscribe to Twitter mentions notifications. When they do, they'll receive one SMS for each mention of their username.

The Twitter state of a particular client (identified through their phone number) is longer-lived than that of a particular Telnet connection for that client (they may disconnect and reconnect later on and expect to be able to use the service), so it needs to be kept in a longer-lived actor. The `ClientCommandHandler` keeps the state and handles all commands for one particular client.

`ClientCommandHandler` instances are created by the `CQRSCommandHandler` parent, which also forwards all the commands received from the `SMSHandler`. Both `ClientCommandHandler` and `CQRSCommandHandler` are persistent actors, which means that they'll keep their state when the JVM is restarted. In our application, the state will be persisted to MongoDB.

QUERY HANDLING

A Telnet client can also issue queries to the service, asking for information such as how many times their Twitter username has been mentioned in one day. These queries are forwarded by the `SMSHandler` to the `QueryHandler`, which will query the data in PostgreSQL.

EVENT SOURCING

To be able to answer client queries, our PostgreSQL database needs to be provided with data. Each `ClientCommandHandler` will emit events for each valid command related to a client, such as when a client subscribes to mentions or when a new tweet mentions the username. Those discrete events are broadcast over the Akka event bus. The `CQRSEventHandler` listens to the bus and decides to act on some of those events, which it transforms and writes to PostgreSQL, hence making them available to be queried through a relational database model suited to advanced reporting, as shown in figure 7.4.

The `CQRSEventHandler` plays a central role in the CQRS/ES architecture: it translates discrete events from the event model into data that may spread over several tables in a relational model. Querying the event store directly would be impractical

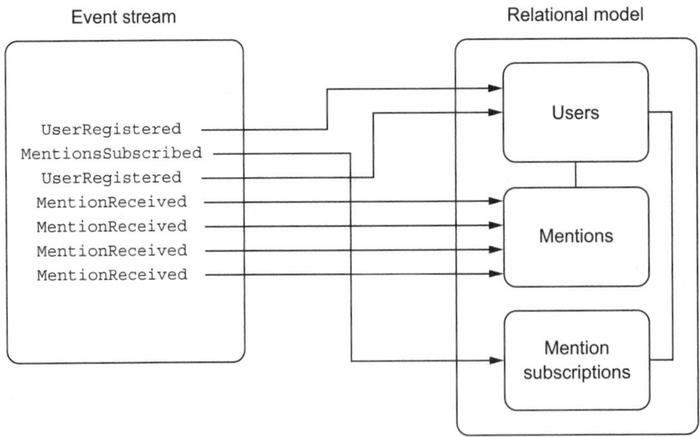

Figure 7.4 Mapping the Event Stream to the relational model with the `CQRSEventHandler`

because the data model would likely not be appropriate for advanced reporting. More importantly, it would impact the performance of the system by creating read/write contention in the event store.

We'll start by building our "fake" SMS gateway, and then move on to create persistent actors backed by MongoDB for handling incoming events. Finally we'll write those events into PostgreSQL.

7.2.2 *Setting up the SMS gateway*

To interact with users by Telnet SMS, you'll to need to listen to incoming connections and handle them. Start by adding the necessary libraries to your application in build.sbt:

```
libraryDependencies ++= Seq(
  // ...
  "com.ning" % "async-http-client" % "1.9.29",
  "joda-time" % "joda-time" % "2.7",
  "com.typesafe.akka" %% "akka-persistence" % "2.4.0",
  "com.typesafe.akka" %% "akka-slf4j" % "2.4.0"
)
```

As in chapter 6, you now need to make sure logging works correctly. Adjust the logging configuration by adding the following bit of configuration in conf/application.conf.

Listing 7.14 Configuring logging bindings

```
akka {
  loggers = ["akka.event.slf4j.Slf4jLogger"]
  loglevel = "DEBUG"
  logging-filter = "akka.event.slf4j.Slf4jLoggingFilter"
}
```

Next, you need to add the required configuration in conf/logback.xml to enable the `DEBUG` log level for the `actors` package. Add the following `logger` element:

```
<logger name="actors" level="DEBUG" />
```

Next, you need an actor for listening to incoming connections. Create the file app/actors/SMSServer.scala with the following contents.

Listing 7.15 Implementation of a server actor listening to incoming connections

```
package actors

import java.net.InetSocketAddress
import akka.actor.{Props, ActorLogging, Actor}
import akka.io.Tcp._
import akka.io.{Tcp, IO}

class SMSServer extends Actor with ActorLogging {
```

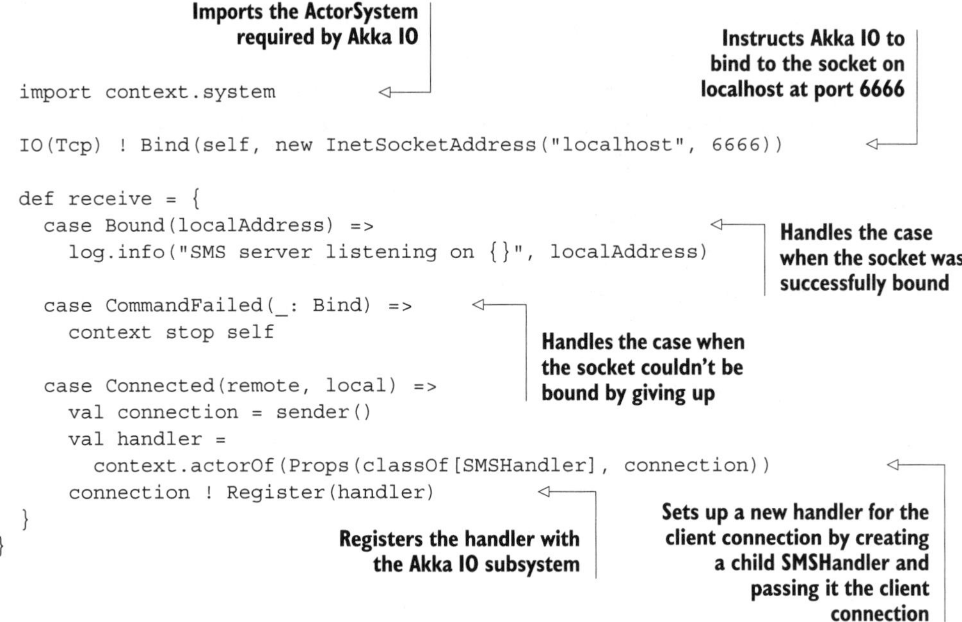

```
import context.system

IO(Tcp) ! Bind(self, new InetSocketAddress("localhost", 6666))

def receive = {
  case Bound(localAddress) =>
    log.info("SMS server listening on {}", localAddress)

  case CommandFailed(_: Bind) =>
    context stop self

  case Connected(remote, local) =>
    val connection = sender()
    val handler =
      context.actorOf(Props(classOf[SMSHandler], connection))
    connection ! Register(handler)
  }
}
```

Imports the ActorSystem required by Akka IO
Instructs Akka IO to bind to the socket on localhost at port 6666
Handles the case when the socket was successfully bound
Handles the case when the socket couldn't be bound by giving up
Sets up a new handler for the client connection by creating a child SMSHandler and passing it the client connection
Registers the handler with the Akka IO subsystem

Akka IO abstracts over low-level components such as channels and selectors to provide lock-free IO connectivity, in our case over TCP/IP. We're just setting up a server here that listens on port 6666 on localhost so we can connect to it later on.

Now that you can accept connections, you need an `SMSHandler` to deal with incoming client messages (the handler deals with all the messages of one connection). Create the file app/actors/SMSHandler.scala as follows.

Listing 7.16 Actor to handle incoming SMS messages

```
package actors

import akka.actor.{ActorLogging, Actor}
import akka.io.Tcp._

class SMSHandler(connection: ActorRef)
  extends Actor with ActorLogging {

  def receive = {
    case Received(data) =>
      log.info("Received message: {}", data.utf8String)
      connection ! Write(data)
    case PeerClosed =>
      context stop self
  }
}
```

Handles the reception of data

Prints out the received data (encoded as ByteString), assuming it's a UTF-8 String

Echoes the incoming message back to the connection

Handles the disconnection of the client

This first version of the handler doesn't do anything interesting other than print the incoming message and send it back to the sender. Data is encoded as `ByteString`, which is an immutable data structure aimed at reducing the copying of arrays when slicing and dicing the incoming data.

You can now test this out—create an `SMSService` actor that initializes the `SMSServer` on prestart and doesn't do anything with any incoming messages it may get for the time being.

To use the `SMSService`, we'll let Play inject it with dependency injection. Alongside your `SMSService` in app/actors/SMSService.scala, create the module shown in the following listing.

Listing 7.17 Letting Play instantiate the `SMSService` actor with dependency injection

```
package actors

import javax.inject.Inject

import akka.actor.{ActorLogging, Actor, Props}
import com.google.inject.AbstractModule
import helpers.Database
import play.api.libs.concurrent.AkkaGuiceSupport

class SMSService @Inject() (database: Database)
  extends Actor with ActorLogging {
  // the implementation is left to the reader
}

class SMSServiceModule extends AbstractModule with AkkaGuiceSupport {
  def configure(): Unit =
    bindActor[SMSService]("sms")
}
```

Uses dependency injection to wire dependencies in the actor's constructor

Mixes in the AkkaGuiceSupport trait to provide the dependency injection tooling for actors

Declares the binding for the SMSService actor with the name "sms". The name will be used for naming the binding as well as the actor.

Don't forget to declare this module in application.conf, as you did in chapter 6, by adding the following line:

```
play.modules.enabled += "actors.SMSServiceModule"
```

Because the actor system we use in this example is standalone, we don't need to inject this actor anywhere—it will be eagerly instantiated by Play as a singleton when the application starts up. But if you ever needed to get a reference to the `SMSService`, you could do so by using the `@Named` annotation:

```
import javax.inject._

class SomeService @Inject() (@Named("sms") sms: ActorRef)
```

Once the application is running (don't forget to open it in the browser, or it won't start!), you can connect to the server using Telnet and send a message like so:

```
» telnet localhost 6666
Trying 127.0.0.1...
Connected to localhost.
Escape character is '^]'.
Hello from the desert
Hello from the desert
```

Alright! It's time to move on to the next step and persist some data!

7.2.3 Writing the event stream with persistent actors

The underlying idea of the CQRS model is to turn commands into events once they've been validated. Only when an event has been written should the state of the in-memory representation of the domain be changed. This way, by replaying all the events in order, the same state can be restored.

Akka persistence offers an extension to the actor model that implements this principle. The two modes of operation of a persistent actor are shown in figure 7.5.

A persistent actor functions like a normal actor in that it sends and receives messages and has a few extensions to handle persistence. It has a `persistenceId` that must be unique for the entire application, and that's used to store and retrieve persisted events.

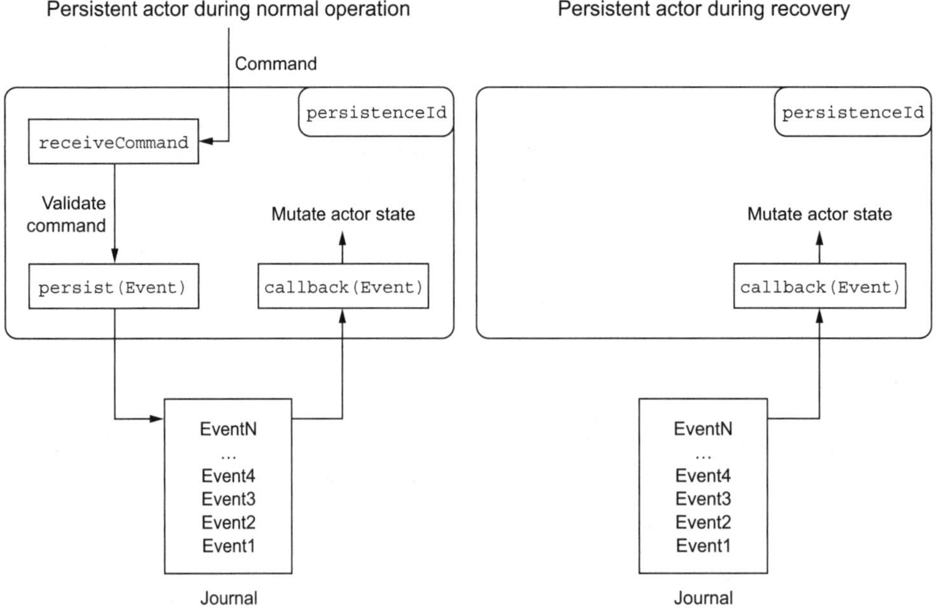

Figure 7.5 Persistent actor in action

During normal operation, a persistent actor receives commands through its `receiveCommand` method, validates them, and then calls the `persist` method with the following signature:

```
final def persist[A](event : A) (handler : A => Unit): Unit
```

When an event is persisted successfully to the event journal, a callback handler is called for the event and then reacts, such as by changing the state of the persistent actor. This way you're ensured that only events that have been written to the journal have any impact on the state of an actor.

This mechanism makes it possible for the persistent actor to recover its state if it crashes. After having been restarted, a persistent actor goes into recovery. During recovery, all the events from the journal are replayed in order, enabling the actor to re-create its internal state.

In terms of supervision, these persistent actors themselves need to be supervised by an actor capable of re-creating them in case of failure or system restart.

> **STATE SNAPSHOTS** To speed up recovery for actors that have already received many events, you can take snapshots of the persistent actor's state. The most recent snapshot is replayed during recovery, followed by any events that took place after the snapshot was taken. We won't use snapshots in this book, but it's useful to know of their existence.

In our example, `CQRSCommandHandler` and `ClientCommandHandler` are two persistent actors. We'll first define the commands and events that model our domain and then move on to implementing the persistent actors.

Start by defining the `Command` and `Event` traits in the app/actors/Messages.scala file, as well as a first command-event pair, as shown in the following listing

Listing 7.18 Command and event definition

```
package actors

import org.joda.time.DateTime

trait Command {
  val phoneNumber: String
}
trait Event {
  val timestamp: DateTime
}

case class RegisterUser(phoneNumber: String, userName: String)
  extends Command
case class UserRegistered(
  phoneNumber: String,
  userName: String,
  timestamp: DateTime = DateTime.now) extends Event

case class InvalidCommand(reason: String)
```

Next, set up the `CQRSCommandHandler` supervisor as a persistent actor. This actor is in charge of forwarding messages to the `ClientCommandHandler` responsible for a given phone number, or for creating it if it doesn't exist.

Listing 7.19 Implementing the `CQRSCommandHandler`

```
package actors

import akka.actor._
import akka.persistence._
import scala.concurrent.duration._

class CQRSCommandHandler extends PersistentActor with ActorLogging {

  override def persistenceId: String = "CQRSCommandHandler"

  override def receiveRecover: Receive = {
    case RecoveryFailure(cause) =>
      log.error(cause, "Failed to recover!")
    case RecoveryCompleted =>
      log.info("Recovery completed")
    case evt: Event =>
      handleEvent(evt)
  }

  override def receiveCommand: Receive = {
      case RegisterUser(phoneNumber, username) =>
        persist(completed(phoneNumber, username))(handleEvent)
      case command: Command =>
        context.child(command.phoneNumber).map { reference =>
          reference forward command
        } getOrElse {
          sender() ! "User unknown"
        }
    }

    def handleEvent(event: Event, recovery: Boolean): Unit =
      event match {
        case registered @ UserRegistered(phoneNumber, userName, _) =>
          context.actorOf(
            props = Props(
              classOf[ClientCommandHandler], phoneNumber, userName
            ),
            name = phoneNumber
          )
          if (recoveryFinished) {
            sender() ! registered
          }
}
```

Annotations:
- Handles the failure of recovery by logging it out
- Handles the end of recovery
- Handles events that are replayed during recovery
- Persists the registration of a user as a UserRegistered event, and calls the handleEvent function in the callback
- Forwards the message to an existing ClientCommand Handler
- Returns an error if the phone number is unknown, which is when there's no child actor with that identifier
- Creates the ClientCommand Handler as a child actor
- Passes the phone number and username as constructor parameters to the ClientCommandHandler
- Informs the client that registration worked if you're not in recovery

During recovery (in the `receiveRecover` method) you receive a few different types of messages, such as recovery failure notifications, a notification that the recovery is completed, and most importantly, the events that are being replayed. Chances are you'll react to these events much like you reacted to them when they were created in the first place, which is why you define the `handleEvent` method to do event handling in one place.

You only proceed to creating the child `ClientCommandHandler` actor in the callback of the `persist` method by calling the `handleEvent` callback, thus making sure that this event has been saved to the journal. In case of a crash, this event will be replayed, causing the child actors to be created again, and they can in turn run through their own journal to recover their state.

> **MESSAGE RECEPTION GUARANTEES** Akka persistence will ensure that no other external messages will reach your actor while the `persist` call is made. This means it's safe to call `sender()` in the callback of the `persist` function if needed.

Don't forget to instantiate `CQRSCommandHandler` as a child of the `SMSService` actor, giving it the name `commandHandler`.

7.2.4 Configuring Akka persistence to write to MongoDB

Our events are written into a journal managed by Akka persistence, which provides a plugin interface for supporting different kind of stores. Let's use the akka-persistence-mongo plugin (https://github.com/ironfish/akka-persistence-mongo) to write events to MongoDB.

Start by doing the following:

- Add the plugin to build.sbt by adding the dependency to `"com.github.ironfish" %% "akka-persistence-mongo-casbah" % "0.7.6"`
- Remove the previous dependency on `akka-persistence` (the correct version will be selected as a transitive dependency).
- Remove the previous dependency on `akka-slf4j` (the `akka-persistence-mongo-casbah` plugin doesn't yet use Akka 2.4.0, which means the logging configuration doesn't require this library).

Now that you have the library in place (don't forget to reload the project), all that's left is to configure it in conf/application.conf:

```
akka.persistence.journal.plugin = "casbah-journal"
casbah-journal.mongo-journal-url =
  "mongodb://localhost:27017/sms-event-store.journal"
casbah-journal.mongo-journal-write-concern = "journaled"
```

That's about it! With this setup, the events will be written in MongoDB's `sms-event-store` database, into the `journal` collection. The `journaled` `write-concern` means that MongoDB will consider an insertion successful once it has been written into MongoDB's journal without replication (you may want to increase this level depending on the system you're building).

7.2.5 Handling an incoming command: subscribing to user mentions

We're now ready to get to the core of our service. One of the basic functions we'd like to offer the user is the option to turn on SMS notifications for mentions on the timeline. Add the following command to app/actors/Messages.scala:

```
case class SubscribeMentions(phoneNumber: String) extends Command
```

Next, let's upgrade the `SMSHandler` to be a bit more useful.

Listing 7.20 Enhancing the SMS handler to parse and relay messages

```
class SMSHandler(connection: ActorRef)
  extends Actor with ActorLogging {

  implicit val timeout = Timeout(2.seconds)
  implicit val ec = context.dispatcher

  lazy val commandHandler = context.actorSelection(
    "akka://application/user/sms/commandHandler"
  )

  val MessagePattern = """[\+]([0-9]*) (.*)""".r
  val RegistrationPattern = """register (.*)""".r

  def receive = {
    case Received(data) =>
      log.info("Received message: {}", data.utf8String)
      data.utf8String.trim match {
        case MessagePattern(number, message) =>
          message match {
            case RegistrationPattern(userName) =>
              commandHandler ! RegisterUser(number, userName)
        case other =>
          log.warning("Invalid message {}", other)
          sender() ! Write(ByteString("Invalid message format\n"))
      }
    case registered: UserRegistered =>
      connection !
        Write(ByteString("Registration successful\n"))
    case InvalidCommand(reason) =>
      connection ! Write(ByteString(reason + "\n"))
    case PeerClosed =>
      context stop self
  }
}
```

Annotations:
- Declares the pattern for matching incoming messages (`MessagePattern`)
- Declares the pattern for matching a valid registration command (`RegistrationPattern`)
- Sends a RegisterUser command to the command handler
- Answers with success if the registration succeeded
- Relays results of invalid commands

From now on you're only going to accept messages that have a valid format and reject all others. A valid registration attempt will be sent to the command handler, which will then act on it by subscribing the client to mentions from Twitter.

EXERCISE 7.2

It's now your turn to implement the `ClientConnectionHandler`, and especially its capability to properly deal with a mention subscription request. Here's a possible plan for achieving this:

1. Handle the `SubscribeMentions` command in the `SMSHandler` as you did user registration. It will be forwarded to the corresponding `ClientConnectionHandler` by the `ConnectionHandler` as a result.
2. Implement the `ClientConnectionHandler` as a persistent actor, passing the phone number as a constructor argument and using it as `persistentIdentifier`.
3. Persist the `MentionsSubscribed` event (after verifying that the client isn't already subscribed—if it is, the received `SubscribeMentions` command is invalid) and proceed to the next steps only once the event has been persisted.
4. Because it isn't possible to get push notifications from Twitter, you'll need to query Twitter at regular intervals for the mentions by using a scheduler that sends a specific message to the `ClientConnectionHandler` at regular intervals, such as every 10 seconds (you saw how to use a scheduler in chapter 6).
5. Use Twitter's search feature (https://api.twitter.com/1.1/search/tweets.json) to retrieve Tweets in which the user has been mentioned (don't forget to add the WS library to the project build and to use the Twitter authentication credentials as you've done previously). You're only interested in new mentions, so you need to keep track of when you first subscribed or last fetched mentions in a dedicated field, and compare it against the creation date of a mention tweet. To parse the time format returned in a tweet's `created_on` field, you can use Joda-Time's `DateTimeFormat` like so: `DateTimeFormat.forPattern("EEE MMM dd HH:mm:ss Z yyyy").withLocale(Locale.ENGLISH)`.
6. Persist each new mention as a new event, and only once it's persisted, inform the `SMSHandler` about the new mention. The `SMSHandler` in turn has to forward it to the client connection.
7. If you want to go even further, simulate SMS delivery acknowledgment by having the `SMSHandler` respond to each new mention with an `AcknowledgeMention` message, and persist a `MentionAcknowledged` event reflecting the acknowledgment. Introduce the `ConnectUser` command, reflecting the fact that the mobile phone has connected to the network, and send all unacknowledged mentions upon connection. You'll need to keep a list of unacknowledged mentions as state to get this to work.

Grab a nice cup of coffee (or tea), and go ahead! This exercise is a bit longer and harder than others, but by the end of it you'll have a good appreciation for what it means to work with persistent actors and their environment. If you're feeling completely stuck, you can always check this chapter's source code on GitHub.

At the end of this exercise, you should be able to register to the service and be notified of new mentions, like so:

```
» telnet localhost 6666
Trying 127.0.0.1...
Connected to localhost.
Escape character is '^]'.
+43676123456 register elmanu
Registration successful
mentioned by @elmanu: @elmanu Testing Twitter mentions
```

7.2.6 Transforming the event stream into a relational model

The *Q* in CQRS stands for *query*, and we're going to look next at how to set up everything we need to perform queries against our data without impacting the write side of things. Separating the write model from the read model has a few interesting advantages.

First, should our service become extremely successful (and why wouldn't it, with such a bulletproof business case?), the queries against the read side won't impact our system's ability to write data—the read-write contention is significantly reduced by this architecture.

If necessary, we can change our minds as to how the read model looks, without endangering the running system. All we need to do is set up a means to replay the event logs we're interested in and write it into our new read model. Only once it's set up will we switch to it, which gives us a graceful upgrade path. In fact, several different read models can coexist side by side, specializing on various aspects of the domain.

Note that the trade-off of this approach is that the read side is delayed. As already mentioned, queries that require real-time data will need to be performed directly against the in-memory persistent actors that hold the latest state. But many types of queries, especially ones related to reporting and analytics, will be just fine if the data is not 100% up to date.

In what follows, we'll use Akka's built-in `EventStream` to transfer the events into our relational database. Depending on your requirements, this approach can be supplemented with another message queue, such as RabbitMQ (www.rabbitmq.com).

We'll track three types of events: registrations of new users, subscriptions to our mentions delivery service, and the mentions themselves. For the latter two events, we need to provide some metadata before publishing them to the bus, namely the phone number and user handle, which are not part of these events.

Start by adding the following new event type to Messages.scala:

```
case class ClientEvent(
  phoneNumber: String,
  userName: String,
  event: Event,
  timestamp: DateTime = DateTime.now
) extends Event
```

Next, we want to publish those events on the global event bus. This is easy, so I'll show you just one example—the `RegisterUser` event. In the `CQRSCommandHandler`, adjust the `handleEvent` method as follows.

Listing 7.21 Publishing an event on Akka's built-in event stream

```
def handleEvent(event: Event): Unit = event match {
  case registered @ UserRegistered(phoneNumber, userName, _) =>
    // ...
    if (recoveryFinished) {
      sender() ! registered
```

```
      context.system.eventStream.publish(registered)
    }
  }
```

Publishing the event as is on the event stream

Go ahead and do the same for the `MentionsSubscribed` and `MentionReceived` messages, after wrapping them in a `ClientEvent` wrapper (you didn't need this wrapper for `Registered` because that message already contains the phone number and Twitter username).

Next, we need to build the relational schema in which we want to represent our data. Create the file conf/evolutions/default/2.sql as shown in the following listing, and then restart and access the application to apply it.

Listing 7.22 Evolution script for creating the read model

```
# --- !Ups

CREATE TABLE "twitter_user" (
  id bigserial PRIMARY KEY,
  created_on timestamp with time zone NOT NULL,
  phone_number varchar NOT NULL,
  twitter_user_name varchar NOT NULL
);

CREATE TABLE "mentions" (
  id bigserial PRIMARY KEY,
  tweet_id varchar NOT NULL,
  user_id bigint NOT NULL,
  created_on timestamp with time zone NOT NULL,
  author_user_name varchar NOT NULL,
  text varchar NOT NULL
);

CREATE TABLE "mention_subscriptions" (
  id bigserial PRIMARY KEY,
  created_on timestamp with time zone NOT NULL,
  user_id bigint NOT NULL
)

# --- !Downs

DROP TABLE "twitter_user";
DROP TABLE "mentions";
DROP TABLE "mention_subscriptions";
```

Last but not least, we need to write the values coming down the event stream into the database. Start by creating a new `withTransaction` helper method in app/helpers/Database.scala, which does the same thing as the existing `Database.query` method that we defined in listing 7.11 but calls the underlying `DB.withTransaction` method instead, and which has the advantage of automatically committing the transaction before closing it.

Once you have this helper method ready, you need to build the `CQRSEventHandler` that will write the relevant events to the database. Create the file app/actors/CQRSEventHandler.scala with the following contents.

Listing 7.23 Writing the events to a relational model in the `CQRSEventHandler`

```
package actors

import java.sql.Timestamp
import akka.actor.{Actor, ActorLogging}
import helpers.Database
import generated.Tables._
import org.jooq.impl.DSL._

class CQRSEventHandler(database: Database)
  extends Actor with ActorLogging {

  override def preStart(): Unit = {
    context.system.eventStream.subscribe(self, classOf[Event])
  }

  def receive = {
    case UserRegistered(phoneNumber, userName, timestamp) => // TODO
    case ClientEvent(phoneNumber, userName,
      MentionsSubscribed(timestamp), _) =>
        database.withTransaction { sql =>
          sql.insertInto(MENTION_SUBSCRIPTIONS)
            .columns(
              MENTION_SUBSCRIPTIONS.USER_ID,
              MENTION_SUBSCRIPTIONS.CREATED_ON
            )
            .select(
              select(
                TWITTER_USER.ID,
                value(new Timestamp(timestamp.getMillis))
              )
              .from(TWITTER_USER)
              .where(
                TWITTER_USER.PHONE_NUMBER.equal(phoneNumber)
                .and(
                  TWITTER_USER.TWITTER_USER_NAME.equal(userName)
                )
              )
          ).execute()
      }
    case ClientEvent(phoneNumber, userName,
      MentionReceived(id, created_on, from, text, timestamp), _) =>
        // TODO
  }
}
```

Callout annotations:

- `preStart` subscription line: **Subscribes to all messages that match the Event trait and delivers them to this actor**
- `sql.insertInto(...)`: **Creates an INSERT INTO ... SELECT statement**
- `select(...)`: **Creates the SELECT statement (the select method is provided by the wildcard import of the DSL class)**
- `value(new Timestamp(...))`: **Inserts the timestamp as a constant value using the value method**

This code writes each received event directly into the appropriate table. In this example, we have a rather simple domain, but you could have a more complex one involving writing into several tables. In any case, jOOQ does a great job at helping you write valid SQL along the way.

To get the `CQRSEventHandler` to work, you'll need to pass an instance of the `Database` helper down the actor hierarchy and inject it in the `Actors` module.

> **JOOQ DATA CONVERTERS** jOOQ allows you to define custom converters for data types, such as for the timestamp. See the "Data type conversion" page in the jOOQ documentation: http://mng.bz/URIA.

> **SQL ADVANTAGE IN ACTION** By using an `INSERT...SELECT` statement, we've just saved ourselves a round trip from the database to the application. The entire process of copying data takes place inside the database, avoiding the latency cost of a round trip between application and database. This decreases thread utilization and overall load.

EXERCISE 7.3

Write the missing insertion statements for the `UserRegistered` and `MentionReceived` events.

7.2.7 *Querying the relational model*

Using our brand-new relational database model, we're now able to get more information out of our service:

- Count of mentions today or in the past week
- Ranking of most-mentioned user among users of the service
- Interconnectedness of two individual users
- Busiest mention time of the day, week, or month
- Subscriptions to the mentions service over time
- Frequency of connections to the service

Let's go ahead and provide users with the ability to find out how many mentions they got recently. Start by adding the following `Query` messages to the app/actors/Messages.scala file:

```
trait Query
trait QueryResult
case class MentionsToday(phoneNumber: String) extends Query
case class DailyMentionsCount(count: Int) extends QueryResult
case object QueryFailed extends QueryResult
```

Next, create the app/actors/CQRSQueryHandler.scala actor.

Listing 7.24 The `CQRSQueryHandler` interacting with Postgres

```
package actors

import akka.actor.Actor
import helpers.Database
import generated.Tables._
import org.jooq.impl.DSL._
import org.jooq.util.postgres.PostgresDataType
import akka.pattern.pipe
import scala.concurrent.Future
import scala.util.control.NonFatal

class CQRSQueryHandler(database: Database) extends Actor {

  implicit val ec = context.dispatcher

  override def receive = {
    case MentionsToday(phoneNumber) =>
      countMentions(phoneNumber).map { count =>
        DailyMentionsCount(count)
      } recover { case NonFatal(t) =>
        QueryFailed
      } pipeTo sender()
  }

  def countMentions(phoneNumber: String): Future[Int] =
    database.query { sql =>
      sql.selectCount().from(MENTIONS).where(
        MENTIONS.CREATED_ON.greaterOrEqual(currentDate()
          .cast(PostgresDataType.TIMESTAMP)
        )
        .and(MENTIONS.USER_ID.equal(
          sql.select(TWITTER_USER.ID)
            .from(TWITTER_USER)
            .where(TWITTER_USER.PHONE_NUMBER.equal(phoneNumber)))
          )
      ).fetchOne().value1()
    }
}
```

Recovers from any query failure by emitting a QueryFailed message

Pipes the result to the requesting SMS handler

Fetches all of today's mentions

Casts the variable type

Uses a subquery to retrieve the user's database identifier, given their phone number

The resulting query will have the same semantics as the following native PostgreSQL query:

```
select count(*)
from mentions
where created_on >= now()::date
and user_id = (select id from twitter_user where phone_number = '1')
```

As you can see, creating subqueries and using the native cast functionality is not a problem with jOOQ's DSL.

EXERCISE 7.4

Plug the `CQRSQueryHandler` into the communication chain through the `SMSHandler`:

1. Initialize the actor in `SMSService` and give it the name `queryHandler`.
2. Handle the reception of the `MentionsToday` query in the `handleMessage` method of the `SMSHandler`, such as by reacting to the message "mentions today."
3. Handle the reception of `DailyMentionsCount` in the `receive` method by relaying the answer to the `connection`.

That's it! When you're done, you should be able to SMS the service and retrieve the number of mentions you've gotten during the day:

```
~ » telnet localhost 6666
Trying 127.0.0.1...
Connected to localhost.
Escape character is '^]'.
+43650123456 mentions today
2 mentions today
```

What we have now is an application that separates the write (command) side from the read (query) side, effectively removing one of the most important contention points in high-throughput applications. As we've discussed, one of the side effects of this approach is eventual consistency, but in the case of this service, we should be fine with a small delay between those two sides.

7.2.8 A word on eventual consistency

Eventual consistency has gained popularity and is used in many social network applications that have massive numbers of users. For this domain, the side effects of eventual consistency are acceptable because temporarily missing posts or comments may not have a very profound impact. (That being said, the alternative model of causal consistency[7] depicts some examples of unfortunate side effects thereof.) For domains wherein strong consistency needs to take place at the core (bank accounts, order placement, execution systems, and so on), eventual consistency is a suboptimal solution. But it's important to have a good definition of what parts of a system require strong consistency—in the banking world, ATMs are an example of eventual consistency coupled with policies that make it acceptable (the withdrawal limit).

With increasingly cheaper RAM available, it has also become realistic to hold most of an application's state in main memory and to query live application state when necessary, overcoming the limitations of eventual consistency for those cases that require access to the latest state. Generally speaking, eventual consistency is a good fit for performing near-real-time analytics on highly available systems.

[7] "Don't Settle for Eventual Consistency," *acmqueue*, vol 12, 3 (April 21, 2014), https://queue.acm.org/detail.cfm?id=2610533.

7.3 Summary

In this chapter, we've looked at working with state in a stateless Play application. In particular, we have talked about

- Configuring Play for relational database access
- Handling client-side state with the Play session
- Using memcached for server-side replicated caching
- Using jOOQ to interact with the database using type-safe SQL

Furthermore, we built a small application using the CQRS/ES architecture:

- We built a command-handling mechanism using Akka IO
- We persisted events into MongoDB using Akka persistence
- We streamed those events into a relational database using Akka's event bus
- We built the query side and implemented a simple query with jOOQ

In the next chapter we'll add a user interface to this application, allowing us to visualize its usage in real time.

8 Responsive user interfaces

This chapter covers

- Setting up a Play project to work with Scala.js
- Integrating the AngularJS framework with Scala.js
- Writing your own integration of JavaScript libraries with Scala.js
- Best practices for building responsive user interfaces

To monitor the Twitter SMS service from chapter 7, we now need an administrative dashboard that will allow us to visualize a few key performance indicators of the service.

To increase our developer happiness, we'll employ Scala.js (http://scala-js.org), which will allow us to work in a type-safe fashion. Scala.js allows us to write Scala code that compiles down to JavaScript and to leverage existing JavaScript libraries. We'll also use the AngularJS framework (http://angularjs.org). Figure 8.1 shows how all these parts fit together.

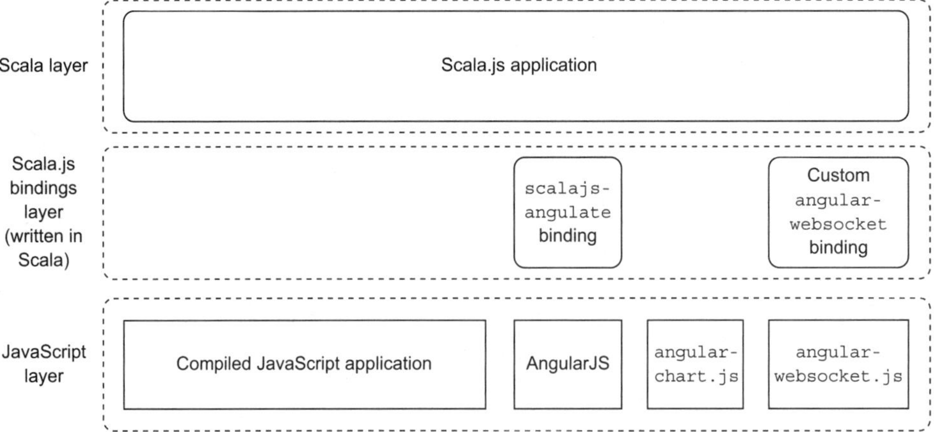

Figure 8.1 The Scala.js application is written in Scala, leverages existing JavaScript libraries through bindings, and compiles down to JavaScript.

Why go through the trouble of using Scala.js and AngularJS, and not simply write the application directly in JavaScript without any library? Indeed, for a simple dashboard application, this approach might look like overkill, but the aim of this chapter is to show you how to use Scala.js together with an existing JavaScript framework, as it helps to increase productivity considerably in the long run. Scala.js enables you to write the entire application in one language (Scala), and it results in more-robust client-side code because the Scala compiler will check it at compile time. Type-safety helps to get rid of many issues that would go unnoticed when writing plain dynamic JavaScript code and makes it possible to refactor the application code with an IDE such as IntelliJ IDEA or Eclipse.

Additionally, a framework such as AngularJS helps you build a single-page web application and organize the client-side code as well as reuse many existing components of the framework. We could use any other JavaScript framework for building this dashboard (there are plenty available), but the relatively more complex MVC architecture of AngularJS lets us look into more-advanced use cases.

> **LEARNING JAVASCRIPT** I'll guide you through this chapter on how to use Scala.js as an alternative to writing JavaScript, but if you plan on writing applications in this fashion on your own, I recommend that you get your hands dirty with plain old JavaScript first, to get a deeper understanding of what's going on. For learning JavaScript, I recommend taking a look at Douglas Crockford's *JavaScript: The Good Parts* (O'Reilly, 2008).

8.1 Integrating Scala.js and Play

The first thing we need to do to get our application going is integrate Scala.js source code generation into the flow of our Play application. We'll also need to configure Play to serve the correct assets depending on whether we run the application in development or production mode, as the assets will be different in those modes (unoptimized during development, and optimized for production use).

8.1.1 The application structure

Our application will be divided into two logical parts: the server-side Play application and the client-side Scala.js application. A Scala.js application needs to be in its own sbt project for the compilation lifecycle to function properly, so we'll set up the application so that the client module is a subproject of the main Play application.

Furthermore, because the AngularJS framework follows the MVC pattern, the client side will be split into three parts, as shown in figure 8.2. The client-side application will be loaded through a regular template of the main Play application, including all JavaScript dependencies it needs.

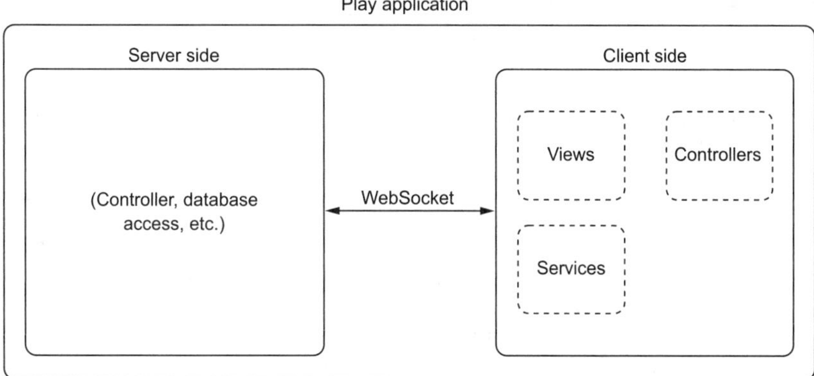

Figure 8.2 Structure of the Play Scala.js application

Let's get started by setting up the build pipeline for this structure.

8.1.2 Setting up the build process

The primary task of Scala.js is to compile Scala into JavaScript code and to provide for good interoperability with existing JavaScript libraries. In addition, it provides a few very useful features, such as generating source maps that help with debugging in the browser, and making it possible to configure dependencies on JavaScript libraries in the sbt build file. JavaScript libraries that are published through npm and Bower can be included in the build as JAR files by using James Ward's WebJars (www.webjars.org).

To set up the Play project, create it using the simple Activator template, as you did in chapter 2. This will create the scaffold of view templates that you'll use. Then create the necessary directories for the following project structure:

```
├── app
│   ├── controllers
│   └── views
```

```
├── conf
├── modules
│   └── client
│       └── src
│           └── main
│               └── scala
├── project
└── public
```

To integrate Scala.js and Play, we'll use the sbt-play-scalajs plugin (https://github.com/vmunier/sbt-play-scalajs), which leverages sbt-web to provide all the configuration needed to neatly combine both technologies. Start by adding this plugin to the project/plugins.sbt file.

Listing 8.1 Adding the sbt-play-scalajs plugin to the project

```
resolvers += "Typesafe repository"
  at "https://repo.typesafe.com/typesafe/releases/"

addSbtPlugin("com.typesafe.play" % "sbt-plugin" % "2.4.3")

addSbtPlugin("com.vmunier" % "sbt-play-scalajs" % "0.2.6")

addSbtPlugin("org.scala-js" % "sbt-scalajs" % "0.6.3")
```

- The standard Play sbt plugin
- The sbt-play-scalajs sbt plugin that combines Play and Scala.js
- The Scala.js sbt plugin

Next, go ahead and set up the build.sbt file.

Listing 8.2 Defining the build for a Play-Scala.js client-server application

```
lazy val scalaV = "2.11.6"

lazy val `ch08` = (project in file(".")).settings(
  scalaVersion := scalaV,
  scalajsProjects := Seq(client),
  pipelineStages := Seq(scalaJSProd),
  libraryDependencies ++= Seq(
    "com.vmunier" %% "play-scalajs-scripts" % "0.2.2"
  ),
  WebKeys.importDirectly := true
).enablePlugins(PlayScala).dependsOn(client).aggregate(client)

lazy val client = (project in file("modules/client")).settings(
  scalaVersion := scalaV,
  persistLauncher := true,
  persistLauncher in Test := false,
  libraryDependencies ++= Seq(
```

- Defines the sbt-web pipeline stages: in this case, the generation of optimized Scala.js artifacts for production
- Defines the root Play project
- Indicates which projects are Scala.js projects
- Includes a library that helps with referencing Scala.js artifacts in Twirl templates
- Directly imports the artifacts of the client module without wrapping it in an intermediary WebJar
- Defines the client Scala.js project

```
    "org.scala-js" %%% "scalajs-dom" % "0.8.0"
  ),
  skip in packageJSDependencies := false
).enablePlugins(ScalaJSPlugin, ScalaJSPlay, SbtWeb)
```

Includes the scalajs-dom library for DOM manipulation

Loads the scalajs, scalajs-play, and sbt-web plugins

Scala.js compiles the application code written in Scala into JavaScript code and also generates an optimized version of the generated JavaScript code for production deployments. The sbt-play-scalajs plugin takes care of handling the asset pipeline for these special Scala.js assets so that the correct assets are available when Play runs in development or production mode.

INCLUDING ARTIFACTS FROM THE CLIENT MODULE You'll later want to access some of the artifacts in the client module from the root module (such as partial HTML views for AngularJS), so you explicitly instruct sbt-web to import the entire client module directly, using the `WebJars.importDirectly` module. This module can leverage the classpath dependency established through the `dependsOn(client)` instruction to directly include artifacts that are part of the client project, and not just generated ones.

Using Node.js

To reduce JavaScript compilation time, it's recommended that you install Node.js (http://nodejs.org). Otherwise, the Rhino JavaScript interpreter is used, and it has rather poor performance.

Once you've installed Node.js, add the following setting to the root project definition in build.sbt:

```
scalaJSStage in Global := FastOptStage,
```

This will cause Scala.js to use Node.js for JavaScript compilation, which should significantly speed things up.

8.1.3 Creating a simple Scala.js application

Now that we have the application structure in place, let's do something with it, such as displaying some text. In the app/views/main.scala.html file that's generated in the default application scaffold, add the following line before the closing `</body>` tag:

```
@playscalajs.html.scripts("client")
```

This will include the correct JavaScript artifacts that result from the Scala.js compilation, and it will switch to the optimized version of those artifacts if you run the application in production mode. More specifically, there are three files generated in the modules/client/target/scala-2.11/ folder for use in development mode:

- `client-fastopt.js`—The optimized version of the application created rapidly during development (a smaller version can be produced but takes longer)
- `client-jsdeps.js`—The JavaScript dependencies (libraries)
- `client-launcher.js`—A snippet of JavaScript that runs the `main` method in `JSApp` (as you'll see later)

As a next step, let's display some simple HTML to test Scala.js. Create (or replace) the `index` action in the `Application` controller so as to display the app/views/index.scala.html file with the following content:

```
@main("Twitter SMS service dashboard") {
  <div>Hello from Twirl!</div>
  <div id="scalajs"></div>
}
```

The second `div` is left empty on purpose—we'll populate it using Scala.js. Create the file modules/client/src/main/scala/dashboard/DashboardApp.scala with the following contents.

Listing 8.3 Bootstrapping the Scala.js application

```
package dashboard

import scala.scalajs.js.JSApp
import org.scalajs.dom._

object DashboardApp extends JSApp {
  def main(): Unit = {
    document.getElementById("scalajs").innerHTML =
      "Hello form Scala.js!"
  }
}
```

Defines the application that extends the JSApp trait as entry point

Imports the Scala.js wrapper that allows JavaScript DOM manipulation

Implements the main method, which is called by default

Redefines the content of the scalajs div

If you now reload the application, you should see both `div`s populated—one directly through the Twirl template, and one through JavaScript. The `DashboardApp` is the entry point to the application, and its `main` method will be invoked when the page is loaded.

The Scala.js DOM wrapper is a type-safe *facade* around the native DOM. It provides a statically typed interface for manipulating the DOM from Scala.[1] Feel free to play around with it to get a feel for developing JavaScript with Scala—in my opinion this is a quite refreshing experience.

> **IMPROVING THE USER INTERFACE** To make the application look a little bit nicer, you can use Bootstrap. The starter template (http://getbootstrap.com/examples/starter-template) is simple but powerful, and it gives a nicer look.

[1] See the scala-js-dom page at http://scala-js.github.io/scala-js-dom.

DEBUGGING SCALA.JS APPLICATIONS IN THE BROWSER Scala.js creates source maps that allow for easy debugging of Scala.js applications in the browser's developer console. You can test this in the example from listing 8.3 by throwing an exception in the `main` method (simply writing `throw new Exception("boom")` will do). If you load your browser's development console, you should now see a reference to `DashboardApp` with the line at which the exception was thrown. Some IDEs, such as IntelliJ IDEA, also offer support for debugging on the client side in the IDE using plugins, which further eases the development of client-side applications written this way.

8.2 Integrating Scala.js and AngularJS

The next step in building the dashboard application is to integrate the AngularJS framework with appropriate Scala.js bindings.

8.2.1 Setting up the AngularJS bindings

The scalajs-angulate project (https://github.com/jokade/scalajs-angulate) provides bindings that simplify the development of AngularJS applications with Scala.js. More specifically, it provides *facade traits* for type-safe access to the library (we'll talk about these traits in depth later) as well as a few macros for declaring AngularJS controllers, services, and other components in a Scala-like style. This is the glue code we need to easily use AngularJS in combination with Scala.js. We could also opt to not use bindings, but that would make the whole experience awkward at best.

To integrate scalajs-angulate, you need both the scalajs-angulate library and the original AngularJS JavaScript library. Edit the build.sbt file and add the following library dependency to the `client` project:

```
libraryDependencies ++= Seq(
  // ...
  "biz.enef" %%% "scalajs-angulate" % "0.2"
)
```

Then add the following `jsDependencies` setting to the `client` project:

```
jsDependencies ++= Seq(
  "org.webjars.bower" % "angular" % "1.4.0" / "angular.min.js",
  "org.webjars.bower" % "angular-route" % "1.4.0" /
      "angular-route.min.js" dependsOn "angular.min.js"
)
```

The `jsDependencies` setting allows you to define dependencies on JavaScript libraries. Libraries published through npm and Bower are automatically available as WebJars. The last parameter allows you to define a file that's part of the WebJar to be loaded in the project when it's run. (The WebJars website lists which files the WebJars contain so you can figure out the name of the JavaScript artifact to load.) The `dependsOn` notation helps you indicate dependencies between JavaScript libraries so that the load order is correct.

THE %%% NOTATION The `%%%` notation in the `libraryDependency` on scalajs-angulate allows you to encode the current Scala.js version into the dependency, enabling you to cross-compile Scala.js libraries across several Scala.js versions. It also distinguishes these special libraries (which essentially contain code meant to be compiled down to JavaScript) from other kinds of JVM libraries.

8.2.2 Creating the AngularJS application

Let's create a simple AngularJS application that will, for now, just display some text that comes from a controller. An AngularJS application is structured as shown in figure 8.3.

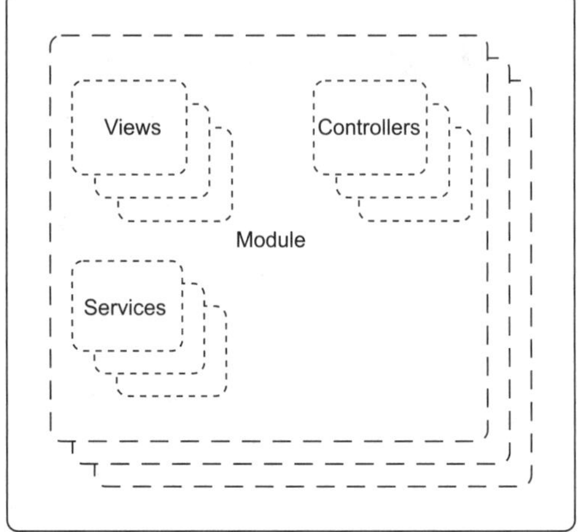

Figure 8.3 Structure of an AngularJS application

An AngularJS application consists of several parts:

- One or more modules that tie together controllers, views, services, and more
- Controllers that encapsulate the logic underlying the manipulation of the view
- Views or partial views that display data and allow user input
- Services to take care of specialized tasks, encapsulating advanced business logic

Scopes enable two-way binding between views and controllers and ensure a good separation of concerns between those two elements.

ANGULARJS SCOPES AND TWO-WAY BINDINGS Scopes allow you to bind views and controllers by having a view-controller pair share the same scope. In itself, this mechanism is fairly popular in MVC frameworks. Typically these bindings are one-way bindings, which means that the controller sets the properties of the scope and the view only reads from them. In the case of AngularJS, the view can also set properties and influence their values, which is why the binding is called a two-way binding. Changes in the view are propagated to the controller, which can then react to those changes and trigger the appropriate logic without you having to do any additional programming. AngularJS takes care of propagating those scope changes in two directions, keeping the data in controllers and views synchronized.

The data flow of our simple AngularJS application is shown in figure 8.4. We'll start by defining a `hello` variable in the controller, which gets bound to the scope ❶, and

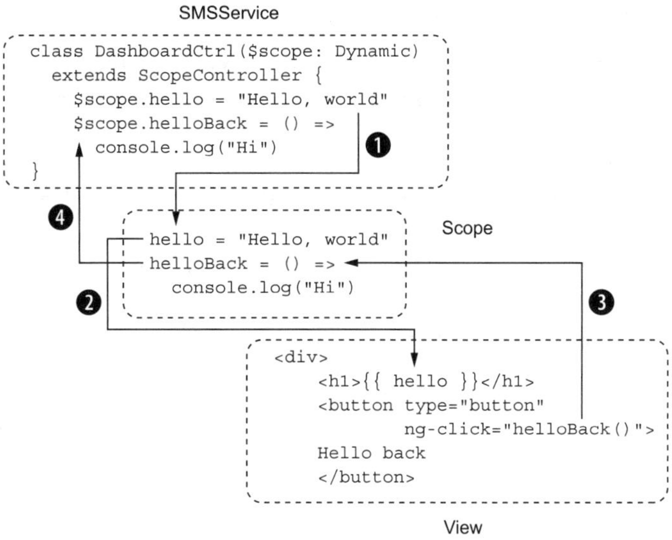

SMSService

```
class DashboardCtrl($scope: Dynamic)
  extends ScopeController {
    $scope.hello = "Hello, world"
    $scope.helloBack = () =>
      console.log("Hi")
}
```

❶ ❹

Scope

```
hello = "Hello, world"
helloBack = () =>
  console.log("Hi")
```

❷ ❸

```
<div>
    <h1>{{ hello }}</h1>
    <button type="button"
            ng-click="helloBack()">
    Hello back
    </button>
```

View

Figure 8.4 Data flow in the two-way binding of the AngularJS scope

we'll display it in the view ❷. In the view, when you click on the Hello Back button ❸, the scope's `helloBack()` method is invoked, leading to its execution inside the controller ❹, which in turn will log the message "Hi" on the browser's JavaScript console.

Let's start by defining the application module. Adjust the `DashboardApp` as follows.

Listing 8.4 Initializing the AngularJS application module

```
package dashboard

import biz.enef.angulate.ext.{Route, RouteProvider}
import biz.enef.angulate._
import scala.scalajs.js.JSApp

object DashboardApp extends JSApp {
  def main(): Unit = {
    val module = angular.createModule("dashboard", Seq("ngRoute"))
    module.controllerOf[DashboardCtrl]
    module.config { ($routeProvider: RouteProvider) =>
      $routeProvider
        .when("/dashboard", Route(
          templateUrl = "/assets/partials/dashboard.html",
          controller = "dashboard.DashboardCtrl")
        ).otherwise(Route(redirectTo = "/dashboard"))
    }
  }
}
```

Defines the dashboard AngularJS module, depending on the ngRoute service

Declares the DashboardCtrl controller

Configures the routes service

This example illustrates a few of the core mechanisms of AngularJS. Now let's look at it in detail.

8.2.3 Initializing the AngularJS dashboard module and its dependencies

The entry point of an AngularJS application is a module. In listing 8.4 you start by declaring the `dashboard` module with a dependency on the `ngRoute` service, which you need to configure routes.

AngularJS routes bind a client-side URL to a view and a controller, so that when the URL is accessed, the controller is loaded and the view displayed with the data provided by the controller. This mechanism is very similar to normal routes that you'd use in Play (through the conf/routes file), with the difference that client-side routes employ "hashbang" URLs such as http://localhost:9000/#/dashboard to perform routing on the client side. This is an essential part of applications that rely on a single page of server-side HTML to be deployed (the browser only loads a page once, and everything else happens through JavaScript).

8.2.4 Initializing the Dashboard controller

In the second part of listing 8.4, you use the `module.controllerOf` macro provided by scalajs-angulate to initialize the `DashboardController`. This macro expands into a slightly more complex definition and takes care of naming the controller for you.

You then use the `$routesProvider` (provided by your dependency on the `ngRoute` service) to declare that `dashboard.DashboardCtrl` will be responsible for rendering the `dashboard.html`*partial view.*

Implement this controller in the file modules/client/src/main/scala/dashboard/DashboardCtrl.scala.

Listing 8.5 Implementation of the `DashboardCtrl`

```
package dashboard

import biz.enef.angulate._
import org.scalajs.dom._
import scalajs.js.Dynamic

class DashboardCtrl($scope: Dynamic)
  extends ScopeController {
    $scope.hello = "Hello, world"
    $scope.helloBack = () => console.log("Hi")
}
```

- **Extends the ScopeController trait, which represents controllers with explicit scope** (`extends ScopeController {`)
- **Declares the controller, taking as a constructor parameter the $scope** (`class DashboardCtrl($scope: Dynamic)`)
- **Defines the hello variable on the scope** (`$scope.hello = "Hello, world"`)
- **Defines the helloBack function on the scope** (`$scope.helloBack = () => console.log("Hi")`)

In this example we declare the scope explicitly. As I already mentioned, AngularJS relies on mutable scopes to provide two-way bindings between views and controllers. The `$scope` is injected by AngularJS, and we represent it as a `Dynamic` value. The `Dynamic` type, as its name indicates, lets you dynamically read and write values, which is very close to writing JavaScript. We could have defined the scope explicitly, as you'll see later, but we'll use a dynamic type here.

8.2.5 *Creating the partial view*

The next piece we need for our example to work is the view. Create the file modules/client/src/main/public/partials/dashboard.html with the following content.

Listing 8.6 Creating a partial view with AngularJS

```
<div>
    <h1>{{ hello }}</h1>
    <button type="button" ng-click="helloBack()">Hello back</button>
</div>
```

Displays the contents of the hello scope variable in the view

Registers the ng-click event handler to execute the helloBack() scope method when the button is clicked

The syntax with double-curly brackets makes it possible to access any value on the scope and to execute simple JavaScript expressions (although these should be encapsulated inside methods defined in the scope, for better readability). Any variable or method declared in the controller's scope can be accessed this way, and when its value changes, those changes are reflected in the view automatically.

8.2.6 *Loading the AngularJS application in HTML*

The last thing we must do for our AngularJS application to function properly is tell it in which part of the DOM tree it should be running. Adjust the `<body>` tag in the main.scala.html Twirl template as follows:

```
<body ng-app="dashboard">
```

This will tell AngularJS which application to look for when loading the page.

Finally, edit the app/views/index.scala.html template to instruct it to display partial views in a special part of the page by appending the `ng-view` attribute to a container, as in the following listing.

Listing 8.7 Declaring where the partial views will be loaded in the HTML structure

```
@main("Twitter SMS service dashboard") {
  <div class="container" ng-view>
  </div>
}
```

If you run the application now, you should see the contents of the `hello` variable that you just defined in the controller printed on the screen. Clicking the Hello Back button will print a message in the browser console.

Custom scope types for Scala.js integration

It's possible to define custom scope types, which may be useful if you want a more strongly typed representation of scopes. All you need to do is extend the `Scope` trait and use the custom trait in the controller's constructor:

```
trait DashboardScope extends Scope {
  var hello : String = js.native
  var helloBack: js.Function = js.native
}
class DashboardCtrl($scope: DashboardScope)
  extends ScopeController {
  ...
}
```

8.3 Integrating existing JavaScript libraries with Scala.js

There are two main ways of interacting with JavaScript from Scala.js: dynamically (using the `Dynamic` type you just saw) or by providing the facade traits necessary for wrapping the dynamically typed JavaScript functions with statically typed interfaces. This latter mechanism isn't specific to Scala.js; it's also used in other technologies that provide a static type system on top of JavaScript, such as TypeScript (http://typescriptlang.org), which has a curated repository of *type definitions* for JavaScript libraries (http://definitelytyped.org).

In this section we'll integrate an existing JavaScript library into our Scala.js application by writing our own facade, and then make use of it to fetch data from the back end.

8.3.1 Wrapping an existing JavaScript library as an AngularJS service

To exchange data with our client-side application, we'll use WebSockets. Rather than writing the connection-handling part ourselves, we'll delegate this job to the angular-websocket library (https://github.com/gdi2290/angular-websocket), which uses exponential back-off during reconnections.[2]

Let's write our own facade! The first thing we need to do is decide how we'd use the library from JavaScript. What we'd primarily like to do with this library is establish a new WebSocket connection, send messages to the server, and handle messages sent from the server. In JavaScript, that would look like this:

```
var ws = $websocket('ws://localhost:9000');
ws.send('hello');
ws.onMessage(function(event) {
  console.log(event.data);
});
```

[2] See Douglas Thain's "Exponential Backoff in Distributed Systems" blog entry (Feb. 21, 2009), http://dthain.blogspot.co.uk/2009/02/exponential-backoff-in-distributed.html.

In a first version of our facade, we'd need to wrap three methods:

- The constructor that gives us back an established WebSocket connection.
- The `send` method, which returns an AngularJS promise.
- The `onMessage` method, which optionally takes a JavaScript options object to filter messages. The callback specified in `onMessage` is given a `MessageEvent`.[3]

To build a good facade, we therefore also need to provide facades for related types. Luckily for us, we can reuse existing facades that have already been created. The AngularJS promise is wrapped by scalajs-angulate as `HttpPromise`, and the `MessageEvent` has been wrapped as part of the Scala.js DOM library. For the options object of the `onMessage` method, we'll simply use a dynamic object now, because we're not sure whether we're going to use the filter feature.

Add the following JavaScript dependency to the `jsDependencies` of the `client` project:

```
jsDependencies ++= Seq(
  "org.webjars.bower" % "angular-websocket" % "1.0.13" /
    "dist/angular-websocket.min.js" dependsOn "angular.min.js"
)
```

Because we intend to use this library, we also need to tell AngularJS about it. In `DashboardApp`, add the dependency on `ngWebSocket` when creating the module, like so:

```
val module =
  angular.createModule("dashboard", Seq("ngRoute", "ngWebSocket"))
```

Next, create the file modules/client/src/main/scala/dashboard/WebsocketService.scala with the following contents.

Listing 8.8 Implementing the Scala.js facade for the WebSocket service

```
package dashboard

import biz.enef.angulate.core.{HttpPromise, ProvidedService}
import org.scalajs.dom._
import scala.scalajs.js
import scala.scalajs.js.UndefOr

trait WebsocketService extends ProvidedService {
  def apply(
    url: String,
    options: UndefOr[Dynamic] = js.undefined
  ): WebsocketDataStream = js.native
}

trait WebsocketDataStream extends js.Object {
```

Extends the ProvidedService helper trait provided by scalajs-angulate so this service will be marked as automatically provided by AngularJS

Uses the apply method to mimic the JavaScript constructor of angular-websocket

Defines a facade for the underlying object returned by the service constructor

[3] See the `MessageEvent` page on the MDN site: https://developer.mozilla.org/en-US/docs/Web/API/MessageEvent.

```
  def send[T](data: js.Any): HttpPromise[T] = js.native
  def onMessage(
    callback: js.Function1[MessageEvent, Unit],
    options: UndefOr[js.Dynamic] = js.undefined): Unit = js.native
}
```

Defines a type-safe wrapper to the send method that returns an HttpPromise

Specifies the callback parameter of the onMessage method as a function that takes a MessageEvent and returns nothing

Specifies the optional options parameter as a Dynamic value

As you can see, defining the facade itself isn't very complicated—the most important part of the job is to identify which types make sense being associated with the methods. The only thing specific to AngularJS in this facade is the use of the `ProvidedService` trait, which eases service discovery—to wrap any JavaScript library it's sufficient to extend `js.Object`.

It's also not compulsory to wrap all the methods if you only plan to use a subset of the functionality of the wrapped library. To get a good idea of the types that Scala.js uses to represent JavaScript types, have a look at the Scala.js documentation on the subject.[4]

8.3.2 Creating a service to fetch data for a graph

In the next step we'll display data using the Chart.js library (www.chartjs.org) in combination with its AngularJS wrapper `angular-chart.js` (http://jtblin.github.io/angular-chart.js/).

We'll also need some data. For this purpose, we'll create the `GraphDataService` AngularJS service, which makes use of our newly created `WebsocketService`.

But before we build this service, you'll need to do a bit of work to get everything ready. To draw a line chart, `angular-chart.js` expects a JSON object with the following structure:

```
{
  "graph_type": "MonthlySubscriptions",
  "labels": ["January", "February", "March", "April", "May", "June"],
  "series": ['Series A', 'Series B'],
  "data": [
    [65, 59, 80, 81, 56, 55],
    [28, 48, 40, 19, 86, 27]
  ]
}
```

The line graph has a number of labels for the X axis, a number of series (two in this example), and some data for each of the series. Note that the `graph_type` field isn't

[4] See the "Type Correspondence" section in the Scala.js documentation: www.scala-js.org/doc/js-interoperability.html.

expected by the library, but we'll need it to know how to display the graph on the client side.

Create a WebSocket endpoint in the `Application` controller that listens to incoming messages and returns this type of graph when asked for a string message of kind `MonthlySubscriptions`.

EXERCISE 8.1

Fetch the monthly subscriptions from chapter 7's Twitter SMS service using jOOQ. You'll need to establish a database connection as in chapter 7, and you'll need to query the `SUBSCRIPTIONS` table to return daily aggregates for the past month.

Once your WebSocket endpoint is ready and providing data in the right format, you can go one step further and define a `GraphDataService` that will leverage the `WebsocketService`, as shown in the following listing.

Listing 8.9 Implementation of an AngularJS service that retrieves and graphs data

```
package dashboard

import biz.enef.angulate._
import org.scalajs.dom._
import scala.scalajs.js.{Dynamic, JSON}
import scala.collection._

class GraphDataService($websocket: WebsocketService) extends Service {
  val dataStream = $websocket("ws://localhost:9000/graphs")

  private val callbacks =
    mutable.Map.empty[GraphType.Value, Dynamic => Unit]

  def fetchGraph(
    graphType: GraphType.Value,
    callback: Dynamic => Unit
  ) = {
    callbacks += graphType -> callback
    dataStream.send(graphType.toString)
  }

  dataStream.onMessage { (event: MessageEvent) =>
    val json: Dynamic = JSON.parse(event.data.toString)
    val graphType = GraphType.withName(json.graph_type.toString)
    callbacks.get(graphType).map { callback =>
      callback(json)
    } getOrElse {
      console.log(s"Unknown graph type $graphType")
    }
  }
}

object GraphType extends Enumeration {
  val MonthlySubscriptions = Value
}
```

Declares a dependency on the WebsocketService in this service's constructor

Obtains a WebSocket connection using the service

Creates an empty map for keeping callbacks

Fetches monthly subscriptions by remembering the callback and sending a message

Reads the graph type from the JSON

Attempts to find the appropriate callback for a message and calls it with the data

Encodes the different graph types in an Enumeration

The GraphDataService declares a dependency on the WebsocketService using the AngularJS notation $websocket (it's customary in AngularJS to prepend a dollar sign to provided utility services that aren't part of the core application logic itself). As you're making asynchronous calls, you need to employ a callback mechanism to pass the resulting graph data to the caller. Furthermore, this mechanism enables you to continuously push new graph data to the client from the server if necessary, which could become useful for near-real-time reporting.

There's an important thing to take away from listing 8.9. As you may have noticed, the implementation of this service feels very close to writing a plain Scala class. There are only a few types that indicate that the code will be running on the client side in the browser, such as the use of the js.Dynamic type. Other than this, you couldn't really distinguish it from a normal server-side Scala service running on the JVM. And even though the onMessage method of WebsocketService expects a js.Function1[MessageEvent, Unit] (as you defined it earlier in listing 8.8), you don't really get to see any of this. Thanks to the implicit conversions that Scala.js provides, you can write out the function expected as a parameter of onMessage using Scala's normal syntactic sugar for defining anonymous functions.

You could even go one step further and get rid of js.Dynamic by using the Scala.js Pickling library (https://github.com/scala-js/scala-js-pickling) and parse the graph data into a case class shared between client and server, thus enjoying compile-time type-safety from end to end. If you want to, go ahead and give it a try!

There are only a few more steps necessary to get the data to the controller.

First of all, you need to register the GraphDataService with AngularJS in the DashboardApp. Use the module.serviceOf method to do this, like when you registered DashboardCtrl.

Next, declare a dependency on the GraphDataService in the DashboardCtrl constructor and call the fetchGraph method. At this stage, you can just print the resulting data out in the JavaScript console.

Done? Great! Let's move on to displaying the graph on the screen.

8.3.3 Displaying metrics using the Chart.js library

To display the graph using the Chart.js library, we need to do a few things:

- Declare the necessary dependencies in build.sbt
- Declare the dependency on the angular-chart.js service in the AngularJS application
- Define the chart HTML markup and load the data
- Set up the WebJars mechanism for Play so that we can load the CSS stylesheets associated with the library

In build.sbt, start by adding the following two jsDependencies:

```
"org.webjars.bower" % "Chart.js" % "1.0.2" / "Chart.min.js"
"org.webjars.bower" % "angular-chart.js" % "0.7.1" /
    "dist/angular-chart.js" dependsOn "Chart.min.js"
```

In the DashboardApp, add a dependency on the angular-chart.js service in the module declaration:

```
val module = angular.createModule(
  "dashboard", Seq("ngRoute", "ngWebSocket", "chart.js")
)
```

The name of the service is usually to be found in its documentation. Many services have names starting with "ng" (shorthand for Angular), but there are exceptions as you can see here.

Now, let's set up a line chart to show the data. Adjust the dashboard.html partial view as follows.

Listing 8.10 Markup for a line chart using Chart.js

```
<div>
    <canvas id="line"
        class="chart chart-line"
        data="monthlySubscriptions.data"
        labels="monthlySubscriptions.labels"
        series="monthlySubscriptions.series"
        legend="true">
    </canvas>
</div>
```

In listing 8.10 you read data out of the monthlySubscriptions variable. Make sure that you set this variable in the scope when you make the controller call that fetches data from GraphDataService.

At this point, you're almost set to load the graph. There's just one more thing needed for it to look nice: you need to load the stylesheet provided by the angular-chart.js library. Go back to build.sbt and add the following dependencies to the libraryDependencies of the main project:

```
libraryDependencies ++= Seq(
  // ...
  "org.webjars" %% "webjars-play" % "2.4.0",
  "org.webjars.bower" % "angular-chart.js" % "0.7.1"
)
```

There's again a dependency on the angular-chart.js library, because you want to load the stylesheet that it provides, so it needs to be available in the root's project classpath. Loading artifacts provided by WebJars requires a route to be added to conf/routes:

```
GET     /webjars/*file              controllers.WebJarAssets.at(file)
```

Finally, you can load the stylesheet in app/views/main.scala.html:

```
<link
  rel="stylesheet"
  href="@routes.WebJarAssets.at(
```

```
    WebJarAssets.locate("angular-chart.css")
  )"
>
```

The `WebJarAssets` helper allows you to specify a filename in the classpath, allowing it to be loaded by the `WebJarAssets.at` action.

That's it! Upon loading the application, you should now see a beautiful graph of subscriptions to chapter 7's SMS service. It should look something like figure 8.5.

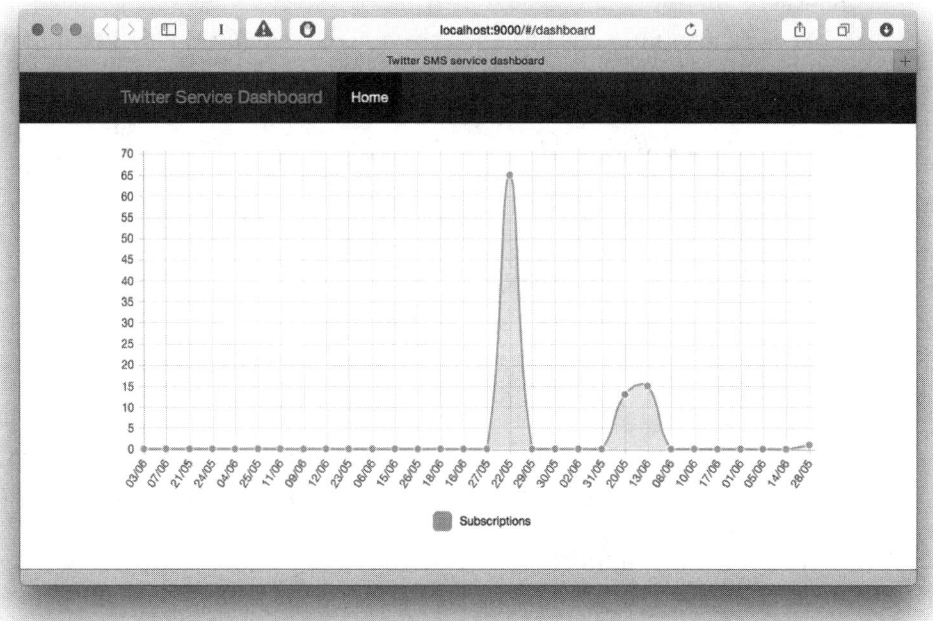

Figure 8.5 Graph of last month's subscriptions to the Twitter SMS service

8.4 Handling client-side failure

Apart from all the technical challenges involved in implementing a responsive web application, one of the hardest tasks is keeping users happy. This not only entails creating an intuitive user interface but also keeping the user up to date about what's going on with the task at hand, especially if things aren't going well. Depending on what your application is doing, some user actions may take a little longer to execute, and rather than keeping the user waiting for a result, it may be better to let them work on other things (if the workflow permits) and notify them once their action has been processed.

Ideally you should keep your users happy by building relatively bug-free client-side applications. Scala.js can help you do so, as it combines the advantages of a type-safe language with a powerful type system on the client side.

Let's look at the ways you can detect issues and inform users about them with the Twitter SMS service dashboard.

8.4.1 Preventing bugs with tests

The first line of defense against failures is to create automated tests that will detect bugs before the application is deployed. The test infrastructure in Scala.js is still developing, but there are already a number of testing frameworks available. It isn't possible to use server-side frameworks such as ScalaTest or Specs2 with Scala.js on the client side, because those are heavily interleaved with JVM dependencies, so we'll use the µTest library (https://github.com/lihaoyi/utest).

Start by adding the `"com.lihaoyi" %%% "utest" % "0.3.1" % "test"` library dependency to the `client` project in build.sbt, and add the framework as a test framework with the setting `testFrameworks += new TestFramework("utest.runner.Framework")`. If you haven't done so already, you should now switch to using Node.js, because running the tests on Rhino won't work too well.

To run the tests, you'll also need to install PhantomJS, which enables headless website testing (testing without running an actual browser window). You can find the installation instructions at http://phantomjs.org.

Next, create the file modules/client/src/test/scala/services/GraphDataServiceSuite.scala with the following contents.

Listing 8.11 Testing the GraphDataService

```
package services

import biz.enef.angulate.core.HttpPromise
import dashboard._
import org.scalajs.dom._
import utest._
import scala.scalajs.js
import scala.scalajs.js.UndefOr
import scala.scalajs.js.annotation.JSExportAll

object GraphDataServiceSuite extends TestSuite {
  val tests = TestSuite {
    "GraphDataService should initialize a WebSocket connection" - {
      val mockedWebsocketDataStream = new WebsocketDataStreamMock()
      val mockedWebsocketService: js.Function = {
        (url: String, options: js.UndefOr[js.Dynamic]) =>
          mockedWebsocketDataStream.asInstanceOf[WebsocketDataStream]
      }

      new GraphDataService(
        mockedWebsocketService.asInstanceOf[WebsocketService]
      )

      assert(mockedWebsocketDataStream.isInitialized)
    }
  }
}
```

Extends the TestSuite trait to be discovered by the test runner

Declares a test

Mocks the WebsocketService constructor using a native JavaScript function

Initializes the real GraphDataService with the mocks

Checks whether the WebsocketDataStream has been initialized

```
@JSExportAll
class WebsocketDataStreamMock {
  val isInitialized = true
  def send[T](data: js.Any): HttpPromise[T] = ???
  def onMessage(
    callback: js.Function1[MessageEvent, Unit],
    options: UndefOr[js.Dynamic] = js.undefined
  ): Unit = {}
  def onClose(callback: js.Function1[CloseEvent, Unit]): Unit = {}
  def onOpen(callback: js.Function1[js.Dynamic, Unit]): Unit = {}
}
```

Exports all public members of the mocked class to JavaScript

Because there's no mocking library that runs with Scala.js yet, you need to mock the dependencies on your service by hand. Mocking facade traits isn't a straightforward process and requires a bit of preparation. You can't simply extend the existing facade traits and override the implementation because of the way Scala.js compilation is designed. Instead, you need to create the mock classes as standalone Scala classes that you export to JavaScript using the `JSExportAll` annotation, and cast them back to the facade trait.

The `WebsocketService` itself only defines a constructor (the `apply` method), so to mock it you need to implement a constructor mock as a native JavaScript function and have it return a mock of `WebsocketDataStream`, which contains all of the interesting functions.

This manual approach to testing is certainly not as convenient as the current JVM tooling, but chances are that a mocking library will be available for Scala.js projects soon.

If you now run `test` in the sbt console, you should see the test running and succeeding.

8.4.2 Detecting WebSocket connection failure

The internet is a shaky place, and if you build an application using a persistent connection with WebSockets, chances are that you'll be disconnected from time to time. The angular-websocket library has a mechanism for reconnecting automatically should the connection be closed unexpectedly. You just need to enable it first.

In the `GraphDataService`, the only thing you need to do is initialize the WebSocket connection a little differently:

```
val dataStream = $websocket(
  "ws://localhost:9000/graphs",
  Dynamic.literal("reconnectIfNotNormalClose" -> true)
)
```

Once you've enabled this option, you can watch it in action: open the developer console of your browser and then kill the Play process. Simply pressing Ctrl-D in the sbt console won't be enough, as this will shut down Play gracefully and therefore close the WebSocket connection—you'll need to forcefully quit the process, such as by calling `kill -9 <PID>` on a Unix-based OS. Once you've done so, you'll be able to observe the library attempting to reconnect with an increasingly large back-off delay. This mechanism of exponential back-off is particularly useful in networked applications, because other approaches would flood an already busy server should all clients attempt to reconnect at the same time.

> **WEBSOCKET DISCONNECTIONS** The `CloseEvent` specified in the WebSocket API (https://developer.mozilla.org/de/docs/Web/API/CloseEvent) provides different codes characterizing why the connection was closed. These codes can be used (and are used by angular-websocket) to decide whether to attempt an automated reconnection to the server.

8.4.3 Notifying users

If your tests didn't prevent the application from failing, the next best thing is to tell the user that something is wrong. To notify users about connection failures, we'll use the `angular-growl` library (https://github.com/JanStevens/angular-growl-2), which displays notifications of various kinds (information, warning, error, success) at the upper-right side of the screen.

EXERCISE 8.2

At this point you should have a good sense of how to integrate an existing JavaScript library with Scala.js and AngularJS, so it's your turn to visit the library's site and integrate it:

- Add the WebJar dependencies to the library in build.sbt, including the repeated dependency in the main project to fetch the stylesheets.
- Load the `angular-growl` stylesheets in main.scala.html using the WebJar assets loading mechanism.
- Write a wrapper for the Growl library's four main methods (`info`, `warning`, `success`, `error`).
- Add the `angular-growl` service dependency in the module declaration in `DashboardApp`.

Once you're done integrating the library, add the `onClose` method to the `Websocket-DataStream` facade trait. This method takes a callback from `org.scalajs.dom.CloseEvent` to `Unit` and allows you to run code when the server connection is interrupted, like this:

```
dataStream.onClose { (event: CloseEvent) =>
  growl.error(s"Server connection closed, attempting to reconnect")
}
```

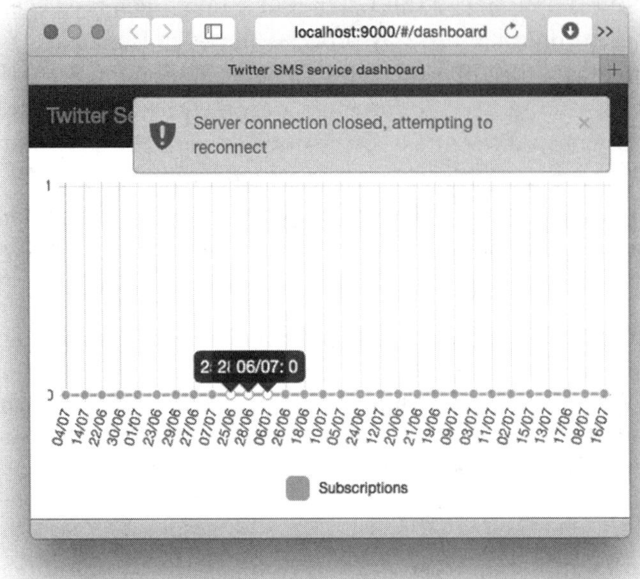

Figure 8.6 Notification shown to the user if the client-side application can't interact with the server

If the user just went offline because their free 10 minutes of airport wifi expired, they'll welcome the kind of notification shown in figure 8.6, rather than having to wonder why the application starts behaving in mysterious ways.

> **CONSISTENT NOTIFICATIONS** No matter which notification style you adopt, be consistent in the implementation across the application, and always use the same channel, or at least the same small set of channels. It's fine to use several types of interaction mechanisms—you may, for example, choose to use modal windows to prompt the user if you can't reestablish the connection after one minute—but do keep the number of different types as low as possible. If you are developing an application in a larger team, it's a very good idea to agree on the notification channels up front, so as to avoid presenting users with a multitude of different notification mechanisms, ranging from elaborate modal dialogs with shadows to crude JavaScript `alert()` boxes.

8.4.4 Monitoring client-side errors

You might usually work on the back end of your applications rather than the client side. If this is the case, you'll nonetheless be interested in the impact that client-side failure can have on the overall perception of your applications.

Error handling on the client side often comes as an afterthought, with a suboptimal or simply nonexistent implementation. It doesn't matter if the whole back end is scalable, resilient, and self-healing if the client side is broken. If the user doesn't get notified that the application is misbehaving, their perception of the entire application will be negatively impacted.

It's easy to not implement the `onFailure` handler of a JavaScript call on the client side, or to implement it with `console.log`, but this won't help the user, let alone yourself when the application is in production, as you won't get to see client-side logs. Tools such as JSNLog (http://js.jsnlog.com) enable you to propagate client-side errors to the server, so you know that something is going wrong on the client side and can act on it. Specialized services such as TrackJS (https://trackjs.com) and Sentry (www.getsentry.com) go one step further and provide you with advanced reporting on your application's client-side errors.

8.5 Summary

In this chapter we looked at building a client-side application with Scala.js. In particular:

- We set up a Play project with Scala.js.
- We integrated an existing JavaScript framework, AngularJS, and Scala.js using the scalajs-angulate library.
- We created our own facade traits to draw a graph with data retrieved via a WebSocket connection.
- We looked at ways to reduce failure on the client side and to notify users about issues.

You now have a good idea of the reactive web application landscape on both the server and client sides. Let's next look into the exciting topic of asynchronous streams with nonblocking back pressure.

Part 3

Advanced topics

This part introduces advanced topics related to building reactive web applications. You'll learn how to use Akka Streams, an implementation of the Reactive Streams standard, to perform asynchronous and fault-tolerant stream processing. We'll then talk about what's necessary to deploy a reactive web application built with Play. Finally, we'll discuss how to test a reactive web application to see if it behaves under load as you'd want it to.

9 Reactive Streams

This chapter covers

- Reasons for defining a Reactive Streams standard
- The building blocks of the Akka Streams library that implements Reactive Streams
- Using Akka Streams in combination with iteratees and building a simple flow graph
- Observing reactive back pressure in action

The Reactive Streams standard (www.reactive-streams.org) defines the interfaces, methods, and protocols necessary for building interoperable libraries that enable asynchronous stream processing with *nonblocking back pressure*. There are already a few implementations of this standard, and in this chapter we'll take a look at the Akka Streams library (http://doc.akka.io/docs/akka-stream-and-http-experimental/current). We'll start by asking why Reactive Streams is useful at all, and then we'll move on to exploring a few of the basic building blocks of Akka Streams. Finally, we'll get our hands dirty revising and extending our application from chapter 2 with Akka Streams.

9.1 Why Reactive Streams

There are two major motivations behind the development of the Reactive Streams standard, both stemming from the fact that there's an increased need for transferring large quantities of data across asynchronous boundaries—boundaries between different applications, different CPUs, or different networked systems. These quantities of data may be so large, in fact, that they can't always be processed at full speed by the system on the receiving end.

The first motivation is technical: there needs to be a means to transport and process those streams of data without running the risk of overwhelming the involved parties because of a processing speed mismatch.

The second motivation is somewhat more human in the sense that the tooling available for developers to manipulate those streams needs to be interoperable. Different libraries already exist to address the problem of manipulating asynchronous streams on a higher level of abstraction, and those libraries should be able to work with one another because it's otherwise not possible to stream data across systems that use different tools.

Let's take a closer look at those two motivations.

9.1.1 Streaming with nonblocking back pressure

Reactive Streams defines a standard useful for building libraries that provide a high level of abstraction for manipulating asynchronous streams of data. *Back pressure* means that *publishers* and *subscribers* of streaming data don't get overwhelmed when the subscriber is slower at processing incoming elements than the publisher is at producing them. This unfortunate case is shown in figure 9.1.

In a system without back pressure, if the subscriber is slower than the publisher, then eventually the stream will stop—either because one of the parties runs out of memory and one of its buffers overflows or because the implementation can detect this situation but doesn't know to stop sending or accepting data until the situation is resolved (if it can be resolved at all). Although the latter scenario is somewhat more positive than the former, blocking back pressure (the capability of a system to detect when it must slow down and to do so by blocking) brings with it all of the disadvantages of a blocking system, which occupies resources such as thread and memory usage.

Reactive Streams defines a methodology for allowing nonblocking back pressure: subscribers communicate with publishers to prevent the system as a whole getting overwhelmed without holding on to precious resources to do so.

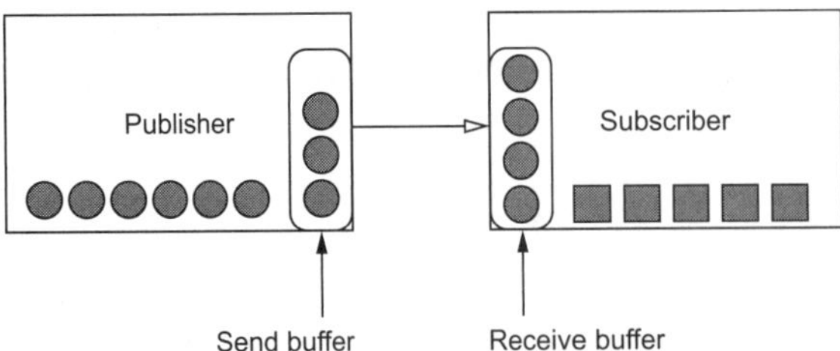

Figure 9.1 Subscriber being slower than the publisher of data, resulting in both send and receive buffers filling up

Let's take a quick look at the core of Reactive Streams—the API for publishers and subscribers, which is defined in Java for interoperability across all kinds of JVM languages. Don't worry, you won't have to implement this API or work directly with it because it's aimed at creators of libraries that implement the Reactive Streams standards, not at its users. But given that it's rather simple, it won't hurt to peek under the hood:

```
public interface Publisher<T> {
    public void subscribe(Subscriber<? super T> s);
}
public interface Subscriber<T> {
    public void onSubscribe(Subscription s);
    public void onNext(T t);
    public void onError(Throwable t);
    public void onComplete();
}
public interface Subscription {
    public void request(long n);
    public void cancel();
}
```

At first, the communication between publisher and subscriber is set up via the publisher's `subscribe`, through which the two parties are introduced to each other. After successful initialization of the communication, the subscriber gets to know about a `Subscription` (which models the established connection) via a call to its `onSubscribe` method.

At the core of the Reactive Streams mechanism is the `request` method of the `Subscription`. Through this method, the subscriber signals to the publisher how many elements it's ready to process. The publisher communicates every element one by one to the subscriber via its `onNext` method, as well as fatal stream failures through the `onError` method. Because the publisher knows exactly how many items it's expected to publish at any time (it has been asked for a number of elements in the `Subscription`'s `request` method), it's able to produce as many elements as required without producing too many for the subscriber to consume, eliminating the need to block while waiting for the subscriber. Additionally, the subscriber is called by the publisher for each published element through the `onNext` method, meaning that it does not explicitly need to block while waiting for new elements to be available.

> **ENTIRELY ASYNCHRONOUS API** As you can see, all methods of the Reactive Streams API are of type `void`, so they don't return any useful information. Instead, the different callback methods (`onSubscribe`, `onNext`, and the like) are used, ensuring an entirely asynchronous workflow.

9.1.2 Manipulating asynchronous streams

In chapter 6 we quickly looked at a way to implement back pressure in actors by using control messages that have a higher priority than normal messages. As you saw, even a rudimentary implementation of a back pressure mechanism turns out to be quite a bit of work as there are many special cases to be aware of and deal with.

Although the actor system does a good job of letting you model and implement asynchronous processes, implementing stream processing with back pressure can quickly become a complicated task, because the loss of a message, the overflow of an actor's mailbox, and other errors all need to be dealt with.

This is where libraries built on top of the Reactive Streams standard come in: they take care of all those low-level concerns and provide the tools necessary for more advanced stream-processing scenarios, such as grouping, concatenating, merging, and broadcasting streams. As this may sound a little theoretical, let's look at a concrete example of stream processing that we've already done in this book.

In chapter 2, we were retrieving tweets from Twitter for a given topic, and then we used iteratees, enumeratees, and enumerators to parse and broadcast the stream of tweets to clients connected via WebSockets, as shown in figure 9.2.

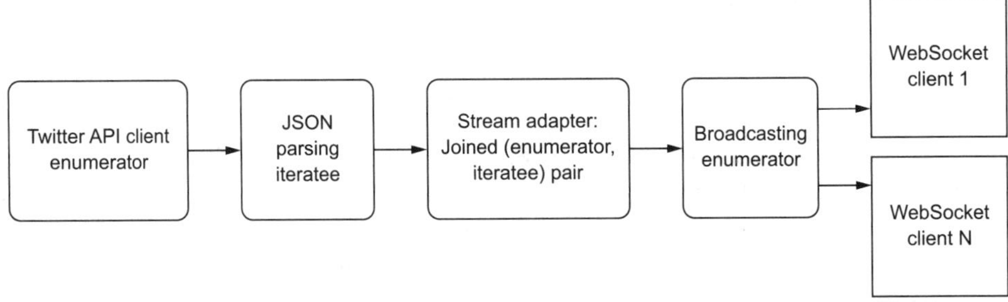

Figure 9.2 Tweet stream processing: parsing the JSON stream and broadcasting it to WebSocket clients

This application may have seemed quite complicated when you were implementing it in chapter 2, but the flow of the stream itself isn't really that elaborate. Indeed, this example is very linear, insofar as the entire transformation takes place on one track of transformation stages, without any junctions. It's only at the very end, when we want to direct the transformed stream toward client browsers, that we used a broadcast operation to cater to more than one client. In this chapter's example, we'll look at a more advanced type of stream manipulation and build a *flow graph*.

First we'll learn a bit more about the library that we're going to use to manipulate our asynchronous stream of tweets with nonblocking back pressure: Akka Streams.

9.2 Introducing Akka Streams

Akka Streams builds on the idea of *flows* and *flow graphs* that define how a stream is being processed. In this section we'll first look at the core concepts you need to know to use Akka Streams, and then we'll use them to build this chapter's example.

9.2.1 Core principles

There are four major building blocks, or *processing stages* in Akka terms, that make a stream-processing pipeline:

- A *source* has exactly one output and is responsible for producing streaming data. This is the equivalent of an enumerator.
- A *sink* has exactly one input and is responsible for consuming streaming data. This is the equivalent of an iteratee.
- A *flow* has exactly one input and exactly one output and usually transforms streaming data in one way or another. This is the equivalent of an enumeratee.
- A *junction* can have multiple inputs and multiple outputs. In the former case, we talk about *fan-in* operations, in the latter of *fan-out* operations. There isn't an exact equivalent of this type of element in the iteratee realm, but the library provides several helper methods to provide a few junction types.

These processing stages are illustrated in figure 9.3.

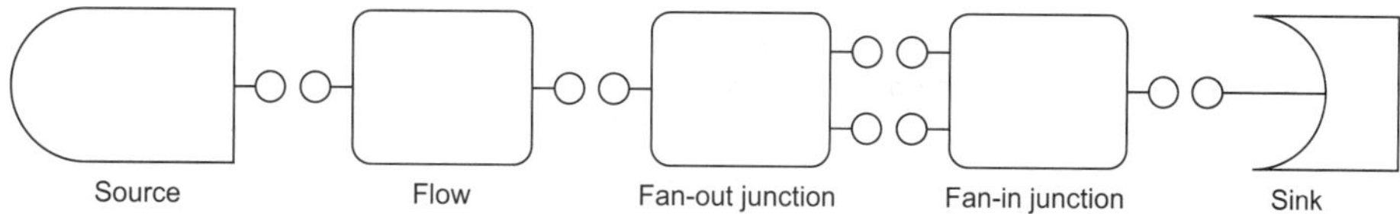

Figure 9.3 The four types of processing stages: source, sink, flow, and junction

A flow can involve more than one processing stage—as long as there's one input and one output, any concatenation of simple processing stages forms a flow. When a flow gets more complicated than a simple, linear processing pipeline and has junctions, we then talk about a flow graph.

When a flow is both connected to a source and to a sink, it's called a *runnable flow*. This means that it can effectively be started to process data. The process of running a flow is called *materialization*: a runnable flow or a runnable flow graph on their own are just definitions of how the stream will be processed (think of it as a blueprint) but in themselves don't actually do anything. When the flow is being materialized, all the necessary resources (buffers, thread pools, underlying actors, and so on) are allocated to finally run the construct. This also means that the definitions can be reused, and it's possible to build a runnable flow graph in multiple steps or even in multiple places, sending it around until it's finished. In that case we talk about *partial flow graphs*.

You now have enough theory to get started building your own runnable flow graph. Let's started with a new project to get some hands-on experience with Akka Streams!

9.2.2 Manipulating streaming tweets

In this section we'll build a graph that involves splitting the stream by the topic of each tweet, and then grouping together a specified number of tweets from each topic stream to simulate a "digest" for each topic, as shown in figure 9.4.

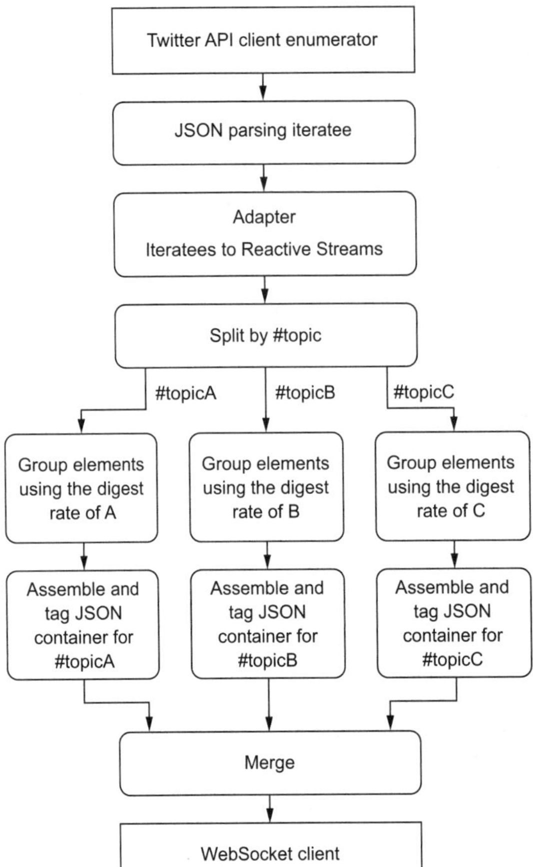

Figure 9.4 Splitting the stream by tweet topic and delivering a digest for each stream

As you can see, we'll start fetching and processing the stream as in chapter 2, but we'll then switch over from iteratees to Reactive Streams to continue processing the stream. We'll then fan out the stream, demultiplexing it into multiple substreams by using the topic of each tweet (in other words, a hashtag), group the tweets on each substream using different rates for each topic to simulate a digest of tweets, merge them again into one single stream, and then deliver each topic to clients. If the digest rate for a topic is 1, then each tweet will be delivered instantly to the client, whereas if the digest rate is 10, tweets with that topic will only be pushed to the client once 10 of them have appeared on the stream.

We now have the following tasks to take care of:

1. Set up the project
2. Set up the stream from Twitter using the WS library and transform it, producing an enumerator
3. Convert the enumerator into an Akka Streams source

4 Create a custom fan-out element that will split the stream into topics
5 Set up the graph
6 Wire the different elements of the graph
7 Deliver the stream to the client
8 Run the graph and observe back pressure

Ready? Go!

SETTING UP THE PROJECT

Start by setting up a new project using an Activator template. You'll need to add the following dependencies to build.sbt.

Listing 9.1 Library dependencies required for using Akka Streams with Play

```
libraryDependencies ++= Seq(
  ws,
  "com.typesafe.play.extras" %% "iteratees-extras" % "1.5.0",
  "com.typesafe.play" %% "play-streams-experimental" % "2.4.2",
  "com.typesafe.akka" % "akka-stream-experimental_2.11" % "1.0"
)
```

FETCHING THE STREAM FROM TWITTER

As a first step, you'll fetch your stream from Twitter. Create the file app/services/TwitterStreamService.scala as follows.

Listing 9.2 Fetching the Twitter stream using the WS library

```
package services

import javax.inject._
import akka.actor._
import play.api._
import play.api.libs.iteratee._
import play.api.libs.json._
import play.api.libs.oauth._
import play.api.libs.ws._
import play.extras.iteratees._
import scala.concurrent.ExecutionContext

class TwitterStreamService @Inject() (
  ws: WSAPI,
  system: ActorSystem,
  executionContext: ExecutionContext,
  configuration: Configuration
) {
  private def buildTwitterEnumerator(
    consumerKey: ConsumerKey,
    requestToken: RequestToken,
    topics: Seq[String]
  ): Enumerator[JsObject] = {
    val (iteratee, enumerator) = Concurrent.joined[Array[Byte]]
```

Defines the method for building the enumerator that streams the parsed tweets

Creates a linked pair of iteratee and enumerator as a simple adapter in the pipeline

```
    val url =
      "https://stream.twitter.com/1.1/statuses/filter.json"
    implicit val ec = executionContext

    val formattedTopics = topics
      .map(t => "#" + t)
      .mkString(",")

    ws
      .url(url)
      .sign(OAuthCalculator(consumerKey, requestToken))
      .postAndRetrieveStream(
        Map("track" -> Seq(formattedTopics))
      ) { response =>
        Logger.info("Status: " + response.status)
        iteratee
      }.map { _ =>
        Logger.info("Twitter stream closed")
      }

    val jsonStream: Enumerator[JsObject] = enumerator &>
      Encoding.decode() &>
      Enumeratee.grouped(JsonIteratees.jsSimpleObject)

    jsonStream
  }
}
```

Formats the topics you want to track

Sends a POST request and fetches the stream from Twitter. This method expects to be fed a body as well as a consumer.

Passes in the iteratee as a consumer. The stream will flow through this iteratee to the joined enumerator.

Transforms the stream by decoding and parsing it

Returns the transformed stream as an enumerator

This code may look vaguely familiar to you. Indeed, we wrote something very similar in chapter 2. Back then, we also included a broadcasting mechanism to allow multiple clients to connect to the stream, but we won't do this here because we want to focus on manipulating the stream with Akka Streams.

Don't forget to add the workaround to the OAuth bug in build.sbt:

```
libraryDependencies += "com.ning" % "async-http-client" % "1.9.29"
```

CONVERTING THE ENUMERATOR TO A SOURCE

To be able to use your enumerator with Akka Streams, you'll need to convert it first. Create a new helper method as part of the `TwitterStreamService` as follows.

Listing 9.3 Defining a helper method to convert from enumerator to source

```
import play.api.libs.streams.Streams
import org.reactivestreams.Publisher

private def enumeratorToSource[Out](
  enum: Enumerator[Out]
): Source[Out, Unit] = {
  val publisher: Publisher[Out] =
    Streams.enumeratorToPublisher(enum)
  Source(publisher)
}
```

Turns the enumerator into a Reactive Streams publisher

Turns the publisher into an Akka Streams source

The Play Streams library provides the tools necessary to interface between iteratees, enumerators, and their Reactive Streams–equivalent publishers and subscribers. You can use this to build the plumbing necessary for converting from one realm to another.

> **PRESERVATION OF NONBLOCKING BACK PRESSURE** Iteratees provide non-blocking back pressure and the Play Streams library makes sure that this property is preserved when converting to or from a publisher.

CREATING A CUSTOM FAN-OUT JUNCTION USING FLEXIROUTE

We've now reached the point where we need to split the stream into substreams, one per topic. For this purpose, we'll use `FlexiRoute`, which lets us define custom route junctions. The shape of our splitter will depend on the topics we want to track, so we have to define it on the fly as part of the function that we'll call to produce and run the graph.

Start to build the `stream` method of the `TwitterStreamService` as follows.

Listing 9.4 Creating the `SplitByTopic` junction using `FlexiRoute`

```
def stream(topicsAndDigestRate: Map[String, Int]):
  Enumerator[JsValue] = {

  import FanOutShape._

  class SplitByTopicShape[A <: JsObject](
    _init: Init[A] = Name[A]("SplitByTopic")
  ) extends FanOutShape[A](_init) {
    protected override def construct(i: Init[A]) =
      new SplitByTopicShape(i)
    val topicOutlets = topicsAndDigestRate.keys.map { topic =>
      topic -> newOutlet[A]("out-" + topic)
    }.toMap
  }

  class SplitByTopic[A <: JsObject]
    extends FlexiRoute[A, SplitByTopicShape[A]](
      new SplitByTopicShape, Attributes.name("SplitByTopic")
    ) {
    import FlexiRoute._

    override def createRouteLogic(p: PortT) = new RouteLogic[A] {
      def extractFirstHashTag(tweet: JsObject) =
        (tweet \ "entities" \ "hashtags")
          .asOpt[JsArray]
          .flatMap { hashtags =>
            hashtags.value.headOption.map { hashtag =>
              (hashtag \ "text").as[String]
            }
          }
```

Defines the stream function that you'll feed with the topics and their associated rates

Specifies that you want to get an enumerator as a result to feed it into a WebSocket connection.

Defines the shape of the custom junction by extending FanOutShape. Because this is a fan-out junction, you only describe the output ports (outlets) because there is only one input port.

Creates one output port per topic and keeps these ports in a map so that you can retrieve them by topic later

Defines the custom junction by extending FlexiRoute

Defines the routing logic of the junction where you'll define how elements get routed

Extracts the first topic out of a tweet. You'll split using only the first topic in this example.

```
      override def initialState =
        State[Any](DemandFromAny(p.topicOutlets.values.toSeq :_*)) {
          (ctx, _, element) =>
            extractFirstHashTag(element).foreach { topic =>
              p.topicOutlets.get(topic).foreach { port =>
                ctx.emit(port)(element)
              }
            }
            SameState
        }
      override def initialCompletionHandling = eagerClose
    }
  }

  Enumerator.empty[JsValue] // we need to continue implementing here
}
```

Specifies the demand condition that you want to use. In this case you trigger when any of the outward streams is ready to receive more elements.

Uses the first hash of a tweet to route it to the appropriate port, ignoring tweets that don't match.

This listing looks somewhat daunting—indeed, there's quite a bit of boilerplate associated with creating a custom junction. But the general mechanism by which you define your custom junction shouldn't be too complicated to understand. You start by defining the shape that the junction has. In this case it will have one input port (you don't need to specify this, since this is already defined by `FlexiRoute`), and a specified number of output ports, depending on how many topics you want to track.

An interesting aspect of the routing is the specification of a *demand condition.* Because Akka Streams have nonblocking back pressure, your element needs to be aware of upstream demand and specify how it wants to react to that demand. In this example, you want to continue processing as soon as demand is available on one of the output ports, so you use the `DemandFromAny` condition. There are two other demand conditions you could use: `DemandFromAll`, which will wait until there is demand on all ports before triggering the routing, and `DemandFrom`, which will trigger when there is demand on the specified port.

Finally, you may have noticed that you only look at the first hashtag to decide how to route a tweet. You also discard (don't emit) any element for which the first hashtag isn't one of the expected topics. This could be improved on by emitting the element on all streams for which there are matching topics.

ALTERNATIVE SPLITTING STRATEGY In this example we used a custom element to split the stream. Akka Streams also provides a `groupBy` operation that lets you group elements of a stream by topic, effectively producing a stream of streams. The advantage of this approach over ours is that you wouldn't need to know beforehand which topics to expect. There's one catch: at present the only means to flatten this stream of streams back into one stream is to concatenate all streams. This doesn't work very well when the streams are potentially infinite (only the first stream would be visible). Future versions of the Akka Streams library will provide the `FlattenStrategy.merge`, which will allow you to interleave elements from multiple substreams.

STARTING TO BUILD THE FLOWGRAPH

Let's build our graph. The first step is to add all elements to the graph, as follows.

Listing 9.5 Adding all required elements to the graph with the `FlowGraph` builder

```
def stream(topicsAndDigestRate: Map[String, Int]):
  Enumerator[JsValue] = {

  // ...

  implicit val fm = ActorMaterializer()(system)

  val enumerator = buildTwitterEnumerator(
    consumerKey, requestToken, topicsAndDigestRate.keys.toSeq
  )
  val sink = Sink.publisher[JsValue]
  val graph = FlowGraph.closed(sink) { implicit builder => out =>
    val in = builder.add(enumeratorToSource(enumerator))
    val splitter = builder.add(new SplitByTopic[JsObject])
    val groupers = topicsAndDigestRate.map { case (topic, rate) =>
      topic -> builder.add(Flow[JsObject].grouped(rate))
    }
    val taggers = topicsAndDigestRate.map { case (topic, _) =>
      topic -> {
        val t = Flow[Seq[JsObject]].map { tweets =>
          Json.obj("topic" -> topic, "tweets" -> tweets)
        }
        builder.add(t)
      }
    }
    val merger = builder.add(Merge[JsValue](topicsAndDigestRate.size))

    // TODO: here we will need to wire the graph
  }
  val publisher = graph.run()
  Streams.publisherToEnumerator(publisher)
}
```

Annotations:
- Defines a sink that the data will flow to. Uses a sink that will produce a Reactive Streams publisher, which you'll later turn back into an enumerator.
- Creates a FlowMaterializer that you'll need to be able to run the graph flow
- Builds the enumerator source. Building the OAuth consumerKey and requestToken is left as an exercise.
- Creates the builder for a closed FlowGraph, passing in the sink as an output value that will be materialized when the flow runs
- Adds the source to the graph
- Adds the custom splitter to the graph
- Adds the groupers to the graph, one for each topic. These will group the specified number of elements together, depending on the rate of each topic.
- Adds the taggers to the graph, one for each topic. These will take the grouped tweets and build one JSON object out of them, tagging it with the topic.
- Adds a merger to the graph to merge all streams back together
- Runs the graph. The materialized result will be the publisher, which you can convert back to an enumerator.

You start by creating a `Source` based on the enumerator you built previously, and you define a `Sink` to which all the data will flow. Because the Play Streams library provides a method to turn a Reactive Streams `Publisher` into an `Enumerator`, you create a publisher `Sink` and pass it in as an argument to the `FlowGraph` builder. The result is that once this graph runs, the `Publisher` will be materialized, allowing you to turn it back into an `Enumerator` that you can use to feed the data to a WebSocket.

Inside the `FlowGraph.closed(sink)` block, you add the individual flow elements to the graph using the following building blocks:

- `in`—A `Source` that you obtain from converting the enumerator
- `splitter`—The `SplitByTopic` junction
- `groupers`—A map of `Flow[JSObject].grouped()` flows that groups elements together, producing elements of type `Seq[JSObject]` as output
- `taggers`—A map of `Flow[Seq[JSObject]].map()` flows that builds one wrapper JSON object containing the topic and the grouped tweets
- `merger`—A `Merge` junction that will merge back the streams that you fanned out in the `splitter`

As a next step, you need to wire your graph or you won't be able to run it.

WIRING THE GRAPH

Everything is in place for wiring your graph. Complete the `FlowGraph` block as follows.

Listing 9.6 Wiring the graph using the `FlowGraph` builder

```
builder.addEdge(in, splitter.in)
splitter
  .topicOutlets
  .zipWithIndex
  .foreach { case ((topic, port), index) =>
    val grouper = groupers(topic)
    val tagger = taggers(topic)
    builder.addEdge(port, grouper.inlet)
    builder.addEdge(grouper.outlet, tagger.inlet)
    builder.addEdge(tagger.outlet, merger.in(index))
  }
builder.addEdge(merger.out, out.inlet)
```

- Connects your source to the splitter's inlet (`builder.addEdge(in, splitter.in)`)
- Repeats the wiring for each of the outlets of the splitter (`.foreach { ... }`)
- Connects the outlet of the splitter (the substream) to the grouper for this topic (`builder.addEdge(port, grouper.inlet)`)
- Connects the outlet of the grouper to the inlet of the tagger (`builder.addEdge(grouper.outlet, tagger.inlet)`)
- Connects the outlet of the tagger to one of the ports of the merger (`builder.addEdge(tagger.outlet, merger.in(index))`)
- Connects the outlet of the merger to the inlet of the output publisher (`builder.addEdge(merger.out, out.inlet)`)

That's all! You've added all the required wires for your graph. If there's a problem with your wiring, you'll be notified at runtime.

Indeed, the `FlowGraph` isn't capable of knowing at compile time whether the graph makes sense. In our case, this is easy to understand—if, for example, we didn't provide any topics, the resulting graph wouldn't be complete or connected, but this piece of information would only be available at runtime.

> **DSL FOR GRAPH WIRING** Akka Streams provides a DSL for drawing a graph using the `~>` and `<~` operators. We can't use this DSL for this example, or rather, it wouldn't be very elegant to use it because we don't have a fixed set of topics. If we could use it, however, this is what our code would look like:

```
val f = FlowGraph.closed(publisher) { implicit builder => out =>
  import FlowGraph.Implicits._
  val in = ...
```

```
    val splitter = ...
    val grouper1, grouper2, grouper3 = ...
    val tagger1, tagger2, tagger3 = ...
    val merger = ...

    in ~> splitter ~> grouper1 ~> tagger1 ~> merger ~> out
          splitter ~> grouper2 ~> tagger2 ~> merger
          splitter ~> grouper3 ~> tagger3 ~> merger
  }
```

As you can see, this syntax is much more elegant and should be preferred when building graphs that have a well-defined set of elements.

DELIVERING THE STREAM TO THE CLIENT

The hardest part is done. Now we just need to send the stream to the client via WebSockets. As a rudimentary user interface, we'll use the query string to let the user specify the topics and the desired rate, like so:

```
http://localhost:9000/
  ?topic=akka:5
  &topic=playframework:1
```

Each `topic` query parameter holds a specific topic and the desired rate, separated by a colon.

This simple user interface will work as shown in figure 9.5.

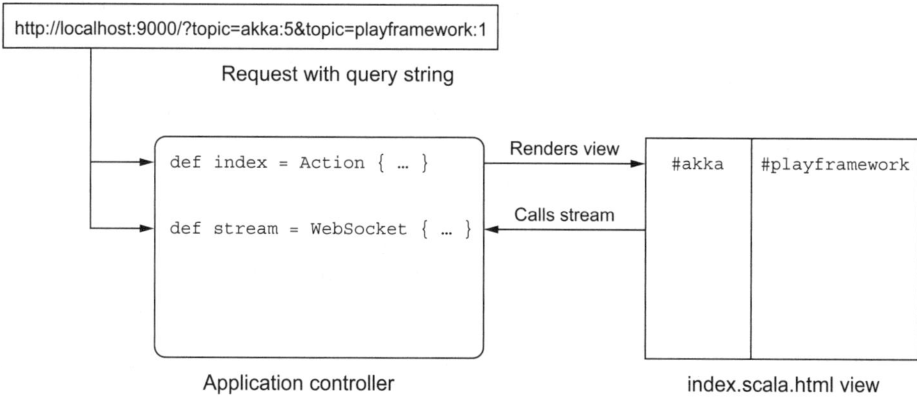

Figure 9.5 Simple user interface to trigger the stream

This is how it works:

- The `index` action of the `Application` controller will parse the query string into a `Map[String, Int]`, and then call an `index` view, passing it the parsed map of topics and rates as well as the raw query string (you'll need this one to initiate a WebSocket connection from the view).

- The `stream` action of the `Application` controller will also parse the query string into a `Map[String, Int]`, and then use the service you just built to establish the stream, using it to feed a WebSocket.
- The view will have one column per topic and append each new digest object to the right column. It will do so after opening a WebSocket connection to the server.

Create (or replace) the file app/views/index.scala.html with the following.

Listing 9.7 Building a view that splits the topics by column

```
@(topicsAndRate: Map[String, Int], queryString: String)
 (implicit request: RequestHeader)
 <!DOCTYPE html>
<html>
  <head>
    <title>Reactive Tweets</title>
    <script src="//code.jquery.com/jquery-1.11.3.min.js"></script>
    <link
      rel="stylesheet"
      href="http://maxcdn.bootstrapcdn.com/bootstrap/3.3.5/css/
                 bootstrap.min.css">
  </head>
  <body>
  @if(topicsAndRate.nonEmpty) {
    <div class="row">
      @topicsAndRate.keys.map { topic =>
        <div
          id="@topic"
          class="col-md-@{ 12 / (topicsAndRate.size) }">
        </div>
      }
    </div>
    <script type="text/javascript">
      function appendTweet(topic, text) {
        var tweet = document.createElement("p");
        var message = document.createTextNode(text);
        tweet.appendChild(message);
        document.getElementById(topic).appendChild(tweet);
      }
      function connect(url) {
        var tweetSocket = new WebSocket(url);
        tweetSocket.onmessage = function (event) {
          var data = JSON.parse(event.data);
          data.tweets.forEach(function(tweet) {
            appendTweet(data.topic, tweet.text);
          });
        };
      }
      connect(
        '@routes.Application.stream().webSocketURL()?@queryString'
```

Lays out the columns using Twitter Bootstrap, the grid having 12 as the largest width (annotates the `class="col-md-@{ 12 / (topicsAndRate.size) }">` line)

Defines a function that appends a tweet to a given topic column (annotates the `function appendTweet(topic, text) {` line)

Appends the tweet to the right column (annotates the `appendTweet(data.topic, tweet.text);` line)

```
    );
  </script>
} else { No topics selected. }
</body>
</html>
```

To establish the WebSocket connection based on an enumerator, we'll use a slightly different approach than the one we've used so far with an actor. It's possible to create a WebSocket connection directly using an enumerator-iteratee pair that models the downstream and upstream components of a two-directional WebSocket connection. Not only is this more convenient in our case, but it also brings with it automatic back pressure on the server side (in this example, we won't make use of this because the client side is only consuming data and not producing it, but in other cases this could be useful).

Create the `Application` controller as follows.

Listing 9.8 Creating a WebSocket using an enumerator as source stream

```
package controllers

import javax.inject.Inject

import play.api.libs.iteratee._
import play.api.libs.json._
import play.api.mvc._
import services.TwitterStreamService

class Application @Inject() (twitterStream: TwitterStreamService)
  extends Controller {
  def index = Action { implicit request =>
    val parsedTopics = parseTopicsAndDigestRate(request.queryString)
    Ok(views.html.index(parsedTopics, request.rawQueryString))
  }
  def stream = WebSocket.using[JsValue] { request =>
    val parsedTopics = parseTopicsAndDigestRate(request.queryString)
    val out = twitterStream.stream(parsedTopics)
    val in: Iteratee[JsValue, Unit] = Iteratee.ignore[JsValue]
    (in, out)
  }
  private def parseTopicsAndDigestRate(
      queryString: Map[String, Seq[String]]
    ): Map[String, Int] = ??? // TODO
}
```

Creates a WebSocket; the channels will use JsValue as the format

Creates the output enumerator using the streaming service you've built

Ignores any messages coming from the client

Returns the pair of input and output channels required to build the WebSocket

With this approach, the WebSocket is modeled as a bidirectional communication channel, each direction being represented by one stream: an iteratee on the consuming end that receives messages from the client, and an enumerator on the producing end, sending the stream to the client.

EXERCISE 9.1

Implement the `parseTopicsAndDigestRate` method. Each topic value should be split using a colon as separator, and the second part should be parsed as Integer.

Finally, don't forget to define the necessary routes in conf/routes:

```
GET       /                   controllers.Application.index
GET       /stream             controllers.Application.stream
```

RUNNING THE GRAPH AND OBSERVING BACK PRESSURE

Once you're done implementing the user interface, it's time to run the stream pipeline. To truly see it in action, I recommend you take a look at https://twitter.com/search-home to see what topics are trending, so you get a lively set of streams. Be careful not to call the stream too frequently, or Twitter will limit your access (you'll notice this if you get back a status code of 420, which stands for "Enhance your calm").

As you'll see if you use different rates for each topic (for example, one topic at 1, one at 5, and one at 20), the different columns fill up at different speeds.

Let's check if the flow is indeed capable of back pressure by introducing an element that will slow down processing a little. At the very end of the flow, right before you pass the stream to the sink, introduce a stage that will sleep for a while, as follows.

Listing 9.9 Slowing down the flow

```
val sleeper = builder.add(Flow[JsValue].map { element =>
  Thread.sleep(5000)
  element
})
builder.addEdge(merger.out, sleeper.inlet)
builder.addEdge(sleeper.outlet, out.inlet)
```

Start the stream again and observe it for a moment. It's helpful if at least one of the observed topics has a rate of 1, giving you the chance to see that it indeed takes 5 seconds for the elements to arrive.

After a moment you should be disconnected by Twitter:

```
[info] - application - Twitter stream closed
```

This behavior is new. Before, we could let our stream run for a long time without disconnection. As stated in the Twitter Streaming API documentation (https://dev.twitter.com/streaming/overview/connecting), slow clients are disconnected after a bit, because Twitter doesn't want to have to buffer for them. You can conclude from this result that your stream is indeed capable of back pressure, from the very end up to Twitter where it hits a hard limit.

9.3 Summary

In this chapter we took a crash course in manipulating asynchronous streams with Akka Streams. In particular:

- We discussed the benefits of having the Reactive Streams standard describing a low-level interface for asynchronous flows with nonblocking back pressure.
- We introduced Akka Streams and the components that make a flow graph.
- We built a flow graph using the streaming Twitter API, employing a custom routing junction to split the source stream by topic.

Reactive Streams is a very promising standard, and its implementations, although fairly young, are already showing how easy stream manipulation can be, given the right tooling.

As we're getting closer to the end of the book, let's now look at one very important aspect in the lifecycle of reactive web applications that we haven't yet talked about at all: deploying them!

10 Deploying reactive Play applications

This chapter covers

- Preparing a Play application for production deployment
- Setting up a continuous integration server and running integration tests with Selenium
- Deploying a Play application to the Clever Cloud PaaS and to your own server

One of the most critical aspects of building a reactive web application is deploying it correctly. If, for example, you deploy the application on a traditional application container, it may not have the capability to scale in and out automatically, hence losing the elastic aspect of a reactive application. It's therefore important to be well aware of what happens with the application once deployed and whether it is implemented in such a way that it can meet the requirements necessary for a truly reactive deployment.

In this chapter we'll take a simple Play application, make it ready for production, and then see how to build and test it using the Jenkins CI (continuous integration) server (https://jenkins-ci.org) to finally deploy it. We'll use two deployment

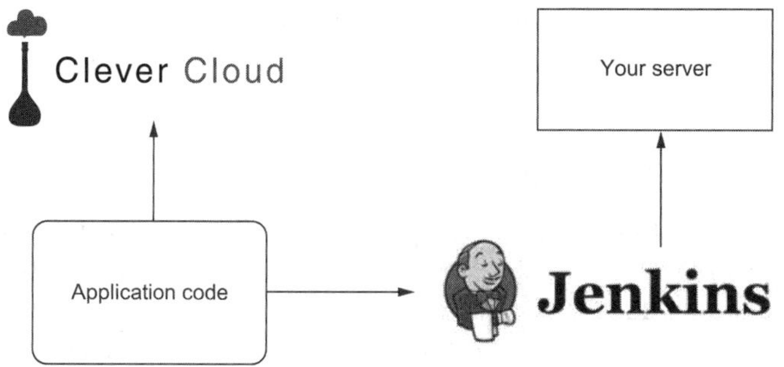

Figure 10.1 The two deployment models explored in this chapter: fully managed with Clever Cloud and self-managed with Jenkins and your own server

methods: the managed Clever Cloud PaaS (Platform-as-a-Service: http://clever-cloud.com) and your own server, as shown in figure 10.1.

> **WHY CLEVER CLOUD?** We're using Clever Cloud as a PaaS in this chapter because it provides autoscalability, which is core to the idea of reactive web applications. Other PaaS platforms such as Heroku don't presently offer this capability, and Infrastructure-as-a-Service providers such as Amazon Web Services don't offer a fully managed deployment flow (you have to set up everything on your own).

In this chapter we'll explore two models of deployment: one that we take care of ourselves and that has a continuous integration step versus one that is fully managed and doesn't include continuous integration. If you want to use a fully managed flow including continuous integration, you could look at services such as Travis CI (http://travis-ci.org) or CloudBees (https://www.cloudbees.com), which provide fully managed continuous integration solutions.

> **WHY IS CONTINUOUS INTEGRATION PART OF THIS CHAPTER ON DEPLOYMENT?** You may be wondering why we're addressing the topic of continuous integration as part of this chapter on deployment. After all, continuous integration is often thought of as being part of testing. As it turns out though (and as you'll see later in this chapter), continuous integration servers play an increasingly important role in software projects beyond merely running tests. In fact, they're at the core of many deployment strategies, and in some cases the deployment of entire, complex applications is completely automated through these tools (this process is then appropriately called *continuous deployment*). In the case of reactive applications, you want to make sure that whatever you deploy works, and hence it's a good idea to set up a continuous integration server that performs all the tests and deploys a test environment, and then to use the same build to deploy the production deployment.

10.1 Preparing a Play application for production

The first step toward deploying an application to production is to fine-tune a number of settings that will improve its performance in a production environment, and also to configure it in such a manner that it can be easily monitored and errors can be diagnosed. Let's start with creating a sample application that we'll then make ready for production.

10.1.1 Creating a simple application to deploy

In the previous chapters we built fairly elaborate example applications to explore the concepts presented in those chapters. For the purpose of deploying an application, we'll use a simple example. There's no need to have a complex application at hand for its deployment since the principles used for deployment of a Play application should always be similar.

Create a new empty application by using the Activator as we've done previously. We'll create a simple application that, upon the click of a button, will fill a `div` with some text, all of this being done by JavaScript.

As a first step, add the dependency on the jQuery WebJar as well as to the `webjars-play` library itself in build.sbt:

```
libraryDependencies ++= Seq(
  "org.webjars" %% "webjars-play" % "2.4.0-1",
  "org.webjars" % "jquery" % "2.1.4"
)
```

Also add the following route to conf/routes to ease the discovery of WebJars in the application:

```
GET     /webjars/*file     controllers.WebJarAssets.at(file)
```

The `WebJarAssets` controller is provided by the `webjars-play` dependency. This in turn makes it possible to resolve the path to the jQuery dependency in app/views/main.scala in the following manner:

```
<script
  type='text/javascript'
  src='@routes.WebJarAssets.at(WebJarAssets.locate("jquery.min.js"))'>
</script>
```

Once you're done setting up WebJars, create the file app/assets/javascripts/application.js with the contents of listing 10.1.

Listing 10.1 Simple JavaScript file that populates a `div` when a button is clicked

```
$(document).ready(function () {
    $('#button').on('click', function () {
        $('#text').text('Hello');
    });
});
```

Now, adjust the app/views/index.scala.html file to contain what is necessary for this to work.

Listing 10.2 Creating the HTML layout for the application

```
@(message: String)
@main(message) {
    <button id="button">Click me</button>
    <div id="text"></div>
}
```

Finally, load the application.js file in main.scala.html:

```
<script
  type='text/javascript'
  src='@routes.Assets.versioned("javascripts/application.js")'>
</script>
```

And that's it for our simple example application!

> **COMPILING JAVASCRIPT CODE** Assets that are placed in the app/assets directory are automatically managed by a few `sbt-web` plugins, one of which is `sbt-jshint`, which is included in the default `activator` template and runs JSHint (http://jshint.com) to check your code.
>
> To see it in action, remove the semicolon on line 4 of listing 10.1 and reload the application. You'll be presented with a compilation error, pin-pointing the missing semicolon in application.js.

EXERCISE 10.1

To make the application a bit more interesting and have a look at configuration management, fetch the text to be deployed from the server via an AJAX request and pass in a value from application.conf.

You'll need to take the following steps:

- Create a `text` action in the `Application` controller that reads the "text" configuration parameter from application.conf. For this purpose, use dependency injection to `@Inject` an instance of `play.api.Configuration`.
- Create a reverse JavaScript route to access the route from the JavaScript file. You can embed the reverse routes in main.scala.html using the helper syntax `@helper.javascriptRouter("jsRoutes")(routes.javascript.Application.text)`.
- Make the AJAX call to retrieve the text parameter. The generated router already includes a mechanism for this, and you can call the method `jsRoutes.controllers.Application.text().ajax({ success: …, error: … })` for this purpose.

If you have any trouble with this, you can always peek at the resources that come with this chapter.

10.1.2 Writing and running integration tests with Selenium

To see whether our application is behaving correctly, we can write an integration test that will emulate the behavior of a user and test the entire application using a browser. If you're aiming at a continuous delivery lifecycle for your application, then making it possible to run these tests is part of your deployment (and writing them becomes part of writing your application). We'll revisit the topic of testing in chapter 11 where we'll focus on testing the reactive properties of an application. In this section you'll see how to configure your deployment to enable running Selenium browser tests, which are a powerful tool but not always straightforward to set up in practice.

With the help of ScalaTest and the ScalaTest + Play library (http://scalatest.org/plus/play), it's easy to integrate the Selenium WebDriver automation library (http://www.seleniumhq.org). Selenium lets you remotely "drive" a browser and emulate what a user would do—read text, click on buttons, and so on—in order to check if the application behaves as it should from the user perspective. This type of testing is pretty powerful, as it tests the entire (integrated) application as opposed to single components, and can detect errors that occur when those components interact with each other.

Start by adding the following dependencies in build.sbt, after removing the automatically generated dependency on `specs2`:

```
libraryDependencies ++= Seq(
  // ...
  "org.seleniumhq.selenium" % "selenium-firefox-driver" % "2.53.0",
  "org.scalatest" %% "scalatest" % "2.2.1" % "test",
  "org.scalatestplus" %% "play" % "1.4.0-M4" % "test"
)
```

> **FIREFOX DRIVER VERSION** The version of the Selenium Firefox driver needs to be compatible with the version of Firefox you're using. If you run into problems while trying to run the tests, make sure to use the latest version of the driver. You can find a list of available versions at http://mvnrepository.com/artifact/org.seleniumhq.selenium/selenium-firefox-driver.

As a next step, create the file test/ApplicationSpec.scala with the contents of listing 10.3 (if you used the `activator` template, a few tests were already created—make sure to remove those).

Listing 10.3 Testing the application with a Selenium integration test

```
import org.scalatest._
import play.api.test._
import play.api.test.Helpers._
import org.scalatestplus.play._

class ApplicationSpec
  extends PlaySpec
  with OneServerPerSuite
  with OneBrowserPerSuite
```

Extends the PlaySpec, which provides Play-specific context to a ScalaTest spec

Uses the same test Play server for the whole test suite

Uses the same browser instance for the whole test suite

```
with FirefoxFactory {                    <-- Uses Firefox as a web browser
"The Application" must {
  "display a text when clicking on a button" in {
    go to (s"http://localhost:$port")    <-- Navigates to the index page
    pageTitle mustBe "Hello"
    click on find(id("button")).value    <-- Clicks on the button
    eventually {                         <-- Tells ScalaTest that this check isn't immediate since asynchronous behavior is involved
      val expectedText = app.configuration.getString("text")
      find(id("text")).map(_.text) mustBe expectedText   <-- Tests if the displayed text corresponds to the expected one from the configuration file
    }
  }
 }
}
```

For this test to run smoothly, you'll need to have Firefox installed on your computer. You then can run the test using the `test` command in the sbt console; this should open a Firefox browser window and you should see the button being clicked and the test displayed.

> **RUNNING TESTS AGAINST MULTIPLE BROWSERS** Play also has built-in support for running other browsers such as Chrome, Safari, and Internet Explorer (and HTMLUnit—but HTMLUnit doesn't really support JavaScript). It's possible to have tests run on multiple browsers instead of just one using the `AllBrowsersPerSuite` trait, which lets you specify which browsers should be used.

We now have an application and are checking its functionality using an integration test—the next step is to make it ready for production!

10.1.3 Preparing the application for production

Before deploying an application to production, several steps need to be taken.

SETTING THE APPLICATION SECRET

The application secret is stored in conf/application.conf; a new one can be generated using the `playGenerateSecret` command in the sbt console. Note that this command won't replace the value in application.conf, but simply print out a generated value. If you want to save it as well, you should use the `playUpdateSecret` command.

For production deployment, it's normal to set values such as passwords or keys using an environment variable. You can pass the configuration value of the Play secret via environment variables in two ways:

- By launching the Play script and passing the property with the `-Dplay.crypto.secret` flag if you're running the script on your own
- By telling application.conf to read the value from an environment variable of your choice

Since we're going to deploy the application to a PaaS, the second option fits our purpose best. Edit appliction.conf and extend the `play.crypto.secret` definition:

```
play.crypto.secret="changeme"
play.crypto.secret=${?APPLICATION_SECRET}
```

If the environment variable `APPLICATION_SECRET` is set, then `play/crypto.secret` will get its value; otherwise, `play.crypto.secret` will remain as is.

Previously, you created a configuration setting for specifying the text to be displayed when a button is clicked. Make sure to also add an optional override as you've done for `play.crypto.secret` to allow for provisioning the value of your configuration parameter through an environment variable.

CUSTOMIZING LOGGING

By default, Play provides an optimized version of the configuration that, for example, takes care of automatic log rotation (you can check the Play reference documentation [https://www.playframework.com/documentation/latest/SettingsLogger] for details). If you have the need to customize it even further, check out the Logback (http://logback.qos.ch) documentation.

If you'd like to specify your own Logback configuration for production, you can use the `-Dlogger.resource` or `-Dlogger.file` flags when launching the application.

OPTIMIZING WEB ASSETS

Chances are that a larger web application will have a number of JavaScript and CSS assets. Loading them quickly is crucial, as this makes a big impact on the speed of the application, especially on mobile devices. Since we have sbt-web at our disposal to customize the pipeline for handling assets, let's use it.

One of the first steps is to set up RequireJS optimization (http://requirejs.org). RequireJS provides dependency management to JavaScript applications and also provides a pipeline that combines and minimizes all JavaScript assets. The `sbt-rjs` plugin (https://github.com/sbt/sbt-rjs) is already loaded in `project/plugins.sbt` as it's part of the activator template; all we need to do is to activate it. In this section we'll look at a basic setup of RequireJS for our small application. If you're interested in a more advanced example, check out the Play-Angular-Require seed (https://github.com/mariussoutier/play-angular-require-seed) by Marius Soutier that provides a template for building a project with Play, RequireJS, WebJars, and AngularJS.

Point your editor at build.sbt and edit the application.js file to look like the following listing.

Listing 10.4 Configuring the build pipeline for RequireJS optimization

```
name := """ch10"""

version := "1.0-SNAPSHOT"

lazy val root = (project in file(".")).enablePlugins(
  PlayScala
)

scalaVersion := "2.11.7"
```

Enables the PlayScala plugin. It has a dependency on SbtWeb, so we don't need to specify that one explicitly.

```
libraryDependencies ++= Seq(
  "org.webjars" %% "webjars-play" % "2.4.0-1",
  "org.webjars" % "jquery" % "2.1.4",
  "org.scalatest" %% "scalatest" % "2.2.1" % "test",
  "org.scalatestplus" %% "play" % "1.4.0-M4" % "test"
)

routesGenerator := InjectedRoutesGenerator

pipelineStages := Seq(rjs)

RjsKeys.mainModule := "application"

RjsKeys.mainConfig := "application"
```

Adds rjs as first stage of the assets pipeline

Specifies that the main RequireJS module is called "application" (this will resolve to our application.js file)

Specifies that the configuration for RequireJS is located in the application module

By default, RequireJS expects the entry point to be called `main.js`; since we've used a different name, we need to declare that. In principle we could've just used the `main.js` name, but it's good to know about this convention to avoid pitfalls.

As a next step, we need to load RequireJS in `main.scala.html`. Add the following line to the `<head>` section before loading any other script:

```
<script
  data-main="@routes.Assets.versioned("javascripts/application.js")"
  src="@routes.WebJarAssets.at(WebJarAssets.locate("require.min.js"))">
</script>
```

Since the play-webjars library has a dependency on the RequireJS WebJar, we can load RequireJS by using the WebJars mechanism.

You'll need to make one more change to `main.scala.html`: remove the `<script>` tag that loads jQuery. Now that RequireJS is in place, it'll take care of loading the library, as you'll see in a bit.

Finally, we need to configure and use RequireJS. Edit the application.js file to look like the following listing.

Listing 10.5 Using RequireJS to tie together JavaScript dependencies

```
(function (requirejs) {
    'use strict';
    requirejs.config({
        shim: {
            'jsRoutes': {
                deps: [],
                exports: 'jsRoutes'
            }
        },
        paths: {
```

Wraps the entire configuration in a function to avoid polluting the global JavaScript namespace

Configures RequireJS

Tells RequireJS about jsRoutes, which is generated on-the-fly in main.scala.html, by telling it the name of the var that defines it

```
            'jquery': ['../lib/jquery/jquery']
        }
    });
    requirejs.onError = function (err) {
        console.log(err);
    };
    require(['jquery'], function ($) {
        $(document).ready(function () {
            // ...
        });
    });
})(requirejs);
```

Configures the path of the jQuery dependency; this is the resulting path for WebJar dependencies

Configures an error handler in order to be made aware of problems

Uses RequireJS to depend on the jQuery dependency, and executes our initial code

The initial configuration of RequireJS is a bit tiresome, but once it's set up there are major benefits to it. As you can see, we need to configure aspects related to our application, such as the use of the generated `jsRoutes` variable, as well as the exact location of the jQuery library.

In the sbt console, run the `stage` command, which is one way of preparing the application for production deployment. You'll see that RequireJS is now optimizing all the output and running all JavaScript files (including jQuery itself) through an optimization process using the UglifyJS library (https://github.com/mishoo/UglifyJS2) that minifies and compresses JavaScript code. (Also this makes it entirely unreadable for humans, which is something you may want when you publish your JavaScript code on a server, depending on whether you were in a hurry while writing it.)

> **MORE OPTIMIZATIONS** Using RequireJS is just one of the many things you can do to customize the assets pipeline. For example, the sbt-gzip plugin applies gzip compression on top of all assets, the sbt-digest plugin computes checksums for assets and prepends them to the name (this is useful for assets fingerprinting and ETag values), and so on. Check out the sbt-web documentation[1] to get a list of all the possible plugins.

USING A CDN FOR PROVIDING COMMON WEB ASSETS

Content delivery networks (CDNs) are frequently used in web applications to off-load the provisioning of common libraries such as jQuery. CDNs have servers around the globe that serve those assets in an optimal fashion depending on the geographical location of the client. The good news is that WebJars is available via the jsDelivr CDN (http://www.jsdelivr.com), and the sbt-rjs plugin takes care of mapping WebJar libraries to their CDN URL for deployment. Therefore, to use the CDN URLs for the libraries in our application in production, we only need to lean back and let the tooling take care of the rest.

10.2 Setting up continuous integration

If you're aiming to build an application that serves a real-life purpose, a continuous integration server is a must. It eliminates all the hassle of running the build by hand,

---

1 https://github.com/sbt/sbt-web

and most importantly runs all the tests for you automatically, in a clean environment created for this purpose and without blocking your computer while running the tests (which may take increasingly more time as your application and test suite grow).

10.2.1 Running Jenkins via Docker

If you're familiar with the Jenkins CI and have a server or a virtual machine at your disposal for running it, you may skip this section. If not, then let's use Docker (https://www.docker.com) and the Docker Jenkins image (https://registry.hub.docker.com/_/jenkins/) to get started quickly.

> **WHY DOCKER?** Docker offers a mechanism for provisioning and running *containers* with a given application or set of applications. Rather than starting a virtual machine emulator, creating a new virtual machine, installing an operating system, and finally installing the application, container platforms such as Docker make it possible to do all of this using container *images*. These images are meant to be simply downloaded and run with a minimal configuration effort. There are plenty of preconfigured images available ready for use, just as for Jenkins in our case.

You'll first need to install Docker itself (check the Docker website for instructions). If you're developing on OS X, you'll also need to install boot2docker (http://boot2docker.io). Detailed installation instructions as well as an installer can be found on the Docker website at https://docs.docker.com/installation/.

Then, you'll need to fetch and clone a modified version of the Jenkins Docker image that also installs additional components necessary for running the integration tests. In a command line shell in the directory of your choosing, run the following:

```
git clone https://github.com/manuelbernhardt/docker.git
docker build -t docker-jenkins docker
```

This will clone the modified Docker Jenkins build and build it with the tag "docker-jenkins." Next, we need to run this new image in such a way that the sources of the application can be available within the Docker container. For this purpose, create a directory somewhere on your computer, for example, in the ~/jenkins folder, and launch the image with the command shown next.

Listing 10.6 Running the Jenkins Docker image

```
docker run
  --name chapter10-jenkins
  -p 8080:8080
  -v ~/reactive-web-applications/CH10:/var/jenkins_home/ch10
  docker-jenkins
```

- `--name chapter10-jenkins`: Gives a name to the container, which makes it persistent so the settings won't be lost on next start
- `-p 8080:8080`: Maps port 8080 from the host to port 8080 of the container, where Jenkins is running
- `-v ...`: Maps the directory with the sources of this chapter inside of the Jenkins home directory so we can access it from within the container
- `docker-jenkins`: Indicates that we would like to run the image that we just built

Be patient; it may take some time to start up at first!

> **FIGURING OUT THE IP ADDRESS OF THE DOCKER CONTAINER** Normally, the Docker port forwarding should make it so that Jenkins is accessible on port 8080 of your localhost—127.0.0.1. But this may not always work; for example, it doesn't readily work on OS X. You can use `docker ps` to inspect which ports and IP addresses should be in use, and on OS X with boot2docker, you can use the command `boot2docker ip` to figure out which IP address you need to access the docker container.

At this point, Jenkins should be up and running and you should be able to access it at http://localhost:8080 (or at a different IP address, depending on your setup), as shown in figure 10.2.

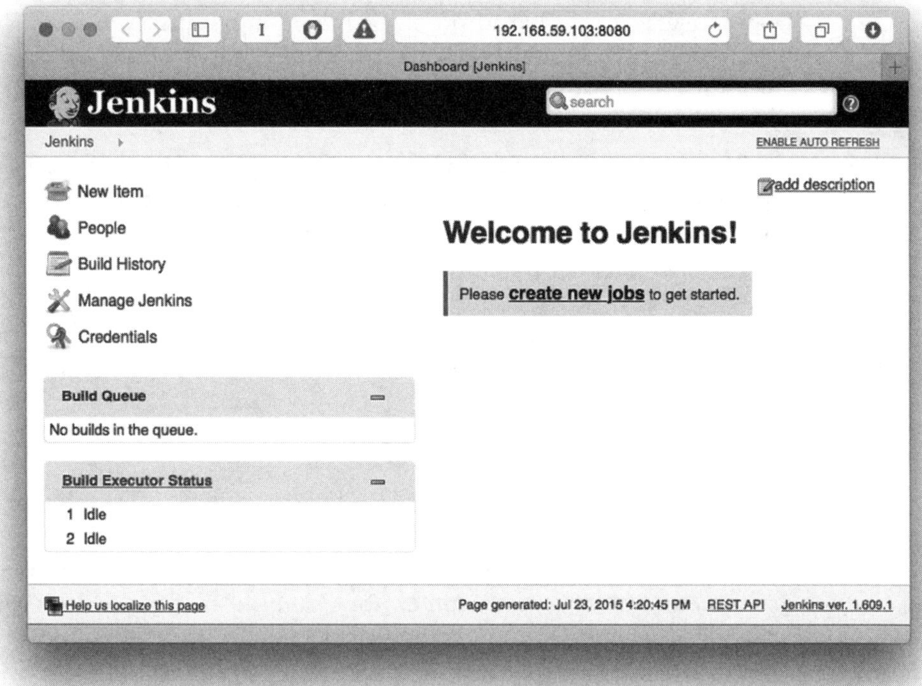

Figure 10.2 Accessing the freshly created Jenkins deployment

10.2.2 *Configuring Jenkins to build our application*

You'll need to take a few steps to configure Jenkins for building the application.

INSTALLING THE NECESSARY PLUGINS

On the left menu, click on Manage Jenkins, then Manage Plugins, and then select the Available tab. We'll need two plugins:

1. The sbt plugin for running our build.
2. The Xvfb plugin for running Firefox inside of a frame buffer for the integration tests. Since the server runs in a "headless" mode (without screen attached), we need a way to emulate a screen that the browser can run in.

Select those plugins and click Download Now and Install After Restart. On the page that shows the progress of the installation, make sure to tick the check box "Restart Jenkins when Installation Is Complete and No Jobs Are Running" for Jenkins to restart right away and activate the new plugin. You may need to refresh the page after a minute if it doesn't do so automatically.

Then, go again to Manage Jenkins, click Script Console, and run the following command in it:

```
hudson.model.DownloadService.Downloadable.all().each {
  it.updateNow()
}
```

This workaround enables you to install sbt automatically.

Next, go again to the Manage Jenkins menu and select the first entry, Configure System. On this page, scroll down to the SBT section and add a new sbt installation. Name it, for example, "default" and select the option Install Automatically with the version 0.13.8. You also need to do the same thing for Xvfb, where you only need to give the installation a name.

CREATING AND RUNNING THE JENKINS JOB

On the main page, click Create New Jobs and create a new freestyle project, naming it, for example, "simple-play-application." Normally, we'd configure the project to be fetched from a version control system such as Git, but since we're running this locally, we'll copy the sources by hand.

As a first step, tick the box "Start Xvfb Before the Build, and Shut It Down After" for the frame buffer to run during the build.

In the Build section, add a new "Execute shell" build step with the following command:

```
rm -rf ${WORKSPACE}/*
cp -R ${JENKINS_HOME}/ch10/* ${WORKSPACE}
```

Then, add a "Build using sbt" job with the actions `compile test dist`.

Finally, in the Post-build Actions section, add the step "Publish JUnit test result report" with the path target/test-reports/*.xml for Jenkins to know where to look for test reports.

Save the configuration and run the build using the menu entry on the left, and be patient—the first execution will need to download quite a number of libraries including sbt itself. You can check the logs during the build and see the test results once it is done, as shown in figure 10.3.

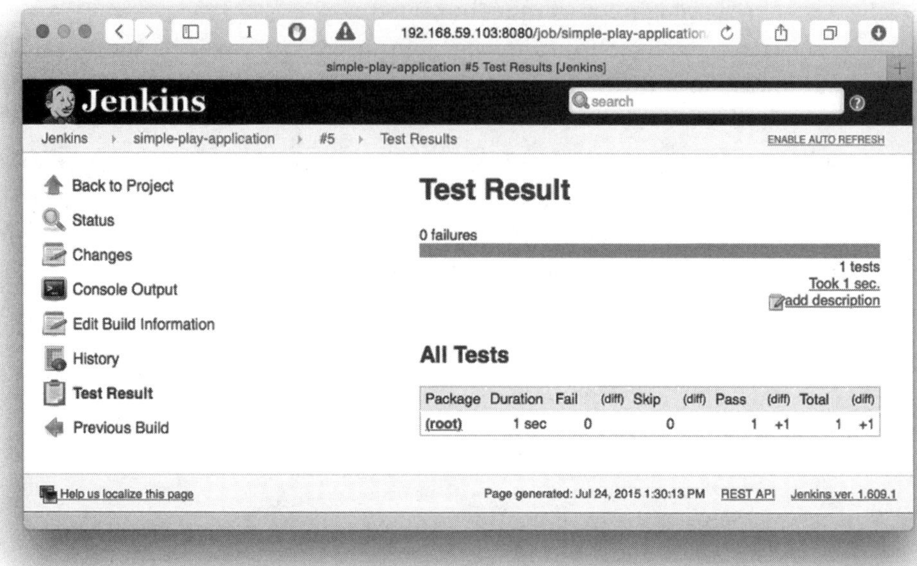

Figure 10.3 Checking the test results in Jenkins

10.3 Deploying the application

We (and our application) are ready to go live! Since we're likely to deploy it often, this process should be as simple as possible. Let's explore two of the many alternatives for deploying an application: the Clever Cloud PaaS and your own server.

10.3.1 Deployment on Clever Cloud

Clever Cloud is a service that takes care of managing and scaling up the necessary server infrastructure required for your application to work. Point your browser to http://clever-cloud.com and create an account. (Clever Cloud will also ask you for SSH keys to let you deploy via Git in a secure manner.) You'll get 20€ of credit for free, which should be sufficient to run our simple application.

Once you're logged in, go to your personal space, click Add an Application, and pick Scala + Play! 2. Give it a name such as "simple-play-application" and create it. At this point you don't need to specify any database to deploy with it because our simple application doesn't use one.

CONFIGURING THE ENVIRONMENT VARIABLES

Clever Cloud lets you configure the environment variables you'd like to see exposed to your application. Make three entries:

1. `JAVA_VERSION`: 8
2. `APPLICATION_SECRET`: Use `playGenerateSecret` command on the sbt shell to get a random value
3. `TEXT`: "Hello from Clever Cloud"

PUSHING THE CODE

Once you're done setting up the application, it's time to push the code. You should see the commands required for this purpose, and will need to run the following command in the directory in which you keep the sources of this chapter:

```
git init
git add .
git commit -m "Initial application sources"
git remote add clever
  https://console.clever-cloud.com/
  users/me/applications/<application-name>/information
git push -u clever master
```

That's it! On the Clever Cloud console you'll now see the logs of the deployment as shown in figure 10.4—although you'll have to be patient at first, as in the beginning the only thing you'll see is a message informing you that your application is currently deploying.

It may take a while until all dependencies are fetched during the first deployment, but once it's done, you should receive an e-mail that the deployment succeeded and be able to access the application.

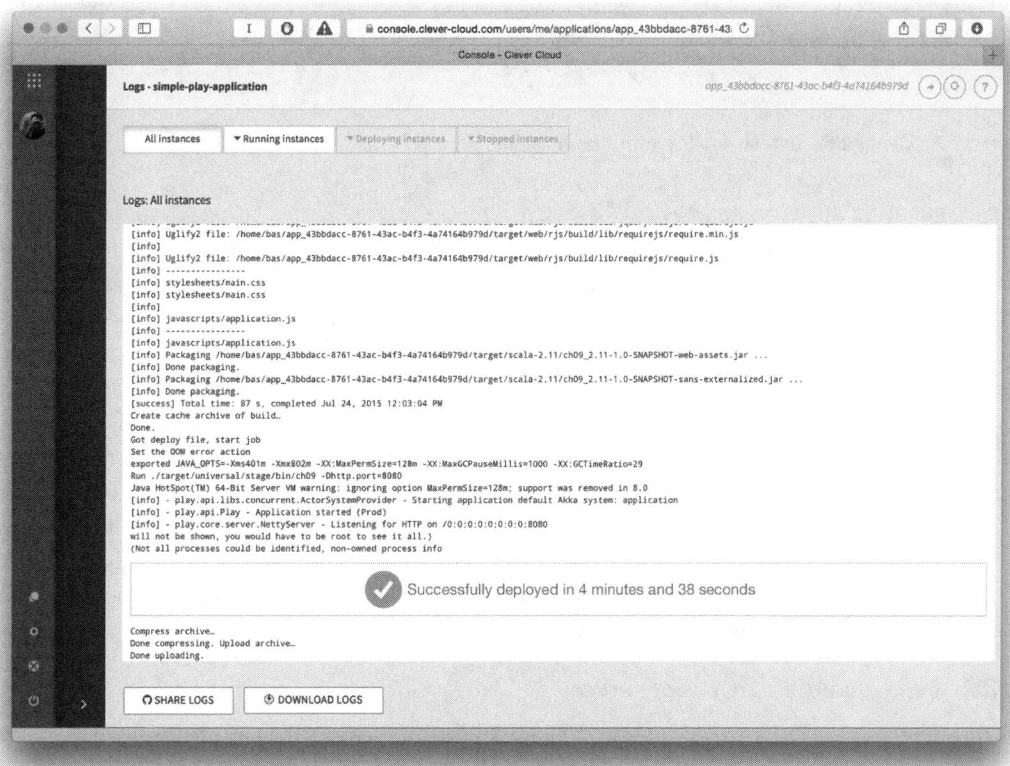

Figure 10.4 Watching the application deploy itself on Clever Cloud

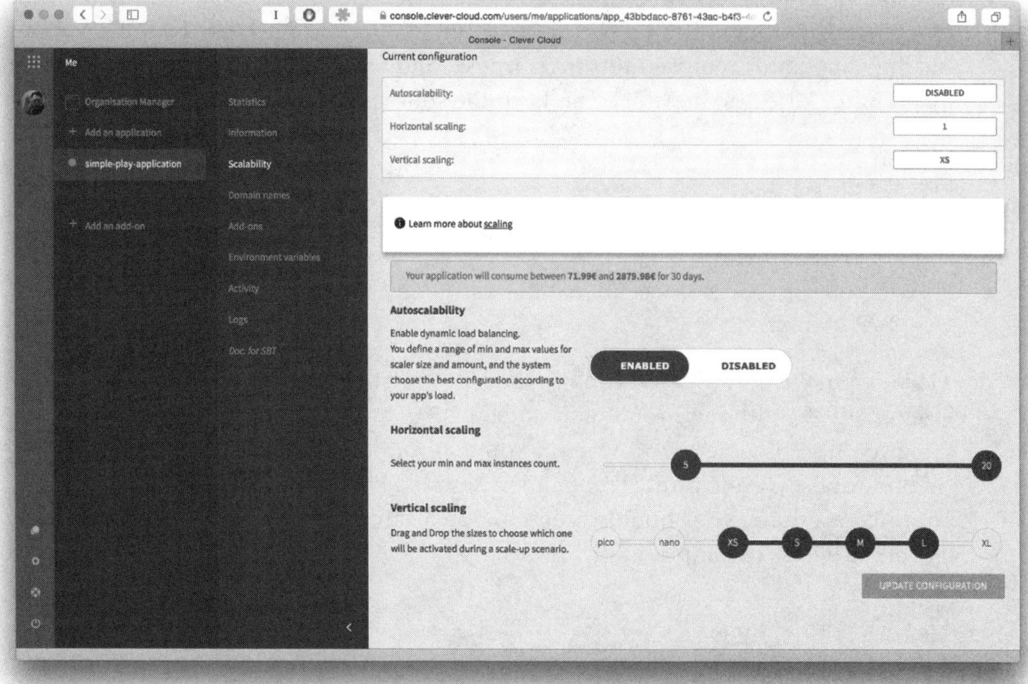

Figure 10.5 Configuring autoscalability with Clever Cloud

ENABLING AUTOSCALABILITY

Clever Cloud can take care of automatically handling horizontal scalability, depending on the current needs of the application. As we discussed at length in chapter 1, this is one of the core features of a reactive web application, and one of the most challenging aspects of operating this type of application.

In the settings of your application on the Clever Cloud console, navigate to the Scalability menu entry and scroll down to Autoscalability. There you'll be able to enable autoscalability and configure both horizontal and vertical scaling. Horizontal scaling specifies the range of nodes you want your application to run on, and vertical scaling specifies the range of instance types you want to use, as shown in figure 10.5. Depending on the load of your application, Clever Cloud will automatically figure out which is the most cost-effective combination of vertical and horizontal scalability to use to operate your application.

10.3.2 Deployment on your own server

There are so many options for packaging and deploying Play applications that it isn't always easy to figure out which approach to take. In fact, the best approach is highly specific to the environment to which you're deploying the application and to the preferences and skills of the operations team taking care of it. Let's explore together three deployment scenarios: a straightforward deployment using a generated script (Play's default), deployment using a generated Debian distribution package, and deployment as a Docker container.

PREPARING THE SERVER

In this step you're free to set up your own server or virtual machine if you have access to one; the only thing you should be aware of is that we'll be using Debian in one of the deployment examples. If you don't have a server or virtual machine at your disposal, no need to worry: since you already went through the trouble of setting up Docker, let's just use a Docker image for running the examples.

Fetch the latest version of a Docker image with Java using the command `docker pull java`. Then, run the Docker container so that there's a shared directory between your host machine and the container through your host's play-docker-home directory (you'll have to create it first):

```
docker run
  9000:9000
  -v ~/play-docker-home:/home/play
  -i -t java:8 /bin/bash
```

This will launch the container and connect you to its shell, from where you have root access. If you use your own server, you'll have to transfer files in a way that suits you best (SCP or any other tool).

Before getting started, let's create a user for the Play application:

```
root@41111c604022:~# adduser --gecos "" play
Adding user `play' ...
Adding new group `play' (1000) ...
Adding new user `play' (1000) with group `play' ...
The home directory `/home/play' already exists.
  Not copying from `/etc/skel'.
adduser: Warning: The home directory `/home/play' does not belong
  to the user you are currently creating.
Enter new UNIX password:
Retype new UNIX password:
passwd: password updated successfully
```

Install `zip` which, we'll need later:

```
apt-get install zip
```

Finally, switch to this user for running our examples:

```
su - play
```

DEPLOYING WITH THE STANDARD DISTRIBUTION BUNDLE

This method of deployment is probably the preferred one if you want to be entirely in control of the lifecycle of the application. The generated script only makes sure to run the application and provides the necessary context for feeding in environment variables.

On your host computer, in a separate shell window, run the sbt console and run the `dist` command. The `dist` command will generate a ZIP archive containing the application ready to be deployed. At the end of the output, you should see a line that looks as follows:

```
[info] Your package is ready in
  /Users/<user>/work/ch10/target/universal/ch10-1.0-SNAPSHOT.zip
```

Copy this file to your ~/ubuntu-home directory to make it available to the Docker container that we use to simulate our container.

Switch back to the Docker container and extract the archive with `unzip ch10_1-1.0-SNAPSHOT.zip`. You can now run the application like so:

```
cd ch10-1.0-SNAPSHOT/bin
./ch10 -DTEXT=Hi
```

You can access it on the IP address of your Docker container on port 9000.

CREATING AND DEPLOYING A DEBIAN PACKAGE

Play uses the sbt-native-packager (http://www.scala-sbt.org/sbt-native-packager) to build the distribution package (including the artifact we used previously by running the `dist` command). This plugin provides many different formats and is easy to configure. Let's create a native Debian package (in essence, a `.deb` file) from our application.

Edit the build.sbt file and make the following changes:

- Add the `DebianPlugin` and `JavaServerAppPackaging` plugins to the list of enabled plugins of the `root` project. The Debian plugin takes care of native Debian packaging, whereas the `JavaServerAppPackaging` takes care of loading the archetype that, among other things, generates the startup scripts.
- Configure the minimal Debian package information as shown in the following listing.

Listing 10.7 Configuring for Debian packaging

```
maintainer := "John Doe <john@doe.com>"
packageSummary in Linux := "Chapter 10 of Reactive Web Applications"

packageDescription :=
"This package installs the Play Application used as an example
  in Chapter 10 of the book Reactive Web Applications"

serverLoading in Debian := ServerLoader.Systemd
```

- Names the maintainer of the package
- Short summary of the package
- Long summary of the package
- Sets the service loading system to SystemD, which is the default in Debian Jessie

You can now build the package with `debian:packageBin` and, once copied over to the shared directory of the Docker container or to your server, install it with `dpkg -i ch10_1.0-SNAPSHOT_all.deb`.

INSTALLING REQUIRED BUILD PACKAGES You'll need to have the packages `fakeroot` and `dpkg` installed to do this build. If you're running OS X, you can install them using Homebrew (http://brew.sh).

CREATING AND RUNNING A DOCKER IMAGE

Creating a Docker image out of your application is simple. Given the existing configuration, just add this line to build.sbt:

```
dockerExposedPorts in Docker := Seq(9000, 9443)
```

This will open up ports 9000 and 9443 for HTTP and HTTPS.

Then, in the sbt console, run the command `docker:publishLocal`. This will build the image and publish it locally to Docker.

Finally, run the image with the following command:

```
docker run -p 9000:9000 ch10:1.0-SNAPSHOT
```

And there you go, the application is running with Docker. From this point on, you can use the image on your own container deployment platform or on a cloud service such as AWS Elastic Beanstalk (http://aws.amazon.com/de/elasticbeanstalk).

DEPLOYING THE APPLICATION AS A WAR PACKAGE Although fairly popular in traditional Java EE environments, deploying a Play application as a WAR package (web application archive) is not recommended, since with this deployment option you lose some of the characteristics of a reactive application. (Depending on the version of the Servlet Standard supported by the application server, this means limited WebSocket support, undependable asynchronous request processing, and so on.) Sometimes, especially in corporate environments with strict deployment policies, it isn't possible to do otherwise though, in which case you can look into using the WAR Plugin (https://github.com/play2war/play2-war-plugin).

10.3.3 Which deployment model to use

As you've seen, there are many different ways in which to deploy a Play application—from a fully managed environment such as Clever Cloud where everything including the build is taken care of, to a bare-metal server setup using a packaged ZIP artifact. What we haven't discussed in terms of custom server deployment is scaling the application. This topic itself is vast and complex enough that it would likely require a book on its own. If you want to start with a simple setup that has two nodes, I invite you to read the official Play documentation, which provides a few example configurations for setting up a load balancer with, for example, Nginx.

Deciding which deployment model to use is more of a business discussion than a technical one, and is somewhat outside the scope of this book. But before making this decision, you should be aware that there is more to it than deploying the application: you also need to monitor it and be able to introspect the logs to analyze error cases. Again, there are managed and self-hosted solutions for these concerns and you (or someone in your organization) will have to make a choice as to which approach to use.

I can't really help you with this decision, as it depends a lot on the environment and organization you're in—I've worked with both fully managed and fully self-hosted operation environments, and both have their upsides and downsides. The only advice I would give is to make an *informed* decision and to take into account the entire set of implications an operational infrastructure has. It's easy to overlook a part of the work that needs to be done or to be seduced by a trend, especially in the ever-evolving technological landscape we live in.

10.4 Summary

In this chapter we've looked at a few aspects of deploying a reactive Play application. In particular, we've talked about

- How to prepare the application and optimize some of the aspects prior to deployment, such as web assets
- How to set up the Jenkins CI server to test your application with Selenium browser tests
- How to deploy and set up scalability for the application using Clever Cloud, and how to package and deploy the application on your own server

The topic of operations is vast and complex. The most important message from this chapter probably is that Play tends to keep up to date with deployment trends and can cater to all kinds of packaging and deployment technologies. Let's now get to the last, and possibly most interesting, part of building reactive web applications: testing them!

11 Testing reactive web applications

This chapter covers

- The various reactive traits you can test
- How to test asynchronous components of your application
- How to test whole applications for resilience, scalability, and responsiveness

Testing web applications is hard, and testing reactive web applications is even harder. Next to all client-side concerns such as browser compatibility and execution on a plethora of mobile devices under varying connection speeds and connection quality, we must also concern ourselves with the guarantees that a reactive web application promises to deliver—being able to react to load by scaling out (and back in), offering a degraded execution rather than complete outage under failure, as well as responding to the user as quickly as possible—with the smallest possible latency.

We've already peeked at various techniques for testing specific parts and behaviors of a reactive application in previous chapters. In this chapter we'll start by taking a high-level look at what exactly needs testing before moving on to how we can achieve some of those tests. Since testing is such a vast topic, this chapter won't attempt to cover the entirety of the topic but will instead focus on giving you a sense of what it means to test a reactive application as opposed to testing only "nonreactive" properties. In the spirit of the previous chapters, you'll also get a chance to get a hands-on experience by, among other things, subjecting an application to copious amounts of load.

11.1 Testing reactive traits

We often think of tests as a way to find out if a piece of code or a component does what it's intended to do, in terms of giving a correct result. When it comes to testing reactive web applications, there's more to it than testing for correctness—we need to additionally ask the following questions about our application or components, in direct connection with the reactive traits:

- *Responsiveness*—Does it produce results in time?
- *Resilience*—When it fails, does it do so gracefully and does it degrade as we intend it to?
- *Elasticity*—Does it scale according to load?

Let's discuss what testing those aspects entails in more detail.

11.1.1 Testing responsiveness

When we want to test responsiveness, what we really want to do is to get a sense of the latency of a specific portion of our application. You may remember our discussion on the subject of latency in chapter 5; if not, here's a quick reminder: Latency is the duration it takes to provide a result to a client and is calculated by taking the sum of all the sequential steps that are taking place during a process. More often than not, it's expressed in milliseconds. If the latency of a component reaches the scale of seconds, chances are that you're in trouble.

We can test for responsiveness at different scopes: at the scope of an individual component, at the scope of an API, and at the scope of the application (by executing a request from the viewpoint of the client). Just as when testing for correctness, testing at different levels of scope makes it easier to identify which part of the computation chain fails to comply with the responsiveness constraints of the application.

Unlike tests that seek to check for correctness, tests that check for responsiveness need to be executed many more times and with different concurrency levels (for example, 10 concurrent users versus 10,000 concurrent users). Only then can we get a good impression (in the form of a histogram) of whether the application responds with the latency we'd like it to.

11.1.2 Testing resilience

When testing resilience, we want to make sure that the different strategies that we've defined in our various components do indeed function as intended if things go wrong.

At this point it's important to make the distinction between failure and error (as defined in the *Reactive Manifesto*: http://www.reactivemanifesto.org). Our application should have a number of error-handling processes in place as part of the normal application logic (for example, a user entering an invalid email address should be tested for, and the error condition should be displayed to the user in return). In contrast, a failure is a rather unexpected condition that may lead to the service becoming unavailable unless you have a failure recovery mechanism in place, hence giving an application its resilient behavior.

Testing if our application is resilient is not the same thing as testing if our application deals correctly with erroneous input or data, which would also be done for "non-reactive" applications. Instead what we want to test for is whether our circuit breakers, control flow messages, and other failure-handling mechanisms are behaving as we want them to, which can be more or less difficult depending on what kind of failure we'd like the application to be able to handle.

11.1.3 Testing elasticity

Elasticity defines the capability of a deployed application to automatically react to increasing load by scaling out horizontally and/or vertically (depending on the scaling mechanism in place). Testing this property means that we need to first be capable of generating enough load for the scaling process to be triggered, and then to be able to check whether there are indeed more nodes running our application.

If you're really serious about testing for elasticity, this entails triggering a small Distributed Denial of Service (DDoS) attack on your own application and seeing if it indeed scales out and the latency is minimally affected. Since we're really serious, we'll see how to make this happen later on.

11.1.4 Where to test?

Though it's common to run unit tests on your own laptop during development, it may not be such a great idea to test for aspects such as responsiveness or elasticity on that machine—this isn't the machine you'll use to run your production environment (I hope). It arguably may also not be a good idea to run those tests against your continuous integration server, since it may have a different infrastructure than the one place you really want to know all about: your production environment.

That being said, testing against your production environment may be somewhat problematic, and chances are that you may have trouble selling this approach to the management of your company or organization. Therefore I'm not going to suggest you run various load and failover tests against your production environment, but instead against an environment that has an identical infrastructure. Only this way will you know that the platform you're running your application on does behave as you'd like it to.

> **THE COST OF TESTING** The advice in this section regarding the infrastructure associated with running tests may raise legitimate questions as to the costs associated with testing. The larger your infrastructure, the larger these costs will be. The question you or the decision makers need to ask yourselves is this: how much does it cost not to perform the appropriate tests?
>
> If you plan on saving some time (or money) on tests, it may be worth considering writing them at a higher level of granularity than unit tests. Even though proponents of test-driven development (TDD) may disagree at this point, if your resources are limited, then unit tests themselves don't necessarily add more value to your application, as all they will do is help you to identify regressions introduced during development faster (and this only if there is a unit test covering the affected bit of code).

This has been enough theory for this chapter; let's move ahead and test things in practice, starting with testing reactive components.

11.2 Testing individual reactive components

In this section you'll see how to test individual components for responsiveness and resilience. We'll take a close look at how to achieve this when working with two of our favorite tools for manipulating asynchronous computations: futures and actors.

11.2.1 Testing individual components for responsiveness

When testing for responsiveness, we need to provide the testing framework with a time-out in terms of how long we expect our asynchronous computation to take. It would be unwise to wait indefinitely for the computation to complete; after all, it may just be that we forgot to complete a future or reply to a message! As we'll see, test frameworks do provide the necessary tooling for providing fine-grained control over the expected latency.

TESTING FUTURES FOR RESPONSIVENESS

Let's use the simple example of a `RandomNumberService` to illustrate the testing of futures. As we've already used specs2 in chapter 5 to illustrate testing, let's use ScalaTest this time.

Start by creating a new Play application (we'll continue building it throughout this chapter) and include the ScalaTest dependencies in build.sbt:

```
libraryDependencies ++= Seq(
  "org.scalatest" %% "scalatest" % "2.2.1" % Test,
  "org.scalatestplus" %% "play" % "1.4.0-M3" % Test
)
```

Let's define our simple service and an implementation thereof in app/services/RandomNumberService.scala as shown in the following listing.

Listing 11.1 Definition of a service that provides random numbers

```
package services

import scala.concurrent.Future

trait RandomNumberService {
  def generateRandomNumber: Future[Int]
}

class DiceDrivenRandomNumberService(dice: DiceService)
  extends RandomNumberService {
  override def generateRandomNumber: Future[Int] = dice.throwDice
}

trait DiceService {
  def throwDice: Future[Int]
}
class RollingDiceService extends DiceService {
  override def throwDice: Future[Int] =
    Future.successful {
      4 // chosen by fair dice roll.
        // guaranteed to be random.
    }
}
```

- Defines our component as a trait to ease testing (`trait RandomNumberService`)
- Defines an implementation of our component depending on a DiceService (`class DiceDrivenRandomNumberService`)
- Defines the DiceService implementation as a trait as well (`trait DiceService`)
- Defines a simple but powerful implementation of a DiceService (`class RollingDiceService`)

You should by now recognize the usual pattern for defining services and their implementation. Declaring all the contractual obligations of a service in a trait and using constructor injection in its implementations as a provisioning mechanism for dependencies guarantees that we'll have no problem testing the component in isolation.

Let's now get to the interesting part—the test. Create the file test/services/DiceDrivenRandomNumberServiceSpec.scala with the contents of the following listing.

Listing 11.2 Testing a dice service for responsiveness with ScalaTest

```
package services

import org.scalatest.time.{Millis, Span}
import org.scalatest.{ShouldMatchers, FlatSpec}
import org.scalatest.concurrent.ScalaFutures
import scala.concurrent.Future

class DiceDrivenRandomNumberServiceSpec
  extends FlatSpec
  with ScalaFutures
  with ShouldMatchers {

  "The DiceDrivenRandomNumberService" should
    "return a number provided by a dice" in {

    implicit val patienceConfig =
      PatienceConfig(
        timeout = scaled(Span(150, Millis)),
```

Annotations:
- Uses the FlatSpec specification style that allows you to define one case after another (`extends FlatSpec`)
- Mixes in the ScalaFutures trait that provides support for futures (`with ScalaFutures`)
- Uses the ShouldMatchers as a flavor for expressing assertions (`with ShouldMatchers`)
- Provides a custom PatienceConfig (`implicit val patienceConfig`)
- Specifies how much time a future will be given to succeed before giving up (`timeout = scaled(Span(150, Millis))`)

```
      interval = scaled(Span(15, Millis))
    )
  val diceService = new DiceService {
    override def throwDice: Future[Int] = Future.successful(4)
  }
  val randomNumberService =
    new DiceDrivenRandomNumberService(diceService)

  whenReady(randomNumberService.generateRandomNumber) { result =>
    result shouldBe(4)
  }
 }
}
```

Specifies how much time to wait between checks to determine success when polling

Implements a simple DiceService to know exactly what to expect

Instantiaties the RandomNumber-Service we want to test

Invokes the service method we want to test and passes it to ScalaTest's whenReady function

Verifies the correctness of the result

ScalaTest provides the `ScalaFutures` trait for testing futures. This trait provides the `whenReady` method, which allows you to wrap a future and check the expected result in the body, and a default `PatienceConfig`, which allows you to configure the maximum amount of time a future runs, as well as how long you should wait between subsequent attempts to query the future for completion. Though the body of a `whenReady` method should check for the correctness of a result, the `timeout` and `interval` values should be tailored to check for the expected responsiveness. In this example we expect our future to succeed within 150 milliseconds, and we check if it has completed every 15 milliseconds. Note that we could also pass the `timeout` and `interval` values directly in the `whenReady` method invocation—the implicit `patienceConfig` merely allows us not to repeat ourselves (which makes sense, since we'll expect that a number of calls will probably have the same kind of time constraints).

TESTING ACTORS FOR RESPONSIVENESS

Akka provides a TestKit (http://doc.akka.io/docs/akka/2.3.11/scala/testing.html) for testing actor systems. The TestKit provides the necessary tooling for testing actors in two ways: either in isolation (when we'd like to peek inside an individual actor and check its state in response to different events) or when working together with several actors and where multithreaded scheduling comes into play. Let's look at how to use the TestKit for testing time constraints on an individual actor.

Include the TestKit in your project by adding the following dependency in build.sbt:

```
libraryDependencies += Seq(
  // ...
  "com.typesafe.akka" %% "akka-testkit" % "2.3.11" % Test
)
```

Time constraints and differences in hardware

In listing 11.2 we use the default values of `PatienceConfig`. You may notice that they're wrapped within the `scaled` function that multiplies all time constraints with a scaling factor (`1.0` by default). This mechanism becomes interesting when you're running the tests on different environments, as you're most likely going to do—the computer used for development, the continuous integration server, or even the replica of your production environment.

Chances are that the test you're running will be influenced by the underlying hardware and network connectivity—after all, you may want to test more-elaborate processes than this simple dice roll—such as a more realistic dice roll involving a Raspberry PI, a camera, an image recognition process, a robotic hand, and an actual dice—in which case, the network would be involved. But even with less-exotic test cases that, for example, only require disk access, there can be significant differences in execution times. A the time of writing this book, SSD drives are ubiquitous on laptops but not yet on servers, so the execution time of tests that involve disk access may vary significantly between test environments.

You can configure the scaling factor in build.sbt to be read from an environment variable like so:

```
testOptions in Test += Tests.Argument(
  "-F",
  sys.props.getOrElse("SCALING_FACTOR", default = "1.0")
)
```

Let's create a test actor that will also produce a random number.

Listing 11.3 Implementing an actor that computes a random number

```
package actors

import actors.RandomNumberComputer._
import akka.actor.{Props, Actor}
import scala.util.Random

class RandomNumberComputer extends Actor {
  def receive = {
    case ComputeRandomNumber(max) =>
      sender() ! RandomNumber(Random.nextInt(max))
  }
}

object RandomNumberComputer {
  def props = Props[RandomNumberComputer]
  case class ComputeRandomNumber(max: Int)
  case class RandomNumber(n: Int)
}
```

Returns a random number in the range from 0 to max when asked to

Defines a helper method for creating the props

This actor in itself isn't spectacular compared to what we've done in the previous chapters. But our test will be more interesting, as shown in the next listing.

Listing 11.4 Testing an actor for responsiveness using the Akka TestKit

```
package actors

import akka.actor.ActorSystem
import akka.testkit._
import scala.concurrent.duration._
import org.scalatest._
import actors.RandomNumberComputer._

class RandomNumberComputerSpec(_system: ActorSystem)
  extends TestKit(_system)
  with ImplicitSender
  with FlatSpecLike
  with ShouldMatchers
  with BeforeAndAfterAll {

  def this() = this(ActorSystem("RandomNumberComputerSpec"))

  override def afterAll {
    TestKit.shutdownActorSystem(system)
  }

  "A RandomNumberComputerSpec" should "send back a random number" in {
    val randomNumberComputer =
      system.actorOf(RandomNumberComputer.props)
    within(100.millis.dilated) {
      randomNumberComputer ! ComputeRandomNumber(100)
      expectMsgType[RandomNumber]
    }
  }
}
```

Extends the TestKit class that provides testing functionality

Mixes in implicit sender behavior that sets the test actor of the TestKit to be the target of sent messages

Mixes in the FlatSpec behavior using the FlatSpecLike trait

Tells ScalaTest that we'd like support for optionally executing custom code before and after all cases

Defines a default constructor that provides an ActorSystem

Shuts down the ActorSystem after all cases have run

Initializes the actor we'd like to test

Uses the TestKit's within method to check whether we get a result within 100 ms, taking into account optional time scaling

Expects a message of type RandomNumber to be returned (we don't know which number it will be)

The TestKit sets up a `testActor` actor directly available in the test cases, able to receive messages sent to actors under test. This is how methods such as `expectMsgType` can work—they just wait for the `testActor` to receive a message of a certain kind.

As you can see, there's a bit of work to do to set up our testing facility with the Akka TestKit. We need to extend from it, and also use the `ImplicitSender` trait (which does nothing other than declare an implicit actor reference and point it to the test actor created by the TestKit) to get going.

The `within` function allows you to define a time constraint and to run code within this block, checking for its timely execution. It can also be given a minimum value, if we'd like to check that an actor doesn't reply too fast.

> **Time constraints and differences in hardware**
>
> Just as for futures, your actors may have a different responsiveness depending on the underlying hardware. We use the implicit conversion provided by the `dilated` method of the `akka.testkit` package to be able to customize scaling.

(continued)

To customize the scaling factor, you have to provide a configuration value for the key `akka.test.timefactor`. You could, for example, initialize the `ActorSystem` in the test class to reuse the same time span provided through an environment variable, like so:

```
def this() = this(
  ActorSystem(
    "RandomNumberComputerSpec",
    ConfigFactory.parseString(
      s"akka.test.timefactor=" +
        sys.props.getOrElse("SCALING_FACTOR", default = "1.0")
    )
  )
)
```

11.2.2 Testing individual components for resilience

Next to responsiveness, we'd like to be able to check whether the components we've written are resistant to failure—or at least can be resistant to failure when we'd like them to! Luckily for us, the testing tools that we've used for testing for responsiveness can also help us with this.

TESTING FUTURES FOR RESILIENCE

In chapter 5 you saw how to recover failed futures with the `recover` and `recoverWith` methods. Let's now adjust the implementation of the `DiceDrivenRandomNumberService` to be resilient against problems with the implementation of the dice.

Let's add a test case to our `DiceDrivenNumberServiceSpec`, this time using a die that falls off the table one out of two times.

Listing 11.5 Implementing a test case for a service, by calling it with a flaky dependency

```
class DiceDrivenRandomNumberServiceSpec
  extends FlatSpec
  with ScalaFutures
  with ShouldMatchers {

  // ...

  it should "be able to cope with problematic dice throws" in {
    val overzealousDiceThrowingService = new DiceService {
      val counter = new AtomicInteger()
      override def throwDice: Future[Int] = {
        val count = counter.incrementAndGet()
        if(count % 2 == 0) {
          Future.successful(4)
        } else {
          Future.failed(new RuntimeException(
            "Dice fell of the table and the cat won't give it back"
          ))
        }
```

Implements a DiceService that will fail one time out of two, including the first time it's executed

```
      }
    }

    val randomNumberService =
      new DiceDrivenRandomNumberService(
        overzealousDiceThrowingService
      )

    whenReady(randomNumberService.generateRandomNumber) { result =>
      result shouldBe(4)
    }
  }
}
```

Expects to receive a result nonetheless

The `DiceService` that we feed to our `DiceDrivenRandomNumberService` will fail every second time, including the first time it's run. If you run the tests at this point, you'll be out of luck and the test will fail, as it should. Let's now make our service resilient.

Listing 11.6 Making the `DiceDrivenRandomNumberService` component resilient

```
import scala.util.control.NonFatal
import scala.concurrent.ExecutionContext.Implicits._

class DiceDrivenRandomNumberService(dice: DiceService)
  extends RandomNumberService {
  override def generateRandomNumber: Future[Int] =
    dice.throwDice.recoverWith {
      case NonFatal(t) => generateRandomNumber
    }
}
```

Recovers failure using the recoverWith handler

Simply invokes the method again until it works

This failure recovery mechanism is naive in that it will infinitely attempt to get a working dice roll out of the `DiceService`, but it will suffice in our case.

As you can see in our test case of listing 11.5, we haven't really invoked the service much differently than in the previous example, except that we have fed it with a special `DiceService`. This is in line with our component being resilient—failure isn't visible outside of the component and is dealt with internally.

> **WRITE THE SPEC FIRST AND FIX THE BEHAVIOR AFTERWARD** In line with best practices from test-driven development, you should first create a spec that will demonstrate that your component isn't resilient and only then alter it to make it resilient, not the other way around. You can use this technique to treat various edge cases; in our example we could check that the service will eventually use another strategy if there are too many failed attempts with the dice and, for example, switch to another set of dice.

TESTING ACTORS FOR RESILIENCE

As you saw in chapter 6, resilience in actor systems is typically achieved by using supervision. Though we probably don't need to test that the supervision mechanism offered by Akka itself works as intended (this is likely thoroughly tested by Akka's test suite itself) or whether a `SupervisorStrategy` is defined correctly (it is, after all, a rather simple partial function), what we may want to test is whether a child actor fails with the appropriate exception.

The problem with wanting to test whether the child behaves correctly lies in that Akka won't let us peek into the supervision process itself. An actor that's created directly through the `ActorSystem` will be supervised by the user guardian, and we have no way to know what happens in case of child failure, thus making it rather difficult to test the behavior of a child. This is where the StepParent pattern (https://groups.google.com/d/msg/akka-user/HIM2LW0BiiQ/FUraKN5QMFIJ) comes in. The way this pattern works is simple: instead of directly creating the actor to be tested in our test case, we use an intermediary "step parent" actor that will instantiate the actor for us and return the reference to it, hence becoming the parent of the actor we want to test. We can then customize the supervision strategy of this parent to check if the child fails as we'd expect it to.

Let's add a new test case to our `RandomNumberComputerSpec`.

Listing 11.7 Testing the failure of an actor using the StepParent pattern

```
it should "fail when the maximum is a negative number" in {

  class StepParent(target: ActorRef) extends Actor {
    override def supervisorStrategy: SupervisorStrategy =
      OneForOneStrategy() {
        case t: Throwable =>
          target ! t
          Restart
      }
    def receive = {
      case props: Props =>
        sender ! context.actorOf(props)
    }
  }

  val parent = system.actorOf(
    Props(new StepParent(testActor)), name = "stepParent"
  )
  parent ! RandomNumberComputer.props
  val actorUnderTest = expectMsgType[ActorRef]
  actorUnderTest ! ComputeRandomNumber(-1)
  expectMsgType[IllegalArgumentException]
}
```

Defines the StepParent helper actor that takes an actor to communicate with as parameter

Defines a custom supervision strategy to intercept child failures

Communicates failures to the target actor by sending them

Creates a child actor when receiving its Props and sending back its reference

Creates a StepParent actor and passes in the testActor as target for communication

Sends the StepParent the Props of the actor we want to test (the RandomNumberComputer)

Retrieves the reference to the actor we want to test by expecting a message of type ActorRef

Tests the RandomNumberComputer with a message that should provoke a failure

Checks whether the actor did indeed fail by expecting an IllegalArgumentException

In this example, we first create a `StepParent` and pass in the `testActor` provided by the TestKit as a target for all communication, allowing us to use all the helper methods. We then ask it to initialize our `RandomNumberComputer` by sending it the props and retrieve the reference by expecting a message of type `ActorRef` to be sent back.

Now comes the interesting part: provoking the failure of the actor under test. Since the method `Random.nextInt()` expects a positive number, passing it a negative one should make it fail. We can test this by sending a message with a negative number and expecting the `StepParent` to forward us a `Throwable` of kind `IllegalArgumentException`.

As you can see, this pattern is powerful. More-advanced implementations of the `StepParent` actor could allow it to react differently to different types of failures by, for example, resuming the child actor instead of restarting it and verifying that it works as intended.

Now that we've looked at ways of testing smaller asynchronous components, let's test the entire application!

11.3 Testing the entire reactive application

In what follows, we'll test our entire application for resilience and then see if it scales when the load increases. To do this, we first need to create a simple web application to be tested. As you may have guessed, it'll have something to do with generating random numbers.

11.3.1 Creating a simple application to generate random numbers

We'll create a simple application that, upon the click of a button, will generate a random number. To make our application a bit more interesting, we'll fetch the random number from RANDOM.ORG (http://random.org) and get some real network traffic going. You'll need to request an API key at https://api.random.org.

Start by creating a new actor that will be in charge of talking with RANDOM.ORG, as shown next.

Listing 11.8 Creating an actor that fetches a random integer from RANDOM.ORG

```
package actors

import actors.RandomNumberFetcher._
import akka.actor.{Props, Actor}
import play.api.libs.json.{JsArray, Json}
import play.api.libs.ws.WSClient
import scala.concurrent.Future
import akka.pattern.pipe

class RandomNumberFetcher(ws: WSClient) extends Actor {
  implicit val ec = context.dispatcher

  def receive = {
    case FetchRandomNumber(max) =>
```

```
      fetchRandomNumber(max).map(RandomNumber) pipeTo sender()
    }

    def fetchRandomNumber(max: Int): Future[Int] =
      ws
        .url("https://api.random.org/json-rpc/1/invoke")
        .post(Json.obj(
          "jsonrpc" -> "2.0",
          "method" -> "generateIntegers",
          "params" -> Json.obj(
            "apiKey" -> "00000000-0000-0000-0000-000000000000",
            "n" -> 1,
            "min" -> 0,
            "max" -> max,
            "replacement" -> true,
            "base" -> 10
          ),
          "id" -> 42
        )).map { response =>
          (response.json \ "result" \ "random" \ "data")
            .as[JsArray]
            .value
            .head
            .as[Int]
        }
  }

  object RandomNumberFetcher {
    def props(ws: WSClient) = Props(classOf[RandomNumberFetcher], ws)
    case class FetchRandomNumber(max: Int)
    case class RandomNumber(n: Int)
  }
```

Pipes the result of the future call to RANDOM.ORG to the sender, requesting a random number

Makes a call to the RANDOM.ORG API to fetch a single random integer

Passes the API key; make sure to replace this value with your key

Extracts the result in an unsafe manner to trigger a failure of the future if anything goes wrong

At this point in the book, the preceding actor should look pretty familiar to you. All we do is to place a remote call against RANDOM.ORG and extract the result. After being wrapped into a `RandomNumber`, the future holding this result is piped to the actor requesting the random number. Note that we don't take care of handling failures of this actor—yet.

Next, we'll create the controller that we'll use in app/controllers/Application.scala.

Listing 11.9 Controller showing the random number computation result

```
package controllers

import javax.inject.Inject
import scala.concurrent.duration._
import scala.concurrent.ExecutionContext
import play.api.mvc._
import akka.actor._
import akka.util.Timeout
import akka.pattern.ask
import actors._
```

```
import actors.RandomNumberFetcher._
import play.api.libs.ws.WSClient

class Application @Inject() (ws: WSClient,
                             ec: ExecutionContext,
                             system: ActorSystem) extends Controller {

  implicit val executionContext = ec
  implicit val timeout = Timeout(2000.millis)

  val fetcher = system.actorOf(RandomNumberFetcher.props(ws))

  def index = Action { implicit request =>
    Ok(views.html.index())
  }

  def compute = Action.async { implicit request =>
    (fetcher ? FetchRandomNumber(10)).map {
      case RandomNumber(r) =>
        Redirect(routes.Application.index())
          .flashing("result" -> s"The result is $r")
      case other =>
        InternalServerError
    }
  }
}
```

Wires in dependencies using dependency injection

Sets timeout at 2 seconds

Creates one single RandomNumberFetcher actor

Fetches a random number with a maximum value of 10

Passes the result to the flash scope available in the response

If we don't get a RandomNumber back, simply fails

The compute action will call our actor and request a random number using the ask pattern. If a random number is returned in time, then it will pass it in the response using the flash scope; otherwise it will simply fail.

Finally, let's create the simple user interface for our test application.

Listing 11.10 Simple view with a button to generate a random number

```
@()(implicit flash: Flash)
@main("Welcome") {
    @flash.get("result").map { result =>
        <p>@result</p>
    }
    @helper.form(routes.Application.compute()) {
        <button type="submit">Get random number</button>
    }
}
```

Expects the flash scope as implicit parameter

Displays the result if there is any

Gives the user a button to obtain a random number

That's it! Or almost: don't forget to add the adequate routes to `conf/routes` (for this example, make it a `GET` request—this will simplify load testing later on).

Now that the application is available, deploy it to Clever Cloud (we did this together in chapter 10) and test it in your browser. Don't yet enable any kind of scaling strategy—this example uses an XS instance (1024 MB RAM, 1 CPU). You should now have access to your application and be able to get random numbers by clicking the Get Random Number button.

Now that our application is ready, let's test it!

11.3.2 Testing for resilience with Gatling

Gatling (http://gatling.io) is a load-testing framework that makes it possible to test advanced interaction flows to simulate real users, and many of them. It's built with Scala, Akka, and Netty, and provides a useful scenario recorder that makes it easy to create various user interaction scenarios.

We want to subject our application to load testing to quickly and automatically spot problems that occur under heavy load. To get a realistic idea of what happens when many users hit the site at once, it's not enough to just generate a lot of requests—we also need to take into account varying load scenarios. Gatling makes it possible to simulate the behavior of many users in many different ways.

RECORDING A SCENARIO

Start by downloading the Gatling bundle on the homepage and extract it, then run the recorder with the command `<gatlin-directory>/bin/recorder.sh` (or `recorder.bat` if you use Windows). You'll be presented with a GUI through which you can configure the recorder, as shown in figure 11.1.

The Gatling Recorder works by acting as a proxy to a browser, hence being able to capture all interactions a real user does with a remote system. It also remembers the time interval at which those actions are performed, which means that it can optimally mimic the behavior of a real user navigating a website.

Configure your browser to use the Gatling Recorder as a proxy (by default the address is `localhost` and the port `8000`) and then click the Start button on the recorder. Navigate to the application you've just deployed on Clever Cloud and click on the button a few times and then stop the simulation.

If you've used the default parameters, then the simulation will be recorded into the file <gatlin-directory>/user-files/simulations/RecordedSimulation.scala. You can run this simulation with `<gatlin-directory>/bin/gatling.sh`. Follow the instructions on the screen to run the simulation. An HTML report is generated at the end of the run, giving you detailed information about the simulation and its performance.

SIMULATING CONCURRENT USERS AND WATCHING THE APPLICATION FAIL

If you edit the file RecordedSimulation.scala, you'll notice this line at the end of the file:

```
setUp(scn.inject(atOnceUsers(1))).protocols(httpProtocol)
```

Figure 11.1 The Gatling Recorder GUI

This is where the simulation run is configured, and as you can see, the default simulation is gentle on the application. Let's spice things up a little: replace the setup line with the simulation setup shown in the following listing.

Listing 11.11 Configuring a simulation run with increasing load on the server

```
setUp(
  scn.inject(
    nothingFor(4 seconds),
    rampUsers(50) over(10 seconds),
    atOnceUsers(10),
    constantUsersPerSec(2) during(15 seconds) randomized,
    splitUsers(50) into (
      rampUsers(10) over(10 seconds)
    ) separatedBy(5 seconds)
  ).protocols(httpProtocol)
)
```

- **Does nothing for 4 seconds** (`nothingFor(4 seconds)`)
- **Ramps up 50 users over 10 seconds** (`rampUsers(50) over(10 seconds)`)
- **Injects 10 users at once** (`atOnceUsers(10)`)
- **Injects 2 users per second over a duration of 15 seconds at randomized intervals of time** (`constantUsersPerSec(2) during(15 seconds) randomized`)
- **Repeats a ramp-up of 10 users over 10 seconds until reaching 50 additional users in total, with 5-second intervals** (`splitUsers(50) into (...) separatedBy(5 seconds)`)

These *injection steps* are executed sequentially (for a detailed description, check the Gatling documentation). As you can see, the configuration options for injecting users are pretty versatile, so it's possible to configure various load scenarios and see how your application reacts. Rerun the simulation with these parameters—and make sure to have a good internet connection.

This simulation will take some time to get started. Behind the scenes, Gatling prepares an army of actors ready to be launched against your application. As you may expect, the simulation, or rather our application, fails miserably and returns an embarrassingly high number of 500 Internal Server Errors (I got, for example, 71% of requests failed).

Now it's time to prepare a cup of coffee, sit down, and take a more detailed look at the report to figure out what's going wrong. One graph that is particularly interesting in our case is the one showing the number of responses per second, as shown in figure 11.2.

As you can see, once we start ramping up the number of users, the amount of failed requests increases dramatically. What is interesting to observe is that even when the number of users goes down, the number of failed requests is still significantly higher than the number of successful ones, even more so than at the beginning of our simulation.

So what's going on? Well, we made a few choices in the first iteration of our application that in hindsight may not be wise:

- We blatantly ignored any consequence of a timed-out `ask` future in the `Application` controller.
- What's even more shameful, we let the `RandomNumberFetcher` crash when RANDOM.ORG returned anything other than the expected result. But if you now go and check out the application logs on Clever Cloud, you'll see them full of indications that something isn't quite right ("The operation requires 1 requests, but the API key only has 0 left").

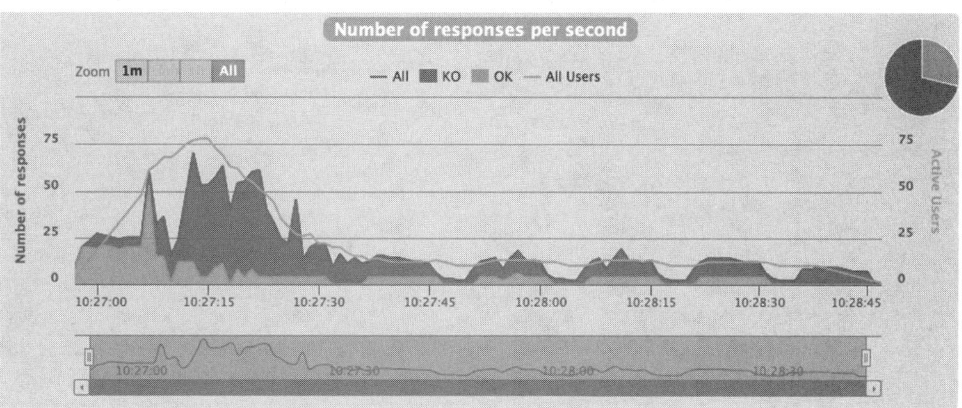

Figure 11.2 Graph showing the number of responses per second

Now it's your turn, dear reader, to make this application resilient to the increased load:

- If the `ask` call in `Application` times out, show the user a page in which you state that you're sorry but the application is currently overloaded. In a real-world application, this is where you can let your creativity shine (http://oatmeal.tumblr.com/post/2910950328/dear-tumblr).
- Protect RANDOM.ORG against massive calls on our side by wrapping the call to `fetchRandomNumber` in the `RandomNumberFetcher` by using a circuit breaker.
- In the `RandomNumberFetcher`, recover from JSON parsing failures (`play.api.libs.json.JsResultException`) and circuit breaker trips (`akka.pattern.CircuitBreakerOpenException`) by falling back to calling `scala.util.Random.nextInt()`.

Once you've made those changes, redeploy the application and run the simulation again. This time, the result should look much better, as shown in figure 11.3.

As you can see, there are no more failures—all requests are satisfied. In this simulation, the 95th percentile global response time is 474 ms and the 99th percentile is 819 ms. When thinking in terms of performance, it's important to look at response time distributions—the more users there are, the more those higher percentiles matter, since the number of users that will be affected by poor performance will increase.

RUNNING LOAD TESTS WITH JENKINS There's a Gatling plugin for Jenkins (https://wiki.jenkins-ci.org/display/JENKINS/Gatling+Plugin) that you can use to run a number of scenarios along with the rest of your test suite on your continuous integration server. This lets you know if a change causes the application to have worse performance than before.

So far, by taking the appropriate measures, we've made our application resilient—100% of the requests of our simulation have succeeded. But to be honest, there weren't many users. The maximum number of concurrent users reported by Gatling is 78, which isn't

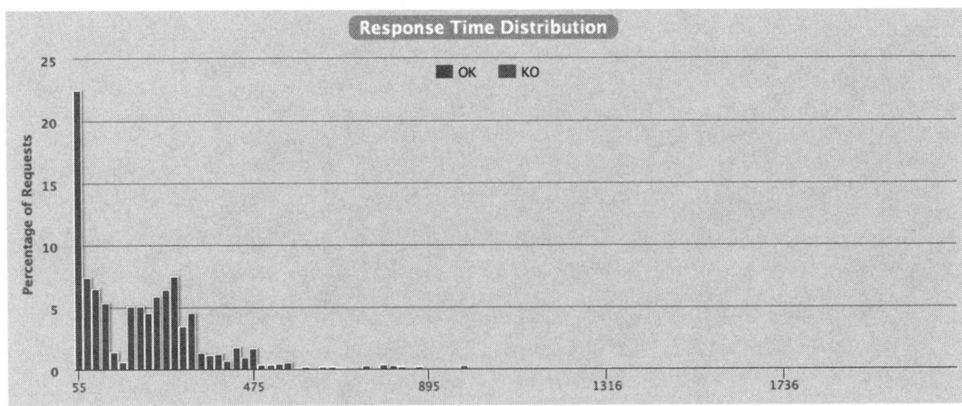

Figure 11.3 Graph showing the response time distribution of all requests

exactly something we can be proud of yet. To get a deeper understanding of how well our application responds under high load and how well it can scale, Gatling won't be enough, as it runs from one single computer. Let's take out the big guns!

11.3.3 Testing for scalability with Bees with Machine Guns

Bees with Machine Guns (https://github.com/newsapps/beeswithmachineguns) is "a utility for arming (creating) many bees (micro EC2 instances) to attack (load test) targets (web applications)." If you want to run the following load tests yourself, you'll need to get an Amazon AWS (Amazon Web Services) account at http://aws.amazon.com as well as a bit of money (running the EC2 instances will cost a bit).

Though Gatling does a good job of defining various load testing scenarios and exerting massive concurrent pressure against our application, it still only operates from one machine. In contrast, Bees with Machine Guns gives us the opportunity to attack our application from many networked machines and see how it behaves.

INSTALLING BEESWITHMACHINEGUNS

Beeswithmachineguns is a Python application, so before you can run it you'll need to install Python (https://www.python.org).

Once python is installed, just use `pip` to install the package:

```
pip install beeswithmachineguns
```

Now you need to set up the necessary credentials so that beeswithmachineguns can fire up nodes at will. This involves the following:

- Creating an AWS user
- Creating and downloading an EC2 key pair
- Creating a security group that makes it possible to open connections via SSH on port 22
- Configuring beeswithmachineguns with the user's key

> **DEFAULT ZONE AND AVAILABILITY REGION** The default region used in Bees with Machine Guns is `us-east-1`. If you want to save yourself some headaches while configuring the EC2 credentials, I strongly suggest you create the EC2 key pair and security group in this region.

First, create a new AWS user to obtain an access key ID and secret access key. You can do so in AWS Identity and Access Management (IAM) in the AWS Console.

Now you'll need a key pair to access EC2. Go to https://console.aws.amazon.com/ec2 and create a key pair, naming it, for example, `beeswithmachineguns`. Move the downloaded key file to ~/.ssh/beeswithmachineguns.pem.

Next you'll need to create a new EC2 security group via the EC2 dashboard. Call it `public` and create a new rule, selecting `SSH` in the Inbound tab and using any IP address to access incoming connections (or specify your current IP address).

Finally, create the file ~/.boto with the contents of listing 11.12 (boto is an AWS library for Python: https://github.com/boto/boto).

Listing 11.12 Configuring EC2 access

```
[Credentials]
aws_access_key_id = <your access key id>
aws_secret_access_key = <your secret access key>
```

DEBUGGING BOTO OUTPUT If you find yourself having trouble connecting to AWS, enable debug messages by appending the following section to the ~/.boto file:

```
[Boto]
debug = 2
```

ATTACKING OUR TARGET

All right, we're now ready to fire up a few bees. Run the following command in a shell:

```
bees up -s 20 -g public -k beeswithmachineguns
```

This command starts up the bees, which is to say the Amazon EC2 micro-instances that will attack our server. We'll use these parameters:

- `-s`—The size of the swarm of bees: how many micro-instances we want to use
- `-g`—The security group to use (we use the `public` group that we've just created to have SSH access)
- `-k`—The name of the key to access EC2

You should see the following output on the screen:

```
Connecting to the hive.
Attempting to call up 20 bees.
Waiting for bees to load their machine guns...
.
.
Bee i-8a7f812a is ready for the attack.
.
Bee i-577c82f7 is ready for the attack.
...
The swarm has assembled 20 bees.
```

A WORD ON ATTACKING A TARGET Be aware that this kind of performance test is very close to a Distributed Denial of Service attack. As long as you're doing it against your own application for educational or testing purposes, this is fine—but do not be tempted to join the dark side and attack other sites (needless to say, it would be easy to trace the attack back to your AWS account)! Before running this example, make sure that you're using the circuit breaker to protect RANDOM.ORG from getting too many requests.

All right, we're now ready to attack! Run the following command:

```
bees attack
  -n 10000
  -c 1000
  -u http://app-<your-app-id>.cleverapps.io/
  -k beeswithmachineguns
```

This will instruct the bees to attack the base URL of our application. We'll use these parameters:

- -n—The number of total requests
- -c—The concurrency of requests
- -u—The URL to attack
- -k—The name of the key to access EC2

Bees with Machine Guns uses Apache Bench (http://httpd.apache.org/docs/2.4/programs/ab.html) to attack a target. Apache Bench is a benchmarking tool that launches a number of requests against a URL and gives statistics as to how it performs.

You should now get an output along the following lines:

```
Read 20 bees from the roster.
Connecting to the hive.
Assembling bees.
Each of 20 bees will fire 500 rounds, 50 at a time.
Stinging URL so it will be cached for the attack.
Organizing the swarm.
Bee 0 is joining the swarm.
...
Bee 13 is firing his machine gun. Bang bang!
...
Bee 7 is out of ammo.
...
Offensive complete.
     Complete requests:          10000
     Requests per second:     739.540000 [#/sec] (mean)
     Time per request:         1352.514700 [ms] (mean)
     50% response time:         817.450000 [ms] (mean)
     90% response time:         2779.350000 [ms] (mean)
Mission Assessment: Target wounded, but operational.
The swarm is awaiting new orders.
```

As you can see, the application takes a hit—the mean time per request is above 1 second and the 90th percentile is nearly 2.8 seconds—but the application is still responding. That being said, we've only directed our bees at the main page, which only displays an HTML page.

Rerun the attack and point it to the more sensitive URL that computes a random number at /compute (or whatever you called the route). This time our server should be in trouble:

```
Offensive complete.
     Complete requests:          10000
     Requests per second:      433.080000 [#/sec] (mean)
     Time per request:          2309.822450 [ms] (mean)
     50% response time:          2340.950000 [ms] (mean)
     90% response time:          2950.200000 [ms] (mean)
Mission Assessment: Swarm annihilated target.
```

Attacking this URL overwhelmed our deployment. What this means is that the application ran out of resources and couldn't respond to all requests—also, the mean response time is poor. Let's see if we can remedy this unfortunate situation by scaling up and out.

AUTOMATICALLY SCALING UP AND OUT WITH CLEVER CLOUD AUTOSCALABILITY

Go to the Clever Cloud control panel and select the Scalability menu item. There, you can enable autoscalability and select a range of horizontal and vertical scaling options, as shown in figure 11.4.

Once you're done, rerun the attack and watch the Clever Cloud activity log: you'll see that a new deployment is being triggered. You can run more and heavier attacks (with a higher concurrency level) to see how the new deployment performs and to force it to scale up and out more.

If we were to run this kind of performance test automatically, it would be useful to have a means to check if our deployment does indeed upscale automatically. Luckily Clever Cloud has an API (https://www.clever-cloud.com/doc/api/) that allows as to do this.

We're interested in checking how many instances of our application are deployed so as to know whether the application scaled up and/or out. If you're deploying an

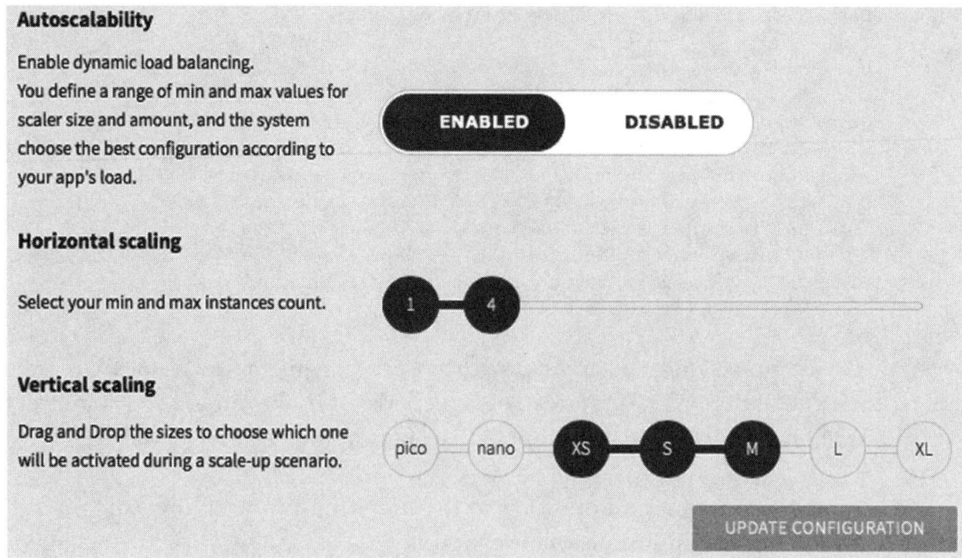

Figure 11.4 Configuring Clever Cloud autoscalability

application yourself (like we've done) and not on behalf of an organization, the interesting API endpoint is /self/applications/{appId}/instances. You can check this endpoint directly on the Clever Cloud API documentation site and test it with your application ID. This should give you a result that looks as follows:


```
[
  {
    "id": "d56b8cef-b6df-46c3-0000-6110201a0000",
    "appId": "app_9b93e68e-c291-4852-0000-48f6462a1d56",
    "ip": "xx.xxx.xx.xxx",
    "appPort": 1706,
    "state": "UP",
    "flavor": {
      "name": "M",
      "mem": 4096,
      "cpus": 4,
      "price": 1.7182
    },
    "commit": "fc4bc0da7382dafaabc4822c52348152d6dd1ded",
    "deployNumber": 10
  },
  {
    "id": "09ca5e98-56af-4c71-97be-8be526820000",
    "appId": "app_9b93e68e-c291-4852-0000-48f6462a1d56",
    "ip": "xx.xxx.xx.xxx",
    "appPort": 1710,
    "state": "UP",
    "flavor": {
      "name": "M",
      "mem": 4096,
      "cpus": 4,
      "price": 1.7182
    },
    "commit": "fc4bc0da7382dafaabc4822c52348152d6dd1ded",
    "deployNumber": 11
  }
]
```


As you can see, there are two nodes running, each of them being an "M" node—our application has indeed scaled up (from XS to M) and out (from one node to two)!

If you wait some time, you'll notice in the Clever Cloud activity log an activity with the title "DOWNSCALE Successful"—when there's no more need for the increased resources, the additional nodes will automatically shut down and the instance will revert to a smaller configuration.

> **DON'T FORGET TO CALL OFF THE SWARM** Once you're done with the attacks, don't forget to shut down the EC2 instances by running `bees down`—otherwise, they will keep humming along, slowly but steadily increasing the amount of your AWS bill.

11.4 Summary

In this chapter we've discussed methodologies and practical tools for testing a reactive web application; we

- Discussed the various scopes at which an application can be tested and the various reactive traits to be tested
- Created tests for asynchronous components built with futures and actors using ScalaTest and the Akka TestKit
- Built a small application and tested it for responsiveness, resilience, and scalability with Gatling and with Bees with Machine Guns

This concludes our common journey through the wonderful world of building reactive web applications using Scala, the Play Framework, Akka, and many other tools and libraries. I hope you had as much fun reading this book as I had writing it and will be able to use some of it to build real-world reactive web applications!

appendix A Installing the Play Framework

The first thing you need to do to install the Play Framework is download it. There are several ways of working with Play: downloading a bootstrap utility called *Activator* or using it directly as a dependency in a standard sbt project. *sbt* is the build tool for Scala projects, and Play runs as an sbt plugin. The Activator utility is a thin wrapper around sbt that offers a few convenience features, such as creating new projects based on templates, or running a user interface to explore the possibilities offered by the Ligthbend technology stack (hence its name, as it activates the use of the technology stack).

To get started quickly, we'll use the Activator utility.

PREREQUIREMENTS Make sure that you have Java 8 installed on your system. Check your version by typing `java -version` in your terminal.

Downloading and installing Play

Point your browser to https://www.playframework.com/download and download the latest version. You'll get a zip file called typesafe-activator-1.3.10-minimal.zip (or a newer version thereof).

You'll need to extract this file somewhere. For the purpose of this example, let's assume that you've created a workspace directory to work from somewhere on your computer (for example, in your user's home directory). Move the downloaded file to this directory and extract it there. You now should have a directory called workspace/activator-1.3.10-minimal containing three files: a JAR file (the Activator launcher) and two scripts, respectively activator and activator.bat (one for Linux/OS X and the other for Windows).

To use the Activator utility from anywhere, and to run it correctly, add it to your `PATH` environment variable. Additionally, it's a good idea to set up the environment so that there is enough memory assigned to the JVM when the `activator` command is being used.

Setting up the environment on Linux or Mac OS X

If you're using Linux or Mac OS X, edit your shell's profile file—the ~/.bashrc or ~/.bash_profile file (or ~/.zshrc if you're using the excellent zsh as shell: http://www.zsh.org). Assuming that you're running OS X and that your username is john, you'd then add the following line at the end of the file:

```
export PATH=$PATH:/Users/john/workspace/activator-1.3.10-minimal
```

If you're running a Linux distribution, the path would look like /home/john/workspace/activator-1.3.10-minimal.

At this point, you can verify that the path is correctly configured by opening a new terminal window and typing `activator - help` (see figure A.1).

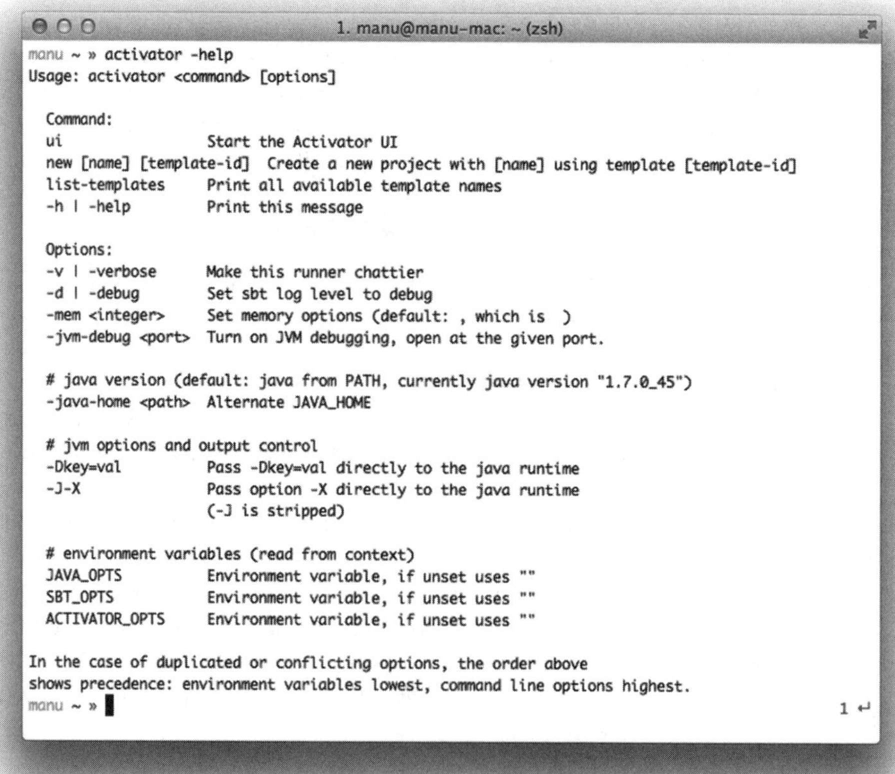

1. manu@manu-mac: ~ (zsh)
manu ~ » activator -help
Usage: activator <command> [options]
Command:
ui Start the Activator UI
new [name] [template-id] Create a new project with [name] using template [template-id]
list-templates Print all available template names
-h | -help Print this message
Options:
-v | -verbose Make this runner chattier
-d | -debug Set sbt log level to debug
-mem <integer> Set memory options (default: , which is)
-jvm-debug <port> Turn on JVM debugging, open at the given port.
java version (default: java from PATH, currently java version "1.7.0_45")
-java-home <path> Alternate JAVA_HOME
jvm options and output control
-Dkey=val Pass -Dkey=val directly to the java runtime
-J-X Pass option -X directly to the java runtime
(-J is stripped)
environment variables (read from context)
JAVA_OPTS Environment variable, if unset uses ""
SBT_OPTS Environment variable, if unset uses ""
ACTIVATOR_OPTS Environment variable, if unset uses ""
In the case of duplicated or conflicting options, the order above
shows precedence: environment variables lowest, command line options highest.
manu ~ »
1 ↵

Figure A.1 Checking if the PATH is set up correctly on Linux or OS X

Setting up the environment on Windows

If you're running Windows, you'll need to set up the `PATH` environment variable. Select Computer from the Start menu, left-click in the window and select Properties, and then select Advanced System Settings. In the Advanced tab, click Environment Variables and edit the `PATH` environment variable to add `C:\workspace\activator-1.3.10-minimal` to the path (don't forget to add a semicolon as a separator), as shown in figure A.2.

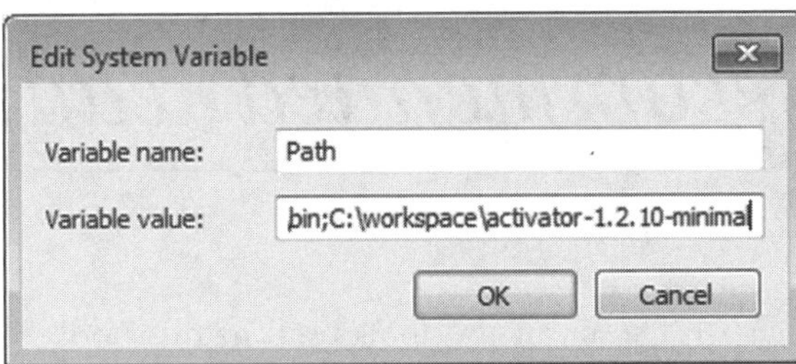

Figure A.2 Editing the `PATH` environment variable in Windows

You can now verify that the path is set up correctly by running `activator help` as shown in figure A.3.

```
C:\Windows\system32\cmd.exe

C:\workspace>activator help

Usage activator [options] [command]

Commands:
ui                    Start the Activator UI
new [name] [template-id]  Create a new project with [name] using template [templ
ate-id]
list-templates        Print all available template names
help                  Print this message

Options:
-jvm-debug [port]  Turn on JVM debugging, open at the given port.  Defaults to 9
999 if no port given.

Environment variables (read from context):
JAVA_OPTS             Environment variable, if unset uses ""
SBT_OPTS              Environment variable, if unset uses ""
ACTIVATOR_OPTS        Environment variable, if unset uses ""

C:\workspace>_
```

Figure A.3 Checking if the PATH is set up correctly on Windows

appendix B *Recommended reading*

If you're not already familiar with some of the tools used in this book, you'll be interested in these resources that will boost your experience with Reactive Web Applications.

Scala

In order to make the most out of this book, you should be comfortable with the basics of the Scala language, since you'll be reading a lot of it and writing a bit of it throughout the book.

- The e-book *Scala By Example* by Martin Odersky is available for free at http://www.scala-lang.org/docu/files/ScalaByExample.pdf. It gives an example-driven introduction to the Scala programming language.
- *Scala for the Impatient* by Cay Horstmann is a compact introduction to Scala, and you can get the first set of chapters for free at https://www.lightbend.com/resources/e-book/scala-for-the-impatient.
- *Scala in Action* by Nilanjan Raychaudhuri (https://www.manning.com/books/scala-in-action) offers a more complete resource for learning the language.

Functional programming

Chapter 3 provides an introduction to the functional programming concepts used in the book. If you want to get a longer and more complete discussion, I recommend you have a look at *Grokking Functional Programming* by Aslam Khan (https://www.manning.com/books/grokking-functional-programming), which offers an introduction to functional programming concepts for object-oriented developers.

appendix C Further reading

The following is a list of resources that can help you further your understanding of the topics covered in the book.

- The official documentation of the Play Framework (https://www.playframework.com/documentation) is an invaluable resource when it comes to exploring what the Play Framework has to offer.
- The official documentation of Akka (http://akka.io/docs) is a must-read if you want to stay up to date with what Akka has to offer.
- *Functional Programming in Scala* by Paul Chiusano and Rúnar Bjarnason (https://www.manning.com/books/functional-programming-in-scala) is an in-depth tutorial on functional programming, from the basics up to advanced concepts.
- *Reactive Design Patterns* by Roland Kuhn with Brian Hanafee and Jamie Allen (https://manning.com/books/reactive-design-patterns) introduces fundamental patterns for building message-driven distributed systems that are resilient, responsive, and elastic.
- *Functional and Reactive Domain Modeling* by Debasish Ghosh (https://www.manning.com/books/functional-and-reactive-domain-modeling) helps you think in terms of domain models with a focus on reactive modeling, covering patterns such as event sourcing and CQRS.
- *Angular 2 in Action* by David Aden, Jason Aden, and Jeremy Wilken (https://www.manning.com/books/angular-2-in-action) introduces the second version of the AngularJS framework used to illustrate the examples in chapter 8.
- *Docker in Action* by Jeff Nickoloff (https://www.manning.com/books/docker-in-action) covers managing applications using Docker containers, which you explored in chapter 10.

index

Symbols

Numerics

A

D

K

L

M

N

O

P

Q

R

S

T

MORE TITLES FROM MANNING

Reactive Design Patterns

by Roland Kuhn
with Brian Hanafee and Jamie Allen

ISBN: 9781617291807
325 pages
$49.99
October 2016

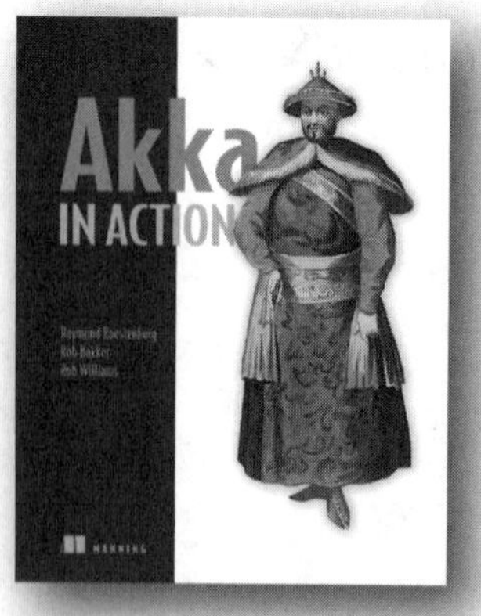

Akka in Action

by Raymond Roestenburg, Rob Bakker,
and Rob Williams

ISBN: 9781617291012
475 pages
$49.99
October 2016

Functional Programming in JavaScript

by Luis Atencio

ISBN: 9781617292828
272 pages
$44.99
June 2016

For ordering information go to www.manning.com